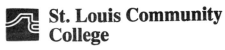

St. Louis Community College

Forest Park
Florissant Valley
Meramec

Instructional Resources
St. Louis, Missouri

GAYLORD

INFORMATION TECHNOLOGY AND SOCIETY

INFORMATION TECHNOLOGY AND SOCIETY

A Reader

Edited by Nick Heap, Ray Thomas,
Geoff Einon, Robin Mason
and Hughie Mackay

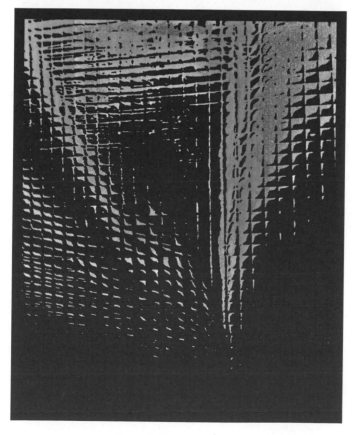

Sage Publications Ltd.
in association with the Open University

SAGE Publications Ltd
6 Bonhill Street
London EC2A 4PU

SAGE Publications Inc
2455 Teller Road
Thousand Oaks, California 91320

SAGE Publications India Pvt Ltd
32, M-Block Market
Greater Kailash - I
New Delhi 110 048

British Library Cataloguing in Publication data

A catalogue record for this book is available from the British Library

ISBN 0 8039 79800

ISBN 0 0839 79819   (pbk)

Library of Congress catalog card number   94-069677

Printed in Great Britain by The Cromwell Press Ltd., Melksham, Wiltshire

CONTENTS

Acknowledgements 7
Introduction *Nick Heap* 9

PART 1
DIFFERING PERSPECTIVES
Introduction *Ray Thomas* 11
The Social Shaping of Technology *David Edge* 14
The Hacker Crackdown: Evolution of the
US Telephone Network *Bruce Sterling* 33
Theorising the IT/Society Relationship *Hughie Mackay* 41
The Roots of the Information Society Idea *David Lyon* 54
A Gendered Socio-technical Construction:
the Smart House *Ann-Jorunn Berg* 74
Access and Inequality *Ray Thomas* 90

PART 2
IT IN THE WORKPLACE
Introduction *Geoff Einon* 101
Robotics, Automation and a New
Industrial Revolution *Paul Kennedy* 103
The Pursuit of Flexible Specialization in
Britain and West Germany *Christel Lane* 114
Computerized Machine Tools, Manpower
Consequences and Skill Utilization: A Study of
British and West German Manufacturing Firms
*Gert Hartmann, Ian Nicholas, Arndt Sorge
and Malcolm Warner* 126
Technological Change and the Future of Work *Peter Senker* 135
Technological Change at Work *Ian McLoughlin and Jon Clark* 149

PART 3
IT AND LEARNING
Introduction *Robin Mason* 179
Do Companies Need Technology-based
Training? *David Hawkridge* 182
Computer Supported Collaborative Learning *Anthony Kaye* 192
The Educational Value of ISDN *Robin Mason* 211
Access to Books for Visually Impaired Learners
- An Investigation into the use of Compact Disc
Technology (CD-ROM) *Tom Vincent and Mary Taylor* 224
Supporting Resource Based Learning
Josie Taylor and Diana Laurillard 237
Constructivist Learning Theories and IT *Ann Jones* 249

PART 4
IT AND THE HOME

Introduction   *Hughie Mackay*   267
Conceptualizing Home Computing:
Resources and Practices   *Graham Murdock,*
Paul Hartmann and Peggy Gray   269
The Feminine Culture of the Telephone:
People, Patterns and Policy   *Ann Moyal*   284
Patterns of Ownership of IT Devices
in the Home   *Hughie Mackay*   311

PART 5
IT FUTURES

Introduction   *Nick Heap*   341
Extra Terrestrial Relays: Can Rockets give
World-wide Radio Coverage?   *Arthur C. Clarke*   344
Iridium: A High Flying Phone System
Lawrence W. Lockwood   352
No Silver Bullet: Essence and Accidents
of Software Engineering   *Frederick P. Brooks*   358
There is a Silver Bullet   *Brad J. Cox*   377
Virtual Reality in the Real World:
History, Applications and Projections   *Ralph Schroeder*   387
Telework and the Changing Relation
of Home and Work   *Leslie Haddon and Roger Silverstone*   400
The New Space Race: Satellite
Mobile Communications   *David B. Crosbie*   413

Index   421

ACKNOWLEDGEMENTS

PART 1

Edge, D., 'The social shaping of technology' from Edinburgh PICT Working Paper Series, 1988.

Sterling, B., 'The evolution of the US telephone network', pp. 4-15 from *The Hacker Crackdown*, Bantam Books, USA, 1992, Viking, Great Britain, 1993 and Blake Friedman Literary Agency, London. Copyright © Bruce Sterling 1992.

Lyon, D., 'Introduction: the roots of the information society idea' from *The Information Society*, Basil Blackwell Ltd., 1988.

Berg, A.-J., 'A gendered socio-technical construction: the smart house' from Cockburn, C and Furst-Dilic, R (eds.) *Bringing Technology Home: Gender and Technology in a Changing Europe*, Open University Press, UK and Philadelphia, 1994.

PART 2

Kennedy, P., 'Robotics, automation and a new industrial revolution', pp. 82-94, Chapter 5, from *Preparing for the Twenty-first Century*, Harper Collins, 1993.

Senker, P., 'Technological change and the future of work', this article was first published in *Futures* Vol. 24, No. 4, May 1992, pp. 351-363, and is reproduced here with the permission of Butterworth-Heineman, Oxford, UK for text and Elsevier Science Publishers BV (North Holland) for CD ROM.

McLoughlin, I. and Clark, J., 'Technological change at work', Chapter 3, pp. 47-70, Open University Press, Milton Keynes and Philadelphia, 1988, Copyright © Ian McLoughlin and Jon Clark. Table 1 Daniel, W.W., *Work Place Industrial Relations and Technical Change*, p. 109, Francis Pinter 1987 © HMSO, Policy Studies Institute, ESRC. Figure 2 taken from Figure 3.1 'Flexible manning - the way ahead', IMSO Report No. 88, Sussex University, Institute of Manpower Studies and Manpower Ltd., 1984. Figure 3: Rothwell, S. 'Summary of Rothwell's cast studies' from 'Company employment policies and new technology in manufacturing and service sectors' in Warner, M. (ed) *Microelectronics, Manpower and Society*, Gower Publishing, 1984.

Lane, C., 'The pursuit of flexible specialization in Britain and West Germany', Vol. 2, pp. 141-8; 153-5; 157-65; 167, *Work Employment & Society*, British Sociological Association, 1985.

Hartmann, G., Nicholas, I., Sorge, A., Warren, M., 'Computerized machine tools, manpower consequences and skill utilization: a study of British and West German Manufacturing Forms, pp. 388-397 *British Journal of Industrial Relations*, Vol. 21, No. 2 (1983), Basil Blackwell Ltd.

Part 4

Murdock, G., Hartmann, P., Gray, P., 'Contextualizing home computing resources and practices', Chapter 9 from Silverstone, R and Hirsch, E (eds.) *Consuming Technologies: Media Information in Domestic Spaces*, Routledge, 1992.

Moyal, A., 'The feminine culture of the telephone, people, patterns and policy' from *Prometheus*, Vol. 7, No. 1, June 1989, Australia National University.

Part 5

Clarke, A.C., 'Extra terrestrial relays - Can rockets give world-wide radio coverage?', pp. 305-308, *Wireless World*, 1945. Reproduced with permission from David Higham Associates and Scoval-Chichak-Galen Literary Agency Inc.

Lockwood, L. W., 'Iridium: a high flying phone system', pp. 28-30 from *International Cable*, November 1992.

Brooks, F., 'No silver bullet: essence and accidents of software engineering', from Kugler, (ed.), *Information Processing*, 1986, Elsevier Science Publishers BV (North Holland) IFIP 1986.

Schroedor, R., 'Virtual reality in the real world: history, applications and projections', first published in *Futures*, Vol. 25, No. 9, November 1993, pp. 963-973 and is reproduced here with the permission from Butterworth Heinemann, Oxford UK and Elsevier Science Publishers BV (North Holland).

Haddon, L. and Silverstone, R., 'Telework and the changing relationship of home and work', presented to PICT National Conference 19-21 May 1993. Reproduced with permission of PICT, Brunel University.

Crosbie, D.B., 'The new space race: satellite mobile communications' *IEE Review*, pp. 111-114, May 1993, Institution of Electrical Engineers.

Cox, B.J., 'There is a silver bullet'. Reprinted with permission from the October 1990 issue of *BYTE Magazine*. © by McGraw-Hill, Inc., New York, NY. All rights reserved.

INTRODUCTION

Homo sapiens survived for over 300,000 years by napping flint into tools for hunting, processing food and building shelters. Metal tools fulfilled the same role for a little more than 10,000 years. The industrial revolution started around the mid-eighteenth century, just over 200 years ago. The information age is barely thirty years old. Whether you believe in revolutions or not, it is clear that the rate of social change is increasing and currently the greatest influence on change is our ability to process information.

As we approach the end of the twentieth century, the impact of information technology is apparent in many aspects of our daily lives - at home and at work, in shops and banks, in schools, colleges and universities. New uses of information processing and automation are spreading, while people are wondering how best to use them and how they or their children will be affected by them.

This book explores some of the social, political and technological impacts of this technology. In doing so it explores both the social and technological issues associated with IT developments. How are these developments controlled? By whom? Are they inevitable? Are IT innovations driven by technology or by social factors? Who has access to the technology? Who benefits?

The collection is divided into five subject areas. In Part 1, *Differing Perspectives,* the authors insist on the adoption of a critical attitude to developments in IT. This approach recognises that the ways in which technological advances are used are not shaped by technical factors, but by social influences that determine both the design and implementation of IT innovations. The readings in Part 1 discuss the ways in which this social shaping of technology occurs, and the ideologies and motivations which underlie it.

Discussion about the nature of the impact that IT has had in the workplace hinges on whether this transformation represents a 'technology-driven revolution'. The scope of IT at work is certainly broad, spreading as it does beyond the production process to encompass clerical work, distribution, retail, design, and management. But if this is a technological revolution, there is a significant debate underway about its nature, scope and impact. Part 2, *IT in the Workplace,* presents contemporary ideas in industrial sociology which have developed from studies of the uses of IT in manufacturing. These ideas challenge the Marxist and Taylorist theses of the nature of the labour process which see the role of automation as being to increase control over labour and, through de-skilling, to reduce labour costs. Here a broader and more pragmatic approach is taken to explanations of the role and effect of IT at work.

The readings selected for Part 3, *IT and Learning,* each address the question of why IT is used in education and training. Education is rightly no longer seen as a process that ends in early adult life, and training is likewise recognised as being of value throughout a working lifetime. The impact of IT in the workplace has contributed to this recognition that training is a continual process. IT can also provide the tools for training and education, and for assessing their success. Thus the papers in Part 3 deal with IT both as the subject and the means of learning.

In doing so they elaborate a number of themes: resource-based learning - its potential and facilitation with IT; collaboration and interactivity - learning through communication; the effectiveness of IT; the increased flexibility of access to education for the disabled and for remote learners, and the decentralisation of training. Against these advantages many early critics set fears that IT in education would lead to a large-scale replacement of teachers by machines, and to the humanistic approach to learning being overshadowed by a mechanistic approach. These fears can now be judged to have been largely unfounded. Though IT may change the teacher's role, it has not been supplanted, and telecommunications has opened up new opportunities for peer-to-peer co-operation, particularly in distance education.

Until recently, the home was not considered an arena for serious study compared to the 'real' world of paid employment. This attitude has changed as the importance of housework and domestic consumption have been recognised. In the area of IT as well the home is seen as far from marginal. The home is an important location for our use of IT equipment and services. The readings in Part 4, *IT and the Home,* introduce a range of issues and debates about IT in the home which have been developed in cultural and media studies. Two of the readings focus on specific technologies: the home computer, and the telephone. The third draws on quantitative marketing and government data to review the take-up and usage levels of a number of key IT devices in the home.

The final Part, *IT Futures,* draws together a disparate set of essays that touch on a number of issues relating to future developments of IT. Teleworking offers the promise of idyllic freedom whilst virtual reality is set to create entirely new modes of interacting with information. Both will benefit from the new software production tools and mobile communication systems waiting around the corner. Can we deliver such promise or is it just more hype? The reader should not look to find answers, and in some cases not even questions. But put together the authors provide a provocative interpretation of the directions technology is taking.

In compiling this selection of readings we have tried to give a wide representation of the major issues, including examples of different theoretical perspectives and contrasting views, from the pessimistic to the enthusiastic. In the case of students studying the Open University course *Information Technology and Society,* this set of articles is complemented by a range of other teaching materials, including study guides, software, teleconferencing, and television programmes. However, we hope that this collection of papers will also prove to be a useful resource in any study of the social impact of information technology.

PART 1 DIFFERING PERSPECTIVES

Ray Thomas, Faculty of Social Sciences, The Open University

INTRODUCTION

Technology is about how society uses science. The study of IT developments belongs as much to the social sciences as it does to technology, and the social sciences insist on the adoption of a critical attitude to IT developments. This insistence starts with the assertion that technical factors do not determine how the advances of science are used. Social factors shape both the design and implementation of IT developments.

The readings by Edge, Sterling, and Mackay discuss ways in which the design of IT products and services are shaped by social factors, and the reading by Lyon explores the ideologies and motivations which underlie this social shaping. The readings by Berg and by Thomas indicate, in very different ways, how social shaping can bring about unexpected or unintended consequences.

Edge provides a conceptual framework for the creation of new technology with a model of the interaction between scientific and technical factors on one side, and economic, social, and political factors on the other. Edge identifies four stages – the generation of basic knowledge, the design of products and services, the introduction of the first prototypes and tests, and the diffusion of the technology throughout the market. At each stage the nature of technology being developed is subject to modification in the light of social factors – such as what is believed to be market responses, or by whatever is believed to give the appropriate effects to the product or service.

Sterling provides an unexpectedly relevant illustration of these processes in an historical sketch of the development of the telephone system. Sterling's account identifies the same kind of stages of development as that of Edge. At the generation of basic knowledge stage in the 1860s (Sterling's Golden Vapourware stage) what later become known as the telephone was a plaything for Graham Bell and his brother. When Bell produced the first working models (Sterling's Goofy Prototype/Rising Star stage) Bell, and others, believed that the telephone would be used primarily for broadcasting. But social and market considerations determined otherwise and helped create the handset, duplex transmission and the switchboard.

The diffusion of the telephone service (Sterling's Cash Cow stage) could have taken many different organizational forms. The particular forms taken in the United States depended upon the interaction of human considerations – such as the personality of people employed as telephone operators and that of Theodore Vail who took over the Bell Company- with the many technical developments which came to be incorporated into the system.

These developments supported the extension of the telephone network to provide near universal service in the US. These developments also support, but have not determined, the current transformation of the telephone network from one wholly devoted to the transmission of analogue voice signals, to one which is increasingly being used to support the transmission of information expressed in digital form.

Sterling's account of the development of the telephone system could well be kept in mind to provide supporting evidence for Mackay's essay on Theorising the IT/Society Relationship. Mackay reviews the theories which, implicitly or explicitly, deal with the relationship between technological developments and society. He notes the crude technological determinism evident in many vox pop declarations – important not for their clarity but for their influence. Mackay contrasts the common assumption of technological determinism to that of Raymond Williams and others who emphasise the flexibility of technology and the influence of society in determining the nature of the technology which is actually developed and marketed.

Mackay discusses a number of approaches which deal with the social shaping of technology in different ways, and drawing on ideas developed in the area of cultural studies, puts forward an approach which takes into account the full production/consumption life cycle of information technology developments. Mackay's own approach encompasses the interaction processes between producers and the market identified by Edge. It takes into account ways in which users give their own meanings to the use made of IT products and services, and ways in which IT products and services are adapted to users' own purposes.

Mackay's broadening of the role of shaping of technology by the user sets the stages for the later readings. This broadening supports Lyon's equivocal answer to the question 'What sort of society will this bring?' The technology itself is flexible. It can be used to liberate and to suppress. It can be used to promote interpersonal communication and for surveillance. And different groups in society will use IT, or will try to use IT, in all these kinds of ways. The outcome – 'The Information Society' – is not predetermined by technical advances. Binary code can be thought of as a piece of pure science which can be considered independently of the human minds which invented and use it. But the information society is an artefact which encompasses a range of applications of binary code which reflect the complexity and dominant interests of society.

Lyon, consistently with Mackay, argues that the nature of the information society will largely reflect whatever the dominant influences in society believe the information society should be. The optimists, the pessimists, those who believe that IT will help create centralised states, and those who believe that IT will promote decentralisation may all be right. Lyon argues that it is important for social scientist not to promote IT developments uncritically, but to subject IT developments to critical analysis to help citizens exercise their power and responsibility to influence the pattern of developments.

The last two readings in Part 1 illustrate the importance of Lyon's prescription. They focus on the kind of social shaping that limits the impact of IT developments and which can give the social shaping quite unintended consequences. The technology may be potentially revolutionary, but human and organizational influences do not change as quickly as the technology, or do not change at all. Just as the early readings in this part demonstrate that social considerations commonly shape the nature of the new technology, so Ann-Jorunn Berg, with a case study of proposals for 'smart' houses, provides a dramatic example of what might be called perverse social shaping – a failure to take into account the needs of the principal users.

Berg's study may also illustrate why particular proposed IT developments fail because they do not give proper consideration to the needs of users. But, more relevant to the main themes of this book, Berg's study illustrates how IT developments can reflect and perhaps reinforce divisions in society. In a household which actually came to live in one of these 'smart' houses the traditional gender roles could well be strengthened. Berg's study poses questions, raised in other areas such as employment, as to whether the introduction of IT generally tends to maintain, reinforce, or magnify the traditional gender roles.

Thomas puts questions of these kinds into context by providing an antidote to the technological optimists who see IT developments as contributing to more egalitarian societies. Thomas does not deny the liberating influence which many find in the use of new technology, but argues that, when the full canvas is examined, that the overall picture is one of growing inequalities. The rapid pace of technological development, hand-in-hand with capitalism, will generally be exploited by the already privileged groups in relatively wealthy societies. Taking a national view and a global view the general influence of new technology will be to reinforce existing inequalities – and create new inequalities.

The questions asked and the views put forward in this group of readings have aimed to identify important questions. They are intended to be used as tools for further investigation of IT developments. They aim to provide a basic theory kit which can be applied for further investigation of specific IT developments and to help identify generalisations about broad categories of IT development. They are perspectives subject to competition from other perspectives, and are subject to modification and elaboration in the light of their application and in the light of new IT developments.

THE SOCIAL SHAPING OF TECHNOLOGY

David Edge

Reader in the Social Sciences Unit at the University of Edinburgh

This paper was originally drafted in 1987, to stimulate discussion among the Edinburgh Group about the social shaping perspective. It broadly expresses, as far as is possible, the views of the Group's original members, and the research that informed them. We have not attempted to update the document to incorporate our subsequent findings and the perspectives of the new members of Edinburgh PICT. It is, therefore, an historical document that captures the starting point for the Edinburgh research.

The paper defines and illustrates the so-called 'social shaping of technology' perspective. It starts with a brief critique of traditional approaches to the social analysis of technical change, emphasising the extent to which such approaches imply a *technological determinism*, use a simplified *linear model* of the innovation process, tend to treat the technology as a 'black box', and are preoccupied with the 'social impacts' of a largely pre-determined technical 'trajectory'. In contrast, an alternative approach is described, which 'opens up the black box', asking questions about the *origin* and *evolution* of the technology itself. This is illustrated with a simplified model, adapting the old 'linear' version. Such analysis draws attention to the *flexibility* of the innovation process, and the extent to which *choices* and 'feedback' are endemic to it. It exposes the range of 'social' (i.e. economic, cultural, political, organisational) factors which help to 'shape' that process with both theoretical and policy implications. The paper presents case studies of innovation in statistics, radio astronomy, missile guidance systems, CNC machine tools and robotics to illustrate these themes, and closes with some more speculative reflections.

INTRODUCTION

Traditionally, social research on technology has tended to focus on the 'effects of technology on society', its 'impact', its 'implications', and so on. These phrases reflect a widely-held commonsense belief (often referred to as 'technological determinism') which holds that technical change is a prime cause of social change, and that technical innovations are themselves *'uncaused'* – in the sense that they arise only from the working out of an intrinsic, disembodied, impersonal 'logic', and not from any 'social' influence [1]. In this view, human and social factors merely mediate, and can perhaps control the timing of, developments that are essentially inevitable. The emphasis of research and policy therefore shifts to attempts to understand and predict the likely *consequences* of evolving technologies, so that the more negative effects might be ameliorated. Such studies might cover the impact on organisational structures,on the structure of industry and the allocation of resources, the implications for markets, and so on.

The importance of posing these kinds of questions about any radical set of technologies which are likely to have a substantial impact on many aspects of our society and economy cannot be doubted. But, valuable though much work in 'this tradition is, its assumptions can be criticised. Moreover, in leaving unasked (and therefore unanswered) a basic question – namely, 'what is shaping the technological changes that are having these "effects"?' – it provides, at best, an incomplete picture of the social processes it studies. In brief, it tends to take technical innovation as a 'given', a 'black box'. The purpose of this paper is to show how that black box may, in principle, be opened, so as to allow exploration of the social processes which mould the form and content of technical knowledge itself – what 'causes' the 'cause', the factors that shape the evolutionary paths of technologies.

SOCIAL SHAPING

In this alternative approach, researchers may ask what factors are influencing both the *rate* of technological change, and the general *directions* that it is taking. They may also ask quite specific questions about the reasons why particular technologies take the form that they do. It is a basic assumption of this approach that the relationship between technology and society is genuinely an *interaction*, a *recursive* process: 'causes' and 'effects' stand in a complex relationship. Obviously, the approach also assumes that *social* shaping is important: technological change is not governed simply by its own 'internal logic'. It is becoming increasingly clear that the answers to these 'shaping' questions – the factors influencing the rate, directions and specific forms of technical change – are *social as well as technical*. The evidence for this is overwhelming: economic, cultural, political and organisational factors – all of which we subsume in the term 'social' – have been shown to shape technological change [2].

In the literature, at least eight types of social influence on technological change are identified: geographical, environmental and resource factors; scientific advance; pre-existing technology; market processes; industrial relations concerns; other aspects of organisational structures; state institutions and the international system of states; gender divisions; and cultural factors [3]. But, at present, research of this kind has two major weaknesses:

(a) Discussion of each type of influence tends to be relatively isolated from discussion of the others. To take just one example, those concerned with the impact of organisational factors on the process of technical change have tended to ignore the importance of market structures and competitive pressures, and vice versa. When more than one influence is discussed, it is often in the form of a simplistic contrast (e.g. 'technology-push' versus 'market-pull'). Much greater integration is needed.

(b) Of equal concern, almost all existing literature lacks a satisfactory conceptualisation of the precise way in which new technological knowledge emerges and evolves over time. Often even the most perceptive authors retreat to rather loose metaphors (such as 'technological trajectories' or 'technological imperatives') [4] when discussing this.

Remedying these defects, while at the same time conserving the insights gained from these existing studies, is a longterm goal of those seeking to understand the social shaping of technology.

TWO APPROACHES

Two broad approaches to the study of the shaping of technological change can be identified. The first is widely used in the history and sociology of science (Shapin, 1982), but has also already been drawn upon in work on technology (e.g. Pinch and Bijker, 1984). Essentially, it consists of studying the development of a scientific or technological field, and identifying points of 'contingency' or 'interpretative flexibility', where, *at the time*, ambiguities are present. These might include experiments that are susceptible to more than one interpretation, or artefacts that could be designed in more than one way. Having identified such 'branch' points, the researcher then seeks to explain why one interpretation rather than another succeeded, or why one way of designing an artefact triumphed. Typically, social factors enter into such explanations. This, for example, is the key to the method employed in Noble's (1984) history of the automatic control of machine tools. Noble distinguishes several different paths the technology could have taken (e.g. numerical control, record-playback), and argues that industrial relations issues, the career interests of the engineers involved, and military concerns were all important in determining the path that was eventually taken. This approach works 'out' from the technology to the context shaping it.

The second approach works 'in' from the context. Here, the starting point is not a particular technological field, but a particular social context within which technical change takes place. Thus researchers have studied markets, organisations, states, and other contexts that shape technology. (Points (a) and (b) above are relevant to this literature.) The social processes, interests and goals typical of the context are identified, and attempts are then made to trace their influence on evolving technology. One particular context that has seen a lot of work of this kind, by economists, economic historians and sociologists of work, is the industrial workplace. Certainly, the recent history of the British car or print industry shows the tight interconnection of technological change with changing patterns of industrial relations. But there is also growing interest in other contexts of technical change, notably the household and home (see Mackenzie and Wajcman, 1985, Part 3; and Gershuny, 1983).

A recent review essay by Powell (1987) illustrates the variety of analyses and explanations that are currently available in studies of technical change in the industrial workplace. Powell considers the work of Hounshell (1984), on the rise of mass production methods, and of Noble (1984) and Shaiken (1986), who discuss automation. Each author offers detailed historical evidence. But, as Powell notes (p.186):

> Where the three authors part company is in their interpretative frameworks. Hounshell offers a remarkable diffusion model of the path of industrial development; Noble makes a forceful argument that the choice of technology reflects business and class interests; and Shaiken's focus ... is the workplace itself, how technology and work are transformed at the point of production. Hounshell considers technology as a form of knowledge, Noble views it as a social production controlled by powerful agents, and Shaiken sees technology to be a process involving negotiating and jockeying by labor and management.

and later (p.193), Powell contrasts Shaiken's 'contingent view' with Noble's more 'grand ... sweeping thesis', and concludes that

> ... it suggests that future research will need to proceed on three levels : the micropolitics of the workplace, the broader social-political context in which technological change occurs, and the organizational and economic factors that shape how work is structured.

Powell is here emphasising the need for integration in this research. His review illustrates some of the rich variety of analytical approaches already available, as resources, for use in studies of the social shaping of production (and, by extension, information) technologies.

INVENTION AND IMPLEMENTATION

This shaping process begins with the earliest stages of research and development. Though 'invention' is at least partially an unpredictable process, extensive studies by historians of technology have demonstrated systematic influences on it. There are cases where a quite specific social influence can be traced – where, say (as in Noble, 1984), inventions are responses to perceived industrial relations problems. In other cases, inventive attention is focused on a particular technical issue (e.g. the high resistance light filament) because that issue is strategic in terms of an expanding technological system. Thus Edison's work on the electric light filament resulted from his identification of the filament as central to electricity's economic struggle with the existing gas light industry (Hughes, 1983).

But, of course, social shaping does not end with 'invention'. There are many more inventions than are ever brought to fruition, and social factors have a demonstrable influence on which are pursued and which are not. The process of *implementing* a technology – for example, an information-technology based automation system – is also crucial to social shaping.

The chosen configuration of such a system will typically reflect organisational and economic interests of various kinds (Shaiken, 1986). The difficulties faced, and opportunities found, in the process of implementation have been shown to be at least as important a source of innovation as formal research and development in production technologies like robotics (Fleck and White, 1987).

'SHAPING' AND 'EFFECTS': A SIMPLE MODEL

There is a high degree of complementarity between research on the consequences of technological change and research on its causes. An examination of the causes of change may well influence the way we understand its implications. It can, for example, indicate whether a particular effect of a technology is inevitable, or whether it is the result of a decision to design the technology in one particular way (see Winner (1980) for instances of both). Conversely, the consequences that a technology has (or might have) often influence future technical decisions (see, e.g., Hughes, 1983). It would be intellectually untenable to concentrate on 'shaping' in isolation from 'effects'. However, specifying precisely the relationship between 'shaping' and 'effects' is currently a *goal* of research: it is not something which has yet been clarified satisfactorily. Indeed, such a specification is almost equivalent to having a satisfactory account of the entire process of technological change! Still, the question of how the two are related demands a better answer than a vague general commitment to consider both. What follows is accordingly an attempt to use a simplistic and unsatisfactory model of technological change to suggest one possible starting-point — a starting-point that will almost certainly have to be discarded as research proceeds. Just how patently unsatisfactory the model is depends on the uses to which it is put. It is obviously unusable for studies adopting our second, 'working inwards' approach (see above); it probably has greater purchase, but is still far from adequate, for the first, 'working outwards' approach.

The model in question is the commonsense 'product-cycle' view of technological change, which divides the process into approximately five phases, in linear sequence:

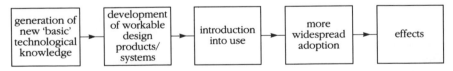

Even when elaborated in the way suggested below, this view is in actuality untenable. A more satisfactory account would have to abandon the separation of the 'boxes', both from each other and from the wider organisational, economic, political and cultural context. It would also have to abandon the suggestion of a necessary 'left-to-right' logical or chronological ordering. Nevertheless, because this view does explicitly or implicitly inform much of the existing literature, it can used to make a few significant points in regard to studies of 'shaping' and 'effects'.

The narrowest 'effects' studies do not simply take this model for granted. They also fail to examine the contents of the first four boxes:

A better, but still inadequate, form of study does examine the processes of adoption of a new technology (its 'diffusion', as it is often called), but still treats the previous phases as a 'black box':

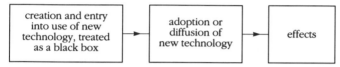

A narrow 'shaping' study, on the other hand, would simply involve opening the boxes on the left-hand side of our diagram. But that would be equally unsatisfactory. For even within the narrow parameters of the 'product-cycle' model, it is essential, both practically and intellectually, to consider the *feedback loops* between the different boxes. What happens in the boxes on the right hand side of the diagram helps to shape what goes on in the boxes on the left.

A simple example of this latter point is indeed recognised by adoption/diffusion studies. The effects that a technology is perceived to have form a major influence on the rate of its adoption. Most obviously, if one of the effects of a technology is seen to have been to raise the profits of those who have adopted it, this will speed its adoption (see, e.g., Griliches, 1957 and 1960). So a feedback loop exists from 'effects' to 'adoption':

What has received much less attention – though there are examples to be found in the literature – are the feedback loops from the boxes on the right to the boxes further to the left. Such feedback loops must exist – the whole point of design, say, is to bring about intended effects. But two interesting points arise: just what are the intended effects and what role do unintended effects play?

There are some intriguing instances where the intended effects are, directly, social objectives. One example emerges from Robert Caro's biography of New York builder and planner Robert Moses (Caro, 1974; see also Winner (1980) and Mackenzie (1984, p.500)). Moses chose to design the overpass bridges for the Long Island parkways with as little as nine feet clearance at the kerb. In doing this, he had in mind a specific effect: keeping commercial vehicles (and especially buses) from being able to use the parkways. By doing so, poor people and blacks could be effectively prevented from gaining access to Moses' treasured recreational areas, suchas Jones Beach. So an explicit social objective was shaping technical design:

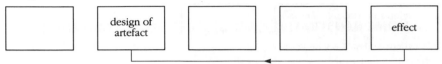

This is, of course, an untypically simple case. But while more typical examples are far more complex, feedback loops certainly have to be seen as existing all the way back into the basic processes of 'invention'. Thomas Hughes' reconstruction of Edison's invention of the modern form of electric light provides a good example. Edison was sharply aware that if his electric light was to be adopted at all widely, it would have to compete economically with the existing gas lighting systems. Examining the likely costs of an electricity supply system, he concluded that the key problem was the high cost of copper for conductors. The new technological knowledge he developed – which crystallised in the form of the high-resistance filament electric light – was structured by the goal of seeking to reduce the amount of copper used in the system as a whole (Hughes, 1983, 1985). So the feedback loop was as follows:

So a minimum necessary revision of the simple product-cycle model – and, as outlined above, we believe that ultimately models based on a wholly different foundation will prove more satisfactory than piecemeal revision of this one – can be produced by redrawing the first diagram with all the feedback loops in place:

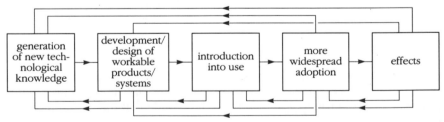

Thought of even in this crude way, the need for an integration of 'shaping' and 'effects' studies (and of the different levels of analysis of the 'shaping') is clear. An understanding of the shaping of a technology will clearly illuminate an analysis of its effects. We may, for example, be able to say whether the effects that a technology is having are intrinsic to *any* use of that technology, or whether they are the consequences of particular design decisions that could have been otherwise (as was patently the case in the instance of Moses' overpasses). Winner (1980) provides a useful discussion of this. But an equally key question for any study of the shaping of technology is the way in which the intended or unintended effects a technology is currently having (or those it is anticipated it will have in the future) are influencing the process of the creation of that technology.

SOME ILLUSTRATIVE CASE STUDIES FROM EDINBURGH

Specifying the forms taken by the social shaping of technology is as difficult as specifying the relationship between 'shaping' and 'effects'. Though again the characterisation is too crude, it may be useful to distinguish four possible ways in which social factors may act in the 'shaping' process:

1 they may influence selection between available technological possibilities. ('Feedback loops' might constitute such factors.)

2 they may permit only one area of 'possible' technical development to be explored, often to the extent that it becomes very difficult to talk of 'alternatives'.

3 they may operate less directly but no less forcefully by creating a particular environment (a market, say, or an intellectual climate) in which only certain technical configurations succeed. Such a state of affairs is particularly characteristic of technologies which require extensive implementation and applications engineering to adapt them adequately to customer requirements.

4 they may shape technical development by the specific embodiment of social models into the technology.

Much research (especially at Edinburgh) has focused on the shaping of *science* by such processes. The Edinburgh 'strong programme in the sociology of scientific knowledge' (for which see Barnes 1974 and Bloor 1976) has sought, in this way, to analyse the shaping of scientific knowledge, irrespective of our present evaluation of such knowledge [5]. Many of us were introduced to the field *via* studies of science, so we will start there.

MATHEMATICAL STATISTICS

Donald MacKenzie's research on the development of the mathematical theory of statistics is one instance of a 'sociology of scientific knowledge' of this kind. It showed how the development of this area of knowledge was shaped by social factors both internal to the scientific community and pertaining to the wider society, its politics and ideologies. MacKenzie identified processes of all four kinds at work. One case in point, where events were perhaps closest to type 1, occurred around 1900. In the previous 15 years, British statisticians had developed the theory of correlation of what we would now call 'interval variables' – those such as height or income, where a unit of measurement is available. While there were differences of interpretation, there was broad consensus about the theory developed by statisticians such as Galton, Pearson, Edgeworth and Yule.

The divergence came when statisticians sought to extend the theory to cover 'nominal' variables – those such as 'dead' or 'alive', or 'vaccinated' and 'unvaccinated' – where the data were simply in the form of *categories*, with no immediate unit of measurement available. To take an elementary example, confronted by a table such as this, linking vaccination and chances of survival in an epidemic, how, *mathematically*, should one produce a measure of the linkage or association?

	vaccinated	unvaccinated	totals
survived	a	b	a + b
died	c	d	c + d
totals	a + c	b + d	N

Two radically divergent schools of thought emerged on this issue, headed respectively by Karl Pearson and George Udny Yule (for full details, see MacKenzie (1978) and (1981a, Chapter 7)). The essential point is that the divergence on the esoteric mathematical issues was wholly interwoven with differing positions on the sociopolitical question of eugenics. Pearson and his followers were proponents of a wholesale programme of 'biological engineering' to improve the inherited makeup of the British population; Yule and his backers were sceptics. In its detailed mathematical development, Pearson's approach was shaped by the needs of his programme of eugenic research. When Yule attacked Pearson's mathematics, he was simultaneously attacking an important plank of the eugenic case that had, for example, been used in an attempt to convince the Government's Committee on Physical Deterioration of the virtues of eugenics [6].

RADIO ASTRONOMY

The case of mathematical statistics involved 'social factors' which concerned preferences and policy options for the entire society. But studies of technical development can highlight the social processes at work *within science*, and include them in an integrated 'multilevel' analysis. A case in point comes from *Astronomy Transformed* (Edge and Mulkay, 1976). This study of the development of radioastronomy compares the instrumental strategies of the pioneer Cambridge and Jodrell Bank groups and shows, in considerable technical detail, how the precise form of the instrumentation devised at these two centres was related to their social group structures and leadership patterns. In particular, the cohesive, integrated group at Cambridge built arrays on the 'aperture synthesis' principle, which they then deployed on an essentially common programme of scientific investigations – while the much more differentiated group at Jodrell Bank relied on multipurpose 'big dishes', deployed by the separate teams on a range of research projects. These two strategies, in turn, make sense when viewed within the national

UK context of astronomical research, and its subsidy by government: they could be seen as sensibly *complementary*. At the 'micro' level, this analysis also helps us to understand individual research choices – e.g. Lovell's decision, in the late 1950s, to embark on a radio search for the emissions from flare stars [7].

MISSILE GUIDANCE SYSTEMS

A study directly concerned with technology, that investigates the processes of selection between technological options, is Mackenzie's work on the design of missile guidance systems, such as the MX/Peacekeeper Advanced Inertial Reference Sphere (MacKenzie, 1987).

Many technical decisions are necessary in designing such a guidance system: what sorts of accelerometers and gyroscopes to use; what accuracy specifications to aim for; whether or not to include a 'star-tracker'; and so on. MacKenzie draws on extensive interviews with those involved in such decisions at organisations such as the Ballistic Missile Office of the US Air Force, the Strategic Systems Program Office of the US Navy, and the Charles Stark Draper Laboratory, Inc., again to show the interweaving of these technical decisions with social and political matters. The process of setting accuracy specifications, for example, which might be thought to exemplify a 'purely technical decision', in fact reflected and subsequently influenced – debate about nuclear strategy: did it, or did it not, enhance US security to build missiles with the capability of destroying Soviet missiles in their silos before they were fired? Matters of bureaucratic politics were also involved: was it in the interests of the US Navy's Fleet Ballistic Missile programme to seek to compete with Air Force missiles in terms of silo-killing capability, or ought the Navy rather play up the distinctive 'ultimate deterrent' features of submarine missile systems? These considerations bore directly on the guidance system design. The technical community, too, was divided. The firm (Kearfott) that had pioneered the ballistic missile boost-phase 'star acquisition' guidance technique pushed for Poseidon and Trident missiles to be equipped with star-trackers. But they and their supporters had to contend with scepticism about the technique – scepticism that came in part from an organisation (the Draper Laboratory) with heavy investment in 'pure inertial' technology not involving star-trackers.

COMPUTER NUMERICALLY CONTROLLED (CNC) MACHINE TOOLS

Fransman's work on the development of CNC machine tools in Japan, South Korea and Taiwan (Fransman, 1986) illustrates the operation of a range of social processes – but, especially, of type 3, the 'selection/environment' kind. Fransman shows the importance of both organisation within the firm and wider environmental factors in shaping the characteristics and design of machine tools. While the former includes organisational forms such as 'just-in-time' production and 'zero-defects' policies, which in turn have generated further forms of technical change, the latter includes the circumstances of users, the extent of competitive pressures on the firm, and the role of the state in assisting in the development of the firm's technological knowledge base, and in helping to restructure the industry. In the United States, for example, the main user of CNC machine tools was the aerospace industry, where the requirement tended to be for large, custom-built machine tools. In Japan, by contrast, the automobile industry (and its system of subcontractors) was the main user of machine tools: accordingly, there was a substantial market for machine tools that would provide flexibility in small batch-produced lots. The small size of the batches was encouraged by just-in-time production requirements imposed by the automobile companies. Japanese machine tool producers (together with firms such as Fanuc, which developed microprocessor-based CNC control systems and servomechanisms) devised CNC machine tools to meet this market. These proved to be suited to parts of the US market particularly in the engineering sector, where there was also a demand for flexible equipment suited to batch production. Accordingly, the Japanese CNC machine tool export drive in the US in the mid-1970s was very successful. By 1981, the Japanese had captured about half of the US CNC machine tool market. This story, however, is not simply one of 'market-pulled' technological evolution. While user requirements played an important role in influencing machine tool characteristics and design, equally important was the development of microprocessor technology by firms such as Fujitsu, Fanuc's parent company. This case illustrates the sophistication with which simple concepts, models and 'feedback loops' have to be deployed if the analysis is to do justice to the reality.

ROBOTICS

Fleck's work on robotics provides examples of all four kinds of processes at work shaping technology.

First, a case of type 1, where social factors influenced selection between available technical possibilities. In the early days of robotics, the programming interface at the development stage would be a standard computer console. However, up to the very early 1980s, such consoles were not acceptable on the shop floor: it was feared that they would cause demand for pay premiums because of the 'white-collar' functions involved; because the keyboard skills were not held by the workforce at that time; and because the consoles were seen as too complex for people to be trained in their use. As a result, the designers explicitly designed hand-held keypads for programming the robots, similar to the existing pads used for controlling other machinery on the shop floor, thus avoiding some of the perceived problems. However, once microcomputers became cheaper and quite widespread (often through the use of home hobbyist computers), these problems of acceptability diminished, and many robots now have the conventional computer console as standard [8].

A second case illustrates type 2, where social factors permitted only one area of 'possible' technological development to be pursued. With the initial development of robotics, it was widely expected that a single anthropomorphic machine could be developed able to perform all functions carried out by human workers, but relatively cheaply because of the large volumes in which it could be produced and sold (by analogy with the mass production of the motor car). But as the field of robotics has developed, expertise in the design of the physical components has progressed to such an extent that the production of quite different physical configurations has become relatively straightforward – and, consequently, relatively cheap in terms of time and personnel effort. In contrast, rapid developments in computer capability have opened up scope for greater sophistication, and made feasible larger scale integration of processes. At the same time, social dynamics have ensured a relatively slow growth in the availability of software expertise, with the result that software development currently requires very much more time and effort than robotics hardware development. Consequently, robotics suppliers now offer large families of quite different physical configurations, each one specifically designed for particular applications, with some measure of common software – quite a different situation from the originally-envisaged 'universal automaton', or general purpose robot.

A third case illustrates type 3, where social factors create particular 'selection environments' that shape technical development. In PhD work co-supervised by Fleck, P.R. Drayson has carried out a set of workplace surveys preparatory to the actual introduction of robots in a particular firm (Trebor). Drayson examined not only obvious sociopsychological factors (such as boredom and the perceived undesirability of certain tasks), but also apparently 'purely technical' factors – such as, for example, whether the work activities were sufficiently simple for robotisation to be feasible. Even these latter turn out to be in large part social, since patterns of work activity are the result of longterm negotiations between workforces and management. The set of surveys then enabled the selection of workplaces where robotisation would be feasible in terms of social desirability, workforce acceptability, technical 'do-ability', and economic viability. This in turn enabled the matching of company requirements with the range of available robot models. The result was, somewhat surprisingly, that no currently available robot model was fully adequate: Drayson therefore went on to derive specifications for the design of two different robot configurations which would meet the requirements for two different broad categories of application within the company. He also articulated the experience of implementing a robot system through to actual production use [9], in a framework which explicitly included organisational and economic as well as technical factors, to produce practical guidelines for robot implementation. In all this, Drayson was both observing and creating a case of type 3: he was mediating the influence of a 'selection environment' on the specific design of a technology.

Finally, Fleck's experience of computer systems and artificial intelligence provides several instances of influences of type 4, where social models are explicitly embodied in technology. This form of shaping is of particular relevance to information and communication technologies, because of the essentially social nature of information and communication. An example is the many cases where patterns of modularization and hierarchical control in computer networks in companies are designed to follow the pre-existing departmental structure and control philosophy of the organisation. Somewhat harder to evaluate, but of significance nevertheless, is the subtler use of metaphors drawn from the social in-fields such as artificial intelligence. For instance, some practitioners talk about 'committees of experts conferring over decisions' to describe the manner in which their programs work. Often, it is interesting to note, such metaphors 'die' – the sense in which they are 'metaphorical' is forgotten, and they become used unselfconsciously as literal descriptions. The term 'computer' itself, of course, is a 'dead' metaphor, which originally referred to people who worked out figures [10].

SOME FINAL REFLECTIONS: SOCIAL SHAPING RESEARCH AND TECHNOLOGY POLICY

The purpose of this paper has been to flesh out what is meant by 'the social shaping of technology', and by the claim that it can, and should, be explored. Some available studies have been summarised: possible models, concepts, approaches and classifications have been described and discussed. It is clear that any research agenda must contain, not only a range of specific projects, at a variety of 'levels', but also a programme aimed at the *integration* of the emerging analyses. The complexity of the process under study demands not only the melding of research at several 'levels' (notably 'macro' and 'micro' studies), but also a realistic response to the challenge of the 'recursive' nature of the process, sensitively allowing for the many 'feedback loops', and transcending some of the cruder categories ('cause' and 'effect'; 'market forces' and 'state intervention'; 'technology-push' and 'market-pull'; and so on).

These are not just 'academic' theoretical and methodological issues: as Drayson's experience illustrates, they involve intensely practical concerns, often with vital policy implications [11]. The social *effects* of technical change are of obvious policy interest – for example, the effects of new information technology on employment. But, more fundamentally, if research is restricted to questions of effects, it can contribute only to what may be called '*reactive*' policy measures designed to cope with, or adapt to, the consequences of technical change, rather than anticipating (and so influencing) these consequences. Even in the reactive mode, policy would probably best be improved by discarding the product-cycle model, which has been overinfluential in recent British information technology policy, and which has many of the characteristics of an inappropriately-extended metaphor. At the very least, if the model is to be retained, *all* boxes and *all* 'feedback loops' must be kept in mind. If the temptation for social scientists is to concentrate exclusively on the two boxes to the right of the diagram, the temptation for technologists is to concentrate exclusively on the two boxes on the left. *Practically successful technology*, no less than intellectually successful socioeconomic studies of technology, *has to consider all the boxes and the connecting feedback loops*. Indeed, MacKenzie (1987) has noted a rough correlation between the worldly success of the engineers he was interviewing and their degree of articulate awareness of the importance of the boxes in the middle and on the right hand side, and of the feedback from them into invention and design. Those who concentrated on nuts-and-bolts, wires-and-equations engineering were often those of whom their colleagues would say : 'X designed a brilliant so-and-so, but somehow it never caught on, nobody took it up'. The engineers whose projects 'took off' were those who, whatever opinions they might have had abstractly about the social sciences, were good practical social scientists!

This experience highlights the inadequacy of a purely reactive policy, and neither governments nor private organisations have been content with such policies: they also seek to shape technological change, to pursue a '*pro-active*' technology policy. This is most obvious in companies which foster technological innovation as a primary concern. But it is also clear for governments. Some, most notably Japan, attempt to develop coherent, centralised policies to shape technological change, such as the Japanese 'Fifth Generation' programme in information technology. Even governments with a greater avowed commitment to *laissez – faire* have felt obliged to embark on major state-sponsored programmes in this area: the UK Alvey Programme, the European ESPRIT and EUREKA initiatives, the US Strategic Computing Plan. We would contend that active technology policy, at both the corporate and governmental levels, could and should interact fruitfully with research on the social shaping of technology. Knowing more about the processes by which technical change is shaped could be invaluable to those who are seeking to foster and guide that change. Conversely, government programmes such as Alvey, the Fifth Generation programme, ESPRIT and the Strategic Computing plan, are in the nature of experiments from which the 'shaping' researcher can learn.

To return to our boxes and feedback loops, the bearing of our discussion of this model upon policy becomes clear when we reflect that, stereotypically at least, the distinction between MacKenzie's 'unsuccessful' and 'successful' engineers corresponds to typical differences between the UK and Japan. In the information and communication technologies field, the UK is very strong in the generation of new technological knowledge (i.e. the left-hand box). There is, for example, no obvious Japanese rival to the Edinburgh group in Artificial Intelligence. But moving to the development and design of workable products and systems, the UK is definitely in a more difficult position – though with some marked strengths, such as the software industry. It is when we move to the boxes further to the right, and particularly to the question of the attention given to the feedback loops from

27

those boxes into the generation of new knowledge, development and design, that Japan's strengths become apparent. To take but one example: the achievements of the Japanese NC and CNC machine tool industry (and the robotics industry) owe a great deal to the effort undertaken to find out what was going to be necessary for the successful use of such machine tools and robots – not just in large sophisticated companies, but also in smaller firms.

How, then, might Britain's performance be improved in this respect? How can we increase attention to the entry into use, and more widespread adoption, of new technologies, and to strengthen the influence of the exigencies of these processes on the generation of new 'basic' knowledge, and the development and design of new products? Exhortations to 'do better', or to be 'more like the Japanese', are simply not going to be enough. For, typically, the different types of knowledge involved in the different phases of the product-cycle model are possessed by different types of people, and there is a hierarchy of prestige that rises as we move from right to left across our diagram. 'Basic research' is more prestigious than development and design, and both are more prestigious than the mundane – but commercially crucial – tasks of implementation, marketing, distribution, maintenance and repair. All these involve technological knowledge, but it is knowledge our culture typically devalues.

So here again the product-cycle critique leads us to the same insistent conclusion: the intimate interweaving of the 'technological' and the 'social' is a practical, policy matter, as well as an engrossing intellectual challenge. Whether the product-cycle model, as it stands, can lead us to satisfactory policy guidance is more questionable. It is here that the insights of a 'social shaping' approach are likely to be crucial. Were it not for the negative connotations of the phrase, one might say that 'social engineering' – in the sense of ensuring the right conditions for the possessors of all the different types of knowledge to work productively together – is as crucial as 'engineering' (in the ordinary sense) in getting technological change to happen, and in reaping its potential benefits. Successful engineers, experience suggests, know this as a matter of commonsense wisdom: social scientists' theoretical understandings of technological change should not lag too far behind them!

NOTES

1   For a discussion of these two aspects of technological determinism, see MacKenzie (1984a); for a more general discussion of the topic, see Winner (1977).

2   For a sample of this evidence, see MacKenzie and Wajcman (1985). Our discussions at Edinburgh have persistently led us to the conclusion that both socioeconomic and scientific/technological factors have to be considered in explaining changes in information and communication technologies: see, e.g., Fleck (1982), Fleck and White (1987), Fransman

(1986), MacKenzie (1986). For a collection of more recent studies, see Bijker, Hughes and Pinch (1987).

3 For a full discussion and bibliographies, see Fransman (1985a, 1985b) and MacKenzie and Wajcman (1985).

4 For 'trajectories', see Dosi (1982); for 'imperatives', see Winner (1977). For the origins and significance of such metaphors, see note 10, below.

5 That is to say, it is not only 'bad', 'ideological' scientific knowledge that is socially shaped (as many scientists would claim), but *all* knowledge.

6 The analysis presented here has been disputed by Woolgar (1981a) and Yearley (1982). For replies and debate, see MacKenzie (1981b and 1984b), Barnes (1981) and Woolgar (1981b). Our reading is that the criticisms raised have not damaged the analysis presented here.

7 For Lovell's decision, see Edge and Mulkay (1976), 324-25. Work on scientific instrumentation forms an important and explicit bridge between studies of science and of technology: see Galison (1985, 1987). For an historical illustration of the way in which a focus on instrumentation can advance the kind of analysis advocated in this paper, see Shapin and Schaffer (1985).

8 Keyboard or console design appears to be an area where socioeconomic shaping is particularly evident. The continuing dominance of the QWERTY layout (with its origins in the need to avoid jamming in mechanical typewriters) over the faster, more efficient DVORAK layout, indicates how the weight of social 'investment' in a particular design may cause it to live on far beyond the circumstances that gave rise to it. Similarly, the decision in the printing industry on whether to design computer typesetting keyboards with QWERTY or with the compositors' traditional 90-key layout is closely interwoven with the socioeconomic issue of the relative roles of the traditional male craftworkers or women with secretarial training in newspaper production. On this latter issue, and for reflections on the role of gender in shaping technological change, see Cockburn (1983).

9 Drayson was responsible for the development and introduction of a robotised jar-capping line.

10 The use of metaphors drawn from social life is, of course, widespread in science, especially in biological sciences such as evolutionary theory and neurophysiology: for one clear and entertaining example, see Miller (1972). Many such metaphors arise from experience with technology: for a discussion of the significance of such 'technological metaphor', and for further references to the literature in this area, see Edge (1974-75).

11 'Policy', in this context, refers not simply to governmental decision-making, but also to the actions of companies and other non-governmental bodies (Melody, 1985).

REFERENCES

Barnes, B. (1974) *Scientific Knowledge and Sociological Theory*, London, Routledge and Kegan Paul.

Barnes, B. (1981) 'On the Hows and Whys of Cultural Change', *Social Studies of Science*, 11, pp. 481-98.

Bijker, W.E., Hughes, T.P. and Pinch, T. J. (eds) (1987) *The Social Construction of Technological Systems: New Directions in the Sociology and History of Technology*, London and Cambridge, MA, MIT Press.

Bloor, D. (1976) *Knowledge and Social Imagery*, London, Routledge and Kegan Paul.

Caro, R.A. (1974) *The Power Broker: Robert Moses and the fall of New York*, New York, Pandom House.

Cockburn, C. (1983) *Brothers: Male Dominance and Technological Change*, London, Pluto.

Dosi, G. (l982) 'Technological paradigms and technological trajectories: a suggested interpretation of the determinants of technical change', *Research Policy*, 11, pp. 147-62.

Edge, D.O. (1974-75) 'Technological metaphor and social control', *New Literary History*, 6, pp. 135-47.

Edge, D.O. and Mulkay, M.J. (1976) *Astronomy Transformed: The Emergernce of Radio Astronomy in Britain*, New York and London, Wiley Interscience.

Fleck, J. (1982) 'Development and establishment in artificial intelligence', in N. Elias *et al.* (eds), *Scientific Establishments and Hierarchies*, Dordrecht: Reidel, *Sociology of the Sciences*, Volume VI, pp. 169-217.

Fleck, J. and White, B. (1987) 'National policies and patterns of robot diffusion: United Kingdom, Japan, Sweden and the United States', *Robotics*, 3, 1, pp. 7- 22.

Fransman, M. (1985a) 'Conceptualising technical change in the Third World in the 1980s: an interpretive survey', *Journal of Development Studies*, 21, pp. 572-652.

Fransman, M. (1985b) 'A biological approach to new technological knowledge', background paper for ESRC Industry and Employment Committee Initiative in New Technology.

Fransman, M. (ed.) (1986) *Machinery and Economic Development*, London, Macmillan.

Galison, P. (1985) 'Bubble chambers and the experimental workplace', in P. Achinstein and O. Hannaway (eds), *Observation, Experiment and Hypothesis in Modern Physical Science*, London and Cambridge, MA: MIT Press, pp. 309-73.

Galison, P. (1987) 'Bubbles, sparks and the post-war laboratory', in L. Brown, M. Dresden and L. Hoddeson (eds), *Elementary Particle Physics in the 1950s*, Cambridge: Cambridge University Press.

Gershuny, J. (1983) *Social Innovation and the Division of Labour*, Oxford, Oxford University Press.

Griliches, Z. (1957) 'Hybrid corn: an exploration in the economics of technological change', *Econometrics*, 25, pp. 501-22.

Griliches, Z. (1960) 'Hybrid corn and the economics of innovation', *Science*, 132, 29 July, pp. 275-80.

Hounshell, D. A. (1984) *From the American System to Mass Production 1900-1932: The Development of Manufacturing Technology in the United States*, Baltimore, MD, Johns Hopkins University Press.

Hughes, T.P. (1983) *Networks of Power: Electrification in Western Society, 1880-1930*, Baltimore, MD, Johns Hopkins University Press.

Hughes, T.P. (1985) 'Edison and electric light', in MacKenzie and Wajcman (1985), pp. 39-52.

MacKenzie, D. (1978) 'Statistical theory and social interests: a case study', *Social Studies of Science*, 8, pp. 35-83.

MacKenzie, D. (1981a) *Statistics in Britain, 1865-1930: The Social Construction of Scientific Knowledge*, Edinburgh, Edinburgh University Press.

MacKenzie, D. (1981b) 'Interests, positivism and history', *Social Studies of Science*, 11, pp. 498-504.

MacKenzie, D. (1984a) 'Marx and the machine', *Technology and Culture*, 25, pp. 473-502.

MacKenzie, D. (1984b) 'Reply to Steven Yearley', *Studies in History and Philosophy of Science*, 15, pp. 251-59.

MacKenzie, D. (1986) 'Why "The Social Aspects of Science and Technology" is not just an Optional Extra', *ACM Computers and Society*, 15, pp. 2-6.

MacKenzie, D. (1987) 'Missile accuracy: a case study in the social processes of technological change', in Bijker, Hughes and Pinch (1987), pp. 195-222.

MacKenzie, D. and Wajcman, J. (eds) (1985) *The Social Shaping of Technology*, Milton Keynes, Bucks., Open University Press.

Melody, W. (1985) 'Implications of the information and communication technologies: the role of policy research', *Policy Studies*, 6.

Miller, J. (1972) 'The Dog Beneath the Skin', *The Listener*, (20 July),pp. 74-76.

Noble, D. F. (1984) Forces of Production: *A Social History of Industrial Automation*, New York, Knopf.

Pinch, T. J. and Bijker, W. E. (1984) 'The social construction of facts and artefacts: or how the sociology of science and the sociology of technology might benefit each other', *Social Studies of Science*, 14, pp. 399-441.

Powell, W. W. (1987) 'Review essay: explaining technological change', *American Journal of Sociology*, 93, 1 July, pp. 185-97.

Shaiken, H. (1986) *Work Transformed: Automation and Labor in the Computer Age*, New York, Holt, Rinehart and Winston.

Shapin, S. (1982) 'History of science and its sociological reconstructions', *History of Science*, 20, pp. 157-211.

Shapin, S. and Schaffer, S. (1985) *Leviathan and the Air-Pump: Hobbes, Boyle, and the Experimental Life*, Princeton, NJ, Princeton University Press.

Winner, L. (1977) *Autonomous Technology: Technics-out-of-Control as a Theme in Political Thoughtt*, London and Cambridge, MA, MIT Press.

Winner, L. (1980) 'Do artifacts have politics?', *Daedalus*, 109, pp. 121-36. Also in MacKenzie and Wajcman (1985), pp. 26-38.

Woolgar, S. (1981a) 'Interests and explanations in the social study of science', *Social Studies of Science*, 11, pp. 365-94.

Woolgar, S. (1981b) 'Critique and criticism : two readings of ethnomethodology', *Social Studies of Science*, 11, pp. 504-14.

Yearley, S. (1982) 'The relationship between epistemological and sociological cognitive interests: some ambiguities underlying the use of interest theory in the study of scientific knowledge', *Studies in History and Philosophy of Science*, 13, pp. 353-88.

THE HACKER CRACKDOWN: EVOLUTION OF THE US TELEPHONE NETWORK

Bruce Sterling

[...]

Technologies have life cycles, like cities do, like institutions do, like laws and governments do.

The first stage of any technology is the Question Mark, often known as the 'Golden Vaporware' stage. At this early point, the technology is only a phantom, a mere gleam in the inventor's eye. One such inventor was a speech teacher and electrical tinkerer named Alexander Graham Bell.

Bell's early inventions, while ingenious, failed to move the world. In 1863, the teenage Bell and his brother Melville made an artificial talking mechanism out of wood, rubber, gutta-percha, and tin. This weird device had a rubber-covered 'tongue' made of movable wooden segments, with vibrating rubber 'vocal cords', and rubber 'lips' and 'cheeks'. While Melville puffed a bellows into a tin tube, imitating the lungs, young Alec Bell would manipulate the 'lips', 'teeth', and 'tongue', causing the thing to emit high-pitched falsetto gibberish.

Another would-be technical breakthrough was the Bell 'phon-autograph' of 1874, actually made out of a human cadaver's ear. Clamped into place on a tripod, this grisly gadget drew sound-wave images on smoked glass through a thin straw glued to its vibrating earbones.

By 1875, Bell had learned to produce audible sounds – ugly shrieks and squawks – by using magnets, diaphragms, and electrical current.

Most 'Golden Vaporware' technologies go nowhere. But the second stage of technology is the Rising Star, or the 'Goofy Prototype' stage. The telephone, Bell's most ambitious gadget yet, reached this stage on March 10, 1876. On that great day, Alexander Graham Bell became the first person to transmit intelligible human speech electrically. As it happened, young Professor Bell, industriously tinkering in his Boston lab, had spattered his trousers with acid. His assistant, Mr Watson, heard his cry for help – over Bell's experimental audio-telegraph. This was an event without precedent.

Technologies in their 'Goofy Prototype' stage rarely work very well. They're experimental, and therefore half-baked and rather frazzled. The prototype may be attractive and novel, and it does look as if it ought to be good for something – or – other. But nobody, including the inventor, is quite sure what. Inventors, speculators and pundits may have very firm ideas about its potential use, but those ideas are often very wrong.

The natural habitat of the Goofy Prototype is in trade shows and in the popular press. Infant technologies need publicity and investment money like a tottering calf needs milk. This was very true of Bell's machine. To raise research and development money, Bell toured with his device as a stage attraction.

Contemporary press reports of the stage debut of the telephone showed pleased astonishment mixed with considerable dread. Bell's stage telephone was a large wooden box with a crude speaker-nozzle, the whole contraption about the size and shape of an overgrown Brownie camera. Its buzzing steel soundplate, pumped up by powerful electromagnets, was loud enough to fill an auditorium. Bell's assistant Mr Watson, who could manage on the keyboards fairly well, kicked in by playing the organ from distant rooms, and, later, distant cities. This feat was considered marvellous, but very eerie indeed.

Bell's original notion for the telephone, an idea promoted for a couple of years, was that it would become a mass medium. We might recognize Bell's idea today as something close to modern 'cable radio'. Telephones at a central source would transmit music, Sunday sermons, and important public speeches to a paying network of wired-up subscribers.

At the time, most people thought this notion made good sense. In fact, Bell's idea was workable. In Hungary, this philosophy of the telephone was successfully put into everyday practice. In Budapest, for decades, from 1893 until after World War I, there was a government-run information service called 'Telefon Hirmondó'. Hirmondó was a centralized source of news, entertainment and culture, including stock reports, plays, concerts and novels read aloud. At certain hours of the day, the phone would ring, you would plug in a loudspeaker for the use of the family, and Telefon Hirmondó would be on the air – or rather, on the phone.

Hirmondó is dead tech today, but Hirmondó might be considered a spiritual ancestor of the modern telephone-accessed computer data services, such as CompuServe, GEnie or Prodigy. The principle behind Hirmondó is also not too far from computer 'bulletin-board systems' or BBS's, which arrived in the late 1970s, spread rapidly across America, [...].

We are used to using telephones for individual person-to-person speech, because we are used to the Bell system. But this was just one possibility among many. Communication networks are very flexible and protean, especially when their hardware becomes sufficiently advanced. They can be put to all kinds of uses. And they have been –and they will be.

Bell's telephone was bound for glory, but this was a combination of political decisions, canny in-fighting in court, inspired industrial leadership, receptive local conditions and outright good luck. Much the same is true of communications systems today.

As Bell and his backers struggled to install their newfangled system in the real world of nineteenth-century New England, they had to fight against skepticism and industrial rivalry. There was already a strong electrical communications network present in America: the telegraph. The head of the Western Union telegraph system dismissed Bell's prototype as 'an electrical toy' and refused to buy the rights to Bell's patent. The telephone, it seemed, might be all right as a parlor entertainment – but not for serious business.

Telegrams, unlike mere telephones, left a permanent physical record of their messages. Telegrams, unlike telephones, could be answered whenever the recipient had time and convenience. And the telegram had a much longer distance-range than Bell's early telephone. These factors made telegraphy seem a much more sound and businesslike technology – at least to some.

The telegraph system was huge, and well-entrenched. In 1876, the United States had 214,000 miles of telegraph wire, and 8,500 telegraph offices. There were specialized telegraphs for businesses and stock traders, government, police and fire departments. And Bell's 'toy' was best known as a stage-magic musical device.

The third stage of technology is known as the 'Cash Cow' stage. In the 'cash cow' stage, a technology finds its place in the world, matures and becomes settled and productive. After a year or so, Alexander Graham Bell and his capitalist backers concluded that eerie music piped from nineteenth-century cyberspace was not the real selling-point of his invention. Instead, the telephone was about speech – individual, personal speech, the human voice, human conversation and human interaction. The telephone was not to be managed from any centralized broadcast centre. It was to be a personal, intimate technology.

When you picked up a telephone, you were not absorbing the cold output of a machine – you were speaking to another human being. Once people realized this, their instinctive dread of the telephone as an eerie, unnatural device, swiftly vanished. A 'telephone call' was not a 'call' from a 'telephone' itself, but a call from another human being, someone you would generally know and recognize. The real point was not what the machine could do for you (or to you), but what you yourself, a person and citizen, could do *through* the machine. This decision on the part of the young Bell Company was absolutely vital.

The first telephone networks went up around Boston – mostly among the technically curious and the well-to-do (much the same segment of the American populace that, a hundred years later, would be buying personal computers). Entrenched backers of the telegraph continued to scoff.

But in January 1878, a disaster made the telephone famous. A train crashed in Tarriffville, Connecticut. Forward-looking doctors in the nearby city of Hartford had had Bell's 'speaking telephone' installed. An alert local druggist was able to telephone an entire community of local doctors, who rushed to the site to give aid. The disaster, as disasters do, aroused intense press coverage. The phone had proven its usefulness in the real world.

After Tarriffville, the telephone network spread like crabgrass. By 1890 it was all over New England. By 1893, out to Chicago. By 1897, into Minnesota, Nebraska and Texas. By 1904 it was all over the continent.

The telephone had become a mature technology. Professor Bell (now generally known as 'Dr Bell' despite his lack of a formal degree) became quite wealthy. He lost interest in the tedious day-to-day business muddle of the booming telephone network, and gratefully returned his attention to creatively hacking-around in his various laboratories, which were now much larger, better-ventilated, and gratifyingly better-equipped. Bell was never to have another great inventive success, though his speculations and prototypes anticipated fiber-optic transmission, manned flight, sonar, hydrofoil ships, tetrahedral construction, and Montessori education. The 'decibel', the standard scientific measure of sound intensity, was named after Bell.

Not all Bell's vaporware notions were inspired. He was fascinated by human eugenics. He also spent many years developing a weird personal system of astrophysics in which gravity did not exist.

Bell was a definite eccentric. He was something of a hypochondriac, and throughout his life he habitually stayed up until 4 am, refusing to rise before noon. But Bell had accomplished a great feat; he was an idol of millions and his influence, wealth, and great personal charm, combined with his eccentricity, made him something of a loose cannon on deck. Bell maintained a thriving scientific salon in his winter mansion in Washington, D.C., which gave him considerable backstage influence in governmental and scientific circles. He was a major financial backer of the the magazines *Science* and *National Geographic*, both still flourishing today as important organs of the American scientific establishment.

There would never be another Alexander Graham Bell, but in years to come there would be surprising numbers of people like him. Bell was a prototype of the high-tech entrepreneur. High-tech entrepreneurs [...] play a very prominent role [...]: not merely as technicians and businessmen, but as pioneers of the technical frontier, who can carry the power and prestige they derive from high-technology into the political and social arena.

Like later entrepreneurs, Bell was fierce in defense of his own technological territory. As the telephone began to flourish, Bell was soon involved in violent lawsuits in the defense of his patents. Bell's Boston lawyers were excellent, however, and Bell himself, as an elecution teacher and gifted public speaker, was a devastatingly effective legal witness. In the eighteen years of Bell's patents, the Bell company was involved in 600 separate lawsuits. The legal records printed filled 149 volumes. The Bell Company won every single suit.

After Bell's exclusive patents expired, rival telephone companies sprang up all over America. Bell's company, American Bell Telephone, was soon in deep trouble. In 1907, American Bell Telephone fell into the hands of the rather sinister J.P. Morgan financial cartel, robber-baron speculators who dominated Wall Street.

At this point, history might have taken a different turn. America might well have been served forever by a patchwork of locally owned telephone companies. Many state politicians and local businessmen considered this an excellent solution.

But the new Bell holding company, American Telephone and Telegraph or AT&T, put in a new man at the helm, a visionary industrialist named Theodore Vail. Vail, a former Post Office manager, understood large organizations and had an innate feeling for the nature of large-scale communications. Vail quickly saw to it that AT&T seized the technological edge once again. The Pupin and Campbell 'loading coil', and the deForest 'audion', are both extinct technology today, but in 1913 they gave Vail's company the best *long-distance* lines ever built. By controlling the links between, over and above the smaller local phone companies, long-distance AT&T swiftly gained the whip-hand over them, and was soon devouring them right and left.

Vail ploughed the profits back into research and development, starting the Bell tradition of huge-scale and brilliant industrial research.

Technically and financially, AT&T gradually steamrollered the opposition. Independent telephone companies never became entirely extinct, and hundreds of them flourish today. But Vail's AT&T became the supreme communications company. At one point, Vail's AT&T bought Western Union itself, the very company that had derided Bell's telephone as a 'toy'. Vail thoroughly reformed Western Union's hidebound business along his modern principles; but when the federal government grew anxious at this centralization of power, Vail politely gave Western Union back.

This centralizing process was not unique. Very similar events had happened in American steel, oil, and railroads. But AT&T, unlike the other companies, was to remain supreme. The monopoly robber-barons of those other industries were humbled and shattered by government trust-busting.

Vail, the former Post Office official, was quite willing to accommodate the US government; in fact he would forge an active alliance with it. AT&T would become almost a wing of the American government, almost another Post Office – though not quite. AT&T would willingly submit to federal regulation, but in return, it would use the government's regulators as its own police, who would keep out competitors and assure the Bell system's profits and pre-eminence.

This was the second birth – the political birth – of the American telephone system. Vail's arrangement was to persist, with vast success, for many decades, until 1982. His system was an odd kind of American industrial socialism. It was born at about the same time as Leninist Communism, and it lasted almost as long – and, it must be admitted, to considerably better effect.

Vail's system worked. Except perhaps for aerospace, there has been no technology more thoroughly dominated by Americans than the telephone. The telephone was seen from the beginning as a quintessentially American technology. Bell's policy, and the policy of Theodore Vail, was a profoundly democratic policy of *universal access*. Vail's famous corporate slogan, 'One Policy, One System, Universal Service', was a political slogan, with a very American ring to it.

The American telephone was not to become the specialized tool of government or business, but a general public utility. At first, it was true, only the wealthy could afford private telephones, and Bell's company pursued the business markets primarily. The American phone system was a capitalist effort, meant to make money; it was not a charity. But from the first, almost all communities with telephone service had public telephones. And many stores – especially drugstores – offered public use of their phones. You might not own a telephone – but you could always get into the system, if you really needed to.

There was nothing inevitable about this decision to make telephones 'public' and 'universal'. Vail's system involved a profound act of trust in the public. This decision was a political one, informed by the basic values of the American republic. The situation might have been very different; and in other countries, under other systems, it certainly was.

Joseph Stalin, for instance, vetoed plans for a Soviet phone system soon after the Bolshevik revolution. Stalin was certain that publicly accessible telephones would become instruments of anti-Soviet counter-revolution and conspiracy. (He was probably right.) When telephones did arrive in the Soviet Union, they would be instruments of Party authority, and always heavily tapped. (Alexander Solzhenitsyn's prison-camp novel *The First Circle* describes efforts to develop a phone system more suited to Stalinist purposes.)

France, with its tradition of rational centralized government, had fought bitterly even against the electric telegraph, which seemed to the French entirely too anarchical and frivolous. For decades, nineteenth-century France communicated via the 'visual telegraph', a nation-spanning, government-owned semaphore system of huge stone towers that signalled from hilltops, across vast distances, with big windmill-like arms. In 1846, one Dr Barbay, a semaphore enthusiast, memorably uttered an early version of what might be called 'the security expert's argument' against the open media.

> No, the electric telegraph is not a sound invention. It will always be at the mercy of the slightest disruption, wild youths, drunkards, bums, etc.... The electric telegraph meets those destructive elements with only a few meters of wire over which supervision is impossible. A single man could, without being seen, cut the telegraph wires leading to Paris, and in twenty-four hours cut in ten different places the wires of the same line, without being arrested. The visual telegraph, on the contrary, has its towers, its high walls, its gates well-guarded from inside by strong armed men. Yes, I declare, substitution of the electric telegraph for the visual one is a dreadful measure, a truly idiotic act.

Dr Barbay and his high-security stone machines were eventually unsuccessful, but his argument – that communication exists for the safety and convenience of the state, and must be carefully protected from the wild boys and the gutter rabble who might want to crash the system – would be heard again and again.

When the French telephone system finally did arrive, its snarled inadequacy was to be notorious. Devotees of the American Bell System often recommended a trip to France, for skeptics.

In Edwardian Britain, issues of class and privacy were a ball-and-chain for telephonic progress. It was considered outrageous that anyone – any wild fool off the street – could simply barge bellowing into one's office or home, preceded only by the ringing of a telephone bell. In Britain, phones were tolerated for the use of business, but private phones tended to be stuffed away into closets, smoking rooms or servants' quarters. Telephone operators were resented in Britain because they did not seem to 'know their place'. And no one of breeding would print a telephone number on a business card; this seemed a crass attempt to make the acquaintance of strangers.

But phone access in America was to become a popular right; something like universal suffrage, only more so. American women could not yet vote when the phone system came through; yet from the beginning American women doted on the telephone. This 'feminization' of the American telephone was often commented on by foreigners. Phones in America were not censored or stiff or formalized; they were social, private, intimate and domestic. In America, Mother's Day is by far the busiest day of the year for the phone network.

The early telephone companies, and especially AT&T, were among the foremost employers of American women. They employed the daughters of the American middle-class in great armies: in 1891, eight thousand women; by 1946, almost a quarter of a million. Women seemed to enjoy telephone work; it was respectable, it was steady, it paid fairly well as women's work went, and – not least – it seemed a genuine contribution to the social good of the community. Women found Vail's ideal of public service attractive. This was especially true in rural areas, where women operators, running extensive rural party-lines, enjoyed considerable social power. The operator knew everyone on the party-line, and everyone knew her.

Although Bell himself was an ardent suffragist, the telephone company did not employ women for the sake of advancing female liberation. AT&T did this for sound commercial reasons. The first telephone operators of the Bell system were not women, but teenage American boys. They were telegraphic messenger boys (a group about to be rendered technically obsolescent), who swept up around the phone office, dunned customers for bills, and made phone connections on the switchboard, all on the cheap.

Within the very first year of operation, 1878, Bell's company learned a sharp lesson about combining teenage boys and telephone switchboards. Putting teenage boys in charge of the phone system brought swift and consistent disaster. Bell's chief engineer described them as 'Wild Indians'. The boys were openly rude to customers. They talked back to subscribers, saucing off, uttering facetious remarks, and generally giving lip. The rascals took Saint Patrick's Day off without permission. And worst of all they played clever tricks with the switchboard plugs: disconnecting calls, crossing lines so that customers found themselves talking to strangers, and so forth. This combination of power, technical mastery, and effective anonymity seemed to act like catnip on teenage boys.

This wild-kid-on-the-wires phenomenon was not confined to the USA; from the beginning, the same was true of the British phone system. An early British commentator kindly remarked:

> No doubt boys in their teens found the work not a little irksome, and it is also highly probable that under the early conditions of employment the adventurous and inquisitive spirits of which the average healthy boy of that age is possessed, were not always conducive to the best attention being given to the wants of the telephone subscribers.

So the boys were flung off the system – or at least deprived of control of the switchboard. But the 'adventurous and inquisitive spirits' of the teenage boys would be heard from in the world of telephony, again and again.

The fourth stage in the technological life-cycle is death: 'the Dog', dead tech. The telephone has so far avoided this fate. On the contrary, it is thriving, still spreading, still evolving, and at increasing speed.

The telephone has achieved a rare and exalted state for a technological artifact: it has become a *household object*. The telephone, like the clock, like pen and paper, like kitchen utensils and running water, has become a technology that is visible only by its absence. The telephone is technologically transparent. The global telephone system is the largest and most complex machine in the world, yet it is easy to use. More remarkable yet, the telephone is almost entirely physically safe for the user.

For the average citizen in the 1870s, the telephone was weirder, more shocking, more 'high-tech' and harder to comprehend, than the most outrageous stunts of advanced computing for us Americans in the 1990s. In trying to understand what is happening to us today, with our bulletin-board systems, direct overseas dialling, fiber-optic transmissions, computer viruses, hacking stunts, and a vivid tangle of new laws and new crimes, it is important to realize that our society has been through a similar challenge before – and that, all in all, we did rather well by it.

Bell's stage telephone seemed bizarre at first. But the sensations of weirdness vanished quickly, once people began to hear the familiar voices of relatives and friends, in their own homes on their own telephones. The telephone changed from a fearsome high-tech totem to an everyday pillar of human community.

THEORISING THE IT/SOCIETY
RELATIONSHIP [1]

Hughie Mackay
The Open University in Wales

Sociologists have, until recently, tended to avoid technology. This began to change significantly in the late 1980s with the growth and development of both (physical) IT and the (social) debate surrounding it. In a broad sense, sociologists of technology are concerned with explaining how social processes, actions and structures relate to technology; and in this are concerned with developing critiques of notions of technological determinism. The theories and concepts which have been developed are increasingly recognised as of value to technologists, notably in the area of information system design.

Technological determinism is the notion that technological development is autonomous of society; it shapes society, but is not reciprocally influenced. Rather, it exists outside society, but at the same time influences social change. In more extreme varieties of technological determinism, the technology is seen as the most significant determinant of the nature of a society. What is remarkable about the notion of technological determinism is neither its theoretical sophistication nor its explanatory utility. Rather, it is important because it is 'the single most influential theory of the relationship between technology and society' (MacKenzie and Wajcman, 1985, p.4).

The reality, of course, is that technologies do not, in practice, follow some pre-determined course of development. Research and development decisions, for example, are significant determinants of the sorts of technologies which are developed. Also, although technologies clearly have impacts, the nature of these is not built in to the technology, but varies from one culture to another, depending on a broad range of social, political and economic factors.

'Symptomatic technology' is the concept Raymond Williams (1974) employs to explain its inverse – that technology is a *symptom* of social change. According to this model, it is quite clearly society which is in the driving seat of history: given a strong social demand then a suitable technology will be found. Williams, explaining the arrival of television, refers to the twin processes of 'mobilisation' and 'privatisation' which have taken place with the onset of industrial society; these led to a demand for the privatised consumption of leisure, and hence to the development of the television. This is the essence of the social shaping of technology approach, which 'serves as a needed corrective' to technological determinism (Winner, 1985, p.26). Whilst not denying that technologies have social effects, the focus, rather, is on the social forces which give rise to particular technologies. Technologies are social in their origins as well as their effects. Choice and social negotiation are involved in the design process.

Within the sociology of technology there are two broad approaches to the social shaping of technology. I shall discuss each; and then – at rather greater length – introduce some key ideas which lie behind a third body of literature (which neither claims nor carries the label 'sociology of technology'), work in media and cultural studies on the domestic consumption of information and communication technologies. Finally, I shall introduce what I see as the most fruitful direction for research in this area, and refer to a fifth body of work which focuses on the *full life cycle* of a technology, from its development to its later consumption. My argument is that a specific synthesis of these approaches is the most fruitful for understanding technology as a social phenomenon.

The first approach focuses on the micro, and can be seen in terms of three schools: the social constructivist, the systems, and the actor network approach. The social constructivist approach (Bijker *et al* ., 1987), draws on the sociology of scientific knowledge (SSK). According to this, scientific facts are socially constructed, rather than residing in the natural world and awaiting discovery. Applying this approach to technological artefacts, social constructivists have argued that these, too, are socially constructed. Technologies emerge out of processes of choice and negotiation between 'relevant social groups'; other key concepts include 'closure' (the process whereby specific design issues are resolved, and this is agreed or accepted to be so) and 'interpretative flexibility' (the different meanings which various 'relevant social groups' hold of a given artefact) (Pinch and Bijker 1984). The focus is on design and development, which are seen as embodying these social processes, as encompassing the social interests which they represent. Clearly such an approach has vast implications for the design of IT systems.

Thomas Hughes' networks, or systems, approach sees system builders – inventors, engineers, managers and financiers – creating and presiding over technological systems: heterogeneous people, organisations and disciplines become part of a 'seamless web':

> system builders were no respecters of knowledge categories or professional boundaries. In his notebooks, Thomas Edison so thoroughly mixed matters commonly labelled 'economic', 'technical' and 'scientific' that his thoughts composed a seamless web (Hughes, 1986, p.285).

It is argued that Hughes' approach is most suitable for large technological systems – Hughes' work is on the electrification of the United States.

The actor network approach differs from the social constructivist agenda in that it collapses any distinction between the 'technical' and the 'social' – and, for that matter, between these and the 'scientific', the 'economic' or the political' (Callon, 1986; Latour, 1987; Law, 1987). Dropping any distinction between animate and inanimate things and forces, these conventional categories are replaced by the notion of 'actors'

– physical and social – which are involved in the development of technological systems. Technological systems, it is argued, are built by the management, or 'enrolment', of both physical and social actors into networks – using 'heterogeneous engineering', the drawing together of heterogeneous elements (Law, 1987). The primacy of human elements in a socio-technical scenario is rejected; rather, the development of a technology is seen in terms of the relationships formed between human and non-human elements of 'actor networks'.

Second is the neo Marxist approach (Braverman, 1984; Russell, 1986). This argues that technological change cannot be fully understood by reference to individual inventions. Rather, it is argued, we need to examine how broader socio-economic forces affect the nature of technological problems and solutions. For example, the need of management to reduce the cost of labour can influence the decision to invest in a particular line of research and development. This approach criticises the social constructivist approach for ignoring the broader political and economic context within which a technology is developed. Technology is designed, consciously or otherwise, to secure particular social or political objectives. In this vein, the labour process approach looks at how the social relations of workers and management affect the nature of technologies. Braverman identified a long-run tendency towards the degradation, or deskilling, of work in capitalist economies; and subsequent contributors to the debate have provided empirical evidence to both support and refute his arguments. However, technologies are not simply direct translations of economic imperatives into tangible machines and operations. Rather, various groups are involved in the processes of technological innovation; hence the more sophisticated, less reductionist focus of much labour process work – on, for example, managerial strategies (Friedman, 1977), organizational contexts (Child and Smith, 1987), and gender (Crompton and Jones, 1984). Much of this work argues that management has many objectives (for example, quality or labour cost), which will be of particular priority in the design or take-up of a given technology.

Clearly, it is no great leap for the social shaping of technology approach from seeing technology as a social product to seeing it as political. 'Do artifacts have politics?' asks Langdon Winner (1985). Winner distinguishes between technologies which are political in that they are designed to achieve political intent (e.g. Moses' low bridges in New York, designed to keep out blacks, who depended on buses), those which are political without intent (e.g. the design of buildings without access for the disabled), and those technologies which either *require* or are *more compatible with* particular social relations (e.g. nuclear power and the strong state, to guard plutonium). In one sense or another, then, *all* technologies are political.

Winner argues that as a 'corrective' of technological determinism, the social shaping of technology approach 'has its own shortcomings' (1985, p.27). For while the social shaping of technology is opposed to technological determinism, it nevertheless shares with it one fundamental concern. In differing ways, both firmly root their focus on the first sphere of a technology – its conception, invention, development and design. Unlike technological determinism, however, it roots this within a complex of social forces, which not only anchor, but mould the inventing process. The social shaping of technology tends to assume that:

Once one has done the detective work necessary to reveal the social origins – power holders behind a particular instance of technological change – one will have explained everything of importance (Winner, 1985, p.27).

To suggest that once a technology is produced, or even sold, it reaches the end of its social shaping, however, is to ignore both its marketing and how the technology comes to be used or implemented; is it 'finished' once it is made? For example, who *does* 'produce' software? Software is malleable through its entire life, through the processes of customisation, modification and maintenance; is the producer the original developer, or the purchaser who customises it, or the software house which maintains it? The reality is that that most technologies never stabilise in the way which so many sociology of technology accounts suggest [2].

A focus on the socially shaped development and production of technology is incomplete because it fails to consider the social forces at work on the other side of the technology: the way that technologies come to be actively appropriated by their users. People are not merely malleable subjects who submit to the dictates of a technology: in their consumption they are not the passive dupes suggested by crude theorists of consumption, but active, creative and expressive subjects.

People may reject technologies, redefine their functional purpose, customize or even invest idiosyncratic symbolic meanings in them. Indeed they may redefine a technology in a way that defies its original, designed and intended purpose. Thus the appropriation of technology is an integral part of its social shaping.

> ...close inspection of technological development reveals that technology leads a double life, one which conforms to the intentions of designers and interests of power and another which contradicts them – proceeding behind the backs of their architects to yield unintended consequences and unanticipated possibilities (Noble, 1984, p.325).

However, the appropriation of a technology cannot be entirely separated from its design and development: technologies are designed for particular purposes. 'Technologies can be designed... to open certain options and close others' (MacKenzie and Wajcman, 1985, p.7). Such options and limitations of use are defined at one level by 'the material, technical possibilities of the object' (Goodall, 1983).

There is a third body of literature which seems to go some way in correcting the limitation of much of the sociology with its concern on the initial stage. Developed in the field of media and cultural studies, and making little reference to the 'social shaping of technology' literature, this is concerned with consumption. If added to the 'social shaping' approach, it allows us the possibility of a more extended account of how technology is social. This work draws on some of the insights that Stuart Hall (1980) and David Morley (1992) have developed in cultural and media studies. Design and development processes may encode preferred forms of deployment in a technology (via its technical possibilities), which are reinforced through marketing. It is in this semiological sense that one might propose that a technology is a form of text.

The way in which a technology is deployed is also determined by its users: this use is not inevitable, built in to the technology, or fixed. 'A new device merely opens a door: it does not compel one to enter' (White, 1978, p.28). Technologies facilitate, they do not determine; and they may be used in a variety of ways. In short, there is a crucial role for the decoder of the text (Hall, 1980). The subjective, social appropriation of a technology is thus a crucial force in the social shaping of technology – one which cannot be 'read off' from either the physical technology or the social forces behind its development.

One can consider any number of instances of technologies which are used for purposes which differ from the intentions of their designers or marketers: home personal computer use has ended up being largely for non-utilitarian purposes (Haddon, 1988; Turkle, 1984): early cassette recorders were intended to be used for playing pre-recorded tapes, but were generally used for recording from records; scratch music involves moving a record deck backwards and forwards at discos; video is used to make films as well as to watch them at home, and even within the home, use goes beyond the designers' intentions in that video is used predominantly to 'time shift' television (Keen, 1987); the Chinese invented gunpowder, but used it only for fireworks; and invented the watchtower, but to watch for the approach of dignitaries so that a proper welcome could be arranged, not to guard prisoners; and the electric telegraph was seen by its inventor in 1787 as useful for besieged towns or distant lovers (Ascherson, 1987). In sum, the character of a technology is complex and contradictory; technology leads a 'double life', or has 'dual effects' (Keen, 1987; Pool, 1976).

Nevertheless, the range of choice in the deployment of technologies is not limitless; our analysis needs to strike some sort of balance, of freedom within constraint, as Featherstone argues; he seeks to develop a perspective which goes beyond

> the view that lifestyle and consumption are totally manipulated products of a mass society, and the opposite position which seeks to preserve the field of lifestyles and consumption ... as an autonomous playful space beyond determination (1987, p.56).

Some technologies are more 'open' than others, more amenable to being used for a range of purposes. A mortar bomb, for example, might conceivably be used as a door stop, but for little more than its intended purpose; whereas a hammer can be used to kill someone, to bang nails into wood, or to mend a car. The PC is a remarkably 'open' technology, in that it can be used for leisure (playing games), education, typing, process control and military purposes, to name but a few uses. The relative 'openess' or 'closure' of a technology will also depend on its interaction with other technologies – for instance in the form of software: a walkman can only play tapes, but these might be radical, traditional, educational, or whatever.

Hall (1980) argues that TV texts are all, to some extent, polysemic: there are always several possible readings of the text. Polysemy, of course, does not mean a pluralist diversity without constraint: there always exists a 'preferred reading'. Morley has discussed how the meaning (of television content) is both structured and open to interpretation:

> The TV message is treated as a complex sign, in which a preferred meaning has been inscribed, but which retains the potential, if decoded in a manner different from the way in which it has been encoded, of communicating a different meaning. The message is thus a structured polysemy. It is central to the argument that all meanings do not exist 'equally' in the message: it has been structured in dominance, although its meanings can never be totally fixed or 'closed' (1980, p.10).

Morley and others accommodate a recognition of the active role of the user of a given technology. The subjective, social appropriation of a technology is thus one key element of a technology – not just how it is used, but the meaning that use has for the user: a technology is not merely a physical object, it carries meanings.

Consumption is of more than use values (which is not to say that it has no utility). Commodities are signs and, as Fredric Jameson argues, 'no society has ever been saturated with signs and images like this one' (1981, p.131). Consumption has come to be about using commodities to express taste and status differences. Contemporary, postmodern, consumer culture thus stands in contrast to mass consumption. We can see such a shift reflected in advertising, which has changed from product information to advertisements which incorporate looser, lifestyle imagery (Leiss, 1983). Miller is a key writer on the symbolic nature of consumption.

> Although functional purpose must impose a certain constraint on the shape and form of an object, that constraint is generally a very loose one for everyday forms (though obviously not for machine parts) (1987, p.116).

He gives the example of the enormous variety of shapes of glass bottles in an off-licence, and argues that there is very little relationship between form and fitness for function.

Douglas and Isherwood take a similar approach. They examine goods in terms of their symbolic or expressive function: goods are used to make 'visible and stable the categories of culture' (1978, p.59). They stress the non-utilitarian character of consumption, examining goods in terms of their expressive, symbolic and orientational function in social life.

> Goods in their assemblage present a set of meanings, more or less coherent, more or less intentional. They are read by those who know the code and scan them for information (1978, p.5).

Choice, and the display of the products of choice, are primary mechanisms for the assertion of identity, as statements about the self; consumption is an activity of self expression, and is concerned with the production of identity. It is a cultural activity, not merely an economic affair. All consumption, then, involves the consumption of meanings; indeed, it involves the production of meanings by the consumer (Featherstone, 1991).

It would seem that there is less scope for a variety of forms of appropriation in work than in the domestic sphere. In the former, users are generally told to use particular technologies, and in particular ways. Even within work, however, there may be possibilities for the subjective appropriation of technologies. At home, however, there is far greater choice – starting with whether or not one buys the product in the first place. The idea, however, is not applicable *only* to the domestic arena. In the work environment, the symbolic value of a technology can be as crucial as its functional attributes; and can be used by management as a part of its management of meaning.

There is work in media and cultural studies which focuses on the domestic consumption of information and communication technologies – on video (Gray, 1987), early radio (Moores, 1988), home computers (Haddon, 1988b; Turkle, 1984) and a range of information and communication technologies in the home (Silverstone and Hirsch, 1992). The use and meaning of information and communication technologies in the home, it is argued, can only be understood within the class, gendered, geographical and generational context of its consumption.

This work seems to me to complement the traditional focus of the 'social shaping of technology' approach, in terms of both a repertoire of concepts and a concern with consumption. By joining the two, we have a more extended version of how technology is socially shaped. I would argue that it is useful to see technology not solely as a process of design, but as a product of three conceptually distinct spheres:

1 conception, invention, development and design;

2 marketing; and

3 appropriation by users.

Such a characterisation is congruent with Richard Johnson's seminal paper (1983) on the nature of cultural studies, in which he stresses the inter-relatedness of the two spheres of production and consumption. I shall discuss each of these three spheres briefly.

Through the notion of encoding we can extend our understanding of social shaping at the first stage in the life of a technology. Technologies are encoded with preferred forms of use, with or without necessary intentionality on the part of producers. Function is not the only medium by which technology may be encoded to advance particular objectives; it may also be encoded symbolically. Any technology is symbolic as well as functional.

Adrian Forty's discussion of the design of contemporary electric shavers illustrates the symbolic encoding of (politics into) a technology (1986, p.63-66). Forty investigates the 1980 range of Phillips shavers and explores the contrasting design of those shavers designed for men and those for women. The Ladyshave (as it is called) is pink, round and decorated with a floral motif; the male shaver, in contrast, is black, angular and robust looking. Clearly this contrast has little to do with function – it has to do with symbolism which serves to confirm and consolidate existing ideologies of gender and patriarchy, which were mobilised by designers in their efforts to develop product designs which would sell.

In practice, the distinction between symbolic and functional encoding is less clear-cut: a fast car embodies both symbolic and functional encoding – the speed and the image. Indeed, it might be argued that the distinction between function and symbol is misleading, in that it implies that there can be some objective need or function, and that this can be separated from the meaning which the object or technology has for its user. And, of course, the aesthetic of a commodity is a part of its function. Nonetheless, the distinction seems a useful heuristic device.

Whereas most literature suggests that the main function of design is to make things beautiful, Forty rejects idealist accounts of design and shows how the designer should not be ascribed the autonomy so often assumed. He explains how design is a social process, arguing that designers work as agents of ideology. He sees their role as serving to condense a complex of ideologies into a singular product. 'In the way it transforms ideas and beliefs successful design is like alchemy: it fuses together disparate ideas' (1986, p.221). Thus Forty contends that ideology is a critical ingredient in technological design; and argues that domestic consumer appliances would never have come to be created 'without the existence of certain ideas about the nature of domestic life and the part that appliances might play in it' (1986, p.221). In particular, their form draws on and embodies specific ideologies concerning the spatial and gender division of labour and the role of the housewife.

Marketing is a part of the social shaping of technology not only in that it informs design, but also in that it plays a part in constructing demand; yet it is missed from many 'social shaping of technology' accounts. Proponents of consumer sovereignty argue that societal members' desires are manifest in their decision to buy or not to buy a given product. 'It is needed because it is bought; if it were not bought, it would not be made' (Williams, 1983, p.27). Obviously, such a decision is dependent on the ability to buy. But, even then, the choice that exists for a consumer is confined by the parameters which determine what comes to be produced. Consumer sovereignty is severely constrained.

Webster and Robins (1986) discuss how manufacturers often regulated consumption by explicitly deploying a similar philosophy to that which they used to organize work processes. The extension of scientific management into regulating the market took two forms: the accumulation of information about potential customers, and the deployment of that knowledge to organize societal needs, desires and fantasies around the commodity form. The latter largely took the form of advertising, although it was also evident in the design, packaging and branding of commodities. Advertising, clearly, is central to the mobilization of meanings and associations, in its selling of commodities. A large part of the advertising industry is devoted to the construction and mobilization of symbolic associations surrounding commodities – especially domestic consumer technologies. These practices of extending scientific management into the broader social sphere began to mature and congeal into a more systematic scientific approach around the 1920s and 1930s: while market research came to emphasize quantification and scientific procedures in its information gathering, advertising began to practice the sample testing of advertisements and the incorporation of psychological research.

'Sloanism' was being developed to create the consumer. Three key elements of this can be identified: first, there was built-in obsolescence, such as annual model changes, which depended on the prior social acceptance of the idea of 'obsolescence'. Second, there was marginal differentiation, to enable personalisation within the context of mass production. For example,

> According to your desire, you can choose your Mercedes-Benz from among 76 different colours and 697 assortments of internal trimmings (Baudrillard, 1970, p.123, cited by Hill, 1988, p.193).

Third, consumer credit – trade-ins and hire purchase – became available. In these various ways, those in control of production sought to generate the demand for their goods. In short, consumption cannot be seen simply as meeting human demand, but is socially constructed.

Surprisingly, there has been little work which has focused on the full life cycle of a technology, as I am proposing. Schwartz Cowan (1987) links most explicitly consumption and production; she sees her work on stoves as extending the social constructivist approach, by applying an actor-network framework to consumers. Haddon's work (1988b) on the home computer is an excellent example of such an approach, though he is dealing with a range of themes at the same time. My own research on the Apple Macintosh is a modest attempt to apply empirically the approach I am suggesting (Mackay and Powell, 1993). And, most recently, Cockburn and others have produced some excellent work on the microwave and other technologies (Cockburn and Ormrod, 1993, Cockburn and Dilic, 1994).

This article has reviewed the social shaping of technology approach and has argued that the various schools within this broad field can be drawn on to understand with greatest complexity and sensitivity how technology is social. I have argued that technologies are functionally encoded to facilitate the achievement of particular ends – by way of the forms of deployment which they encourage. Further, they are symbolically encoded to the same social end – through the practices of design and marketing. Whilst bringing the user preferred forms of deployment, technologies will vary in their degree of openess or closure.

As well as being encoded, technologies constitute a site on which various social forces converge. This is the sphere of appropriation. The user may bring to bear on a technology an intention which was not foreseen by the technology's designer. As well as being encoded, technologies are subjectively deployed; appropriation is the sphere in which these two forces come together. The notion of the (socially constructed) subject is crucial to countering technological determinism: the direction and nature of technology does not follow some inevitable trajectory. By understanding the full scope of social choice that is involved, we are best equipped to counter notions of technological determinism.

NOTES

1 This paper draws on some of the material and arguments developed by the author in Mackay and Gillespie (1992).

2 There are a few exceptions. Bruce and Mole (1987) have referred to the erroneous separation of those who study the creation of a technology from those studying its effects. Hill (1988) has argued for the linking of invention and consumption in accounts of technology. Fleck (1988) is concerned with the impact of technology implementation on technology design, but focuses on a narrow set of technologies, 'configurational technologies'. Latour's approach (Johnson, 1988), although it focuses on ambiguity and solidification at the early stages in the life of a technology, appears implicitly receptive to understanding later stages; and he alludes to processes of technology take-up.

BIBLIOGRAPHY

Arnold, E (1985) 'The Appliance of Science: Technology and Housework', *New Scientist*, 18 April, pp. 12-15

Ascherson, N. (1987) 'Inventions Never Quite Set Us Free', *Observer*, London, 13 December.

Baudrillard, J. (1970) *La Societe de Consommation – ses Mythes, ses Structures*, Paris: Gallimard.

Bijker, W.E., Hughes, T.P. and Pinch, T.J. (eds) (1987) *The Social Construction of Technological Systems: New Directions in the Sociology and History of Technology*, Cambridge, MA, MIT Press.

Braverman, H. (1984) *Labour and Monopoly Capital: the Degradation of Work in the Twentieth Century*, London, Monthly Review Press.

Bruce, M. and Mole, V. (1987) 'Towards a sociology of technology', paper presented to the BSA Annual Conference, Leeds, April.

Callon, M. (1986) 'The sociology of an actor-network: the case of the electric vehicle', in M. Callon, J. Law and A. Rip (eds), *Mapping the Dynamics of Science and Technology*, London: Macmillan

Child, J. and Smith, C. (1987), 'The context and process of organisational transformation: Cadbury Limited in its sector', *Journal of Management Studies*, 24, pp. 565-93.

Cockburn, C. and Ormrod, S. (1993) *Gender and Technology in the Making*, London, Sage

Cockburn, C. and Dilic, R.F. (eds) (1994) *Bringing Technology Home. Gender and Technology in a Changing Europe*, Buckingham, Open University Press

Cowan, R.S. (1976) 'The "Industrial Revolution" in the Home: Household Technology and Social Change in the 20th Century', Technology and Culture, 17 : 1-23;

Cowan, R.S. (1987) 'The consumption junction: a proposal for research strategies in the sociology of technology', in W.E. Bijker, T.P. Hughes and T.J. Pinch (eds) (1987) *The Social Construction of Technological Systems: New Directions in the Sociology and History of Technology*, Cambridge, MA, MIT Press.

Crompton, R. and Jones, G. (1984) *White Collar Proletariat: Deskilling and Gender in Clerical Work*, London, Macmillan.

Douglas, M. and Isherwood, B. (1978) *The World of Goods: Towards an Anthropology of Consumption*, Harmondsworth, Penguin.

Ewen, E. (1976) *Captains of Consciousness*, New York, McGraw-Hill.

Featherstone, M. (1987) 'Lifestyle and consumer culture', *Theory, Culture and Society*, 4, pp. 55-70.

Featherstone, M. (1991) *Consumer Culture and Postmodernism*, London, Sage.

Fleck, J. (1988) 'Innofusion or Diffusation? The nature of technological development in robotics' Edinburgh PICT Working Paper No. 4. RCSS, University of Edinburgh.

Friedman, A. (1977) *Industry and Labour*, London, Macmillan.

Forty, A. (1986) *Objects of Desire: Design and Society 1750-1980*, London, Thames and Hudson.

Frederick, C. (1929) *Housekeeping With Efficiency*, London.

Goodall, P. (1983) 'Design and Gender', Block, 9, pp. 50-62.

Gray, A. (1987) 'Behind closed doors: video recorders in the house', in H. Baehr and G. Dyer (eds) *Boxed in: Women and TV*, London, Routledge, pp. 38-54.

Haddon, L. (1988a) *The Roots and Early History of the British Home Computer Market: Origins of the Masculine Micro*, PhD thesis, University of London.

Haddon, L. (1988b) 'The home computer: the making of a consumer electronic', *Science as Culture*, 2, pp. 7-51.

Hall, S. (1980) 'Encoding/decoding', in Hall *et al.* (eds), *Culture, Media, Language*, London, Hutchinson.

Hill, S. (1988) *The Tragedy of Technology*, London, Pluto.

Hughes, T.P. (1986) 'The seamless web: technology, science, etcetera, etcetera', *Social Studies of Science*, 16, pp. 281-92.

Jameson, F. (1981) 'Reification and mass culture', *Social Text*, 1, pp. 130-48.

Johnson, J. (1988) 'Mixing humans and nonhumans together: the sociology of the door-closer', *Social Problems*, 35, pp. 298-310.

Johnson, R. (1983) 'What is Cultural Studies anyway?' Occasional Paper No. 72, Birmingham: Centre for Contemporary Cultural Studies, University of Birmingham.

Keen, B. (1987) '"Play it Again, Sony": The double life of home video technology', *Science as Culture*, 1, pp. 7-42.

Latour, B. (1987) *Science in Action*, Milton Keynes, Open University Press.

Law, J. (1987) 'Technology and hetereogeneous engineering: the case of portuguese expansion', in W.E. Bijker, T.P. Hughes and T.J. Pinch (eds) *The Social Construction of Technological Systems: New Directions in the Sociology and History of Technology*, Cambridge, MA, MIT Press.

Leiss, W. (1983) 'The icons of the marketplace', *Theory, Culture and Society*, 1, pp. 10-21.

Mackay, H. and Gillespie, G. (1992) 'Extending the social shaping of technology: ideology and appropriation', *Social Studies of Science*, 22, pp. 685-716.

Mackay, H. and Powell, T. (1993) 'Completing the circuit: the meaning of the Mac', Paper presented to ESRC PICT Annual Conference, Kenilworth, May.

MacKenzie, D. and Wajcman, J. (eds) (1985) *The Social Shaping of Technology*, Milton Keynes, Bucks, Open University Press.

Miller, D (1987) *Material Culture and Mass Consumption*, Oxford, Blackwell.

Moores, S. (1988) '"The Box on the Dresser": memories of early radio and everyday Life', *Media, Culture and Society*, 10, pp. 23-40.

Morley, D. (1980) *The Nationwide Audience*, BFI TV Monograph No 11, London, BFI.

Morley, D. (1992) *Television, Audiences and Cultural Studies*, London, Routledge.

Noble, D. (1984) *Forces of Production: a Social History of Industrial Automation*, New York, Knopf.

Pinch, T.J. and Bijker, W.E. (1984) 'The social construction of facts and artefacts: or how the sociology of science and the sociology of technology might benefit each other', *Social Studies of Science*, 14, pp. 399-441.

de Sola Pool, I. (ed.) (1976) *The Social Impact of the Telephone*, Cambridge, MA, MIT Press.

Russell, S. (1986) 'The social construction of artefacts: a response to Pinch and Bijker', *Social Studies of Science*, 16, pp. 331-46.

Silverstone, R. and Hirsch, E. (eds) (1992) *Consuming Technologies. Media and Information in Domestic Spaces*, London, Routledge.

Turkle, S. (1984) *The Second Self: Computers and the Human Spirit*, New York, Simon and Schuster.

Webster, F. and Robins, K. (1986) *Information Technology: A Luddite Analysis*, Norwood, New Jersey, Ablex.

White, L. (1978) *Medieval Technology and Social Change*, New York, Oxford University Press.

Williams, R. (1974) *Television Technology and Cultural Form*, London, Fontana.

Williams, R. (1983) *Towards 2000*, London, Chatto and Windus.

Williamson, J. (1986) *Consuming Passions: the Dynamics of Popular Culture*, London, M Boyars.

Winner, L. (1985) 'Do artifacts have politics?', in D. MacKenzie and J. Wajcman (eds) (1985) *The Social Shaping of Technology,* Milton Keynes, Bucks, Open University Press.

THE ROOTS OF THE INFORMATION SOCIETY IDEA

David Lyon

> People started getting together and exploring the idea that there was going to be a revolution in technology which was going to change society so drastically. Steve Wozniak (1986) [1].

Suddenly, success in just about any field has become impossible without information technology. In farming, manufacture, education, policing, medicine, entertainment, banking or whatever, IT is apparently set to change everything that human beings do in advanced societies. Steve Wozniak, of Apple computers fame, sees the real revolution as putting personal computers into the home. Others see it in direct broadcasting by satellite, automated work opening up new vistas for freed time, or in the potential for push-button democracy. While differing over details, though, many seem to agree that bringing together computing with telecommunications spells the start of a new age.

It appears that this is the only way forward: Initiation in the processes of information handling, transmission, storage and retrieval is the key to future prosperity and to qualitatively different ways of life. Failure to proceed in this direction carries dire consequences. Punishment for national laggards, according to a British National Economic Development Office report, will be relegation to 'Third World' status [2].

Not surprisingly, this 'one way forward' is greeted by others with some sense of foreboding. Cheerful book-titles such as *Silicon Civilization* and *The Mighty Micro* are answered in *Electronic Nightmare* and *Electronic Illusions* [3]. And fears of being sucked into a new transnational empire or being technologically dependent upon the USA or Japan are greater, for some smaller countries, than the threat of impending 'Third World' status. Nevertheless, for better or for worse, the arrival of the information society is felt to be imminent.

Are we at the threshold of a new kind of society? Discussions of the 'wired society' or of the 'wealth of information' certainly imply this [4]. Alvin Toffler's well-known 'third wave' concept is perhaps the clearest example [5]. The first 'wave' is agricultural, the second industrial, and the third, information society. Sociological debate has not yet crystallized around this single concept – the information society – but it is in sufficiently popular and social scientific use to make it the focus of this study. It finds a ready home in accounts of the 'social impact of new technology', is frequently referred to in policy studies, and is strongly related to other emerging concepts such as that of the 'information worker'. But should it be used as a basic means of characterizing 'society' today? [...]

Despite appearances, the idea of the information society is not entirely new. It has its roots in the literature of 'postindustrialism', a popular social science notion of the 1960s and 1970s which heralded the end of the industrial capitalist era and the arrival of a 'service' or 'leisure' society. Although postindustrialism has been subject to damaging criticism, its resilience is shown by the fact that it can be re-cycled as 'the information society'. This article starts by asking what the two concepts have in common, but also the points at which the information society goes beyond postindustrialism. There is more than 'recycling' here. I also set the scene [...] by proposing which analytical avenues are worth following, and what pitfalls must be avoided.

FROM POSTINDUSTRIALISM TO INFORMATION SOCIETY

The roots of the information society idea are intertwined in a complex manner. It is hard to disentangle the diverse strands of attempted social prediction, government policy, futuristic speculation and empirical social analysis. For instance, a Canadian government report, *Planning Now for the Information Society* [6] is clearly geared to identifying a national technology strategy in microelectronics. But it depends upon social scientific concepts such as the 'information economy', indulges briefly in quoted 'predictions' (for instance that by the year 2000 'smart' highways for semi-automated driving will enter development), and refers to empirical studies of the impact of microelectronics on, among other things, women's work.

One readily identifiable strand, on which hopeful accounts of the information society often rely, is the idea of postindustrialism, especially the version associated with Daniel Bell. This is the view that, just as agrarian society was replaced by industrial society as the dominant economic emphasis shifted from the land to manufacturing, so postindustrial society develops as a result of the economic tilt towards the provision of services. The increased part played by science in the productive process, the rise to prominence of professional, scientific and technical groups, plus the introduction of what is now called information technology, all bear witness to a new 'axial principle' at the core of the economy and society. This axial principle, 'the energising principle that is the logic for all the others', is the centrality of 'theoretical knowledge' [7].

Bell argues that the information society is developing in the context of postindustrialism. He forecasts the growth of a new social framework based on telecommunications which 'may be decisive for the way economic and social exchanges are conducted, the way knowledge is created and retrieved, and the character of work and occupations in which men [sic] are engaged'. The computer plays a pivotal role in this revolution' [8].

Bell also sketches other significant features of the information society. IT, by shortening labour time and diminishing the production worker, actually replaces labour as the source of 'added value' in the national product. Knowledge and information supplant labour and capital as the 'central variables' of the economy. He comments on the way that information is being treated as a commodity, with a price-tag on it, and how the 'possession' of information increasingly confers power on its owner. Unlike some postindustrialists, Bell recognizes some of the ambiguities involved in identifying a 'service sector' and proposes that economic sectors be divided into 'extractive, fabrication and information activities'. This way, he claims, one may monitor the penetration of information activities into more traditional areas of agriculture, manufacturing and services.

Bell underlines ways in which these areas are expanding in the wake of IT development. He foresees major social changes resulting from the establishment of new telecommunications infrastructures. Such huge changes will occur as the merging technologies of telephone, computer, facsimile, cable television and video discs lead to a vast reorganization in the modes of communication between persons; the transmission of data; the reduction, if not the elimination, of paper in transactions and exchanges; new modes of transmitting news, entertainment and knowledge [9] and so on. These in turn will intensify concern about population distribution, national planning, centralization, privacy and so on. For Bell, the 'fateful question', or, one might say, the consumerist question, is whether the promise will be realized that 'instrumental technology' will open 'the way to alternative modes of achieving individuality and variety within a vastly increased output of goods' [10].

Without doubt, Bell asks many of the right questions, and indicates worthwhile lines of inquiry. This is why his work deserves to be taken seriously. But it also demands serious critique because, as I shall show, Bell's attempt to find a thoroughgoing alternative to Marxian class analysis underestimates both the resilience of some familiar features of modern societies, and the extent to which new conflicts and struggles could arise within this 'information society'.

Those 'familiar features' include military, commercial and government power. No small significance lies in the fact that it was military requirements which gave birth to modern computers. The massive mainframe, ENIAC, built in 1946 in the electrical engineering department of the University of Pennsylvania, was intended to assist the aiming of guns, and was soon involved in calculations for the atomic bomb. Neither is it irrelevant to note that huge forces of international capitalist commerce are today locked in mortal combat to capture markets and conquer opposition within the lucrative high technology field. Nor is it an accident that governments are so active in promoting IT and purchasing its products. IT is a powerful tool for monitoring and supervising people's activities. In other words, one does not have to look far before this question comes to mind: Does IT bring about a new society without precedent, or does it rather help to intensify certain processes in today's society of which we are all too aware?

What of new 'conflicts and struggles'? Are we entering an era, not of Bell's rather smoothly harmonious information society, but of new social frictions and power alignments within a divided and contradictory 'information society'? Around the same time as Bell's work on postindustrialism was published a European contribution appeared which took account of the same social and economic trends: Alain Touraine's *La Société post-industrielle* [11].

Touraine's study took a quite different tack from Bell's. He challenged the bland postindustrial assumption that class struggle was a thing of the past, although he argued that many class images are too bound up with the 'era of capitalist industrialisation'. He invited readers to consider the 'fundamental importance of class situations, conflicts and movements in the programmed society'. In particular he had in mind a major cleavage between technocrats and a more disparate grouping whose livelihood and lifestyles are governed by them. Property ownership is less a bone of contention than the opposition brought about because 'the dominant classes dispose of knowledge and control information' [12].

So do changing technologies and shifts in educational qualification and skill lead to novel class alignments? [...] This question still concentrates upon the workplace and on production. The analyses of Touraine and others hint at wider movements of power. The use of IT within governments, education, the media and the domestic sphere as well as in the workplace means that more and more social relationships are mediated by machines. What does this imply for power? Mark Poster suggests that because 'new forms of social interaction based on electronic communications devices are replacing older types of social relations' [13], we should speak of a new mode of information'. He too is questioning the relevance today of some Marxian assumptions, but for very different reasons from Daniel Bell's.

SOCIAL FORECASTERS AND SOCIAL PLANNERS

The roots of the information society idea are found not only in sociology. Futurists and 'social impact of technology' commentators also contribute. They tend to share the belief that technology 'shapes' social relationships. One of the many cheerful social forecasts comes from Tom Stonier. 'Living in a postindustrial world', he avers, 'means that not only are we more affluent, more resourceful and less likely to go to war, but also more likely to democratise' [14]. Increasing prosperity is a common information society theme. By 'more resourceful', Stonier means that IT will enable us to overcome the environmental and ecological problems associated with industrialism. Again he touches on a common theme. James Martin, in *The Wired Society,* also stresses the 'non-polluting, non-destructive' quality of IT as a major point in its favour [15].

New communications technologies hold out the next promise – the demise of war ('as slavery disappeared in the industrial era, says Stonier [16]). Some even hold this out as a 'stage' beyond information society:

'communication society' [17]. Lastly, IT ushers in the world of computer democracy. More information availability, plus push-button referenda, open the door for the first time to genuinely responsive participatory government. This, along with the burden of administration being thoroughly automated, is the contented futurist's world of information society.

A short step away from the futurist's vision is the forecaster's proposal. Japan was the first country to produce such a proposal, in the shape of *The plan for information society: a national goal toward the year 2000.* [18]. Lacking natural energy resources, the Japanese were acutely aware of the fragility of their economy in the face of recession. Yoneji Masuda's work, *The information society as postindustrial society* [19] played a significant part in establishing a 'national plan'. He gives the idea of 'computopia' concrete shape, connecting futurist dreams – 'the goal . . . is a society that brings about a general flourishing state of human intellectual creativity, instead of affluent material consumption' [20] – with actual new towns in Japan and 'information society infrastructures' elsewhere.

Japan's Tama New Town, with its built-in network of co-axial cables, Canada's *Telidon* (videotex) programme, and Sweden's *Terese* project, which monitors regional development using new telecommunications, are cited as relevant examples of such infrastructures. They are significant to Masuda as portending 'a new type of human society' in the information society. For him, 'production of information values and not material values will become the driving force'. At the same time, *past* experiences within industrial society may be used as an 'historical analogical model of future society' [21].

This assumption, that the history of industrial society may be used as an analogy for what will happen in information society, brings us back to the core of the sociological question. Is it legitimate to claim that the steam engine (or more properly the clock) was to industrial society what the computer is to information society, so that one, the new technology shapes the resulting social and political relations, and two, a qualitatively different kind of society emerges?

Within the same sociological question lies the problem of exactly what are the social origins and social consequences of the diffusion of information technologies. Though their immediate genesis is important, the roots of the so-called information society are more properly sought in what James Beniger calls the 'control revolution', analysed at the turn of the century by theorists of bureaucracy such as Max Weber [22]. Putting new technologies in a longer historical context helps us understand non-technical aspects of their origins and relativizes claims that technologies themselves cause change.

On the other hand, even if one remains sceptical about the capacity of silicon chips and fibre optics to transform the world in quite the way envisaged by a Stonier or a Masuda, it is clear that IT is a major phenomenon with a broad potential social impact. It is a 'heartland' technology, one which enables the development of many others, more and more cheaply, and using components of shrinking size and expanding power [23].

Critical comments about futurism and social forecasting should not be understood as a denial either that some view of the good society ought to be connected with the social analysis of new technology, or that attempts to discern the direction of social-technological trends are worthwhile. On the contrary. The problem is rather the lack of realism, the items missing from accounts of the information society. Eyes focused on the tremendous technological potential of IT frequently fail to see that countervailing processes – loss of skills, privacy or personal contact, for instance unceremoniously puncture confident predictions.

In other words, social factors of several different kinds tend to be neglected. The nature of Japanese post-war reconstruction, and its reliance upon the experience of other advanced societies, has guided the direction of IT development there. In Britain, the 'Alvey' programme of IT research, weighted in favour of commerce rather than the universities, has served to give a distinct flavour to the sorts of work carried out. And so on. In fact, the further one moves from grand national IT plans and from futuristic forecasts of conditions prevailing within the 'informatizing' society, and the nearer one gets to actual social analysis in which technology is not perceived as a quasi-autonomous force acting upon society, the more questionable the information society concept appears.

THE INFORMATION SOCIETY AS PROBLEMATIC

So what are the prospects for the information society concept? The answer is not straightforward. For one thing, more than one image of the information society is available. The popular image of a social transformation along 'Third Wave' lines is not the same as the fuzzier image produced within more careful social analysis of societies coming to terms with a range of more and less profound political, economic and cultural effects of information technology. In his 'information society' essay Daniel Bell himself has become silent about the affluence and leisure he once associated with postindustrialism. Another complicating factor is that both popular and serious versions of the information society thesis either rely upon or provoke genuine questions of tremendous importance.

The idea of an information society is more than recycled postindustrialism. To be sure, the two concepts do share a number of common features, not to mention several common flaws. Popular versions of information society forecasting, often giddy with the astonishing progress of microelectronics since the late 1970s, are infused with the same technological determinism that informed much postindustrialism. While strong currents of critical social investigation cause some ripples, much present-day research focuses on social *adaptation to* IT, rather than how IT may be designed to suit people, which betrays the extent to which technologically determinist views have been accepted.

[...] Several analyses start by outlining important features of one or another aspect of the information society idea which are then sifted in order to retain what is significant or contrasted with alternative interpretations.

I choose this method because I see little point in summarily discarding the information society as the rotten fruit of futurist fancy or as ideology in the guise of social analysis. Rather, the information society should be granted the status of 'problematic'. According to Philip Abrams, a problematic is a 'rudimentary organization of a field of phenomena which yields problems for investigation' [24]. Without succumbing to the sociological simplism which sees the information society as a 'Third Wave' of evolutionary progress, it is nevertheless true to say that some of the most significant changes in late twentieth-century society are those inherent in, related to, or consequent upon IT. The information society concept points to that cluster of issues and its better exponents already use it in this sense.

As a problematic its components refer to changes in the workplace and employment and also the political, cultural and global aspects of the diffusion of IT. Whether the sum of these changes amounts to a shift beyond industrial capitalism, militarism or male dominance is highly questionable. Important continuities, such as the chronic persistence of inequalities and the growth of state power using IT, seem to suggest that changes may be more of degree than kind. In important respects many supposed changes highlighted by information society theorists originated well before information technology!

At the same time the category of information is undoubtedly becoming vitally important as an economic factor in its own right. The phenomenon of insider dealing on international stock markets is an obvious illustration. While it may not be supplanting property as a key to the social structure of modern societies, information is proving to be a crucially important element in our understanding of social relationships. Certainly at present it lacks adequate definition, let alone incorporation within a coherent theory of contemporary social change. Yet the new technologies which handle and process information simultaneously influence diverse but significant aspects of social, cultural and political reality.

Let me note two other features of the information society problematic. One is that social analysis must grapple with the ramifications of the *fusion* of the technologies which comprise IT. Conventional distinctions between communication and media studies, on the one hand, and studies of the social aspects of computing, on the other, are eroded. For example, implications of the decline in public service broadcasting now extend far beyond traditional concerns for broadcasting as such. In the USA, the dissemination of government data, once a public function, is under increasing pressure as private profit-seeking firms compete to sell repackaged data. Burgeoning communication between computers and the coming of the commercial database brings 'public service' questions into the heartland of computing.

The other noteworthy feature is that as social analysis exposes alternative options in the adoption of new technology that are in fact available to government, industry and the public, discussions of the strategy for shaping new technologies become more relevant. Do government-sponsored slogans such as 'automate or liquidate' represent genuine choices? Is it 'data' or 'persons' that ought to be protected by law? How does one decide what counts as an appropriate technology where microelectronics is concerned? Social analysis can serve to indicate the conditions under which ethical considerations and social hopes might be realized.

INFORMATION SOCIETY: THE MAJOR THEMES

The information society concept inherits several symptoms of the troubles that beset postindustrialism. The postindustrialists largely failed to justify the significance granted to trends such as the growth of theoretical knowledge and of services. A leisured society based on automated manufacture, a vast array of services and a culture of self-expression, political participation and an emphasis on the quality of life does not seem to have materialized – at least, not for the majority of the populations of the advanced societies.

Will this hereditary syndrome prove fatal for the information society? The answer depends upon careful investigation in the following areas.

INFORMATION WORKERS IN AN INFORMATION ECONOMY

It is clear from job advertisements at least that in the late 1980s one's chances of obtaining employment were enhanced by the possession of qualifications in microelectronics, computing, systems analysis, telecommunications, operational research, software design, fibre optics, expert systems and so on. But what does this proliferation of new job descriptions mean? Those that Tom Stonier refers to as 'information operatives' seem to appear in all manner of workplaces. The big questions are: who are these 'operatives', and what contribution do their activities make to the pattern of social relationship?

Central to much information society discourse is the contention that 'information workers' are rising to a majority within the labour forces of the advanced societies. As early as 1967, claims Marc Porat, 50 per cent of American workers were engaged in the 'information sector', and they received just over 50 per cent of total employee remuneration. But just who are these information workers? Unfortunately, because he does not actually explain what information is (he only defines it as 'data that have been organized and communicated') the categories are blurred. Judges and rent-collectors find themselves in this sector, but doctors, for instance, have an 'ambiguous occupation', straddling 'service' and 'information' sectors [25].

Few studies of 'information work' comment on its purpose, function, or content. Without this, however, we cannot know who makes decisions, on what basis, or with what effect. Masses of computer-generated information confers no power whatsoever on those who use it, whereas at certain points within organizations it may be crucial to the maintenance of power. As it happens, postindustrialism also glossed over questions of information, knowledge and power, especially with regard to the social significance of research and development (R&D). The sheer amount of R&D in any given society tells us little. We learn nothing about the social role of scientific and technical knowledge, the price put on it, and the power of those who manipulate it. The fact that R&D is often financed for political rather than social reasons, and developed for military rather than economic purposes, pulls the rug from beneath the (Bell-inspired) idea that universities are crucibles of power in the modern world [26]. The current squeeze on university funding and the politicizing of technology policy makes the idea laughable.

That said, changes are occurring in the occupational structure of the advanced societies. While the relabelling process noted in Krishan Kumar's critique of postindustrialism still occurs – though today it is programmers becoming software architects rather than plumbers becoming heating engineers – there is expansion at managerial, professional and technical levels. There is, moreover, a strong link between innovation and economic growth; hence the frequently expressed British worries about the lack of domestic R&D funding relative to other countries.

Two major questions are raised by the 'discovery' of information work and an information sector in the economy. First, are the apparently new categories of work and occupation leading to shifts in power? Is there an emerging information 'technocracy' which is wresting power from previously dominant classes? What opportunities for women are opened by the spread of IT? What is the likely effect of IT on industrial relations? When British Rail computerized its freight system, for instance, many 'middle managers' found their positions were simply redundant, and personnel in subordinate positions actually discovered they had new powers of control over the work process [27].

The other question is this: how accurate is the idea of an 'information sector', and is there an historical 'march through the sectors' [28] as agrarianism gives way to industrialism, and industrialism to information society? This point affects not only the advanced societies but also those to which the promise is alluringly held out that they may be able to jump straight from a non-industrial to an information society. Is this really possible, or does informatizing' depend upon an already 'advanced' situation? [...].

POLITICAL AND GLOBAL ASPECTS

Echoes of postindustrialism are again heard with respect to the political and global aspects of information society. A common feature of each is that opportunities for political choice and participation will increase. The difference, however, is that the means of implementing these is now visible, particularly in the possibilities of two-way, interactive electronic networks. The extreme case is that of an 'instant referendum' in which voters views are canvassed via cable television which allows people to receive as well as transmit signals from their living rooms. More soberly, IT is seen as a means of enabling an electorate to be more informed, or for decision-making to be more decentralized [29].

Those committed to ideals of democratic participation on both the right and the left of the political spectrum may advocate the harnessing of new technologies to such ends. Without adequate access to modern means of communication, any idea of a just political community is indeed a chimera. But a number of important questions are raised by this, not least how the necessary telecommunications infrastructure is to be set up. While France is establishing a national *telematique system* which could in principle serve such ends, Britain has experienced some difficulties persuading domestic subscribers to pay for a suitable cable television network, whereas in the USA only local experimental systems have been tried. In the absence of a coherent policy which is intended to ensure equal access of all to such a communications network it is difficult to imagine how dreams of electronic democracy could be translated into realities.

The prominent source of anxiety, however, is the threat of an Orwellian society. Does the widespread political and administrative use of extensive databases which allow for the easy storage, retrieval and transmission of personal information portend a future fraught with the dangers of electronic eavesdropping? On the one hand police, defence, social security and other personnel reassure the public that no innocent person need have any worries about improper prying into their private lives. On the other, cases of wrongful dismissal or arrest which are traced to erroneous computer files serve to fuel fears that in fact 'ordinary citizens' may well be at risk.

But are these computerized forms of surveillance an intrinsically new departure? Or do they rather represent an extension of state garnering of information on citizens which has been occurring for many decades? Is it merely the use of these databases by law-and-order agencies which creates potential perils for citizens? Or is a deeper process at work in which more generalized forces of social control achieve more power by computerization? And what exactly are the risks involved, against which 'data protection' laws and policies are directed? Is wrongful arrest the tip of an iceberg, the submerged portion of which conceals a fundamental issue of invaded privacy and impugned integrity?

This of course, is only one aspect of the state-and-IT connection. As I have already mentioned, the connections between government activity and economic-technological developments are numerous and significant. Whereas postindustrialist Bell insisted upon the relatively independent operation of economic and political spheres, this position is exceedingly hard to justify. It is quite clear that polity and economy are interdependent, and that the relationship between the two is far from simple.

Bringing the global situation into focus, however, other connections between the political and the economic become clear. The IT industry, as others, is dominated by giant transnational corporations – IBM, Exxon, Mitsubishi, AT&T, Philips, Siemens and so on – which often call the political tune. Many countries find their national sovereignty, not to mention the position of their workers, threatened by the activities of these 'stateless' economic interests. Such companies increasingly rely upon the free flow of data across national boundaries for financial reporting and management, marketing, distribution, R&D, and order processing.

Labour unions may debate the future of plants in vain if the crucial decisions are made on another continent. National governments may find their attempts to change direction thwarted, as when in 1985 Australian prime minister Bob Hawke tried to stop Australian bases being used to monitor MX missile tests. Dismayed financial and transnational corporate interests withdrew capital, putting pressure on the economy and thus the government [30]. It would appear that Walter Wriston (who seems not to treat this as a matter for regret) is right to claim that 'the ancient and basic concept of sovereignty which has been discussed since the time of Plato is being profoundly changed by information technology' [31].

Of course it is not only the national sovereignty of the larger and more powerful countries which is challenged by the power of transnational corporations. The phenomenon of 'deindustrialization', for example, often viewed in the northern hemisphere in terms of the shrinking proportion of the labour force involved in manufacturing, may be equally well understood as the partial relocation of workers to 'offshore' plants in the south. The information society is not inaccurately depicted as a global phenomenon. The current expansion and development of microelectronics-related industries require a world market.

There is no doubt that the technological potential for beneficial change – 'deserts that bloom' – is tremendous, and nothing in this book should be taken as denying or minimizing that fact. Tom Stonier, Alvin Toffler and Jacques Servan-Schreiber make a lot of this angle. Stonier reports great gains made in the Upper Volta village of Tangaye when a solar photovoltaic-powered grain mill and water pump were installed [32]. (This is an example of what he calls the 'second silicon revolution'.) Such advances, he states correctly, are dependent on technology and information transfer. That such changes will take place and that 'the postindustrial economy will produce the wealth of information to make it all happen' is rather more open to question.

At present, as a matter of fact, things are somewhat different. Despite dreams of poorer countries 'catching up' with richer ones, or 'leapfrogging' the industrial era, the situation is overwhelmingly not just one of interdependence, but of dependence. While the advanced societies produce silicon chips comprising hundreds of thousands of elements, in Africa only one person in eighteen has a radio. Far from narrowing the 'North-South' divide, the evidence suggests that IT helps to widen it. As

Juan Rada sagely observes. 'Technological fixes of whatever nature are nothing but a drop of water in the sea of reality' [33].

No treatment of the political and global aspects of IT can afford to ignore the connections between new technology and the continuing Cold War. Like earlier postindustrialists, Stonier's focus is on the 'wealth of information' that spells 'unprecedented affluence both at the private level and in the public sector' [34]. But as Krishan Kumar laconically notes, 'the science-based "welfare" state can be rapidly reclassified as the science-based "warfare" state, and with greater respect for the actual history of the last fifty years' [35].

For example, the Japanese 'Fifth Generation' computer project, which aims to introduce the world to ordinary language-recognizing 'artificial intelligence' during the 1990s, is ostensibly civil and commercial. But American responses relate to military supremacy. As Feigenbaum and McCorduck put it, 'the Defense Department needs the ability to shape technology to conform to its needs in military systems. A Fujitsu or a Hitachi marches to a different drummer from a Rockwell or a Lockheed. Our defense industry must obtain and retain a strong position in the new advanced computer technologies' [36]. It goes without saying that these are not the kinds of 'needs' which those concerned for a 'welfare state' – or world welfare – have in mind.

AN INFORMATION CULTURE?

The notion of a 'fifth generation' of computers raises another set of questions besides those of military prowess. Unlike previous technological artifacts which typically have augmented human energy with improved sources of power, those spawned by IT augment – and, according to some, transcend – the human capacity to think and to reason. Needless to say, some references to machine intelligence are no more sophisticated than those associated with Hal, the 'thinking' computer from the film *2001, A Space Odyssey*. Others, however, are pointers to a series of profound cultural issues whose analysis could have far-reaching implications.

It must be said, though, that while debate over the workplace and employment aspects of IT is widespread, and awareness of the political and global dimensions is beginning to make itself felt, the cultural questions have not as yet received the attention they deserve. In what follows, therefore, I can do no more than set the scene.

Once again, Bell's thoughts on postindustrial culture make a suitable starting point. For him, 'a new kind of modernity' has been created by the 'revolutions in transportation and communication that have banded together the world society into one great *Oikoumene'*. It represents a break with the past, thus replacing continuity with variety, tradition with syncretism. Its agent is technology, which by 'introducing a new metric and enlarging our control over nature' has transformed our social relationships and our ways of looking at the world' [37].

Bell maintains that technology has been the 'chief engine of raised living standards and reduced inequalities, created a 'new class' of engineers and technicians who plan work-tasks rather than actually performing them, brought about a new functional and quantitative way of thinking, created new economic dependencies and new social interactions', and altered aesthetic perceptions of time and space. While he believes that cultural issues are of the utmost importance, he partially disconnects analysis of them from political or social life. Each sphere has a different 'axial principle'; that of contemporary culture being the desire for fulfilment and enhancement of the self [38].

Of course, when writing of postindustrialism (in the 1960s) Bell could have had little clear idea of the rapidity with which the technologies of computing and telecommunications would move to centre stage (hence his later work on the information society). But other theorists have taken further these kinds of ideas about the relation of IT to culture. Where Bell limited himself to comments about concepts of speed or the view from the air unknown to pre-moderns, writers such as David Bolter have argued that the computer itself is the harbinger of novel cultural transformations including a new human sense of self [39].

Bolter's argument is as follows. Just as the clock is the key symbol of the industrial era, as Lewis Mumford rightly held, so the computer is becoming the key symbol of the present. It is a 'defining technology' which by its impact on certain basic relationships – of knowledge to technical power, and mankind to the world of nature – occupies 'a special place in our cultural landscape' [40]. Thus humans begin to think of themselves as 'information processors' and nature as information to be processed' [41].

Sceptical eyebrows may well be raised about such speculations. Are not those who define themselves as information processors likely to be only a tiny minority of a given population? By what process does the computer become a defining technology? Bolter's thesis is well worth attending to, though not, I shall argue, for the reasons he gives.

Three issues concerning the 'culture of information' should be addressed. First, questions about computing and telecommunications; the fact of technological 'convergence' is a significant one. While Bell's idea of the 'overflowing of all the world's traditions of art, music and literature into a new, universal container, accessible to all and obligatory upon all'[42] is somewhat inflated, it does flag an important phenomenon. A form of cultural 'synchronization' is indeed taking place, as new communications carrying essentially similar messages encircle the globe [43]. Who controls these messages, and what is their content? Does the ownership of the means of (increasingly computerized) communication lead to the cultural dominance of certain elite groups and societies over others?

Secondly, is the 'defining technology' idea an appropriate means of social and cultural analysis? Are the emerging technologies of information and communication indeed shaping the social and cultural experience of those societies affected by them? Do the new technologies not confer on those with access to them considerable power to control not only the processes of production, about which Marx was concerned, but also those of leisure and consumption? Is there more than passing significance in the rise of 'hackers' and computer gamesters, who get totally absorbed in their machines, or in the ways that computers may converse' with each other about human destinies (I am thinking of credit-worthiness or welfare-eligibility)? [44]

Thirdly, consideration of the so-called culture of information is incomplete without reference to its religious and ideological aspects. Do human beings remake themselves in the image of their technology? If so, then there are obvious implications for philosophical debates about the unique place of human beings in the cosmos. Furthermore, there is scope for critique along 'religious' lines, as evidenced by the denunciation of IT as 'silicon idolatry' [45]. It also brings us back, finally, to the over-riding question of this study: does IT usher us into a new kind of society? And at this point a further query is highlighted: what is the social *meaning* of the 'information society'? Is it better understood as a kind of myth' or 'utopia' than the social 'forecast' it is more frequently taken to be?

CRITIQUE OF THE INFORMATION SOCIETY

For the sake of clarity, and oversimplifying, let me make some distinctions. There arc two kinds of information society thesis, each of which makes two kinds of claims. The view popularized in many media and policy accounts stresses the major social changes for the better that follow in the wake of IT. This popular version may well be buttressed by the 'findings of social science'. The other use of the information society concept is more cautious and open-ended. Here it is a 'problematic' rather than a descriptive term. The two images of information society overlap.

The claims made are both analytical and evaluative, and the two kinds of claim are interrelated. Thus both kinds of information society thesis try to anticipate the *sorts of social change* which can be expected as IT is diffused through different economic, political and cultural spheres. And both also provide at least strong clues as to whether such social changes are *desirable*. His book draws together evidence from a wide range of sources in an attempt to assess both the analytical and evaluative claims of each information society thesis.

The information society idea has both utopian and ideological aspects. To put things in focus I comment on some of the dangers associated with using the information society concept, that is, its ideological aspects. Three are prominent.

Firstly, it obscures vested interests that are involved in IT and that in fact do much to shape its overall direction. The concept yields no clues as to who wields power. Repeatedly, for instance, the popular rhetoric assures us that 'everyone can own information' or 'the real revolution is personal computer ownership'. But information is not steadily diffused in a general way through all social echelons. As Cees Hamelink points out, some information is specialist and thus restricted to a few [46]. Intellectual and managerial skills are required to exploit information economically, and these are unevenly distributed in society. Advanced hardware and software for information processing are expensive, and therefore the few who can afford them are scarcely challenged by others using inferior machines.

Such inequalities are felt globally between north and south in the theatre of transnational corporations and military interests, and locally, whether with the word-processor operator's lack of control over her work or the suspected criminal's difficulty in gaining access to information held about him. 'Information power' is only a reality when access exists to the means of collecting, storing, retrieving and communicating the information.

Secondly, the inequalities and conflicts discernible on the surface are often related to underlying contradictions. These too may be disguised by the information society concept. Within capitalism, private gain is constantly set against efforts to 'socialize' production. In the late twentieth century, the latent potential for trade in information – for this entity to become a commodity – is being realized. While many undoubtedly gain from this process, others lose. Public libraries and public service broadcasting are both time-honoured concepts whose 'public' status is under threat as information has a price put on it. Likewise, new integrated services digital networks (ISDNs) mean more efficient information services, but higher costs for ordinary telephone subscribers.

Another discordant element, which may not qualify as a 'contradiction' in the same sense, is the collusion of military with microelectronic interests in the modern world. The same technologies whose avowed purposes (and actual achievement in many cases) are to reduce drudgery, increase efficiency, conserve resources and promote mutual communication are also dedicated to hostile, destructive and lethal ends. Regardless of any justifications which may legitimately be presented for expanding electronically a nation's 'defence' capabilities, most discussions of the information society conceal in the background the huge military impetus to IT research and development.

Thirdly, the arrival of the information society appears as an entirely natural event, the outcome of progressive tendencies within Western industrial societies. It may be 'revolutionary' in its consequences. such that it represents a new era in human history. But it is simultaneously the obvious and logical way forward. Witness the postures struck against any who dare question the ways in which IT is implemented! The chairman of the British Manpower Services Commission provided a clear illustration in a 1986 speech which recommended 'embracing wholeheartedly the new technologies'. He complained that 'We still have latter-day Luddites around in all parts of our society. They threaten our future, and the attitudes they reflect must go' [47].

Very extravagant claims are often made for IT – 'Athens without the slaves' and so on – which suggest that the aura surrounding new technology is not merely that of the 'gee-whiz' variety. Perhaps, as Jacques Ellul and others have suggested [48], new technologies are invested with a 'sacred' quality. The awe and veneration once accorded to the gods who supposedly controlled human destinies now belong to the machine. This dimension – which Michael Shallis refers to as 'silicon idolatry' – would tend to reinforce views of the information society as the obvious scenario.

Against the backdrop of the well-established Western belief in social progress via unlimited economic accumulation, the information society does indeed appear as a natural development. Information technology is its sacred guarantor. But granting it this 'natural' status forecloses debate over and action towards any alternatives to that dominant tendency. As such, it invites critique.

By arguing that the information society has significant ideological aspects I do not for a moment want to suggest that it is some kind of 'dominant ideology', accepted by the 'masses' of any given population [49]. On the contrary, there is plenty of evidence of coolness, fear and resignation towards, as well as sober and realistic acceptance of, the new technologies. Likewise it should be stressed that using the term 'ideological' does not mean that there is a deliberate conspiracy to 'deceive the general public' by using the information society slogan. If the above analysis is correct, however, the *effect* of using it is to disguise the reality of powerful interests and beliefs at work within it.

On the other hand, it is clear that notions like the information society have become a working 'reality' for many. Educational institutions meekly fall in line with pleas for closer ties with industry. Businesses do computerize, some most successfully, some soon discovering they are encumbered with digital white elephants. As Jennifer Slack admits, 'We are buying computers to have fun and to "keep up". And our children who do not learn to operate computers are "falling behind". And information is being developed to be bought and sold and protected like any other kind of commodity. And it *does* make a certain amount of good sense to try to get by in that world.' [50] The point is not to deny that it is happening, but rather to examine how it is orchestrated and by whom, to what purpose, and with what methods and effects.

BEYOND LIBERAL AND LUDDITE CRITIQUE

Just as there are different images of the information society, so critique comes from different angles. What might be called 'liberal' critiques, while refusing to be seduced by the siren songs of high-tech hype, still assume that 'things could go either way'. They issue warnings about the anti-social potential of some IT applications, but maintain that as long as people are alert to them, effective choices can be made to ensure that IT development will be appropriate and socially beneficial. For them, the information society is the outcome of an informed democratic process.

The Luddite would retort quickly that the liberal seems to have swallowed the idea of technological neutrality. The new technologies already express particular values and priorities. Far from choices being relatively free, they are in fact tightly constrained by dominant interest groups, above all by the power of capital. As for being 'informed', this is a sick joke. By insisting on the neutrality of technology, those dominant interests ensure that its 'real' effects and biases are effectively obscured. Thus the exposure of those dominant interests is of prime importance, before any choices can be made.

In so far as it stresses the importance of choice, and therefore of value, priorities and democratic participation, the liberal critique makes a valid contribution. Such an emphasis is a vital antidote to any technological determinism that forecasts that future society will be shaped by new technologies or that ignores social factors in technical change. On the other hand, the Luddite is correct to temper this by drawing attention to the ways in which choice is limited, often severely and systematically, by social, political and economic definition. But the negative image of Luddism is hard to live down. Luddism can be as pessimistic as the popular information society pundits are optimistic [51]. Their future may be similarly foreclosed.

The kind of critique to which this work aspires catches both the sense of potential for socially appropriate development of IT without pretending that it can occur without considerable struggle on several fronts, and the sober realism of the Luddite, without succumbing to sheer negativism or pessimism I do not hide the fact that some alternatives with which I have sympathy – such as partnership between women and men from the design stage onwards, or innovations originating from users needs rather than mere commercial potential – represents a radical departure from present practice. By placing them in the context of a normative and critical social analysis, however, I hope to show both the enormity of the obstacles to be overcome, and possible routes to their realization.

The yawning credibility gap between futuristic forecasts and fantasies and the hard realities of government, transnational and military involvement in IT demands a sense of urgency within the information society problematic. It also points up a vital role for serious social analysis within the policy-making process, analysis which is not simply shut up within either optimistic or pessimistic scenarios.

NOTES

1   Steve Wozniak (1986) *Equinox,* Channel 4 (TV) November.

2   NEDO (1984) *Crisis facing information technology,* London, National Economic Development Office, August.

3   Christopher Evans (1982) *Mighty Micro: Impact Of The Computer Revolution,* London: Gollancz; Geoffrey Simons (1985) *Silicon Shock,* Oxford, Basil Blackwell;John Wicklein (1981) *Electronic nightmare: the home communications set and your freedom* Boston: Beacon Press; Ian Reinecke (1984) *Electronic illusions* Harmondsworth: Penguin.

4   James Martin(1978) *The Wired Society,*Harmondsworth, Penguin.

5   Alvin Toffier (1980) *The Third Wave,* London, Pan.

6   Science Council of Canada (1982) *Planning now for the information society: tomorrow is too late,*Ottawa, Science Council.

7   Daniel Bell (1974) *The coming of postindustrial society: a venture in social forecasting,* Harmondsworth, Penguin, p. 14.

8   Daniel Bell (1980) 'The social framework of the information society' in Tom Forester (ed.) *The Microelectronics Revolution,*Oxford, Basil Blackwell, and also in Michael Dertouzos and Joel Moses (eds) (1980) *The Computer Age: A Twenty Year View,*Cambridge MA, MIT Press.

9   Bell 'Social framework' p. 533.

10   *Ibid.* p.545.

11   Alain Touraine (1969) *La Société post-industrielle,* Paris, Editions Denoël; English translation (1974) *The Postindustrial Society,* London, Wildwood House.

12   Touraine, *The Postindustrial Society,* pp. 28, 61.

13   Mark Poster (1984) *Foucaut, Marxism and History,* Cambridge, Polity Press, p.168

14   Tom Stonier (1983) *The Wealth Of Information,* London, Thames-Methuen, p.202

15   Martin *The Wired Society,* p. 4.

16   Stonier *The Wealth of Information,* p. 202.

17   Jean Voge (1985) 'The new economic information order' in *International Information Economy Handbook,*Springfield VA, Transnational Data Reporting Service, pp. 39-40.

18   Japan Computer Usage Development Institute (1971) *The Plan for Information Society: A National Goal Towards The Year 2000,* Tokyo.

19   Yoneji Masuda (1981) *The Information Society As Postindustrial Society,* Bethesda MD: World Futures Society.

20   *Ibid.* p. 3.

21   *Ibid.* p. 29.

22   James Beniger (1986) *The Control Revolution: Technological and Economic Origins of the Information Society,* Cambridge MA and London, Harvard University Press. Unfortunately Beniger does little to locate this 'control revolution' within a theory of social power relations.

23   This is discussed with particular reference to telecommunications in William H. Dutton, Jay G. Blumler and Kenneth L. Kraemer (eds) (1987) *Wired Cities: Shaping the Future of Communications,* Boston, G. K. Hall.

24   Philip Abrams (1982) *Historical Sociology,* Shepton Mallet, Open Books p. xv.

25 Marc Porat (1977) *The Information Economy: Definition and Measurement,* Washington DC, US Government Printing Office.

26 Krishan Kumar (1978) *Prophecy and Progress: The Sociology of Industrial and Postindustrial Society,* Harmondsworth, Penguin.

27 Patrick Dawson and Ian McLoughlin (1986) 'Computer technology and the redefinition of supervision: a study of the effects of computers on railway freight supervisors', *Journal of Management Studies,* 23(1), pp. 116-32.

28 This phrase comes from Ian Miles and Jonathan Gershuny (1986) 'The social economics of information technology' in Marjorie Ferguson (ed.) *New Communications Technologies and the Public Interest,* London and Beverly Hills, Sage.

29 See, for instance, Ben Barber (1984) *Strong Democracy,* Berkeley CA, University of California Press.

30 This example comes from Herbert Schiller (1986) 'The erosion of national sovereignty' in Michael Traber (ed.) *The Myth of the Information Revolution,* London and Beverly Hills, Sage, p.28.

31 Quoted in Schiller 'Erosion of national sovereignty', p. 23.

32 Stonier, *Wealth of Information* p, 73. See also Toffler *The Third Wave,* and Jacques Servan-Schrieber (1980) *Le défi mondial,* Paris, Fayard.

33 Juan Rada (1982) 'A third world perspective' in Günter Friedrichs and Adam Schaff (eds) *Microelectronics and Society: For Better or For Worse,* London, Pergamon, p.216.

34 Stonier, *Wealth of Information,* p. 32.

35 Kumar, *Prophecy and Progress,* p. 229.

36 Edward Feigenbaum and Pamela McCorduck (1984) *The Fifth Generation,* London, Pan, p. 289.

37 Bell, *Coming of Postindustrial Society,* p. 188.

38 *Ibid.,* pp. 114-15.

39 David Bolter (1984) *Turing's man: Western culture in the computer age* London: Duckworth and Chapel Hill: University of North Carolina Press.

40 *Ibid.,* pp. 8-9.

41 *Ibid.,* p. 13

42 Bell, *Coming of Postindustrial Society,* p.188.

43 See Cees Hamelink (1983) *Cultural Autonomy in Global Communications,* New York, Longman.

44 Such issues are raised by Mark Poster in *Foucault, Marxism and History.*

45 See Michael Shallis (1984) *The Silicon Idol,*Oxford, Oxford University Press.

46 Cees Hamelink (1986) 'Is there life after the information revolution?' in Traber, *The Myth of the Information Revolution*.

47 Bryan Nicholson's speech, recorded in *The Guardian*, 16 September 1986.

48 Jacques Ellul (1976) *The new demons* London: Mowbray or Shallis *The Silicon Idol* .

49 See Nicholas Abercrombie and John Urry (1980) *The Dominant Ideology Thesis*, London, Allen and Unwin.

50 Jennifer Daryl Slack (1984) 'The information revolution as ideology' *Media Culture and Society*, (6)p.250.

51 Pessimistic statements of Luddism include David Noble (1983) 'Present tense technology' *Democracy*, Spring (8-24), Summer (70-82) and Fall (71-93), and Shallis *The Silicon Idol*.

A GENDERED SOCIO-TECHNICAL CONSTRUCTION: THE SMART HOUSE

Anne-Jorunn Berg
University of Trondheim

Technological innovation processes can be *gendered*. In this article I take one example – the so-called 'smart house' [1] – and show the way gender enters into the design of this supposed technological home of the future.

Everyday life and the home have been important arenas for feminist research and feminist politics but, as has been pointed out (Cronberg and Sangregorio, 1983; Cronberg, 1987; Gullestad, 1987), technology has not been of central interest in that context. On the other hand, in the 1980s, popular scenarios of a future shaped by information technology did point to the home as one important field for change (Gorz, 1981; Toffler, 1981). The home is traditionally women's domain. Technology is traditionally men's domain. Consequently technological change in the home will be a gendered process. Does that mean we may anticipate change in gender relations and the domestic sexual division of labour? The research on which this article is based aimed to find out just what is forecast with regard to this in the case of 'the smart house..

It is a widely held popular belief that new technologies in the home have rationalized housework so that it is no longer an important source of inequality between the sexes. Time budget studies however show us another picture (Vanek, 1974, 1978; Boalt, 1983; Cowan, 1983; Hagelskjcer, 1986). The average weekly hours spent on housework have not declined significantly with the introduction of modern equipment, and, since it is still primarily women who do it. Housework remains a significant source of inequality between the sexes (Berg, 1988; Nyberg, 1990). These two questions (how much work? who will do it?) were central to the study of the smart house on which this article is based [2]. Are there any time-saving appliances in the making? Is change in the sexual division of housework anticipated in the design of the house?

The popular technology-based scenarios of the 'new' everyday life perceive technology as an agent of change and a source of 'progress' in modern society. Critical studies of technology have opposed this view by emphasizing instead the degradation of work, increased political and social control, pollution and unemployment. These studies point to important aspects of technological change, but their political implications have left a feeling of political pessimism. Feminist technology studies are pessimistic too, finding little evidence of 'progress' in gender relations or women's lives (Zimmerman, 1986; Lie *et al.*, 1988).

In both cases, this pessimism stems from the theoretical approach adopted. Technology is too often described as a static independent variable which 'has impacts' on social relations. Few questions are asked about what technology really means and what part value conflicts play in technological innovation. In research on the smart house I posed such questions, hoping to throw light on some of the theoretical problems discussed in connection with the 'housework-technology paradox' (Vanek, 1974; Cowan, 1983; Berg, 1988; Nyberg, 1990), the curious fact that so much time continues to be spent on housework in modern households, despite the massive introduction of technology to the home. One of the most interesting aspects of this field of research is the encounter in domestic technology between technology as a masculine domain and the home as a feminine domain (Berg, 1989). Can a focus on conflicting values between *design* and *use* of household appliances show us more of the development of domestic technology as a gendered process?

In the sociology of technology there is very little theorizing about gender in relation to innovation (Wajcman, 1991). Inspiration may be gained from feminist studies of science, which reveal that masculine values, masculine practices and male domination enter significantly into the social construction of scientific facts (Harding, 1986, 1991; Tuana, 1989). What is true for science however is not necessarily true for technology. The construction of facts and artefacts may well differ, and it remains an open question how feminist studies of science and technology may benefit each other.

This article is one example of the latter. It is about the shaping of the innovative home of the future and the importance of gender in that process. For several reasons, my study concentrates on a specific version of the home of tomorrow – the 'smart house'. First, it has information technology, *the* new technology, at its heart. Second, as publicly projected it resembles the popular scenarios of the 1980s in presenting new technologies as gender neutral. Third, several of the big international electronic corporations are already creating prototypes. The smart house is interesting because it is beyond the stage of unbridled imagination. It is already at pre-production stage – a serious IT-home-in-the-making.

From the outset we noticed that the scenarios on which the smart house is based had an astonishing lack of concern with gender (Berg, 1991). Information technology (IT) was perceived and represented as gender neutral. This is common enough, as others have shown, in debates about technology (Cockburn, 1983, 1985; Sørensen and Berg, 1987; Lie *et al.*, 1988). For women, however, IT in the home is not just any technology: it proposes to transform the home and everyday life – and what are these if not women's traditional concern?

In our research project on the smart house I gathered information through the 'snowball' method, one source of information leading to another. The lack of empirical and theoretical social research on gender and innovation, particularly on the smart house [3], made such an exploratory approach appropriate. I interviewed designers and producers, systematically analysed advertisements and other kinds of written material and visited the three North American test houses described here.

I formulated three main questions, answers to which I hoped might reveal the relationship between gender and technology in the design of the smart house. These questions have their origins in the existing sexual division of labour. First, what material appliances are actually in the making today? Scenarios are not always to be trusted as a guide to the future. Second, what kind of household activities are the new artefacts or appliances meant for? Concretely, is housework taken into consideration during the design process? Third, who are the consumers the designers and producers see as their target group? For whom, exactly, are they making this new home? These three topics are addressed in the research in various ways with the aim of exposing to analysis how innovation can be said to be a gendered process, how the smart house can be seen to be a gendered socio-technical construction.

SMART HOUSE PROTOTYPES: MODELLING OUR FUTURES

Two of the three smart house prototypes I analysed are laboratory houses financed respectively by Honeywell and the National Association of Home Builders (NAHB). The third is a commercial show-case named Xanadu, owned by private investors [4].

THE HONEYWELL HOUSE

Honeywell is a multinational corporation producing control systems and services, including thermostats, air cleaners, burglar and fire alarms. The home is not Honeywell's only market, but its various control appliances are already installed in more than 60 million one-family houses in the United States.

Honeywell has been interested in home automation since 1979. Its first laboratory house was built in natural surroundings in a residential area, but it proved too difficult to test and change the infrastructure of the house in such a location. The current Honeywell test house is therefore built inside a laboratory. It embodies the Honeywell products and services linked together through one central programmable communication network: the integration system. Honeywell aims to develop a flexible package that can be adjusted to individual homes to suit different life situations and life styles.

The house, as it was when I visited it, is a life-sized model of a typical North American detached house. The 'Home Automation Test Laboratory' (the house together with two environmental test chambers) is a large research and development project within Honeywell Corporate Systems Development Division. The six-room house is the test site for prototypes of home automation products and the integrated house control systems Honeywell are developing. Apart from the fact that the walls are 'open' to simplify access by the engineers, the house looks like any ordinary house. No fanciful details suggest that this is the home of the future. The R&D team says this is deliberate: Honeywell plan to present home automation as nothing out of the ordinary. Only the control panel, affording central control of all electronic systems, reveals this to be a somewhat special house.

The interior of the house is decorated in a studiedly 'ordinary' style. People from the neighbourhood are sometimes invited along to consumer test Honeywell technologies. To make the test situation as natural as possible, say the producers, the house must resemble a typical home. Of course, they have not fully achieved this, because the many small details and decorations that go to make a house a home are missing.

NAHB SMART HOUSE SYSTEM

The National Association of Home Builders (NAHB) is an association of producers and suppliers of different products for the home. The Association has about 150,000 members which makes them an organization to reckon with in the struggle over standardization to which we shall refer below. It has its own National Research Foundation which fostered the idea of developing a smart house. From 1986 they intensified and restructured their research effort, turning smart house R&D into an independent business, The Smart House Development Venture Inc. (SHDVI).

The NAHB demonstration house is located in a large long-distance truck, so that it can be moved from place to place. From the outside, it resembles less a house than a large caravan. The associated R&D work is carried on in a nearby building, where the house is also modelled in miniature. The house consists of entrance hall, kitchen, living room and bedroom. The rooms, to natural size, are arranged in a linear plan, one adjacent to the next. Each is in fact only half a room, but together they embody all the functions found in a normal house.

The main focus in the NAHB smart house system is on the communication network. The whole infrastructure of the home is going to change, say its designers. Their cable system integrates all kinds of power, independent of the energy source. NAHB are particularly competing to influence standards for signal transmission in networks made for homes.

XANADU

Xanadu is located in Orlando, Florida. It is owned by private investors and used as a show-case for different suppliers to display and demonstrate their various products.

Unlike the other two houses, Xanadu embodies architectural innovations: its external appearance is unique. The unconventional form is supposed to express symbolically the novel thinking in the infrastructure of the house. One of its founding fathers, the architect Roy Mason, invented the term 'architronics', to signify the designed integration of building structure and information technology (Mason, 1983).

Xanadu too has a central control unit that integrates various appliances. It is described as an analogue of the human brain, emphasizing differences in function between left and right hemispheres.

The interior of the house seems unfinished; it has no comprehensive style. Each application stands alone and fails to blend into the futuristic unity promised in the brochures. Whereas in the Honeywell and NAHB houses the control network is designed for application to an existing structure, in Xanadu the net is integral with its innovatory structure and is thought of mainly as applicable to new construction.

TECHNOLOGICAL DEVELOPMENTS: WHAT DO DESIGNERS HAVE IN MIND?

Leaving aside the appliances designers liked to tell us about in futuristic terms, I chose to concentrate on new technologies actually visible or simulated here and now in the smart house prototypes.

TECHNOLOGIES IN THE HONEYWELL HOUSE

The substance of the Honeywell smart house concept is *integration,* the central programming of diversified control and regulation systems. The main R&D effort is directed towards a control system integrating: remote registration of outdoor temperature and humidity, regulation of indoor air quality, temperature and environmental control in specified zones and light regulation. It includes control of an advanced security system, with motion detectors. For instance, a video camera scans the main entrance and shows visitors on a monitor. It also involves service/diagnosis equipment and makes use of voice recognition and voice information. A safety device, for example, detects smoke and alerts the inhabitants, indicating on a video screen both the source of the fire and the appropriate action.

Honeywell pay particular attention to means of reducing energy consumption. With this in mind, they have invested considerable effort in a motion-activated system of light control in which lights switch on and off in response to information from motion detectors as to where people are currently located. (Besides, all lights are automatically switched on if the security alarm sounds.) Honeywell are not very happy with the results so far, however. To try out the system in a natural situation they had invited several people to the test house for dinner. As the guests entered the dining room, the lights obligingly went on. But when everyone had settled around the table and all was still the room was suddenly plunged in to darkness. The Honeywell engineers had to ask their guests to flap their arms to activate the lights again. On consideration, Honeywell now feel voice activation may have more potential, in combination with infrared remote control.

To sum up, the technologies in the Honeywell version of the home of tomorrow are applied to light and heat regulation, to security control and alarm systems. Technologies that have anything to do with *housework* are notably absent.

TECHNOLOGIES IN NAHB'S SMART HOUSE

In today's home we have different cables for different types of power or energy. In 1988 NAHB directed their R&D efforts to the development of a system to make all sources of power available with the same cable and through identical power-points. In such a multi-cable system the microwave oven, the washing machine, the home computer and the telephone may all be plugged into the same socket. This calls for purpose-designed appliances, of course, for only those equipped with the correct microchip will access the new power source. Signals from the microchip in each appliance will be sanctioned by a chip in the control unit.

SHDVI does not see its role as developing new appliances as such. They are, rather, projecting a future in which domestic technology is adjusted to their own project: the new network. The washing machine will signal on the television screen when the washing is ready to be moved to the tumble-dryer. The vacuum cleaner will be programmed to stop when someone is at the door or when the phone rings. When the temperature in the microwave indicates that dinner is almost ready it will signal to the hot-plate to warm the soup and to the stereo to provide the right background music for the meal. In addition to integrating in-house appliances in this way, the house net will also be connected to outside communication networks. It will support telework, telebanking and teleshopping as such services become available to private households.

The appliances displayed in this second smart house, then, are familiar technologies. The only thing that is new is their integration. Again we have to emphasize: the technological changes envisaged here are a long way from being consciously concerned with routine housework.

TECHNOLOGIES IN XANADU

As we saw, Xanadu has rooms with traditional functions: kitchen, bedroom, bathroom, etc. In every room appliances are presented that, claim the designers, are innovatory. In the book about the house, the new appliances are presented in a 'hi-tech' style, and to a certain extent this is carried through in the house itself. Xanadu is represented as a house you can talk to, a house that answers in different voices, where every room can be adjusted to your changing moods, a house that is servant, adviser and friend to each individual member of the household. Controlling all the functions in the home is Xanadu's house-brain.

Xanadu's technologies, with certain exceptions, are not dissimilar from those in the two prototypes already described, though their applications encompass a wider range of activities. These applications, however, have not all yet reached the stage of being prototypes. Some are simulations anticipating future possibilities.

DREAMING OF INTEGRATION

Our first question concerned the appliances in the home of the future. The list of what we found as testable prototypes – disregarding mere future possibilities – is neither extensive nor impressive. The innovations discussed above amount to control of:

- energy (heating and lighting);
- safety (security and fire alarms);
- communication (information and messaging, within the home and between the home and the outside world);
- entertainment (television, compact disc player, video recorder, computer games);
- environment (temperature, air pollution).

None of the technologies on this list differ radically from technologies already in existence (Miles, 1988). All are available – albeit unintegrated – on the market today. All that is new about these 'smart houses' is the *integration* itself, linking different appliances in a central local network, variously called a 'small area network' (SAN), 'homebus', *domotique* or 'house-brain'.

This is the designers' dream, therefore – integration, centralized control and regulation of all functions in the home. This is the core of the smart home as a socio-technical construction. Many different companies and organizations today are engaged in R&D projects for such home networks, and the battle over standards is preoccupying all the big electronic firms and other contenders such as the NAHB. Whoever wins the standardization battle will have a clear advantage in the future market for networks and new appliances.

HOUSEWORK: OUT OF SIGHT, OUT OF MIND

Women and men traditionally have distinct and different work in the home. Housework, still mainly women's unpaid work, comprises the most repetitious and time-consuming tasks in the household – cooking, washing, cleaning, tidying, mending. Turning to the second topic in our research, then, the precise activities preoccupying the designers of smart houses, we must ask: Does housework feature in their thinking about the smart house? What do they seem to know about housework?

HONEYWELL: THE HOUSE WILL 'DO THE JOB FOR YOU'

For Honeywell the main idea about the smart house is, to quote an R&D manager, that 'it does more things for you, the way you would like to have them done, than today's houses'. This means the overall purpose of the smart house is to help the owner so that he (I use the pronoun advisedly) will 'no longer have to think about how things are done'. All he has to be concerned with is 'whether the technologies are simple to use, increase comfort, are pleasant and affordable'. Housework is not mentioned in any way here – though one could imagine that technological solutions that increase comfort could relate to housework somehow. The designers responded to our question as to the *advantages* of the smart house with the following words – listed in order of the priority they felt they would have in the market: comfort, security, convenience, energy saving and entertainment. Labour-saving was not mentioned. Neither was it mentioned when they were asked about any *disadvantages* in the smart house. The main problem pointed out was a new kind of hazard: vulnerability to the 'housebreak'. With all appliances integrated in a single electronic network, a failure due to technical breakdown or human interference would bring down the entire system.

It seems strange that in talk about 'a house that will do the job for you', 'job' does not refer to the actual work that is carried on in a house. Housework is no part of what this house will 'do' for you. This anomaly became yet more obvious when one of our informants went on to tell us how their prototype differed from Japanese home automation. According to him, Japanese systems are designed to leave the finishing of jobs to manual intervention. Japanese culture, he explained, is extremely service minded. In Japanese households women render service to men. Even when technologically possible to eliminate it, the Japanese do not want to change this service relationship. North Americans, he said, by contrast, see the optimal use of technology as full automation of as many activities as possible. Yet he did not see the paradox of Honeywell's own lack of concern with housework.

NAHB: A HOUSE THAT WILL 'TAKE CARE OF ME'

We found the same tendency at the NAHB. They present their smart house as, primarily, 'a house which will take care of me'. This implies the house will do 'anything you want to be done in your home today and in the future'. Such a general concept could, of course, well include housework. On asking for more detail however we were told that it is first necessary to develop a communication network to modernize the basic infrastructure of the house. This network would then act as an invitation to suppliers of domestic technology to intensify their product development with the new network in mind. Housework as such was not NAHB's concern.

When asked more precisely what it means that a house will do 'anything you want done', the NAHB designers signalled as important that the house will be more comfortable, safer and easier to live in. Other advantages cited were better communication with the surrounding world, saving on energy, and enhanced entertainment. Things are vaguely glimpsed as being 'done' in a home, but housework as such is invisible and it has not occurred to the NAHB designers that users might like the house to carry out the time-consuming activities of housework.

XANADU: A HOUSE TO SERVE YOU

Xanadu is somewhat different. Integration in a house network is important here too, but in addition this more social, more imaginative version of the smart house does accommodate (albeit rather elliptical) references to housework. The title page in the book about Xanadu, for example, has a picture of a robot serving mother breakfast. The accompanying text reads:

'We are not replacing Mommy with a robot. We are presenting ideas on how to design, build and use a home in new ways that can reduce drudgery while increasing comfort, convenience and security' (Mason, 1983, p. 1). Housework is not mentioned explicitly, but it is easy to interpolate: drudgery will be reduced. The robot serving mother is a technical solution that serves the traditional server.

Family life is often mentioned, and the house is designed to be a place in which people can live happily together.

> What is really futuristic about an architronic house like Xanadu...is not the way it looks but the way it works. In this sense, the house of the future will be more like the houses of the past than like the houses of today' (Mason, 1983, p. 43).

The house is intended to work in such a way as to give the family more opportunity to spend time together, but the designers say nothing about how work time can be saved to make this a possibility.

Xanadu's message is therefore ambiguous. Women as mothers and housewives are shown as playing an important role in the home. But we are left unclear as to whether it is women's work they mean when claiming the house will reduce drudgery.

IGNORANCE OF HOUSEWORK

During the interviews we pressed the housework issue. When making appointments with informants we told them explicitly that housework would be our main focus. Nevertheless, when it came to it, they seemed surprised to be asked about it, and their answers were imprecise. NAHB said housework was not their concern – they left that to the white goods producers. At Honeywell they said they had paid some attention to housework, but when prompted they gave unconvincing examples such as the automatic light switch. They justified this as facilitating housework by arguing that a housewife entering a room with her hands full of wet clothes would not have to put them down to turn on the light.

In Xanadu one example of a housework appliance was the 'robutler'. This device was said to serve drinks. In fact, someone had to fill the glasses first and place them on exactly the right spot for the robutler to collect them. The machine then required guidance by remote control in serving them. There seemed to be little saving in manual intervention and, besides, serving drinks can hardly be said to be a burdensome task in the average home.

Another instance of Xanadu's insubstantial inventions is the 'gourmet autochef'. It sounds interesting and looks fancy, but on closer inspection is found to do nothing except suggest a menu for the dinner party. The housewife (a woman is shown in the picture) is still responsible for planning, shopping, cooking and all the rest of the work that goes into preparing a meal. The gourmet autochef, when the chips are down, is no more than a computer program.

When reflecting on what goes on in a home the Xanadu designers say 'today home is often little more than a place to sleep, eat a meal or two and store possessions' (Mason, 1983, p. 16). This is a highly misleading description of what takes place in a home (Cowan, 1983). A housewife would certainly ask 'Does nobody change the sheets? Is that meal not cooked and are the dishes not washed up afterwards? Are those possessions never dusted?'

The designers' knowledge of such material realities of housework is scanty indeed. First, the variety and necessity of today's housework is quite overlooked. 'Once household chores were regarded as inescapable duties – like tending animals or crops on a farm. But today they are more often resented as impositions that everyone in the family would like to avoid.' They continue: 'As a result a host of new household appliances are appearing that require less time and physical effort to do unpleasant jobs.' Yet they clearly have no idea of housework's centrally time-consuming tasks for they cite quite peripheral appliances: 'the toilet-bowl cleaner that fits inside the tank, the in-sink garbage disposal, trash compactor etc.' (Mason, 1983, pp. 19-20).

What is more, many of the appliances described in connection with Xanadu, technologies that might seem to promise to reduce household labour, are as yet no more than future possibilities. There are plans, for instance, for a closet that could make the washing machine superfluous. Vapour is distributed inside the closet during the night to clean the clothes where they hang. Despite the fact that a woman, Frances GABe, pioneered such a concept some years ago in her 'self-cleaning house' (GABe, 1983), this cleaning-cupboard does not exist in Xanadu even as a prototype – its control panel is no more than a simulation, the innovation no more than a thought.

In printed publicity about these smart homes, the housewife is sometimes pictured with new technologies. She smiles happily by the computer in her kitchen. Our interviews with the men behind the publicity, however, convinced us that they did not know much about this woman's work and visions for the future.

WOMEN AS A SOCIAL GROUP: RELEVANT BUT ABSENT

I move now to the third question to ask: just whom, then, do the designers have in mind as their target consumer? 'Relevant social group' is a term used by Trevor Pinch and Wiebe Bijker to denote 'institutions and organizations...as well as organized or unorganized groups of individuals' for whom an artefact has a shared 'set of meanings'. They emphasize specifically that the social group of 'consumers' or 'users' fulfils such a requirement and should be included in the analysis of a technological development (Pinch and Bijker, 1987, p. 30).

Women are a relevant social group in the development of the smart house in at least two ways. First, women possess important skills for and knowledge about the home that should be a resource in the design process. Second, since the home is women's traditional domain, women could be seen as an important target in the marketing of the smart house.

Often, when the user-producer relationship is discussed in connection with technical design it refers to a relation where the user's competence, based on task-related experience, knowledge and skills, could guide the development of a new tool or machine for factory or office. In a similar way women's competence in housework could constitute an important innovative resource for the development of home-oriented information technology.

When asked about the relevance of users in the design process, producers said they found it 'an interesting idea'. Such an interest would seem self-evident: after all, how can one expect a product to sell except by ensuring it corresponds to consumer needs and demands? Yet we found evidence of only one actual contact by these designers with potential users: the instance already described when Honeywell invited guests to dinner and left them in the dark. Women's housework skills are being entirely neglected as a design resource.

Who exactly do the producers see as the target purchaser of their smart house? It proved difficult to pin them down. 'Anyone and everyone' seemed to be the answer. NAHB was the most specific: they had at least decided to concentrate on the one-family house. The others had only vague pictures of potential consumers. Honeywell see the user as 'the owner', synonymous with the man of the house. It is 'the owner' who will no longer have to think about 'how things are done'. The 'things' they rank as potentially most important in the house market are male activities and the most important consumer group (they say when pressed) is the technically-interested male.

In Xanadu too the user/consumer is difficult to identify. When the *user* is discussed at all it is in connection with specific appliances. Alleviation of household labour is mentioned as a potential demand in the market but the robutler and the gourmet autochef typify the lightweight response.

When we asked about the *consumer* the designers had in mind, we were answered several times with rather similar stories of individuals that had built and equipped their own houses with new technologies. One example was a Norwegian engineer living in Texas who had built his own private smart house. A detail that fascinated the storytellers was the lighting system he had devised: the lights would dim along the corridor when, for example, the children went to their rooms to sleep. This was the kind of consumer the producers liked and speculated about, one who would share their fascination with electronic or technological gadgets. That this man had been unsuccessful in his attempt to sell his house seemed not to dampen their enthusiasm. It is the technology-as-such, the way artefacts function in technical terms, that fascinates the designers. Again, the target consumer is implicitly the technically-interested man, not unlike the stereotype of the computer hacker.

In summary, then, the men (and it is men) producing prototypes of the intelligent house of the future and designing its key technologies have failed to visualize in any detail the user/consumer of their innovation. In so far as they have one in mind, it is someone in their own image. They have ignored the fact that the home is a place of work (women's housework) and overlook women, whose domain they are in effect transforming, as a target consumer group.

GENDERED INNOVATION PROCESS, GENDERED TECHNOLOGY

Smart house prototypes resemble their literary forerunners, those scenarios of the 1980s that presented home-oriented information technologies as gender neutral. We have seen just how far from reality this is. Nothing could be clearer evidence of the gendering of the technological innovation process than the absence of women we have uncovered in this design and development process – their invisibility, the waste of their housework knowledge.

Smart house prototypes are one of several kinds of attempt to create today the technological home of tomorrow. The nature of that future home has serious implications for women. Technology as an element in social action has the power to change, or to preserve, today's gender relations, including the sexual division of labour. This particular sociotechnical construction is transparently not intended to change gender inequality.

To say the smart house is a masculine construct and leave it at that, however, is unnecessarily defeatist. Technology should not be understood as ready-made artefacts whose use is non-negotiable. A technology's impacts are never entirely determined by its designers' and producers' intentions or inscribed visions (Akrich, 1992). Rather, technology should be seen as *process* – open to flexible interpretation by its various user groups. To look at the eventual application of a technology, to see what users make of it for themselves, is often to dissipate the pessimism. Unfortunately, in the case of the smart house, still at prototype stage, we cannot yet see it in use.

Despite the non-fixed nature of a technology, however, to observe its gendering in those early stages before it reaches the user is of vital importance for understanding what happens subsequently. The smart house is a typical case of 'technology push', in contrast to 'consumer pull'. Its inspiration lies not in the practices of everyday life but in a fascination with what is technically possible.

The gender implications of this are clear. Technology is traditionally a masculine domain and an interest in technology is seen as constitutive of masculinity (Lie, 1991). When technological possibilities lead, as they do in the socio-technical construction of the smart house, the house that results is somewhat like Corbusier's 'machine for living' – a highly masculine concept.

Conversely, decor and style are traditionally a feminine domain, and creative flair in home-making has been described as an important part of feminine identity (Prokopi, 1978; Gullestad, 1989). There is a crucial difference between a house and a home. It is women, in the main, whose work and skills make the former into the latter. Decor and style have no place in these prototypes. The smart house is no home (Miles, 1991).

As we saw, historical studies of housework and domestic technology have disproved the idea that new technologies have reduced the time spent on housework (Boalt, 1983; Cowan, 1983; Hagelskjaer, 1986). None the less, the popular conception of domestic technology remains one of 'time-saving' (Vanek, 1974, 1978), and it seems reasonable to expect to find such a conception among the designers of the smart house. Instead, they manifest neither interest in nor knowledge of housework. The home is acknowledged as an important area of everyday life, yet the work that sustains it is rendered invisible.

To summarize, then, the integrative technology that is the core of the smart home project appears unlikely to initiate any developments that would substitute or save time in housework. As a result we may anticipate that the producers will experience serious difficulties in selling their ideas. This socio-technical construct reflects a male idea of the home and responds to male activities in it. It is gendered in what it leaves out – its lack of support for changes in the domestic sexual division of labour.

There has been no actual user participation in the innovation process of the smart house to date, nor is the anticipated user described in more than hazy outline. Behind the shadowy notion however we can see the consumer these designers really have in mind: a technically-interested man in their own image. Women and men could, at different stages in the development process, 'negotiate'. Here such a negotiation has not taken place. And in women's exclusion from the imagination of its designers, as a 'relevant social group' we see how deeply gendered the nature of an innovation process can be. Is our finding on the smart house cause for hope or fear? For women who may have reckoned on saving themselves time and labour the smart house looks like being a cheat. For techno-freaks who hope for some really interesting and significant inventions the smart house will likewise be a disappointment. On the other hand, for those who may have feared 'technology is taking command' the evidence assembled here should be reassuring. Nothing much, it seems, is going to change because of the smart house – at least not in terms of gender.

NOTES

1 'Smart home', 'intelligent home', 'home automation' and 'computerhome' are synonyms for 'smart house'. The term denotes the extensive application of information technology (IT) to the dwelling of the future. Here, for simplicity, I limit myself to the term 'smart house'.

2 The research project, *From the Home Computer to the Computer Home*, was financed by the Norwegian Research Council (NAVF) programme on *Technology and Society* and was carried out in the Institute of Social Research in Industry (SINTEF-IFIM), Trondheim, during 1988-90. The planning of the project and collection of data were undertaken in

cooperation with my late colleague Elin Hagelskjaer, who died in February 1990.

3   The existing literature on the smart house is mainly concerned with the functions of appliances in technical terms.

4   These three North American houses were chosen because in 1987 when I applied for money for this project they were the ones I knew about. Later I learned of several other prototypes being built in European countries (including a joint project in the European Community) and in Japan, as well as others in the United States. Information about the European houses, and permission to visit them for research purposes, proved difficult to obtain.

REFERENCES

Akrich, M. (1992) The description of technical objects, in Bijker, W.E. and Law, J. (eds) *Shaping Technology/Building Society: Studies in Sociotechnical Change.* Cambridge, MA: MIT Press.

Berg, A.-J. (1988) Husarbeid som et trekkspill om teknologi [Stretch-to-fit housework, adjusts to all technologies], in Lie, *M. et al.* (eds) *I menns bilde: Kvinner-teknologi-arbeid [In the Image of Men: Women-Technology-Work],* Trondheim, Tapir.

Berg, A.-J. (1989) Informasjonsteknologi i hjemmet – den nye hjemmefronten [IT in the home – old or new forms of resistance], in Sørensen, K. and Espeli, T. (eds) *Ny Teknologi en Utfordring for Samfunnsforskning [New Technology – A Challenge to Social Science],* Oslo, NAVF-NTNF-NORAS.

Berg, A.-J. (1991) He, she, and I.T. – designing the technological home of the future, in Sørensen, K. and Berg, A.-J. (eds) *Technology and Everyday Life: Trajectories and Transformations,* Report No. 5: Proceedings from a Workshop in Trondheim, May 1990, Oslo, NAVF-NTNF-NORAS.

Boalt, C. (1983) *Tid för hemarbete. Hur lång tid då? [Time for housework but how much time?],* in Åkerman, B. (ed.) *Den okanda vardagen – om arbetet i hemmen [Unknown Everyday Life – On Housework],* Stockholm, Akademilitteratur.

Cockburn, C. (1983) *Brothers: Male Dominance and Technological Change,* London, Pluto Press.

Cockburn, C. (1985) *Machinery of Dominance: Women, Men and Technical Know-how,* London, Pluto Press.

Cowan, R. S. (1983) *More Work for Mother: The Ironies of Household Technology from the Open Hearth to the Microwave,* New York, Basic Books.

Cronberg, Tarja (1987) *Teknologi og Hverdagsliv [Technology and Everyday Life],* Copenhagen, Nyt fra samfundsvidenskaberne.

Cronberg, T. and Sangregorio, I.-L. (1983) *Fagre nye Hverdag [Brave New Everyday Life]*, Copenhagen, Delta.

GABe, F. (1983) 'The GABe self-cleaning house', in Zimmerman, J. (ed.) *The Technological Woman: Interfacing with Tomorrow*, New York, Praeger.

Gorz, A. (1981) *Farvel til Proletariatet [Adieux au proletariat]*, Copenhagen, Politisk Revy.

Gullestad, M. (1987) *Kitchen-Table Society*, Oslo, Universitetsforlaget.

Gullestad, M. (1989) *Kultur og Hverdagsliv [Culture and Everyday Life]*, Oslo, Universitetsforlaget.

Hagelskjaer, E. (1986) *Teknologiens Tommeliden: Moderne Tider i Husholdningen [The Tom Thumb of Technology Modern Times in Households]*, Aalborg, Aalborg Universitetsforlag.

Harding, S. (1986) *The Science Question in Feminism*, Ithaca, Cornell University Press.

Harding, S. (1991) *Whose Science? Whose Knowledge?*, Milton Keynes, Open University Press.

Lie, M. (1991) *Technology as Masculinity*, Trondheim, SINTEF-IFIM.

Lie, M., Berg, A.-J., Kaul, H., Kvande, E., Rasmussen, B. and Sørensen, K. (1988) *I menns bilde: Kvinner-teknologi-arbeid [In the Image of Men: Women-Technology-Work]*, Trondheim, Tapir.

Mason, R. (1983) *Xanadu: The Computerized Home of Tomorrow and How It Can Be Yours Today!*, Washington, DC, Aeropolis Books.

Miles, I. (1988) *Home Informatics. Information Technology and the Transformation of Everyday Life*, London, Pinter Publishers.

Miles, I. (1991) 'A smart house is not a home?', in Sørensen, K. and Berg, A.-J. (eds) *Technology and Everyday Life: Trajectories and Transformations*, Report No. 5, Proceedings from a Workshop in Trondheim, May 1990, Oslo, NAVF, NTNF, NORAS.

Nyberg, A. (1990) 'Hushallsteknik – mødrars møda och mäns makt [Household technology – mothers' toil and men's power]', in Beekman, S. (ed.) *Teknokrati, Arbete, Makt [Technocracy, Work, Power]*, Stockholm, Carlsons.

Pinch, T. and Bijker, W. E. (1987) 'The social construction of facts and artefacts: or how the sociology of science and the sociology of technology might henefit each other', in Bijker, W.E., Hughes, T.P. and Pinch, T. (eds) *The Social Construction of Technological Systems*, Cambridge, MA and London, MIT Press.

Prokopi, V. (1978) *Kvindelig livssammenherg [Female Life Situations]*, Copenhagen, GMT.

Sørensen, K. and Berg, A.-J. (1987) 'Genderization of technology among Norwegian engineering students', *Acta Sociologica*, Vol. 30, No. 2, pp. 151-71.

Toffler, A. (1981) *Den tredje bçlge [The Third Wave]*, Copenhagen, Politisk Revy.

Tuana, N. (ed.) (1989) *Feminism and Science*, Bloomington, Indiana University Press.

Vanek, J. (1974) 'Time spent in housework', *Scientific American*, Vol. 231, No. 5.

Vanek, J. (1978) 'Housewives as workers', in Stromberg, A. and Harkess, S. (eds) *Women Working, Theories and Facts in Perspective*, Palo Alto.

Wajcman, J. (1991) *Feminism Confronts Technology*, Cambridge, Polity Press.

Zimmerman, J. (1986) *Once Upon the Future*, London, Pandora.

ACCESS AND INEQUALITY

Ray Thomas
Faculty of Social Sciences, The Open University

It is arguable that there has already been an IT revolution, in Britain and in most other advanced industrial societies, over the past decade or so. The large majority of people in employment, for example, now use a computer or some other microprocessor driven device to do their work. This development has in most cases substantially changed the nature of their work, the status of their work, and their future employment prospects. But if this change has constituted a revolution it has not been one which has been widely acknowledged.

The growth in the 1980s of unemployment and of inequalities in the distribution of incomes, for example, are seen as the product of Thatcherism, not of information technology developments. The importance of the influence of the policies of Thatcherism on levels of unemployment and the distribution of incomes cannot be denied. But the political success of Thatcherism in the 1980s may be inseparable from IT developments. The recession of the early 1980s, for example, was associated with a decline in employment in manufacturing of two millions, and poses the question of the extent to which this 'shakeout' be attributed to the adoption of new technology.

Social influences on the nature of new technologies and the social influences of adoption of the new technologies may constitute a more complex area of study than the ideology of Thatcherism. Critical studies such as Webster and Robins (1986) and Lyon (1988) are interpretative and make little attempt to articulate empirical generalisations about recent changes, nor to identify likely future trends. But the dominant tone of most literature on IT developments has been optimistic in tone and geared to the future (e.g. Naisbitt, 1991), and optimistic views of the future assume a positive contribution by IT developments (e.g. Handy (1989), Toffler (1980)). The optimists identify choices, but, implicitly or explicitly, they assert the benign overall influence of the technology and present visions of the world immeasurably enriched by information products and services.

This article does not quarrel with these visions. These visions show how groups of people can enrich their lives by constructively using the new technology within a particular cultural milieu on more or less equal terms with thousands or even millions of others. Most of these visions are well within the bounds of possibility, many of them have already happened for some people, and are likely to happen for many more people in the future.

This article argues however that these visions are distortions because of their egalitarian assumptions. They are selective in their focus on the vanguard of IT developments. These visions focus on the lives of the relatively privileged and affluent members of human societies and on the prospects for IT developments in relatively advanced industrialised countries. They fail to acknowledge that access to new IT developments is not distributed evenly, that access by the underprivileged members of industrial societies, and by nearly all members of non-industrial societies, is limited.

FACTORS MAKING FOR INEQUALITY

The contention of this article is that IT developments, far from creating a more egalitarian world, will bring about a world which is more unequal as well as socially fragmented. IT developments tend to confirm or reinforce existing inequalities, and to create new inequalities. The world of the future is likely to be closer in character to that portrayed in *Neuromancer* and other science fiction novels by William Gibson (1985) who invented the term cyberspace – than to the utopias of the technocrats. Gibson does not write about the rich elites of the future, though he sometimes writes about their children. Gibsons main focus is the extraordinary lives of what we might otherwise regard as ordinary people, living in the debris left behind by industrial societies. Gibson's world is one of a multiplicity of conflicting groups, of short term lifestyles, of people hanging on in desperation to the bits of technology which make their life tolerable.

Gibson is not a social scientist. But there are four reasons why his imaginings, which seem to be consistent with growing inequalities, deserve to be taken just as seriously as the visions of the technological optimists. First, IT developments are the product of capitalism. Their nature is shaped by what is expected to sell, not by what is expected to help produce a utopia or an egalitarian society. Second, the pace of change in IT developments means that, for the foreseeable future the social and cultural gaps between different levels of adoption of IT can be expected to widen – in particular the gap between those who have access to the new technology and those who do not.

Third, new IT developments build upon existing technology, and fourth, those members of society and those countries who are already relatively affluent and educated are better placed to exploit the new technology than those who are poor. These third and fourth factors are likely to work synergistically to reinforce and magnify existing inequalities.

CAPITALISM AND INFORMATION TECHNOLOGY

The rapid rate of technological development in microprocessors and growth in the size of the market disguises the ferocity of competition within IT industries. Growth of employment has softened the social traumas associated with structural changes within the IT industries. But there can be few other industries where competition is more ruthless and which have been subject to more rapid change in terms of required employee skills.

The usual mode of development among the leading players in the computer industry is for a firm to try to kill off competition and to create a near monopoly through establishing a de facto standard. When such a standard is established customers can be charged what they can afford to pay without fear of undercutting. The profits can be used to undercut potential competitors.

IBM held an 80% monopoly of the computer market for decades. According to DeLamarter (1988) the experience of Thomas Watson, who led IBM from the 1920s to the 1950s, was gained with National Cash Register whose unscrupulous methods of business were the main inspiration for US antitrust legislation. IBM established its monopoly position in the interwar period on the basis of selling tabulating card equipment. IBM established its monopoly in computers through its monopoly of punched card mechanisms which were then essential to computers as input devices. IBM maintained its monopoly position by using below-cost pricing to destroy competitors.

Even IBM were unable to respond to the rate of technological progress in the 1980s symbolised by advent of the microcomputer. By the 1990s IBM suffered losses without precedent and was obliged for the first time in its history to enforce heavy redundancy programmes. Wallace and Erickson (1992) and Cringley (1992) give accounts of how Microsoft helped to undermine IBM's position through apparently friendly agreements. But the micro has not heralded an era in which the needs of the users come first. Instead the micro has spawned new monopolies.

At the time of writing (1994), Microsoft's domination of the personal computer software market is actually greater than that ever achieved by IBM in the area of mainframe computers. Microsoft's dominance is achieved by selling low cost suites of programmes based on virtual monopoly of the operating system level set of programs (i.e., at the time of writing, MSDOS and the Windows environment) (see Schofield (1994)). Microsoft's sales strategy involves the supply of new client/server systems to markets previously dominated by IBM or some other major supplier, and the supply of systems to those whose existing microcomputers are already two, or three, or four years old and so can be regarded as obsolescent. Microsoft's sales strategy gets the active support of producers of microcomputers and most kinds of peripheral equipment. Microsoft's new programs are ever more demanding in terms of processor speed and size of memory – which is good for sales of hardware.

There is nothing immoral about Microsoft's marketing strategy. Microsoft have no need to indulge in the kind of competition which IBM used to achieve and maintain its dominance. In terms of performance for cost Microsoft's systems often perform better than the systems they replace. But Microsoft's marketing strategy is designed to achieve dominance, through establishing Microsoft programs as the de facto standard, and selling to major organizations. Meeting users' needs can only be a secondary consideration in such a market-share oriented strategy.

Toffler, writing in the late 1970s, with the invention of the term 'prosumer' identifies a 'blurring of the line that separates producer from consumer' (Toffler, 1980, p. 278). The concept of the prosumer does not capture major features of the market for microcomputers. Far from being prosumers, most users of microcomputers do not have any choice about the nature of the systems they use. Users in organizations have no more choice about their micro systems than users in the 1970s had about the computer terminals which were installed on their work desks. Those who buy for themselves have a choice between different machines running the same Microsoft programmes.

Naisbitt and Burdene writing in the 1980s argue that the new technology represents a triumph of empowerment of the individual. Technology is empowering the individual in the sense that the new programs are more powerful and complex than the old. But it is difficult to identify ways in which such empowerment of individuals is to help create an egalitarian society. The creation of an egalitarian society is certainly not on Microsoft's agenda.

THE PACE OF CHANGE

The perspective of the users of IT systems is often one which encourages a kind of egalitarian optimism. Users can easily identify with other users of the same kinds of system. Use of a system can bring membership of a users group – many of which are international in character. Use of IT systems can bring membership of a global community created by communications systems such as Internet and the Association for Progressive Communication (APC). It is perhaps users perspectives of this nature which have inspired the visions of the optimist summarised in the first section of this article.

Such perspectives fail to take into account the many different levels associated with the pace of IT developments. Underlying the pervasive and variegated pattern of IT developments is a continuous rate of technical progress which has no precedent in human history. Many inventions have triggered further technological advances, but the digital computer seems unique in generating a wide range of advances over a long period of time.

George Moore (cofounder of Intel which made the chip which runs the Microsoft dominated PC market) formulated a 'law' which states that the number of transistors which can be built on the same size piece of silicon will double every eighteen months. The output of Intel, and that of other chip manufacturers, has matched this pace of development up to the time of writing. It is commonly estimated that the cost of semiconductor storage has fallen by about 20% every year over the past two decades, and it is expected that this pace of development will continue for the foreseeable future.

There has been a comparable pace of development in other components of computer systems such as data storage – with the transition from magnetic tape, to floppy disk, hard disk and CD-ROM, which can hold the equivalent of a library of books and costs about £1 to make. The invention of packet switching has supported exploitation of the existing telephone network designed for analogue transmission and the development of optical fibre networks – which promise vast improvements in the capacity of telecommunications systems.

This pace of technical progress is continually changing and extending the nature of IT developments. Until the 1980s the costs of IT devices were relatively high. New IT developments were mostly confined to the commercial sector and were not generally visible to a wide public. But by the late 1980s and 1990s the cost of IT devices had fallen to mass market levels. Already at the time of writing in 1994, a wide range of IT devices and services had become available to a substantial proportion of the population of advanced industrial countries. It is expected that a rapid rate of development will continue until prices fall to levels which will enable a growing proportion of users to treat IT products as if they were disposable.

Such a rate of technical progress supports a multiplicity of IT products and services – and many different levels of usage. At the forefront are a few groups of advanced users of cutting edge technology who upgrade their system every year or so. But the majority of users will be content with what Schofield characterised as 'trailing edge technology' (which he argued usually offered better value for money).

Now that prices have fallen to mass market levels, markets are large enough to support a wide range of trailing edge technologies. For the foreseeable future there will be a growing number of levels of development in IT systems. Advances at the cutting edge will continue to render last years systems out-of-date, but last year's systems will not be obsolescent. Accountants encourage firms to write off systems over a period of three years, but such systems can give good service for as long as there are support services available. IT products and systems become truly obsolescent when the expertise needed to support the users of the systems is dissipated.

Is should be noted that such genuine obsolescence means that there is a limit to any kind of 'trickle down' kind of mechanism in the use of IT developments. The entry level systems tend to maintain their prices in spite of technical advances. This means that the gap between what can be broadly characterised as users and non-users is reinforced rather than softened by the pace of technical progress.

THE DISTRIBUTION OF INFRASTRUCTURE

The systems that support use of the voice telephone (sometimes called POTS – Plain Old Telephone Service) are one of the most important components of the IT revolution. The range of services which can nowadays be delivered via the telephone network using a computer is almost unlimited (sometimes referred to as PANS – Pretty Amazing New Stuff). But the possibilities of participating in the informational panopticon opened up by digital use of the world-wide telephone network varies dramatically between the advanced industrial countries and what used to be called the third world.

The number of telephones per head of population in industrialised countries falls in the range 0.5 to 1, but there is less than one telephone per 100 people in most countries of Africa, India and other countries of South Asia. China does not even get into the charts.

One of the most important groups of optimists about the future use of the world-wide telephone network is represented by the Association for Progressive Communication. Frederick, a spokesperson for APC, points to the ways in which communications can create new communities and to possibilities for global discussions among non-governmental organizations within the fields of 'human rights, consumer protection, peace, gender equality, racial justice, and environment.' (Frederick, 1992, p.. 285).

Looked at from a distant perspective APC represent a new elite – the chattering classes of the turn of the century. Their forebears were those who helped establish the British social survey tradition through the creation of local statistical societies to bear witness to the evils of nineteenth century urbanisation (see, Cullen, 1975). This is not to disparage the work of the APC. Just as statistics collected in the nineteenth century contributed to social reform, so can it be expected that the activities of members of the APC will contribute to the causes of human rights, gender equality, racial justice and environmental protection – and help maintain peace.

But the difference between the life and work styles of the APC elite and that of most of the world's population – the subject matter of many of their messages – will be magnified by these developments in communications. For the foreseeable future most of the world's population will not have easy access to a telephone, let alone digital services, and will not be able to participate in the electronic discussions which may well, ironically, give increased coverage to such topics as third world development.

The major users of the global telecommunications networks are not APC but commercial groups of various kinds. In a study specific to the dominant group of financial services, Wharf points to the importance of higher levels of infrastructure investment in maintaining inequalities, and provides a summary of a pattern which seems likely to be a characteristic of many other forms of IT development.

The comparative advantage of cities such as London, New York and Tokyo was accentuated by the presence of fibre optics networks and teleports. Simultaneously, satellites and fibre optic systems permitted the decentralisation of unskilled back office activities. Both trends have reinforced the transformation of these cities into repositories of skilled white-collar labour and accentuated the bifurcation of the regional labor market. Telecommunications systems, therefore, neither obliterate the importance of space nor iron out uneven development, but serve to replicate both phenomena. (Wharf, 1989, p. 267).

THE DISTRIBUTION OF INCOMES AND WEALTH

The reports of the United Nations Development Programme provide the most systematic approach to the measurement of human equalities at a global scale. The UNDP reports are not limited to consideration of inequalities between nations as measured by economic statistics – such as income per capita. The reports also consider other areas – such as inequalities in the distribution of incomes within nations, expectation of life, education as measured by literacy rates and years of schooling, gender inequalities and basic freedoms.

Real per capita income levels in the advanced industrial countries are more than ten times the level in most countries of Africa and South East Asia. The UNDP reports reject partial measures, such as per capita income, as adequately measuring differences in levels of development. But differences in per capita income do reflect ability to pay for IT products and services. Such differences in per capita income are also closely related to differences in the level of IT infrastructure discussed above. It can be expected that differences in income levels often work synergistically with differences in the level of infrastructure to perpetuate differences in levels of IT development.

Many other dimensions of levels of development are identified in the UNDP reports – including adult literacy, years of schooling, income distribution, and gender inequalities. It can reasonably be assumed that economic growth would often be associated with a reduction of inequalities in these other dimensions. But it cannot be assumed that the introduction of IT will reduce these inequalities.

Inequalities between men and women, for example are characteristic of all societies, but are usually much greater in developing countries than they are for the Scandinavian countries. The UNDP's gender-sensitive indexes of development indicate wider variations between countries than is shown by the unadjusted indexes. It seems likely that where women are treated unequally they will not have equal access to new IT systems. The introduction of IT would then increase the inequalities between men and women.

Differences in educational levels, as measured by the average number of years of schooling and in literacy levels, as measured by the proportion of adults in a society who can read, are indicators or inequality which also tend to reinforce the commonly associated differences in income per capita measures. Variations in access to IT developments can be expected to be associated with variations in levels of literacy.

Gender and educational inequalities illustrate the importance of institutional and cultural factors which have a powerful influence, independently of income levels, on ability to obtain and use IT products and services. But the UNDP reports do not provide evidence or suggest that IT can be used in any way to reduce differences in levels of development. A handful of Pacific rim countries have succeeded in using the manufacturing of IT products as a basis for rapid industrial growth, and Singapore has achieved dramatic advances based on IT services. But these countries are exceptional. In general, because access to IT developments is positively related to level of development in nearly every dimension, it can be expected that existing inequalities, between countries and within countries, will be magnified rather than diminished by IT developments.

THE INFORMATION ECONOMY

One of the major problems presented by the rapid rate of IT developments is, paradoxically, that information is becoming more available. There are doubts that market forces will provide sufficient impetus for sustained economic development if information is too freely available. As Branscomb put it 'information providers are investing both financial and intellectual capital into the production of the their information products. They must, in order to survive in the information economy, be paid fair market value for their work' (Brancsomb, 1986, p. 301)

The interest in the concepts of 'intellectual property rights' and 'the commoditization of information' , and 'information management' indicate a growing emphasis being given to the value of information and the role which information should play in the market place. But the emphasis on the role which information should play in the market provides a sharp contrast with the traditional attitude to information as expressed in education and in the public library system. The traditional function of the education and library sectors has been to provide information without charge, and where users do have to pay charges such as course fees, these are not related in any direct way to the value of the information which has been used.

The extent to which the position of the protagonists of intellectual property rights and the commoditization of information is inconsistent with the tradition of freely available information, and the extent to which these two positions are contradictory, provides the basis for a debate which goes far beyond the concern of this article (see Allott and Thomas (1993)). But the beliefs which are associated with these two positions may have a substantial influence on the degree of inequalities associated with IT developments.

If it is believed that the market should play a dominant role in the distribution of information, then the factors described in the earlier sections of this article which reinforce existing inequalities or create new inequalities may be strengthened. If on the other side the education and library sector traditions prevail it can be expected that there will be some countervailing influences supporting wide access to information services.

Both factors are at work in most kinds of information system. The national flat rate charge for letters irrespective of distance between place of posting and delivery constitutes a classic example of an information service which is both commercially intelligent and which provides near equal access to all. The tension between these two positions is evident in discussions on the future of the Internet which came into existence largely as a means of giving free electronic mail facilities to academics. At the time of writing there are occurring simultaneously proposals to upgrade the capacity of the system which would require increased financial support from governments, and substantial commercial interest in the use of the system.

The traditional information-should-be-free position is sometimes expressed in terms of providing universal access to an information service. In the United States the Communications Act of 1934 articulated in general terms a national goal of 'Universal Service' for telephones, and that kind of principle has also been debated in Britain in recent years. But the clearest recent statement comes from the proposal to create a National Information Infrastructure – the 'information superhighway' – in the United States. The Al Gore inspired Democratic administration has pointed to the dangers of developing inequalities with IT developments, and has proposed aims to counteract the danger:

> A major objective in developing the NII will be to extend the Universal Service concept to the information needs of the American people in the twenty-first century. As a matter of fundamental fairness, this nation cannot accept a division of our people among telecommunications or information 'haves' and 'have-nots.' The Administration is committed to developing a broad, modern concept of Universal Service – one that would emphasise giving all Americans who desire it easy, affordable access to advanced communications and information services, regardless of income, disability, or location. (Brown, 1994)

This expression of this aim is a public and explicit acknowledgement, albeit within the boundary of a single country, of the importance of the problem discussed in this article. This notable acknowledgement may reflect the importance given to the maintenance of a sense of national identity in the United States. Communication is essential to the way human communities are usually created and maintained. Access to IT systems generally promises a sense of national or global identity. But the inequalities prognosticated in this article point to the limitations of access which bode the fragmentation of societies.

REFERENCES

Allott, M. and Thomas, R. (1993) 'Information as a commodity and the information economy', Proceedings of the International Conference on Information Technology and People, May 1993, ICSTI, Moscow, Part I, pp. 30-38.

Branscom, A. (1986) 'Law and culture in the information society', *The Information Society*, Vol 4, No 4, pp. 279-311.

Brown, R. H. (Chair) (1994) Agenda for Information Infrastructure Task Force, Washington, Department of Commerce.

Cringely, R. X. (1992) *Accidental Empires: How the Boys of Silicon Valley make their Millions, Battle Foreign Competion, and Still Can't Get a Date*, Penguin Books.

Cornes, R. (1990) *Business Systems: Design and Development*, Prentice Hall.

Cullen, M. (1975) *The Statitstical Movement in Early Victorian Britain*, Harvester Press.

DeLamarter, R. T. (1986) *Big Blue: IBM's Use and Abuse of Power*, Pan Books.

Frederick, H. (1993) 'Computer networks and the emergence of global civil society' in Harasim, L. (ed.) *Global Networks and International Communication*, MIT Press.

Gibson W. (1987) *Neuromancer.*

Handy, C. (1989) *The Age of Unreason*, Business Books.

Lyon, D. (1988) *The Information Society: Issues and Illusions*, Polity Press.

Naisbitt, J. and Burdene, P.A. (1991) *Megatrends 2000 – The Next Ten Years . . . Major Changes in your Life and World*, Pan Books: London.

Schofield, J. (1994) 'Windows NT – taking on the world', *Online Guardian*, 2 June, pp. 8-9.

Toffler, A. (1980) *The Third Wave*, Pan Books.

United Nations Development Programme (1991) *Human Development Report 1991*, OUP.

Wallace, J. and Erikson, J. (1992) *Hard Drive: Bill Gates and the Making of the Microsoft Empire*, Wiley.

Warf, B. (1989) 'Telecommunications and the globalization of financial services', *Professional Geographer*, 41 (3), pp. 257-271.

Webster, F. and Robins, K. (1986) *Information Technology: A Luddite Analysis*, Ablex Publishing.

PART 2 IT IN THE WORKPLACE

Geoff Einon, Faculty of Science, The Open University

INTRODUCTION

It has been argued that the application of IT at and to work represents a transformation so profound that it can be regarded as a 'technology-driven revolution', (Kennedy) which will have drastic consequences for all aspects of economic life, for all work organisations and for all workers. Not only the processes of production, but also those of clerical work, distribution, retail, design and indeed of management itself have been (or are capable of being) transformed by electronic processes of data collection, analysis, storage, transmission, and application. But if IT at work does represent a revolution, then there is certainly considerable debate about its nature, scope and impact.

The readings in Part 2, *IT in the Workplace* portray contemporary positions in industrial sociology developed from empirical studies of the uses of IT and other new technologies in manufacturing. These studies challenge the dogmatic theses of the nature of the labour process formulated and popular in the first half of this century- and which remained influential through the 1970s and into the 1980s. Marxist and Taylorist positions which view the role of new technologies as being to increase control over labour and, through deskilling, reduce labour costs, have not stood up to close scrutiny. This selection of readings presents a more eclectic and pragmatic approach to explanations of the implementation and impact of IT in the workplace.

In making the selection of readings, our concern for the application of IT in the workplace centres on two main themes. First, why and how is IT used at work? Secondly, what are the objectives of those who install expensive IT systems within organisations? These two questions appear to be straightforward and simple but unmask highly complex issues. For example, are management decisions on IT simply inevitable responses to an awareness of the benefits of the new technology, and thus in a sense technologically determined; or do managers make choices between a variety of technologies and applications? If managers make choices about IT then on what are these choices based and what factors influence the outcome of managerial decision-making and discussion?

The argument that the relationship between new technology is, and the utilisation of labour is not, a matter of technical determinism is at the heart of Lane's article. In her view the growing complexity and integration of new technology calls for an approach that enhances both the skills and autonomy of the workforce. But even though management strategy is not determined by technology, it may nonetheless be dependent on having a tradition of semi-autonomous work groups and, more importantly, on the availability of enough workers of sufficient skill without whom, as Hartmann *et al.* argue, less sophisticated equipment may have to be used or sophisticated equipment is used less effectively.

By the demonstration that Computer Numerical Control (CNC) equipment is adaptable to very different patterns of use and control, Hartmann *et al.* seek to attack the idea that technology is a given. They argue instead that its use reflects, inter alia corporate policy, workplace organisation and workplace skills. By referring to Hartmann *et al.*'s investigation it becomes more accurate to speak of the impacts if IT rather than of a single impact. For example, if deskilling has been common in the UK and the USA as Lane and Senker point out in their articles, in Japan and (West) Germany, work has often been designed to require flexibility and independent thought. In short, the skill implications of IT are complicated and highly variable: a mixture – as Senker puts it – of technology and management policy.

We might expect that decisions about the implementation of IT would be highly rational, based on good data, well analysed around clear objectives. But to assume this is to ignore the reality of organisational decision-making, which is that much decision-making is characterised by a range and variety of motives and principles, assumptions and objectives, some of which may conflict; and that the outcome of the processes of decision is likely to be negotiated and adjusted in the light of organisational cultures and politics. If we wish to study decisions about IT these need to be seen in the context of managerial decision-making as a whole.

Cultural, educational, socioeconomic, political and demographic differences are all seen to contribute to differences in the way that IT is implemented and in the degree and success of implementation. Control over labour is just one factor in decisions to implement IT. More important are strategies which are seen to promote economic survival in the market place in which the implementation of IT makes a contribution by maximising product performance or sales or by reducing production costs. Decisions about IT are also closely related to other change programmes – new products, new business strategies, new forms of organisation, new relationships with clients, suppliers and staff. The articles by Kennedy and by McLoughlin and Clark address these issues. Kennedy explores the issues of management choice with specific reference to robotics and asks why Japan leads the field in the application of robots to manufacture. That different countries should differ in their application of a potentially enormously beneficial form of IT immediately suggests that choice of IT is not simply technologically determined.

The reading by McLoughlin offers a comprehensive overview of the area of management and IT through a consideration of what the available literature from many fields of study tell us about why managers make the sorts of decisions they do about IT. One of the great benefits of the reading, aside from its thoroughness, is that it demonstrates the complexity of managerial motives, and of managerial decision-making. IT itself may represent the supremacy of rationality carried to its logical conclusion; but these values are far less apparent in the way it's used.

ROBOTICS, AUTOMATION AND A NEW INDUSTRIAL REVOLUTION

Paul Kennedy

Steam-driven manufacture that began to spread across northern and central England in the late eighteenth and early nineteenth centuries, naturally attracted the attention of many foreigners. Displaying fascination, enthusiasm, and sometimes apprehension, European and American visitors observed the brave new world of industrial production in which steam engines converted heat into work through machines. What impressed people about these machines was that they were 'rapid, regular, precise, tireless' [1]. Provided the supply of coal was maintained and the machines kept in order, they never flagged in the way that human beings, oxen and horses did when their 'animate' energy was exhausted. Machines could work all day and through the night; they could work nonstop for weeks, if necessary.

But the real significance of the Industrial Revolution – and the reason observers were so awed by it – was that it placed these steam-driven machines and their human attendants within a *factory system*. Hitherto, most forms of manufacture were decentralized, house-based activities, involving everything from urban candlestick makers to rural handloom weavers, usually paid by piecework. Specialist crafts, from potters to haberdashers, were similarly arranged. Even the largest projects – building a warship, or a palace – were in a way idiosyncratic, irregular enterprises, subject to various interruptions. In a factory system, however, workers were assembled together and required to labor in a standardized fashion to a rhythm *set by the machines*; they worked in fixed 'shifts' of ten or twelve or more hours, and were paid an hourly rate. Because the machines' requirements were supreme, the laborers had to live nearby, in employer-provided row houses. The factory system thus begat an urban proletariat, the succeeding generations of which knew less and less of their forebears' pre-industrial way of life.

It is easy to understand why foreign observers viewed the new manufacturing with apprehension as well as fascination. The Industrial Revolution clearly enhanced the power of Great Britain, especially during the Revolutionary and Napoleonic wars, when booming exports sustained the coalition forces in their epic struggle against France [2]. A country capable of imitating the British system would also enjoy a relative rise in productivity and national power, whereas states unable to industrialize would be hurt. Industrialization thus gave a fresh twist to the age-old competition among the Great Powers.

A second and larger reason for apprehension was concern about the effects of industrialization upon one's own society. The clanking, steaming new machines might be marvels to watch, but it was clear that working in a factory was hell – not just because of unhealthy conditions, but because of the strict regimen of work. Could the pre-industrial inhabitants of the Rhineland or Silesia be turned into a city-dwelling proletariat without inviting social convulsions? Worse still, how would one deal with the mass of craftsmen, handloom weavers, and the like who lost their jobs to the factory system, or influential guilds fighting hard against their redundancy? [3] To fail to match English practices was problem enough; to imitate them would mean profound changes in the way one lived, worked, and earned one's keep.

This dilemma is worth recalling because, two centuries later, we may be on the brink of another revolutionary change in how industrial goods are made – a change led this time not by England but by Japan, involving the replacement of human beings in the factory by robots and other automated equipment. For two hundred years, manufacture and assembly have been amended in all sorts of ways; but whatever the innovations of Taylor and Ford, or 'just-in-time' production, the key element was human beings coming together in a place of work. Now we are witnessing a technology-driven revolution which breaks from that process; by replacing factory workers with robots to increase productivity, automation takes more and more human beings *out* of the factory until perhaps only a few supervising engineers remain. If that aim is achieved, the wheel will have come full circle. The industrial 'serfs' of the factory system, whose working conditions appalled foreign observers in the England of the 1820s, will finally have been replaced by robots, whose linguistic root is the Czech word for serf, *robotnik* [4].

Like steam power itself, robotics has many applications, of varying complexity. Apart from simple devices not controlled by a computer and considering only *programmable* machines, there are immense differences of sophistication among industrial robots, field robots, and intelligent robots. The first are fixed machines with manipulators primed to do various tasks automatically, such as spot welding or spray painting. Field robots, by contrast, are designed to operate in an unstructured environment and possess sensors to allow them to move around, respond to an obstacle, and so on; they are often used in operations too difficult or hazardous for human beings, such as mining, fire fighting, treating a contaminated plant, and undersea work; some are steered by teleoperated remote control. Finally, there is the new, exciting field of third-generation intelligent robots, experimental computerized machines designed to use artificial intelligence (the so-called knowledge-based systems) to solve problems as human beings do [5].

Obviously, the more complex and expensive the task, the further robots are from actual replacement of human beings. The majority of industrial robots are employed in automobile plants – cutting pieces of metal, spot welding, painting – since that industry is the classic example of a factory-line production and assembly system requiring its workers to perform uniform, repetitive movements, like automata [6]. The same is true for the assembly of the components of a radio or CD player. Jobs needing independent actions, like schoolteaching or police work, are not going to be accomplished by machines. Lawyers, doctors, and professors will ensure that automatic emulation will not happen in their fields.

Although most of this article discusses the potential impact of industrial robots, it is worth noting that the use of field robots and intelligent robots is also influenced by economic consideration. In the United States, where the costs of long-term medical care are spiraling upward, hospitals are examining the purchase of robots able to move specimens in a laboratory, decontaminate surgical instruments, deliver medications from the pharmacy, and so on. [7] Again, because it will take hundreds of billions of dollars to clean hazardous waste across America, robots are now being recruited; field robots were developed to inspect, take samples from, and clean up the contaminated Three Mile Island plant after its 1979 accident. Other machines have been created for space exploration, for deep-sea mining, and even to act as 'sentry robots' equipped with remote-imaging and intruder-detection sensors as well as alarm/communications systems. [8]

In the United States and Europe, most attention has focused upon exotic robotics: machines that can traverse the moon's surface, or play chess. While that research is very important, the fascination for robots in the Jules Verne tradition distracts from the automation of the manufacturing industry, to achieve improvements in efficiency and productivity. Industrial robots for assembly or metal-cutting may seem less interesting than robots that play chess, but their long-term effects economic, demographic, and upon shares of world output – promise to be more significant.

Before considering those effects, however, we should understand why some industrial societies have embraced the new machines while others have not. Why, especially, has Japan become the world leader in robotics whereas the United States – which created much of the original technology and whose scientists still provide new ideas for the future of robotics – has allowed its share of this industry to be eroded? At first sight, Japan's superiority over America in robotics is a further example of what has occurred in related industries such as microprocessors, computers, and electrical goods. Japan possesses many strengths: a highly educated work force, a long-term commitment to develop key industries, easily available capital at low interest rates, high levels of R&D investment, masses of engineers, and a dedication to top-quality design and efficient production. Cutthroat competition among firms in Japan's automobile and electrical-goods industries drove them to invest in new machines to increase productivity; a government-encouraged leasing company (JAROL) offered advice and machines at low cost; and the robots were carefully integrated into a factory culture already practising 'just-in-time' production techniques. [9]

In the United States, conditions were far less favorable, despite the early breakthroughs achieved by companies such as Unimation and Cincinnati Milacron. The government's hands-off policy toward business meant that no help came from that source. No equivalent body existed to do JAROL's work of leasing, publicizing, and advising upon the use of robots. The costs of raising capital in America were greater than in Japan or Germany, and American companies were under pressure from Wall Street to keep profits high (even if this meant investing less). After initial enthusiasm in automated assembly by the major automobile companies, new investment in manufacturing as a whole fell sharply in the mid to late 1980s. [10] The result was a drastic shakeout of the robotics industry; more than half the fifty or so companies making robots in 1985 disappeared by 1990. [11] Those left were acquired by or forced to merge with foreign companies. By 1991 no independent American robotics manufacturers were left.

While a similar tale can be told of other American industries, the different response of Japan and America to robotics was heavily influenced by a special factor: demography. The chief reason for Japan's commitment to automation has been a serious labor shortage, which existed as long ago as the mid-1960s and threatened to reduce Japan's export-led boom. Demographic changes since then – not to mention those to come – are significantly altering the number of Japanese available for manufacturing work. The economic advantages of employing industrial robots are now overwhelming, as the cost of a robot has decreased sharply and the time needed for a return on investment has shrunk accordingly. 'If a robot replaces one worker for one shift per day, the payout is roughly four years. If a robot is used for two shifts, it will pay for itself in two years, and if used round the clock, in just over one year." [12]

Yet automated production could not have occurred so easily without the special structure of Japanese industry and the state of management-labor relations. Most large companies in Japan have a policy of lifetime employment, so that a worker whose job has been taken over by a robot will not be fired, but retrained and relocated inside the firm or in related companies within these industrial conglomerates. Moreover, robots were initially deployed in repetitive and/or dangerous jobs, such as cutting metal, spot welding, painting and transporting spare parts, which relieved workers of unpleasant tasks *and* promised enhanced productivity to be reflected in annual bonuses. Finally, Japanese trade unions traditionally work with management to enhance quality control and ensure that their company does better than its rivals. If robots helped Toyota or Kawasaki Heavy Industries to crush the competition, they would be warmly welcomed.

Not only did Japanese industry ease its labor shortages without destroying the social peace, it also avoided the path followed by German firms – or, for that matter, companies in New York and California – of importing large numbers of guest workers. Japan's commitment to its racial homogeneity was thus preserved, since mechanical 'serfs' could do the work instead, while Japanese workers were retrained for other tasks. Whatever migration occurs from South to North in the future, therefore, Japan plans to be much less affected than the United States and Europe while still ensuring its industrial competitiveness.

The contrast with the American experience could not be more marked. Although rising labour costs led US automobile companies to invest in robots during the early 1980s, America has no overall labor shortage; in addition, average wages now are considerably less than those in Japan. Moreover, robots often proved disappointing. To make them work effectively requires significant changes in factory layout and in redesigning products so that robots can handle them more easily. The more sophisticated the robot, the more redesign is required, so that many American firms eventually chose to retain the older methods – and the workers – and to sell off their new machines. In other words, there was no compelling demographic reason for companies to embrace robotics, even if the result was smaller productivity increases in the United States than in Japan.

Finally, American unions see robots as a threat to employment, suspicions well justified, for American industry does not usually retrain workers whose jobs have been made redundant. Following the 1981-82 recession, for example, as many as 2 million Americans with outdated skills lost their jobs. In cities like Pittsburgh, where one might imagine that robots would be welcomed to improve productivity, hundreds of thousands of skilled workers were fired as the 1980s unfolded. [13] While machines that replaced such arduous work as welding were tolerated, in general American labor has opposed robots – and the companies know it.

Therefore, the dominant place in robotics is now firmly occupied by Japan, as shown in Table 1.

Table 1   World industrial robot population, end of 1988 [14]

Japan	176,000
Western Europe	48,000
USA	33,000
Eastern, Europe, Southeast Asia, rest of world	23,000
Total	280,000

Because Japan has spent much more than any other country on automation since 1988, its lead has grown further. With only 0.3 percent of the world's land and 2.5 percent of its population, it possessed around 65 or 70 percent of the world's industrial robots, [15] recalling that other island country, mid-Victorian Britain, which produced five-sevenths of the world's steel and half its iron.

How significant are the productivity increases coming from automation? A few years ago Nissan upgraded its automobile plants in the Tokyo area with a highly sophisticated method of assembly, using robots. Formerly it took eleven months and cost Nissan 4 billion yen to retool its body assembly for a new car model; now it takes a quarter the time and costs about a third as much [16] – which is the chief reason that Japanese auto productivity continues to rise. Perhaps the famous FANUC manufacturing plant near Mount Fuji comes closest to representing the 'factory of the future.' Before 1982, a work force of 108 people and 32 robots produced about six thousand spindle motors and servo motors each month. After a radical redesign and further automation of the factory, it now employs only six people and has 101 robots to produce ten thousand servo motors a month – a *threefold* improvement in productivity which handsomely repays the initial investment. Yet even that is regarded merely as an interim step toward full automation by FANUC's management. [17]

Although the increases in productivity are incremental, they become significant over time, producing not only a steady flow of orders for the Japanese robotics industry, but also a cumulative increase in the quality and efficiency of Japanese manufacturing. Robots do not require heating or air-conditioning; they can work in the dark, and save electricity; they do not become sloppy or tired. They contribute to a greater flexibility in manufacturing, since they can be reprogrammed for different tasks or to assemble different models. Because their movements are perfectly controlled, they do not waste materials – robot spray painters, for example, use up to 30 percent less paint than human workers.

All this suggests that we may be witnessing the beginnings of a new industrial revolution, involving the automation of the manufacturing process. In many ways, the similarities between the steam engine and the robot are striking. Both are a new way of making things that simultaneously reduces the physical efforts of workers *and* enhances overall productivity; a process that creates new jobs and eliminates many others; and a stimulus to social change as well as to new definitions of work. [18] Like the steam engine, robotics affect international competitiveness, raising the per capita output of nations that invest heavily in the newer technology and weakening the long-term relative position of those unable to do the same.

Another similarity seems to be the strong impression made upon visitors who witness the new technology for the first time. Like aghast observers at Britain's early steam-driven factories, foreign visitors to the FANUC automated factory appear awed by the sight of robots moving around inside the building, clicking and whirring as they solder circuit boards, examining their work with camera eyes, passing items from one robot to another, work which continues after dark, when the lights are dimmed. [19] Both steam engine and robot, people could sense, brought promise and peril to manufacturing.

Since robotics is still in its early stages and heavily concentrated in one country, less attention has been paid to its implications for developed and developing nations in (say) thirty years' time than has been devoted to biotech or demographic change. Despite the publicity given to FANUC's wonder robots, the use of robotics in Japanese manufacturing is undramatic and incremental as factory after factory installs additional machines. It is also much less headline-catching than breakthroughs in aerospace or supercomputing. Interestingly, although American industry is increasingly dependent upon Japanese robots, few politicians denounce this imbalance as they bemoan America's dependence on foreign-made chips or laptop computers. Even the term 'robotics revolution' may be questioned by American businessmen who have had problems using them or see little advantage in the new machines when labor is relatively cheap.

Within developed nations, robotics is likely to progress most where there exists a strong 'engineering culture,' high per capita average living standards (and therefore high labor costs), and a shrinking pool of skilled workers because of demographic slowdown; after Japan, the leading contenders are Germany and Sweden, each with traditional strengths in machine tools, electrical engineering and high-quality automobiles. Robotics is less likely to progress in countries where investment in manufacturing remains low, or where trade unions fear robots as job-replacers. Robotics is also unlikely to flourish in the states of the former Soviet Union, for, although the USSR claimed to possess tens of thousands of industrial robots, a top-notch robotics industry cannot function efficiently in an economy backward in computers and microprocessors. In any case, with millions of citizens of the erstwhile Soviet Union looking for work, robots are the last thing that is needed. The economics of investing in automation and a country's demographic and social structures always seem to provide the key.

Since automation increases manufacturing productivity, it adds to the relative power of companies and nations which can automate *and* handle the social consequences. In the global scramble for market shares in the three great economic zones of North America, Europe, and East Asia, robotics threatens to widen the already significant productivity gap between the Nissans and Toyotas on the one hand and the Peugeots, Fiats, and Chryslers on the other. As European bureaucrats and American car manufacturers scramble to meet East Asia's challenge in manufacturing and high technology by imposing import restrictions to give themselves a breathing space of five or ten years in which to catch up, robotics makes their task harder, perhaps impossible, so long as Japan's companies invest more than everyone else in the future. A further consequence of robotics, then, could be to shift the global economic balances away from Britain, France, Italy, and the United States and towards Japan and Germany.

If Europe's and America's responses to robotics are sporadic and hesitant, they are much better prepared to compete – at least in terms of physical and intellectual assets – than societies in the developing world. As with global finance, biotechnology, and multinationals, we are once again looking at a technology-driven revolution that could keep poorer countries at the bottom of the heap, or weaken them further.

Since a few developing countries appear to be detaching themselves from the Third World and catching up with the First [Note 1], the following discussion focuses on the fate of the really poor, overpopulated societies of South Asia, Africa, and Central America, not the NIEs of East Asia, which are in a different category. Except for Taiwan [Note 2], figures are not available on robotics in the NIEs, but they will probably reflect a more general technology indicator, such as semiconductor production. In that field, South Korea, Taiwan, Singapore, and Hong Kong are making very swift progress, since their governments have targeted electronics and computers as key industries for export-led growth. Because Japanese competitors have invested heavily in robotics – to beat the low labor cost products of the NIEs – that may encourage the latter to go heavily into automation. Obviously, it is not yet worthwhile in countries where wages remain low; but the explosion of workers' earnings in recent years in (say) South Korea and the steady decline in fertility rates bring automation closer.

To create its own robotics revolution, a developing country needs surplus capital, a large supply of engineers and scientists, and a labor shortage. Alas, countries in the developing world have few capital resources, and interest payments on international debts result in a net outflow of capital each year. They also have relatively few engineers and scientists. Finally, since their major problem is a massive surplus of labor, there is no economic or social rationale – from the viewpoint of their troubled governments, at least – in encouraging *labor-saving* systems of manufacture.

If there is little prospect that an indigenous robotics industry will arise in the developing world, might multinational companies establish automated manufacturing in those countries to obtain low-cost production? After all, some of the less developed and most populous countries of Asia – Indonesia, Thailand, Malaysia, China itself – have experienced rapid industrialization, faster than everywhere else in the world, and now export many manufactured goods. This economic growth is due to the relocation of manufacturing to those countries by firms like Fujitsu and Motorola, to take advantage of lower labor costs. Components of, say, a radio or record player are sent to a company's plant in Southeast Asia, where it is assembled and packaged for re-export. Such work improves the developing country's balance of payments, although it also creates unusual employment patterns, since these electronics companies employ almost entirely unskilled and semiskilled female workers. [20] The problem of young, frustrated men without work remains, and may be compounded. Moreover, such an employment structure creates little incentive for the training of native scientists and engineers.

Nevertheless, industrialization does bring *overall* benefits to Southeast Asia – export-led growth, a higher standard of living, a rising number of consumers of manufactures – especially when compared with Africa or the Middle East, where investment by multinational companies is negligible. Even if these developing countries have been 'relegated to assembling pieces of high-tech equipment largely for consumption in industrial countries,' [21] that is better than no industrial employment at all.

But what prospect is there of a move by multinationals to *automated* assembly, instead of low-labor-cost assembly, in their developing world plants? Given the structure of the robotics industry, that seems unlikely at present, since it would require a skilled work force (systems engineers, trained maintenance crew), which most developing countries do not have;

it would also require adequate infrastructure, power supplies, telecommunications, water, roads and ports, which many poorer countries desperately lack. In any case, why invest in automated assembly in (say) Indonesia if it retains its cheap labor advantage? Moreover, even if automation did occur – despite all the problems noted above – it would then pose the same threat to local factory employment as it does in other parts of the world.

The final irony – and an awful future possibility – is that low-labor assembly plants established by foreign companies in Southeast Asia may one day be undermined by an intensification of the robotics revolution in Japan. This might seem farfetched at the moment, although at least one writer on 'high technology and international labor markets' has argued that labor-saving technology, intensively used, could make the manufacturing of steel, heavy equipment, machines, and even textiles competitive again in industrial countries.[22]

As one indicator of how robotics might permit manufacturing to return to a developed country – or, in this case, not abandon it – consider the remarkable turnaround achieved by a single radio-cassette-recorder factory in Sendai, Japan, in 1985. Suffering from the rise in the value of the yen, acute labor shortages at home, and fierce competition from low-labor competitors in Southeast Asia, the company was in deep trouble. Rejecting the idea of relocating production to cheaper countries, the management embarked upon massive automation – the installation of no fewer than 850 industrial robots. Within a short while, the assembly line required only sixteen workers to reach full production compared with 340 (!) before automation, restoring the company's competitiveness even against Southeast Asian rivals whose wages were a fraction of those in Japan. [23] The 'serfs' in the low-labor assembly plants abroad were outbid by automated 'serfs' at home. If that was already possible in the mid-1980s, what degree of manufacturing efficiency might the robotics revolution achieve by 2020?

Whether or not the members of the Association of Southeast Asian Nations that are the home of foreign-owned assembly plants will escape from this challenge is impossible to judge at present; probably the more adept of them will. The main point is that multinational corporations in certain industries, already switching production from one country to another according to differentiated labor costs, will gain the further advantage of assessing whether developing-world wages are greater or less than the robot's 'costs' in the automated factory back home. After all, the theory of the borderless world encourages managers to be constantly weighing the relative advantage of production in one part of the globe as opposed to others. With the robotics revolution, Fujitsu assembly plants abroad might one day return to Japan and Motorola factories to America. In any event, such decisions will not be made by developing countries or their governments.

The mass replacement of factory workers will not happen overnight. Just as it took decades for the early steam engines to advance from mere curiosities and 'wonder machines' to the center of the manufacturing process, so it may take a generation or more before the robotics revolution makes its full impact; and there is always the increase in cheap labor supplies to slow the pace of automation in many societies. Nevertheless, the longer-term implications are disturbing and threaten to exacerbate the global dilemma. If the biotech revolution can make redundant certain forms of farming, the robotics revolution could eliminate many types of factory-assembly and manufacturing jobs. In both cases, multinational companies become the beneficiaries of the reduced value of land and labor. Marvelous though the technologies behind the new agricultural and industrial revolutions may be, they neither offer solutions to the global demographic crisis nor bridge the gap between North and South. For all the difficulties it faced, Malthus's England perhaps had an easier time of it.

NOTES AND REFERENCES

1   Landes, *Unbound Prometheus*, p. 41.

2   Kennedy, *Rise and Fall of the Great Powers*, pp. 126-39.

3   This is nicely discussed in T.S. Harmerow (1958) *Restoration, Revolution, Reaction Economic and Politics in Germany, 1815-1871*, Princeton, N.J., chaps 2, 5 and 8.

4   According to P. B. Scott (19832) *The Robotics Revolution*, Oxford/New York, p. 10.

5   *Ibid.*; and especially W. B. Gevarter (1985) *Intelligent Machines*, Englewood Cliffs, N.J., p. 161.

6   See the breakdown of the industries using robots in *Annual Review of Engineering Industries and Automation, 1988*, vol. I (UN Economic Commission for Europe, N.Y., 1989), p. 53.

7   Robotics Technology and Its Varied Uses, Hearing Before the Subcommittee on Science, Research and Technology, U.S. Congress, 25 September 1989 (Washington, D.C., 1989), testimony of Mr. K. G. Engelhardt; see also K. G. Engelhardt, 'Innovations in health care: roles for advanced intelligent technologies,' *Pittsburgh High Technology Journal*, vol. 2, no. 5, pp. 69-72.

8   Robotics Technology and Its Varied Uses, pp. 15, 19, 24.

9   J. Baranson (1983) *Robots in Manufacturing*, Mt. Airy, Md., p. 67.

10 *Ibid.*, pp. 39-41, 111-27; Robotics Technology and Its Varied Uses, p. 76; P. T. Kilborn, 'Brave new world seen for robots appears stalled by quirks and costs,' *New York Times*, 1 July 1990, p. 16.

11 Kilborn, 'Brave new world seen...'

12 Baranson, *Robots in Manufacturing*, p. 86.

13 Robotics Technology and Its Varied Uses, p. 172.

14 *Annual Review of Engineering Industries and Automation*, p. 53.

15 'Japan's New Idea: Technology for the 21st Century,' Industry Week Special Report, 5 September 1990, p. 42.

16 'Bodybuilding without tears,' *Economist,* 21 April 1990, p. 38.

17 FANUC's operations have been described in innumerable articles, for example: L. Schodt, 'In the land of robots,' *Business Month,* 132, November 1988, pp. 67-75; F. Hiatt, 'Japanese robots reproducing like rabbits: high-tech capital investment helps fuel economic miracle,' Washington Post, 2 January 1990, pp. Al, A13; and more technically, D. F. Urbanials (1983) 'The unattended factory,' 13th International Symposium on Industrial Robots, and Robots : Conference Proceedings, vol. I, Dearborn, Mich., pp. 1-18 to 1-24.

18 See the extremely stimulating article by M. J. E. Cooley (1985) 'Robotics – some wider implications,' *The World Yearbook of Robotics Research and Development 1985,* pp. 95-104.

19 See again the articles by Schodt and Hiatt (note 17 above).

20 M. Carnoy, 'High Technology and International Labour Markets,' International Labour Review, vol. 124, no. 6 (1985), p. 649.

21 *Ibid.,* p. 650.

22 *Ibid.,* p. 653.

23 'Japan's new idea,' *Industry Week,* p. 69.

THE PURSUIT OF FLEXIBLE SPECIALIZATION
IN BRITAIN AND WEST GERMANY

Christel Lane

INTRODUCTION

Braverman's (1974) work on the labour process introduced the claim that, in advanced capitalist society, the pressure for capital accumulation compels management to assume full control over the labour process in order to enhance economic exploitation. Tayloristic work organisation, entailing the maximum possible division of labour and the minimum possible worker discretion, is regarded as the tool ideally suited to the achievement of management goals. For Braverman, as Wood and Kelly (1982, p. 76) point out, management under capitalism has reached its purest expression in Taylorism. Braverman does not envisage the possibility that capitalist production organisation allows for the development of any alternative strategy of work organisation.

Subsequent critiques have challenged this claim and have shown that the goal of capital accumulation can be pursued by other means or that control over labour can be achieved by a variety of strategies. But most of these critiques still hold the Taylorist model to be the predominant one during the post-war period. The recent books by Sabel (1982) and Piore and Sabel (1984), in contrast, claim that the dominance of the Taylorist approach and of the whole model of industrial production in which it is embedded, is now being challenged and that an alternative manufacturing policy, referred to as 'flexible specialisation', has emerged. They envisage such fundamental industrial change to talk of the occurrence of a second industrial divide'.

THE PIORE AND SABEL THESIS ON 'FLEXIBLE SPECIALISATION'

World-wide economic changes, particularly a shift in the international division of labour, have rendered problematic the old form of industrial development which has prevailed in advanced capitalist societies for most of this century. Greater competition in world markets from newer low-wage industrial countries and a general decrease in market stability and predictability have rendered less viable the established model of mass production of standardised goods with the use of special-purpose machinery and of semi-skilled labour. A search for alternative markets and the emergence, at the same time, of a new and more flexible technology has caused industrial producers to reconsider their strategy of both capital and labour utilisation. The new market strategy aims to compete by offering product diversity and/or high quality, and the new technology facilitates the frequent adaptation to changing market demands as well as the attainment of higher quality standards and smaller batches, without increasing production costs. The advantages of the new technology for the pursuit of the new market strategy can be most fully exploited, Piore and Sabel argue, if it is allied to a new form of labour deployment. The Taylorist strategy of designing high specialisation/low discretion jobs needs to be replaced by one seeking a high degree of overlap between specialisms and flexibility of deployment, as well as the exercise of 'craft' judgement and skill. Lastly, these authors suggest, such a strategy of flexible specialisation is more likely to succeed in industrial communities with systems of industrial relations, based on co-operation, rather than on competition and conflict.

MANAGERIAL PRACTICE IN THE POST-WAR PERIOD

In the more recent past – from 1950 to the middle 1970s – German industry has stood out as being the least penetrated, though by no means unaffected, by Taylorist strategy, whereas British employers have been more receptive to Taylorist techniques. The following examination of the two national patterns of work organisation during this period will utilise Littler's (1982) comparative schema and analyse employer strategies in terms of three dimensions: division of labour/degree of discretion; structure of control; and employment relationship. This analysis, summarised in Table 1, makes it possible to characterise national patterns in ideal-typical form and place them on a continuum from the strategy of 'responsible autonomy' at one end of the pole to that of full Taylorism at the other.

In Germany the craft paradigm and the managerial strategy of responsible autonomy' remained central to the national economy. The first factor predisposing German management towards a strategy of responsible autonomy' in work organisation is the skill profile of the manual working class. All through the post-war period, there has been in German industry a predominance of skilled workers with high, formally labelled and certified qualifications. This proportion has stayed almost constant up to the late 1970s (Mooser, 1984). Although there is not always a correlation between official skill labels and actual skill exercised, in Germany this correspondence is widely held to be close. The expansion of mass production industries has to a large extent drawn on un- and semi-skilled immigrant *(Gastarbeiter)* and female labour but also on skilled workers from economically declining industries and the artisan *(Handwerk)* sector. The nature of the skills imparted to skilled workers is best summed up by the concept of polyvalency, i.e. knowledge and capabilities in two or more areas, acquired through systematic rotation during training. Polyvalency of skill permits a broad and flexible utilization of labour across boundaries between production work, on the one side and technical and maintenance work, on the other. Polyvalency has not, as in the case of British craftsmen, been undermined by the erection of highly formalised boundaries between skills. Polyvalency of the German type also furthers co-operation within work groups across hierarchical divisions and thus provides a natural foundation for the institution of semi-autonomous work groups. German semi-skilled workers' training, although less broad and deep, is nevertheless also systematically oriented towards polyvalency.

This existence of a large pool of skilled, polyvalent workers has predisposed employers to implement the strategy of 'responsible autonomy'. (The concept used here is adapted from Friedman (1977).) It refers to a strategy which allows workers a reasonable scope in utilising their skills and trusting them to use them responsibly, i.e. in the interest of their employing organization. This form of work organization implies a structure of control which minimises task control and instead exerts ideological control. The control process utilises an ideology, inculcated during the training process. Contrary to Friedman, however, the inculcation of the tenets of this ideology does not require a complex ideological apparatus but occurs almost imperceptibly as a by-product of the technical training process. The ideology is based on the idea of a professional community in which superiors are respected as 'experts' rather than as punitive controllers, and a common task orientation dwells on unity of purpose and de-emphasises hierarchical divisions. Reduced task control in German industry is indicated by the facts that the authority over the organisation and monitoring of work in progress is vested in the chargehand and that the foreman is regarded more as a technical expert than as a punitive supervisor. This ideology is also expressed in, and reinforced by, the system of industrial relations which is characterised by a co-operative style. Lastly, the foregoing makes clear that, contrary to Friedman, the implementation of the strategy of responsible autonomy constitutes not merely a management reaction to worker unrest but has been a much more enduring feature of German management control, deeply embedded into the general institutional framework.

In Britain Taylorist employer strategies have become more widely established than in Germany during the post-war period, but they have been applied in a very half-hearted and inconsistent form. Inconsistency or ambiguity flows from two sources. The first, and by now less significant one, is the co-existence in British industry of a small 'craft' sector, in which work is still characterised by a relatively low division of labour and high level of discretion, with a large mass production sector, dominated by semi-skilled workers engaged in monotonous, deskilled detail work. (For examples of work in the craft sector, see accounts of work organisation in the engineering industry in Wood, 1982). The second, and more formidable, inconsistency lies in employer strategy. In the mass production industries, a high division of labour (including that between direct and indirect labour) and a fairly rigid separation of planning and implementation is accompanied by a structure of control which, while eschewing ideological control, is neither fully committed to task control nor to a strategy of 'responsible autonomy'. By international standards British workers have achieved a relatively high degree of control over the organisation of the labour process (e.g. joint regulation in the areas of job definition, task allocation, manning). But this control has not been granted as part of a strategy stressing worker 'responsible autonomy' which, indeed, is quite incompatible with deskilled detail work. This control orientation on the part of British management can be attributed to both the social origins and the relatively low level of technical training managers which foster social distance and hinder the development of a task- and production-orientation among them.

Thus, to summarise, although Fordist employer practices have been widespread during the post-war period in both societies, their penetration has been more thoroughgoing in Britain than in Germany. The differences, it has been argued, are due not only to the differing numerical preponderance in the workforce of skilled workers but also to the differential processes by which skill is produced among all types of workers and the uses to which it has been put. This has, on the one side, led to differing worker identities, expectations and attachments to the employing organisation and, on the other, has channelled employer goals and practices in differing directions. These differences are summarized in schematic form in Table 1.

Table 1 **Capitalist employer strategies on work organization up to the early 1980s**

	Responsible autonomy	Taylorism
	Germany	*Britain*
Division of labour	Large proportion of high skilled	Deskilled (pockets of high skill in craft sector)
	Low formalisation of boundaries	High formalisation of boundaries
	High level of discretion	Low level of discretion
Structure of control	Predominantly ideological control	Weak task control
Employment relationship	High degree of employment security* for the core labour force	Complete substitutability of workers *
	Elements of paternalism	Minimum interaction

Adapted from Littler 1982: 193, Table 12.2

*In 1986, the unemployment rates in Germany and Britain were 7.8 and 12.02, respectively *(CEDEFOP News, 2, 1986)*

FLEXIBLE SPECIALISATION IN GERMANY

The case for an emergent new industrial strategy in German manufacturing has been most cogently stated and most fully supported by empirical evidence in the work of Kern and Schumann (1984a and b). Their theoretical claims and empirical data are based on a follow-up study of several industries – the car, machine tool, chemical and, to a lesser extent, food-producing and shipbuilding industries – which they first investigated in the middle 1960s.

The evidence of industrial transformation in Germany during the late 1970s/early 1980s [...] leaves no doubt that, at least in the core industries. changed market and technology strategies have led to the creation of more flexible production arrangements which have involved job enrichment. enlarged autonomy and upskilling for significant numbers of workers. It is more contentious, however, whether these developments amount to a new industrial strategy or new production concepts, to use Kern and Schumann's term (1984a and b). The latter make it clear that, at the present time, only a minority of production workers in the core industries are engaged in new forms of production work and that the full development of the new production concepts will not occur until the late 1980s/early 1990s. They also suggest that labour needs to exert more influence both management to follow the new strategy more broadly and on the state to distribute the ensuing costs and benefits more widely.

THE IMPLICATIONS

The question, therefore, remains whether the new forms of labour utilisation signal an emergent trend which will eventually become a fully-fledged industrial strategy or manufacturing policy, or whether, as some German commentators suggest (e.g. Düll, 1985), they constitute merely island solutions which will remain confined to small sections of production and leave the overall Taylorist pattern intact. My own view is that in the German industrial context there exist a number of distinctive features which make the Kern and Schumann scenario at least very likely, if not inevitable. Some of these features which support a move towards a broader application of the policy of flexible specialisation and which were not recognised or under-emphasised by Piore and Sabel (1984) will be outlined in the following section.

Firstly, analysis of industrial change in the 1980s requires that a stronger emphasis be put on the key role the new technology plays in the process of change. Kern and Schumann (1984b) and Jürgens et al. (1986, p. 273) make it clear that the new technology is an indispensable factor in realising the new market concept and in facilitating and, sometimes, stimulating changes in work organisation. But this emphasis on new technology is not to be interpreted as the adoption of a stance of technological determinism. Kern and Schumann underline that the new technology can be exploited the more broadly the stronger the policy of labour utilisation has created the preconditions for such an exploitation. The computer-controlled technology has made the enterprise more transparent and hence more amenable to organizational integration. The new flexibility in worker deployment is mainly desired because the complexity and high degree of integration of technology makes machine down-time more disruptive and costly, and upskilling is practised because it is believed that the new technology can only be fully exploited with a skilled, autonomous workforce (*Industriemagazin,* April 1987). In each of the four industries where significant moves away from Taylorist work organisation had occurred, these had been preceded by the introduction of new technological processes. The most highly automated industry – the auto industry – has also been the most innovative one in terms of work organisation.

For German management maximum technical sophistication appears to be a central weapon in all the core industries surveyed. This technology-led competitive strategy presupposes the availability of both a high level of managerial technical competence and of investment resources. Thus, whereas Piore and Sabel (1984) stressed only the availability of worker skill as a precondition for achieving flexible specialisation, the German evidence also highlights the critical importance of managerial competence.

Secondly, German sources stress the situation on the labour market as an equally important intervening variable. The unemployment of even skilled workers guarantees an ample supply of skilled labour. This is further increased by the fact that, to alleviate youth unemployment, employers have yielded to union pressure and have trained apprentices in excess of their own immediate needs. This makes non-Taylorist work organisation a feasible goal and renders the conversion process suggested by the new strategy relatively painless.

German sources see flexible deployment of labour only in functional terms. The pursuit of numerical flexibility, i.e. the adjustment of labour inputs to meet fluctuation in output, receives no mention. [...] The lack of attention to numerical flexibility is probably due to the fact that external numerical flexibility was not very prominent in German industry during the early 1980s. Generally speaking, German employment legislation has made it difficult for employers to solve the problem of fluctuating demand by casualisation of the labour force. The high degree of *de facto* employment security and the strong involvement of works councils in manpower regulation have compelled employers to engage in more careful and long-term manpower planning and to deploy the core labour force flexibly in both functional and numerical terms (Streeck, 1987). But more recent developments suggest that German employers too, are seeking greater numerical and wages flexibility. Although attempts to attain this have so far remained isolated cases they are now seen as the beginning of a more pervasive future trend (Sengenberger, 1984, pp. 331f).

A last important issue to be settled is whether the emergence of a paradigm change is compatible with the capitalist organization of production and, if so, how it fits into Marxian theorisation of the labour process. Kern and Schumann point out that the new industrial strategy is an employer initiative, aimed at adjusting the production process to their changed market strategies, and that the reorganization of work is not a response to worker unrest or demands nor is it based on humanitarian impulses. Thus a non-Taylorist mode of worker deployment is not an end in itself but is a consequence of a different mode of capital utilisation. The new automated technology demands very high rates of capital investment, and the return on that investment is more assured if it is complemented by greater investment in labour. Thus, flexible specialisation is regarded as a capitalist rationalisation strategy which happens to yield considerable benefits also for labour. It tries to increase industrial efficiency through, and not against, worker competence *(Handlungskapazität)*. Often the reorganisation of work is not consciously planned but evolves, after periods of trial and error, as a consequence of other changes in production (Drexel, 1984, p. 108).

The new mode of labour utilisation does, however, constitute a break in capitalist thinking. Labour has long been thought of as a factor disruptive of production, to be substituted as far as possible by machines and restricted and controlled as much as possible. This has been a central tenet of the Braverman thesis on the labour process in capitalist society. The new strategy, in contrast, implies that labour is a valuable resource and that worker skill and initiative are productive forces which should be fully utilised (Kern and Schumann, 1984, p. 149). [...] As Drexel (1985, p. 123) points out, the new attitude to labour deployment implies not *just* a broader utilization of existing labour power but also its greater unfolding and development. The new mode of labour utilization does not represent a one-sided gain by capital but one which has been achieved by developing worker potential to a higher degree. The worker receives a pay-off in terms of higher skill level, greater autonomy and increased satisfaction and material reward. Granted, development of worker potential remains strictly within the limits set by the capitalist enterprise, and the unfolding of the full potential of labour is prevented by the remaining contradictions between the interests of capital and labour.

Achieving domination *(Herrschaftsabsicherung)* is no longer considered such an important goal by German management. This is the case, partly, because automatic control of production processes secures sufficient worker effort. But it is also true that workers are no longer regarded as system opponents. They are viewed as people who are willing to make compromises because their own interests are becoming more closely tied in with those of their employer (Kern and Schumann, 1984, p. 152). But, at the same time, management has become more dependent on the goodwill of workers to keep the new, highly complex and vulnerable apparatus in operation. This is not to say that management control of workers has become unimportant but merely that it no longer takes the old form. As has been pointed out by many of Braverman's critics, subsumption of labour does not necessarily occur by close task control in the labour process. But this relaxation of control in the labour process ... is a peculiarly German phenomenon.

To sum up this section, flexible specialization in Germany is seen to have the following characteristic features. It is, as yet, only an emergent trend.

Taylorism has not been completely abandoned, but fundamental organizational innovation is very much on the agenda; technology is held to play a crucial role in the process of change, and a management committed to, and capable of instigating, far-reaching technological innovation is an integral part of the transformation process; the labour market situation has made available a sizeable pool of skilled polyvalent labour to operationalise the new strategy; the system of industrial relations facilitates relatively smooth technological change and the attainment of functional flexibility; the new 'professional' worker, although sharing some features with the craft worker of old, is not identical to him; the benefits of the new industrial strategy for workers need to be generalized by political means beyond the core industries; the strategy of flexible specialisation is an integral part of capitalist rationalisation but it signifies an important change in capital's attitude to labour deployment which has more positive consequences for labour than the old Taylorist concept.

FLEXIBLE SPECIALISATION IN BRITAIN?

Where the strategy of 'flexible specialisation' is adopted, the British version differs from the German one in several ways. It is rarely conceived of as a comprehensive industrial strategy in which the use of complex new technological systems is integrated with the creation of greater skill resources and the broader deployment of skilled labour on the one side, and a new 'industrial relations' approach, evoking worker commitment and cooperation, on the other. An attempt to adopt such a comprehensive strategy in the British context meets with too many impediments and tends to become unstuck in the pursuit of one or several of its constituent elements. Consequently it is usually the case that the strategy is embraced only partially and is combined with elements of the old Taylorist model of labour deployment into a hybrid type. Alternatively, the pursuit of functional flexibility culminates in a contest between management and labour over the elimination or retention of union control over labour deployment. A preoccupation with industrial relations moves to the centre of the field, and the attempt to realise a comprehensive new manufacturing policy becomes jeopardised.

What then are the impediments in the British industrial context which hinder the successful realisation of the new industrial strategy in a consistent form? One important constituent element of the new model is the reorganisation of the productive apparatus, replacing old special-purpose machinery with new automated equipment of a highly complex type. The degree of flexibility permitted by the new technology increases with the technical sophistication of the equipment and with the degree of integration of individual technical devices into a comprehensive system. Such a reorganization of production requires a management committed to technological innovation, confident to forge ahead, and competent both to acquire the right type of equipment and to put it into operation and maintain it without too much disruption of the productive process. Such energetic technological innovation requires not only the commitment of considerable financial resources but also a high level of technical expertise among management and support staff at all levels. Neither precondition typically exists in British industrial organisations.

Although the high level of unemployment in Britain makes available a large pool of labour, this labour is, on the whole, not of the right type to restructure work organisation in line with the new production concepts. Due to the decline of the apprenticeship system, skilled labour has been declining in relative terms. In the engineering industry, for example, where skilled labour has traditionally been most prevalent, the number of craftsmen undergoing training has halved between 1978 and 1984 *(Skills Bulletin,* 1, 1987, p. 11). Moreover, the traditional skilled worker does not possess the polyvalency which ensures flexible deployment. In those cases where management is committed to operating the new technology with skilled, polyvalent labour – for maintenance such labour is becoming a *sine qua non* – they have had both to invest resources in initial and further or re-training *and* to overcome union resistance to the elimination of demarcation between crafts.

All this is not to say that functional flexibility is rarely sought or obtained by British management. The recent IMS study (1986, p. 8) of this problem found that nine out of ten manufacturing firms in their sample had been seeking to increase functional flexibility of their workforces since 1980. Daniel (1987, p. 168f) established that management had a greater commitment to flexibility in worker deployment and that establishments using microelectronic technology were twice as likely as those not using it to have taken steps to promote it. But 34 per cent of all works managers still felt constrained in their freedom to distribute tasks between different categories of workers. The impediments to the realisation of flexible labour deployment are such that success is often only limited or of short-term duration.

It has already been indicated that 'industrial relations' issues represent an impediment to the attainment of work restructuring in the direction of greater functional flexibility. The new forms of work organisation, it was shown in the German context, require that workers act more autonomously and adopt a greater amount of responsibility for the smooth and continuous functioning of the complex productive apparatus. This exercise of responsible autonomy on the part of workers presupposes that management trusts them to use this autonomy in the interest of the enterprise. A strategy of 'responsible autonomy' assumes that management feels fairly secure and confident about the existing balance of control in the enterprise and is not constantly locked into a contest for control. It also presupposes that workers identify to a large degree with management goals and accept a part of the responsibility for the accomplishment of these goals.

In the British industrial relations context, with its long tradition of 'minimal involvement' and adversarial pursuit of sectional interests, such a climate of mutual trust and co-operation cannot easily develop. Many studies have shown that British management does not and cannot feel confident and relaxed about the existing balance of control. In many instances management has shown itself intent on exploiting labour's current weakness and changing the balance of control in management's favour (IMS, 1986). Instead of seeing the elimination of demarcation as one necessary step in the larger strategy of creating a polyvalent, flexible and more responsible labour force it often becomes a goal in its own right and degenerates into a contest of strength between management and labour.

The foregoing argument has made it clear that although a new market strategy and a quest for the more flexible organization of production are also a lively concern of British management there are formidable impediments in the way of realising a comprehensive and consistent industrial strategy. There exist difficulties about creating the necessary technological foundations. But the more formidable problems appear to be those of achieving a new approach to management-labour relations and a non-Taylorist practice of labour deployment. The example of Britain shows, contrary to the claims of Piore and Sabel (1984), that countries without a pervasive craft ethos will not necessarily remain wedded to the old model of industrial organization. Instead managements in such countries are more likely to develop a hybrid strategy, combining a changed market orientation with a high-tech version of production along the old Taylorist lines. Although greater functional flexibility of labour and upskilling is practised, the pursuit of numerical flexibility and of the greater casualisation of the labour force appears to be the more widely adopted alternative. Although numerical flexibility can successfully cope with uncertainties in demand of a quantitative type it is doubtful whether a casualised labour force can handle other aspects of market uncertainty, such as frequent product changes or product diversification, and the demand for customised high-quality goods.

CONCLUSION

A quest for 'flexible specialisation' has been characteristic of both German and British management during the 1980s. But the attempts to adjust the organisation of production to new and changing market demands have taken different forms in the two societies, and the industrial strategies devised possess different degrees of logical consistency and/or comprehensiveness. [...] Whereas in Germany the new strategy is very much technology-led and -inspired, in Britain the impetus has come more strongly from the relaxation of constraints previously exerted by labour market conditions and the industrial relations system.

German employers, able to draw on a large pool of skilled, polyvalent labour and union cooperation for functional flexibility, have further reinforced and extended functional flexibility. British managements, in contrast, possessing none of these advantages, have made only limited moves in the direction of greater functional flexibility. They have, instead, significantly increased their recourse to numerical flexibility and the concomitant expansion of a peripheral labour force. The German strategy has been consistent with the restructuring of work along non-Taylorist lines and the upskilling of the labour force, albeit only in some industries. The British attempt to gain greater flexibility, in contrast, typically has not been linked to the broader and fuller use of worker capacity. The emphasis has been more on destroying old forms of utilising skill rather than creating new ones. Consequently, the British approach has had ambiguous consequences for skilled labour – some upskilling but the loss of union control over labour deployment. It has had only negative effects for semi- and unskilled labour. For them the Taylorist thrust of work organisation has intensified and employment conditions have significantly deteriorated.

Management efforts to regain control, in order to secure greater workplace discipline, complete the Fordist/Taylorist model. German management have adopted a consistent strategy of flexible specialisation which, on balance, constitutes a progressive move from the point of view of labour. Moreover, it is likely to achieve the successful realisation of the new market strategy. High quality and product diversity can only be obtained with skilled, polyvalent and responsible labour. Whether the British alternative of a high-tech version of Fordism will be able to cope with the new market demands must be regarded as doubtful.

REFERENCES

Braverman, H. (1974) *Labour and Monopoly Capital,* New York, Monthly Review Press.

Daniel, W. (1987) *Workplace Industrial Relations and Technical Change,* London, Frances Pinter.

Drexel, I. (1985) 'Neue Produktionsstrukturen auf Italienisch?', *Soziale Welt,* vol.2, pp.106-27.

Dull, K. (1985) 'Gesellschaftliche Modernisierungspolitik durch "neue Produktions-konzepte"?', *WSI Mitteilungen,* vol.3, pp.141-5.

Friedman, A. (1977) *Industry and Labour. Class Struggle at Work and Monopoly Capitalism,* London, Macmillan.

Institute of Manpower Studies (IMS) (1986) *Changing Working Patterns,* a report for the National Economic Development Office in association with the Department of Employment, London, IMS.

Jürgens, U., Does, K. and Mallet, T. (1986) 'New Production Concepts in West German Car Plants', in Tolliday, S. and Zeitlin, J. (eds) *The Automobile Industry and its Workers,* Cambridge, Polity Press.

Kern, H. and Schumann, M. (1984a) 'Neue Produktionskonzepte haben Chancen', *Soziale Welt,* vol.35, nos.1-2, pp.146-58.

Kern, H. and Schumann, M. (1984b) *Das Ende der Arbeitsteilung? Rationalisierung in der industriellen Produktion,* Munich, Verlag C.H. Beck.

Littler, C. (1982) *The Development of the Labour Process in Capitalist Societies,* London, Heinemann.

Mooser, J. (1984) *Arbeiterleben in Deutschland 1900-1970,* Frankfurt, Suhrkamp .

Piore, M.J. and Sabel, C. (1984) *The Second Industrial Divide,* New York, Basic Books.

Computerized Machine Tools, Manpower Consequences and Skill Utilization: a study of British and West German Manufacturing Firms

Gert Hartmann, Ian Nicholas, Arndt Sorge and Malcolm Warner

Introduction

The impact of new information technology on organization and manpower depends on where and how it is used. A statement such as Rada's to the effect that 'electronics [...] will substantially condition industrial and service activities and the socio-political structure' is at least potentially misleading, for its consequences may be more due to the specific culture prevailing in such societies.[1] It is thus advisable to exercise great caution when examining any prediction of its effects.

Since the 1950s, metal cutting has undergone major technical advances. It has, in the eyes of the layman, been 'automated'. The development of numerical control (NC) of machine tools has been followed gradually by the introduction of computer numerical control (CNC) of such machines, involving the use of microprocessor technology. The microprocessor increases their capabilities from that of merely registering control information and monitoring step-wise applications to providing programming and other control facilities right on the machine. An alleged consequence of both these technical developments has been greater 'deskilling' of shop floor workers, according to writers such as Braverman and others.[2] We argue that this has not been equally true in advanced economies and we have looked at British and German experiences to question this view and theories built upon it, which emphasize 'deskilling' as characterizing the 'labour process' in the twentieth century.

The theoretical significance of the 'deskilling' debate recently discussed critically in the volume edited by Wood cannot, however, be divorced from its practical implications regarding manpower utilization and training.[3] Moreover, we feel that national differences are likely to affect work organization, and hence the relative distribution of skills to be found. We therefore hypothesize that the integration of the new technology into enterprises follows quite different routes in Britain and Germany. British companies will in turn train and use noticeably less skilled workers than German ones, and the difference will be particularly visible in production, as opposed to maintenance jobs.

It may be further hypothesized that the reverse of deskilling may result if 'changing technology (automation) induces a tightening up of selection criteria' because more skilled labour is required on the shop floor as Windolf suggests [4]. We also conjecture that a greater utilization of skilled labour may be anticipated in the future, and stronger in Germany because of a relatively greater supply of trained manpower there at all levels, as indicated by Prais [5]. In Germany, over half the primary work force has gone through a formalized apprenticeship.

Previous machine-tool applications controlled by paper tape programming prepared in the planning department (such as NC) have been to date essentially geared to specialized, homogeneous mass markets, inflexible automation and an erosion of craft skills. In the labour market, there has also been a move towards information processing, administration and different kinds of clerical work, particularly visible in the British experience. Recent directly programmed machine-tool applications, (such as CNC), in our view, may reverse this trend at least in the manufacturing sector, there is now increasingly a focus on craft skills and the levelling-out of the growth of indirectly productive employees very clearly seen in German firms. This consequence basically follows the organizing tradition of the respective national work cultures. It is misleading, we believe, to examine technological change outside this 'societal' context; rather, we see it interacting with it. In so far as the study has implications for organization theory, it argues that technological change needs to be seen as having much more open social implications and leaving organization designers more options than hitherto assumed.

RESEARCH FINDINGS [6]

NATIONAL INSTITUTIONS AND CULTURAL PRACTICES

If CNC exercises different effects according to technology and machine type, it also adapts to different 'societal' environments, namely to *national institutions and cultural practices*.

The German companies, for example, distinguished less than those in Britain between specialized functions and departments for production management, production engineering, work planning and work execution functions. Similarly, there was a consistently greater use of shop floor and operator programming in Germany; programming is seen as the nucleus around which the various company personnel, the managers, engineers, planners, foremen and operators, are integrated. The differences are reinforced by the CNC dimension. Furthermore, the greater separation of programming and operating in Britain ties in with the increasing differentiation of technician and worker apprenticeships, whereas technician training in Germany invariably comes after craft worker training and experience. In addition, whilst in Britain the planning and programming function confers white-collar status, it is much less common in Germany, where blue-collar workers are more extensively used for programming, both on the machine and in the planning department. Rotation between the two groups was frequently observed.

National differences, in turn, interact with company and batch size differences. In Germany, the similarity between organization, labour and technical practices of small and larger companies was greater than in Britain, where there appeared to be a split between pragmatically flexible small plants and organizationally more segmented larger plants. Formal engineering qualifications at various levels were relatively more common in Britain in larger plants, whereas often they were not represented in small British plants. In Germany, by contrast, formal qualifications were common to smaller and larger plants alike.

In both countries, CNC operation was generally seen as exacting less 'informatics' skills than advanced machining talents. Programming aids on the machine or in the planning departments are seen to be tools of increasing facility to control a process which has become ever more demanding from the point of view of precision, machining speeds, tools, fixtures and materials.

SOCIOECONOMIC CONDITIONS

While there was a series of 'logics' moulded by distinct historical, cultural and social developments, there was also a further thrust of CNC application which was *common to Britain and Germany*. This stemmed from the relevant existing macroeconomic factors, including competitive and marketing strategies, which interact with sociotechnical considerations. They incorporate a very broad range of factors which affect enterprises, but which they themselves attempt to influence.

Firms stated that they were keen, or perhaps being forced, increasingly to cater for small market 'niches' rather than for homogeneous mass markets, given that the most generally stated competitive situation was one in which there was static, or more commonly in Britain, negative market growth. More individualized, customized products, with a greater number of product variants were seen as appropriate.

Complex design of components may be consistent with NC application, but the greater variability of products and components was more specifically associated with CNC application. The two most important factors which lead to increasing CNC application within manufacturing were as follows:

1 the demand for more frequent and less time-consuming machine conversion from one batch to another, arising from the increased variability of products and components;

2 the inducement to minimize finished product stocks and work-in-progress which can be substantially reduced when the full potential for manufacturing 'families' of different, but similar, components is realized and/or advantage is taken of the opportunity to produce, in a single manufacturing cycle, those subassemblies which comprise the final product.

Thus, both market-oriented as well as financial considerations point in the direction of smaller batch sizes and more frequent conversion; this has important sociotechnical implications. It is through these developments that we can see the effect on skills. The increased variability of batches is not one which can be handled bureaucratically through a conventional increase in the division of labour. CNC operators are likely to have to deal with a greater and more frequently changing range of jobs; part of this is related to the increased sophistication of the machine control system through which more flexible changeovers and improvements of programmes can be achieved.

The crucial 'bottlenecks', however, may not be information-processing and calculating skills; experience indicates that the most crucial problems refer to tooling, materials, feeds, speeds, faults and breakdowns. Skills in handling these problems are most directly developed on the machine. Thus, while programming skills are required, increasing emphasis must be placed on the maintenance of 'craft' skills on the shop floor, rather than the converse (as implied by the 'pessimists' writing on the subject).

The justification of CNC *ex ante* was however made in rather general terms, often intuitive, through lack of information about skills requirements, down-time, maintenance and service quality, equipment reliability, organizational implications and so on. *Ex ante* and *ex post,* NC uses in general were justified on the basis of the complexity of the geometric design of the components, and the required cutting cycles and sequences. Economic justifications were also discussed by respondents, but were often presented as secondary considerations. This may or may not be the case. Arguments for CNC, however, emphasized increased flexibility coupled with potential increases in productivity in manufacturing. In the past, productivity increases had involved the production process becoming less flexible and less capable of handling variations in component specifications, small batch size, batch conversion and so on.

Differences also existed in the kind of production technologies selected in the German and British plants. It was, for example, rather more difficult in the case of both small and bigger plants to find examples of large batch processing involving CNC equipment in Britain. This may have been because of the recession reducing batch sizes. We do not interpret this wholly as a problem of matching: it would seem that there are different nationally specific overall socioeconomic trends in operation which affect the application of CNC both quantitatively (more CNC turning in Germany) and qualitatively.

ORGANIZATIONAL STRUCTURE

Work shop and operator planning were more widespread in German small batch turning, whereas British plants still followed the more traditional NC organizational view where programmes are made in the programming department and proved on the shop floor by both programmer and the operator. This difference between the two countries also applied to a lesser extent in CNC milling, particularly where automatic tool change facilities were absent. It was however less visible with respect to machining centres, the stronghold of traditional NC philosophy in both countries.

Organizational differences as far as CNC were concerned could be very strong even on the same site. They were related to production engineering practices, but cannot be explained fully without recourse to factors of personal influence and departmental tradition. This was visible in the German large plant-large batch categories – where differences between turning and milling were striking. In the latter case, programming was centrally performed, whereas in turning a high degree of shop floor autonomy was retained.

Within all the cases, British companies used CNC in such a way as either to maintain planning department control and/or autonomy, or to segregate the NC operations from the other sections. In Germany, CNC organization was fashioned so that it linked foremen, charge hands, workers and planners around a common concern. This was particularly apparent in the case of foremen, who in Germany were deeply involved in CNC expertise, but whom in Britain had been largely by-passed, resulting in deskilling of their jobs.

In both countries, the attractiveness of programming-related functions lay less in a formalized language, than in the instrumental value of programming as a means whereby the more demanding part of the task, that of metal cutting, could be more effectively planned and controlled. This diffusion of control to the shop floor depended on the ability to make programmes on the machines without losing too much machining time but more importantly on the accepted view of operator competence in metal-removal technology. This view was more partial to physically locating programme-related functions in the hands of planners in Britain, whereas it was more likely to prefer programming by operators as experts in cutting and setting in Germany.

TRAINING AND EMPLOYEE QUALIFICATIONS

Rather than any one deterministic outcome, there was a striking variety in the training and qualification patterns under CNC application, which was closely related to differences in the organization of the work process.

In both countries, using more skilled people as CNC operators was strongly linked to the integration of the operating and machine-setting activities. Where this existed, operators were more likely to be skilled; where it was absent, operators were unskilled. This relationship, however, was also a function of batch size, and thus it followed that there was also a *differentiation* between semiskilled operators and skilled setters where *large batches* were run. However, more *skilled* operators, who also performed setting functions, prevailed in *small batch* processing.

In small plants, setting and programming-related functions were intimately combined. In the small plant-small batch classification, there was a large overlap of operating, setting and programming-related functions. In the small plant-large batch category, setting and programming were still closely combined, but they were differentiated from the normal running of a batch. Was the policy to encourage – and this is important in the context of the deskilling debate – the development of operator expertise in the programming-relating functions? Would this be an end in itself since the operator was uniquely placed, via the CNC 'electronics' to control and, if necessary, modify the cutting process?

Operators frequently reported that they were more concerned with the problems of metal removal, that is, feeds and speeds, tool selection, tip wear and quality, tool life and so on, than with programming difficulties. Some limitations with machine programming were nevertheless encountered; these were usually associated with the question of reduced machine utilization that might result from the direct programming of geometrically difficult components.

The most pervasive national differences occurred in the small batch-large plant category. German companies allied CNC operations to tradesman status and experience, but British companies did not necessarily do so. Where this happened, however, it was usually recently introduced and not uncontested within the company.

There was a consistently held view in Britain that CNC tended to deskilling and that CNC operation was more routine. The same companies are however planning to introduce skilled tradesmen onto their NC and CNC machines in an attempt to increase machine utilization and, to a lesser extent, improve quality.

There were very different views of the qualifications needed for planning and programming. The higher the skills required of the CNC operators, the less was the demand placed upon the planners-programmers. This proposition held both within countries and between countries, and was linked as before for the setting and operating functions, with the effect of batch size. Thus, the application of CNC fitted with equal ease into strikingly different qualification structures; at one extreme, it could be found, within a polarized qualification pattern with unskilled operators, skilled setters and technician-planners neatly differentiated; at the other, it could be located close to conventional machining, even craftsman activity, involving a skilled, homogeneous work force.

Did this leave national differences between Britain and Germany in vocational training unaffected? There are perhaps even greater differences under CNC, although there was no direct causal connection. One of the more striking was the training of industrial workers. In Britain, there was a split at the beginning of working life, between technician and worker apprenticeships, between programming and planning as opposed to machining occupations. Training for these operated in parallel, whereas in Germany the latter set of skills was an essential prerequisite for the former. This difference appeared likely to persist and in Britain to sustain the more polarized qualification structure; whilst in Germany CNC was more visibly used to reduce training differentials between technical staff and the shop floor personnel, to increase the tradesman's status, to encourage even greater flexibility in production and to reduce the 'decision-making overload' on top management.

PERSONNEL STRUCTURE

Personnel structure, seen in terms of proportions of white-collar staff and worker categories resulted from a complex set of influences which did not necessarily originate from CNC. There was a general tendency in most of the companies investigated, particularly the small British but including most of the German companies, for a merging or blurring of status between the shop floor and the planning functions. The personnel structure remained more or less constant through the action of the status-bound grading policy, and any shift in the distribution of actual functions had limited influence. This merging of status may have even helped advance the utilization of the CNC process.

However this was not the complete story; this process took on very different forms. When craft qualifications were more frequently held on the shop floor, and particularly on the part of the operators, programming and planning functions were often delegated to these workers. Conversely, the weaker the craft qualifications, the stronger was the tendency to reclassify shop floor personnel as white-collar staff. Both effects could be observed in Germany; but their respective incidence depended on batch size which, in turn, was strongly related to operator qualifications. In short batches, operators progressed onto programming tasks without changing status, whilst with large batches white-collar status was extended into the works.

Status up-grading in Britain took place in small companies, but occurred less in larger factories where there was a more consistent distinction between works and staff. This was despite the more legalistic character of the definition of workers and white-collar employees in Germany. Where figures are comparable, Britain used craft workers more *sparingly* than Germany. These differences in personnel structure were related to the degree to which production engineering, work planning and production control tasks were set away from the shop floor. The relationship between white-collar employees in programming and production control, and the shop floor, changed very little even with intensive CNC use. In Germany this was more visible on the shop floor, and the associated functions moved to meet it on the 'home' ground. In Britain, the programming, planning and control staff were seen as the 'proprietors' of such knowledge, but this philosophy is being questioned more and more critically, as in Germany, if not for the same reasons.

CONCLUSION

All our data lead us to stress the extreme malleability of CNC technology; it is inadequate to consider a technology as given and to observe the effects which follow from it. But this is not to say that technology is unimportant; its significance unfolds through a continuous series of 'piecemeal' modifications. As part of a complex pattern of sociotechnical design and improvement, such changes interact with organizational and manpower innovations. Thus, in the company context, the detailed technical specifications of the CNC system adopted may reflect the specific influence of corporate and departmental strategies, and the existing production,' engineering and organizational procedures and the current manpower policies, all of which vary *within* a country and *between* countries and societies when we are considering the 'labour process' in general.

In the study, we found that solutions to CNC applications were alternatively organizationally simple or complex; some stressed functional differentiation, while others emphasized functional integration within positions or departments; in some cases there was a strong element of skill polarization, but with skill enrichment at the shop floor level. None of these contrasting policies can be said to be more 'advanced' from the technical point of view, yet at the same time it cannot be said that the application of CNC was haphazard or the subject of accidental initiatives.

Companies, particularly in Germany, are increasingly seeing the merits of stressing craft skills, as a viable option, when implementing the new technology. This is not because it is a necessary consequence, but because CNC has been developed in a context which links economic success with this process. There is a striking kinship between the increasing use of CNC and the renewed interest by companies in training and employing skilled workers.

Increased programming or programme changing in the workshop may further blur status boundaries for blue- as well as white-collar workers. It would, however, be misleading to interpret this as another step towards the 'post-industrial society', as 'information-processing' work or as a 'service' function, as so often happens. Whilst it is true that workers are dealing with increasingly sophisticated information technology, this may only concern the *tools of their trade* rather than their *working goals*.

ACKNOWLEDGEMENT

We gratefully acknowledge the support of the Anglo-German Foundation for the Study of Industrial Society for this study, as well as the help of CEDEFOP, the European Centre for Vocational Training. For professional dialogue and criticism, we have the pleasure to thank Derek Allen, Georges Dupont, Michael Fores, Donald Gelwin, Jonathan Hooker and Marc Maurice, and many others too numerous to mention.

NOTES AND REFERENCES

1   Rada, J. (1980) *The Impact of Microelectronics*, International Labour Office, Geneva, p. 105.

2   Braverman, H. (1978) *Labour and Monopoly Capital*, The Degradation of Work in the Twentieth Century. Monthly Review Press, New York.

3   Wood, S. (ed.) (1982) *The Degradation of Work?*, Hutchinson, London, ch. 1, pp. 1-10.

4   Windolf, P. (1981) 'Strategies of enterprises in the German labour market', *Cambridge Journal of Economics*, 5 (4), p. 359.

5   Prais, S.J. (1981) *Vocational Qualifications of the Labour Force in Britain and Germany*, National Institute of Economic and Social Research, London, Discussion Paper 43.

6   Information on research methods is given in Sorge, A., Hartmann, G., Warner, M., Nicholas, I.J. (1983) *Microelectronics and Manpower in Manufacturing Applications of Computer Numerical Control in Great Britain and West Germany*, Gower Press, Aldershot.

TECHNOLOGICAL CHANGE AND THE FUTURE OF WORK

Peter Senker

Science Policy Research Unit, University of Sussex

AN APPROACH TO AN ANALYSIS

Information technology, new materials and biotechnology are significant clusters of technologies likely to influence work. In the absence of effective countermeasures, the balance of job creation and displacement resulting from their exploitation is likely to benefit the already richer countries and to be relatively unfavourable to poorer people in developing countries: 'Capitalism Triumphant' is by no means completely successful. Work organization varies from country to country and affects quality of working life. In Anglo-Saxon countries deskilling is common, but Japanese and West German firms more often design work to require flexibility and independent thought. Progress in reducing discrimination against ethnic minorities and women has been slow. Extensive changes in attitudes and policies throughout society as well as reduction in employers' discrimination are necessary. Serious attempts at real solutions would also involve changing the working environment better to meet the needs of the groups concerned.

Except for a few nasty jolts – such as oil shocks, the October 1987 stock market fall, and moments when it seemed that the Third World debt problem could bring the world banking system to the point of collapse – the past few years could be characterized as 'Capitalism Triumphant'.

The success of capitalism, particularly in the West and in some countries adjoining the Pacific Ocean, in producing vast quantities of high-quality products and services for mass markets cannot be denied. In Eastern Europe, and in Russia and the other countries of the former Soviet Union, there is increasing determination to use market forces to overcome the inefficiencies resulting from centralized economic planning.

This article raises some concerns about the implications of 'Capitalism Triumphant' for the worldwide distribution of products, services and work.

The following represents a broad, inevitably crude, classification of some principal factors which affect the quantity and quality of available work:

1 the organization and stage of development of the various economies which comprise the world economy, e.g.. capitalist, centrally planned, advanced industrial, newly industrializing, developing countries;

2 the types, quantity and quality of products and services produced;

3 the technology, methods and materials used in production;

4 the organization of work, itself affected by management traditions, relationship between owners, managers, trade unions and governments.

In addition, a vast range of factors affects the distribution of production and employment around the world, including relative costs and availability of raw materials and labour with various skills.

This article is mainly concerned with the implications of technological change, which exercises a strong, but not overwhelming, influence on work. Even confining the analysis in this way leaves a large number of issues to consider. Moreover, the extent and nature of economic growth may well be affected by environmental considerations such as concern about exacerbating the greenhouse effect. While such problems are undeniably of great potential importance, insufficient data exist to consider them in detail at this stage.

History shows that there are considerable chances of being wrong about the types of products likely to be in use in the future. In the late 1920s, influenced by the huge increase in demand for automobiles in the previous decade, there was a good deal of talk about developing a 'flivver 'plane' – a small 'plane for everyday family use. For example, General Motors were convinced that the 'flivver' was at least a possibility, and this was one of the factors that influenced their investments in aviation companies at that time [1]. It would be optimistic to believe that we are much better now at forecasting the medium- and long-term future than General Motors were 60 years ago.

More important, forecasting the future accurately is impossible because deliberate human action may counteract any trends. It is, however, essential to have some idea of policy objectives to provide a focus for forecasting. Forecasting is essentially about influencing policy:

Ideally, the formulation of goals should precede policy decisions. In the real world ...

> even where long-term goals have been adopted, the lack of visibility of interactions in the complex modern world often makes it impossible to see how an immediate policy decision bears on the long-term goal ... Free from the formidable pressure of daily decision-making, research can ... examine the policy decisions which need to be made in the continuous process of approximating the goal [2].

To meet this need in relation to the future of work, I suggest a crude 'benchmark' long-term goal of attempting to secure economic growth which involves the provision of well paid interesting jobs, distributed as evenly as possible around the world to as many people as want them, regardless of gender, race or geography.

E. H. Carr suggested that 'human beings . . . may be warned in advance, by the prediction of consequences unwelcome to them, and be induced to modify their action, so that the prediction, however correctly based on the analysis, proves self-frustrating' [3]. This article is somewhat pessimistic: at the most, it is hoped that it will play some small part in causing its predictions to be self-frustrating.

A WORLD OF 'MACHINES'

In the second half of the twentieth century, the production and use of 'machines' (broadly defined), the production of the materials and components designed to be incorporated in machines, together with the energy used to power them, dominate the economies of advanced countries and increasing proportions of the economies of developing countries.

In 'machine production' I include anything from vehicles, machine tools, aircraft, missiles and tanks to computers, telecommunications equipment and power stations: the products of the engineering industry broadly defined – clearly important in all advanced industrialized countries [4].

The products of such industries are changing rapidly and playing highly significant roles in both manufacturing and service sectors of the economy – and in international trade and competition. As Schumpeter pointed out: 'The fundamental impulse that sets and keeps the capitalist engine in motion comes from the new consumer goods, the new methods of production or transportation, the new markets, the new forms of industrial organization that capitalist enterprise creates'. These are the basis for 'the competition which counts' [5].

Unlike Schumpeter, most of the classical and neoclassical economists who followed Adam Smith have neglected the profound influence of changing *products* on economic development, and the effects of a changing product mix on the location of industrial activities and employment. The goods with which Adam Smith's analysis was mainly concerned were the basic goods of his time:

> The tailor does not attempt to make his own shoes, but buys them off the shoemaker. The shoemaker does not attempt to make his own clothes, but employs a tailor. The farmer attempts to make neither the one nor the other, but employs these different artificers [6].

One of the most important aspects of the profound economic changes which have occurred in the past 200 years has been the change in the emphasis of production from the basic products such as clothes, food and shoes with which Smith was concerned. Conventional neoclassical economics mainly considers productivity and efficiency. It is not primarily concerned with issues such as what products or services are produced, for whose benefit, or who is employed in production: in that sense, it has not progressed much beyond Adam Smith.

SOME SIGNIFICANT MODERN TECHNOLOGIES

Freeman [7] suggests that changes of technoeconomic paradigm based on combinations of radical product, process and organizational innovations are more or less inescapable. He considers the adoption of Fordist mass production and assembly-line techniques as one paradigm change; and the change to more flexible manufacturing processes involving information technology as a further one.

At present, the most important cluster of technologies in terms of their implications for the future of work are microelectronics and information technologies: these are likely to remain important for several decades. In addition, a vast range of new materials is likely to come into significant use in the next 10 to 15 years. Biotechnology is also likely to begin to become significant in employment terms by the early years of the twenty-first century.

Freeman suggests that competitive pressures in the world economy are so strong that once such a paradigm has crystallized, it is hard for firms and countries to be non-conformist. Technological choices become increasingly constrained, even though an element of social and political choice remains. Even socialist countries which have attempted initially to opt out of a pattern of technology characteristic of the capitalist countries have after a decade or so generally been obliged to fall in with worldwide trends, with relatively minor differences. This was the case with the USSR after intense controversy in the 1920s, which adopted Fordist assembly-line technology and even Taylorism in the attempt to overhaul the capitalist countries.

Before considering the future location of economic activity and its implications for the quality of work it is necessary to outline developments in the 'clusters' of technology which are likely to be most important in the foreseeable future – information technology, new materials and biotechnology.

INFORMATION TECHNOLOGY (IT)

PRODUCTION PROCESSES BASED ON IT

There is widespread speculation that IT will be utilized in the next 10 years or so as the basis for the development of 'automatic factories'. The automatic factory depends essentially on the ability to pass computerized information between various functions – for example between design, production, marketing and information. Kaplinsky has published a wide-ranging and thoughtful survey of automation and its prospects. He points out the need for information to be available in compatible formats for it to be used for the integration of various functions effectively. The harmonization of functions necessary is facilitated by rationalization of design and process. Standardization and group technology (GT) are key to this. GT involves parts being grouped into families, thus simplifying and systematizing design and production.

Kaplinsky suggests that fully automated production – the true factory of the future – will be fairly widespread in the 1990s [8]. There are, however, grounds for believing that he may have overestimated the speed at which these developments will take place and, at the same time, underestimated the skills needed for their achievement [9].

IT PRODUCTS AND SERVICES

IT products include telecommunications equipment, defence and transportation electronics, factory automation and electronics products for use in the home, office and car. Much of the employment growth related to IT arises from the use of IT equipment to provide services, from telecommunications to insurance. Much service production involves the provision of services to manufacturing industry. In addition, the knowledge to provide 'product-based services' tends to be concentrated amongst those who design the products.

NEW MATERIALS

The four areas likely to have the most impact on employment, skills and working life are developments in plastics such as strong engineering plastics, adhesives, composite materials and advanced high-performance technical ceramics. Steel has long been a dominant material, but its dominance is likely to be eroded during the period under consideration. Nevertheless, steel makers are likely to respond to the competitive challenge from other technologies, and some new materials techniques – for example the creation of composites – are likely to be applied to steel as well as to plastic and other materials.

Achievement of forecast growth in advanced ceramics markets depends on *success* in development in a number of directions, including improved reliability and cost reduction in several applications such as cutting tools, turbocharger rotors, mechanical seals and valve guides. Much of the future growth in plastics use is likely to be in the automobile industry, substituting for metals in a wide range of applications including under-bonnet components, leaf springs, the drive train and exterior trim [10].

BIOTECHNOLOGY

During the next 10 years, the increase in employment resulting from the development of biotechnology will probably be relatively small and concentrated on R&D. A recent OECD report [11] suggested that, in the early years of the next century, biotechnology would begin to acquire importance of the same order as that of IT now. In the twenty-first century, biotechnology could become a net creator of employment, creating new (as well as substitute) industrial products and agricultural crops, and creating new means of environmental protection.

LOCATION OF ECONOMIC ACTIVITY

ADVANCED COUNTRIES

IT. US production of IT products is by far the largest in the world at present, but Japan is catching up fast. Japanese competitive strength in world markets is reflected by large exports, and it has been suggested that this strength may well increase – to the point where, in about 15 years, their exports will represent twice the value of their production. Of course, trade barriers may slow the growth of Japanese exports. Total Japanese production could catch up with that of the USA in 15 to 20 years, with both countries employing about five million people each in IT production. While European markets are much larger than Japan's at present, in terms of production and employment, Europe is likely to lag far behind and could experience a growing trade deficit.

It has been suggested that 'skill clusters' – concentrations of expertise – are critical to success in IT. While such concentrations have been created to some extent in Europe, they are not as large or growing as rapidly as in the USA and Japan. Electronics production in other countries is relatively small – perhaps 10% of total production in Japan, the USA and Western Europe [12].

New materials. It appears that the leading countries in the exploitation of new materials are likely to be Japan and the USA, followed by Germany. For example, most estimates and forecasts show Japanese production accounting for about half of a rapidly growing world market for advanced ceramics between 1980 and 2010. The Japanese industry is already well developed. Several manufacturers of more traditional materials, together with firms such as electrical appliance manufacturers which use the new materials, have already started advanced ceramics production and development. A similar pattern has arisen in the USA, but the European industry has progressed less rapidly. The UK industry is still very small. With few exceptions, end-users have not become involved in R&D to the same extent as in other advanced industrial countries: the UK domestic market is minute [13].

While Japan is a major user of advanced plastics, the USA is the leader in advanced plastics such as engineering plastics and advanced composites. The US lead is sustained by large users in aerospace and defence industries, and by their large markets for luxury goods such as speedboats. In Europe, the powerful chemicals companies, and large automotive and electrical user industries contribute to the strength of the German plastics industry, which leads those of France, Italy and the UK.

Biotechnology. R&D and market potentials are concentrated in highly industrialized countries. Several firms hope that microbially produced protein will find markets in OECD countries.

DEVELOPING COUNTRIES

The labour cost advantages of developing countries can be significant in securing employment, but the importance of such advantages can easily be exaggerated. For example, several newly industrializing countries (NICs) have had some success in the motor industry. US manufacturers, unable to compete with Japanese small car imports began to import cars from South Korea, Taiwan, Mexico, Brazil and Thailand. While these countries do have advantages in terms of labour costs, the high productivity achieved by Japanese manufacturers – and later emulated by

US and European manufacturers – reduces these cost advantages. In addition, developing countries have difficulty in producing components and building vehicles of the quality necessary to be fully competitive on world markets [14].

Developing countries are at a disadvantage in relation to securing employment from new technology, because they usually import it: jobs producing the new technology are usually located in advanced countries. Nevertheless, South Korea and Brazil already have electronics capital goods industries [15]. It is too early to forecast the role of developing countries in relation to new materials. Several developing countries may find that the use of these materials threatens jobs in the extraction of traditional raw materials.

Similarly, some companies based in OECD countries intend to exploit opportunities afforded by biotechnology to replace Third World exports with products produced in industrialized countries based on plant cell culture. At present, the cultivation of high-value cash crops, for example coffee, cocoa, vanilla, represents a significant source of revenue and employment for several poorer countries. Biotechnology offers the possibility of producing such products in factories in developed countries. The Third World *needs* for new pharmaceuticals such as diagnostics and vaccines are widely recognized, but nobody yet knows how such developments could be financed [16]. There is at least some tendency for the production of services related to the use of advanced technologies to move nearer to the producers of new technology products. Thus, to some extent, service employment may be expected to follow manufacturing employment in terms of location.

In the absence of deliberate and effective countermeasures, the balance of job displacement and creation resulting from technological change is likely to be relatively unfavourable to developing countries.

IMPLICATIONS OF CHANGING TECHNOLOGY FOR THE QUALITY OF WORKING LIFE

The emphasis here is on automation simply because, at present, any consideration of new materials and biotechnology would have to be relatively pure speculation.

The 'deskilling' tendencies in capitalism have been observed for a long time. In most work activities, deskilling *of the production of existing products and services* could possibly be the general tendency. But this by itself would not provide sufficient reason to believe that the overall tendency in capitalist economies is towards deskilling. At least three major factors counteract overall deskilling in the economy:

1 the production and use of ever more complex products and services;
2 the production of *new* products and services;
3 (a) the increasing use of production equipment (e.g. the substitution of robotic assembly for manual assembly which results in *additional*

equipment which needs to be maintained); (b) the *substitution* of more complex equipment for less complex equipment which requires more skill to maintain.

The upskilling view maintains that economic development involves a process of increased differentiation and efficiency. This process of change invariably requires a broader variety of skills and a higher average level of skills from the labour force.

The downgrading view (propounded mainly by Marxists) draws on studies of the labour process to argue that capitalist industrialization has involved the steady fragmentation and narrowing of tasks and a separation of the planning and conceptual aspects of view from the execution.

The conditional perspective maintains that results are mixed, depending on the level of automation in production, the organizational context in which innovation occurs, and decisions made by management.

The statistical evidence in favour of upskilling is fairly clear. For example, while the total employment in the engineering industry has declined quite sharply in the UK, employment of professional engineers and technologists has increased quite rapidly. Technician and draughtsman employment has fallen quite slowly, while the employment of craftsmen and operators has fallen fast [17]. These tendencies are broadly reflected in other advanced industrial countries.

But this leaves open the question of how the content of jobs has changed. It is conceivable that within several categories, the skills exercised have declined: it is possible, for example, that technician work has been so deskilled that technicians perform less skilled work than craftsmen did a few years ago. Skill changes in the economy as a whole can arise through changes in industrial composition – through the creation and destruction of jobs in various parts of the economy, as well as through changes in the content of specific jobs.

Skill is a multidimensional concept. When new technology is introduced, more skill of one type may be needed and less of another. With the more widespread use of IT, mental and interpersonal skills seem likely to be increasing in relative importance [18]. But the evidence for a general upskilling thesis is tenuous. Empirical research has shown that there are two basic dimensions which differentiate changes in skill levels – substantive complexity and autonomy control. The first refers to 'the level, scope and integration of mental, manipulative and interpersonal tasks in a job'. Complexity is also affected by the cognitive, motor, physical or other demands of the job. Tasks involving the integration of a range of cognitive or physical demands across a wide scope of settings but at a low level on each subdimension may require greater skill than those involving higher levels across a narrow range of settings and with little or no integration. The second, autonomy-control, 'refers to the discretion available in a job to initiate and conclude action, to control the content, manner and speed with which a task is done' [19]. The evidence is that shifts along the autonomy-control dimension can occur in either direction according to circumstances with the introduction of more automated practices. It is, therefore, not always easy to determine whether the net effect of automation on all the jobs affected has been upskilling or deskilling.

Buchanan and Boddy's conclusions from their case-studies are worthy of note in this context: they show in great detail that the skills implications of the introduction of new technology are both complicated and highly variable:

> The changes in job characteristics that accompany technological change reflect partly the capabilities of the technology and partly the objectives and expectations of management. Computing technologies make demands on human information processing and decision making skills, reduce the need for some manual effort and skill and introduce new forms of work discipline and pacing. The extent to which responsibility, discretion, challenge and control increase, however, depends on managerial decisions about the organization of work [20].

Further, there is danger in assuming that managers' strategies are always conscious, rational and coherent. This is certainly not so.

Not only does the process of skills formation differ radically from country to country, but traditions of work organization and attitudes vary from place to place. These have substantial effects on the quality of working life. There is a tendency for managers, workers and trade unions in the Anglo-Saxon countries to assume that the general tendency will be toward deskilling, and to pay insufficient attention to the need for training and retraining and to issues related to the quality of working life.

Japanese, Swedish and German firms are more inclined to design work in such a way that it requires ability to study, think independently, learn quickly, be flexible and work with others [21]. Apprentice training in Germany is more widespread than in France, and much more widespread than in the UK. In the past 20 years, more than half the German apprenticeship syllabuses, covering 96% of all apprenticeships, have been revised – to help workers cope better with new technology. Revised syllabuses also give workers broader basic knowledge, helping them to respond more flexibly to the requirements of changing technology [22].

An extensive review of the literature on new IT and working conditions in the EC found that there was a general trend towards increased occupational safety with the introduction of IT, with workers less often engaged in extreme physical exertion, and less frequently exposed to hazardous substances. But managerial decisions to rationalize and fragment work which involve higher work intensity and fewer interruptions in the work cycle can have severe adverse consequences. In particular, management demands for fast inputting speeds on computer keyboards can lead to muscular-skeletal problems (repetitive strain injury). But, unfortunately, working conditions are usually only considered after the decision to adopt IT has been taken [23].

Managements in the UK and the USA often fail to adopt the organizational and skill changes needed to realize the opportunities afforded by the new technology. Reports of the problems in implementing a computer system to process passports typify the problems which occur in new technology implementation in accordance with the authoritarian style of management prevalent in the UK. An efficiency review of UK passport issuing offices encouraged exaggerated expectations of a five-day turnaround for applications for passports at the same time as making possible 20% staff savings. But little effort was deployed to work out how the computerization programme could be implemented to provide these results. The efficiency review's fundamental weakness was its narrow and unimaginative view of the possibilities of computerization. The result of the administrative system set up by Home Office management was longer delays issuing passports, chaos and strikes which led to the computerization being stopped. The lack of involvement of both the management and the staff of the user organization in implementation and the 'assembly line' process used to issue passports were criticized in a management consultants' report. The report proposed the replacement of the 'assembly line' by group working [24].

DISCRIMINATION IN RECRUITMENT

Having considered in outline some factors affecting the location of jobs and their quality, it is necessary to consider some factors which affect access to those jobs. 'Employers must recognise that women can no longer be treated as second-class workers ... Discrimination against ethnic minorities by employers is not only unlawful [in the UK] but is also against their own commercial interests' [25].

GENDER

It has often been suggested that discrimination against women is encouraged by employers because it provides capitalism with cheap labour. But such analyses can readily be dismissed as naive. The subordination of women started long before capitalism; it occurs in all classes under capitalism; and it has continued in countries that have ceased to be capitalist.

'Equal opportunities' legislation has sometimes been perceived as offering a solution to problems of discrimination against women. Felicity Henwood has shown that the ideology of equal opportunities can actually exacerbate women's problems. It reinforces the idea that 'women's work' is less valuable than men's and encourages them to leave it. It results in women who enter traditional 'women's occupations' being regarded as having chosen them freely – this despite solid evidence that there are considerable obstacles to women who seek to enter non-traditional occupations.

Precisely because 'men's work' carries more status and power than women's work, women aspire to such work. Conversely, as women's work carries lower status and power, men do not normally aspire to do women's jobs. Men's sense of security in relation to their gender and sexuality fits comfortably with work which is valued and rewarded in society and which gives them power. But women have to live with contradictions which men do not have to face: women's sense of security in their gender/sexual identity relates to work that undervalues them. 'Women's work' tends often to value such attributes as sexual attractiveness, discretion, loyalty and subservience [26].

ETHNIC MINORITIES

In the UK, a substantial proportion of young people from ethnic minority groups are keen to persevere with their education and to enter higher education courses which lead to their chosen occupations. But studies have shown that ethnic minority pupils tend to be placed in courses and entered for examinations well below the levels which are appropriate for their abilities and ambitions. Young black people tend to be more persistent than white people in pursuing opportunities for continuing their education after school. But even when black people succeed in getting appropriate qualifications, they do not get their fair share of good jobs [27]. For significant progress to be made in resolving such problems would require extensive changes in attitudes and policies throughout societies – changes in the attitudes of employers and teachers, changes in policies of firms as well as in the education system. Reduction in employers' discrimination would be necessary, but not sufficient. Any attempt at real solutions to such problems could involve the need to consider possibilities of changing the working environment to meet the needs of the groups concerned.

DISCUSSION

The amount and quality of work available to the world's population and its distribution around the world are affected by the types of products and services produced as well as by the quantities.

Mankind has certain basic needs – food, shelter, clothing, health. Today's highly successful capitalist economies can be caricatured as being driven by the production and use of reliable, sophisticated 'machines' – motor cars, aeroplanes, weapons systems, washing machines, video tape recorders, power stations, telecommunications systems, together with the machines and complex systems on which these machines and other products are produced, such as computer numerically controlled machine tools, robots and so on.

The source of this drive is that those people who have already satisfied their basic needs are very open to persuasion of the benefits offered by the ownership and use of such products and services. Any capitalist economy which fails to produce reliable, sophisticated machines at low cost suffers from the effects of the strong import demand deriving from those among its population who can afford to own and use more and better machines. If a country's manufacturing industry fails to produce machines which are as good at as cheap a price as its overseas competitors, then it faces difficult problems in relation to its international balance of payments. The more successful the capitalist economy, the more it 'can afford' to spend in such areas as health, shelter and education.

As they become more affluent, the more powerful and richer citizens in developing countries naturally want to have and use machines just like those used by their brothers and sisters in the capitalist developed world. Similar pressures, therefore, apply worldwide. Changes in the prevailing ideology, for example in Eastern Europe, Russia and the other countries which until recently formed the Soviet Union, serve to intensify the worldwide drive to gain access to machines and the services they provide.

This analysis indicates that, however poor the country or region, a high priority for most governments would be the production and consumption of the benefits which flow from the possession of machines. A quick look round the world is sufficient to indicate that this caricature of the operation of the world economy is not a complete fantasy.

Marxist analysis can be limited by a failure to recognize the extent of the tangible benefits which capitalism has delivered to the majority of workers in several advanced capitalist economies. Modern industrialized economies deliver the goods and services which relatively affluent people in every country want. At present, the nature of work in manufacturing industry worldwide is determined to a considerable extent by the drive to satisfy markets for large volumes of high-performance, reliable machines and the products and services which they provide so cheaply and effectively.

Japan shows every sign of maintaining its technological lead in IT and advanced materials, with the USA following, and, perhaps, a growing gap between Japan and the USA on the one hand and Europe on the other. New technologies are likely to be exploited mainly to provide better paid and more interesting jobs in the countries which dominate their initial development and exploitation. The main benefits in terms of production and employment are likely to accrue to the more advanced countries – in the next few decades a category which may include the advanced regions of some newcomers such as South Korea and Brazil. Nevertheless, many developing countries seem likely to fare relatively badly.

Biotechnology is likely to increase rapidly in significance in the early years of the twenty-first century. It is unlikely that developing countries will benefit disproportionately in terms of employment: indeed, such trends as it is possible to discern indicate that advanced countries may well benefit at the expense of developing countries.

What is produced and how it is produced – the production process – largely, but not entirely determine the skills workers need to acquire and use and the quality of working life. Managements in the UK and the USA often fail to change their organizations and train their workers in the skills needed to secure the benefits offered by new technology. Japanese, Swedish and West German managers are more inclined to design work in such a way that it requires ability to study, think independently, learn quickly, be flexible and work with others; and to train their workers in the necessary skills. The discretion which managers have in the design of work is one of the factors which causes variation in the results of the introduction of new technology in terms of efficiency, skills exercised and quality of work. Worker participation in new technology introduction tends to be beneficial in terms of efficiency as well as humanity.

The dominant world economic system – 'Capitalism Triumphant' – is failing to provide the food, shelter, clothing, education and healthcare which the poorer people of the world want and need but are not in a position to demand. Economic development worldwide is dominated, and seems likely to continue to be dominated for the foreseeable future, by the production and development of products, services and materials which meet the needs of the relatively affluent – which includes the majority of people living in advanced countries. Progress in reducing discrimination against ethnic minorities and women has been slow. Recent research shows clearly that extensive changes in attitudes and policies will be neccessary to secure faster progress.

NOTES AND REFERENCES

1   Sloan, A.P. (1968) *My Years with General Motors,* London, Sidgwick and Jackson, page 363.

2   Encel, S., Marstrand, P. and Page, W. (eds) *The Art of Anticipation: Values and Methods in Forecasting,* Oxford, Martin Robertson, pages 27 and 38.

3   Carr, E.H. (1987) *What is History?,* London, Penguin, 2nd edn.), page 70.

4   Developments in prefabricated construction and 'intelligent buildings' mean that an increasing proportion of the construction industry can be regarded as 'machine production' for the purposes of this article.

5   Schumpeter, J.A. (1954) *Capitalism, Socialism and Democracy,* London, Unwin, 4th edn, pages 83-84.

6   Smith, A. (1910) *The Wealth of Nations,* London, Everyman edn.).

7   Freeman, C. (1987) 'The case for technological determinism', in R. Finnegan, G. Salaman and K. Thompson (eds), *Information Technology: Social Issues, A Reader,* London, Open University Press.

8   Kaplinsky, R. (1984) *Automation: The Technology and Society,* Harlow, Longman, pages 105-107.

9   Senker, P. and M. Beesley, M. (1986) 'The need for skills in the factory of the future', *New Technology, Work and Employment,* 1 (1), Spring, pages 9-17.

10   Rigg, M., Christie, I. and White, M. (1989) *Advanced Polymers and Composites: Creating the Key Skills,* Sheffield, Training Agency.

11   OECD (1989) *Biotechnology: Economic and Wider Impacts,* Paris, OECD.

12 Mackintosh, I. (1986) *Sunrise Europe: The Dynamics of Information Technology,* Oxford, Blackwell, pages 255-263 and 279.

13 Brady, T. (1988) *Advanced Ceramics: Research, Innovation and the Implications for Skills and Training,* Sheffield, Manpower Services Commission.

14 Jones, D.T. (1989) 'Corporate strategy and technology in the world automobile industry', in M. Dodgson (ed.), *Technology Strategy and the firm: Management and Public Policy,* Harlow, Longman, pages 11-24.

15 Schmitz, H. (1985) *Microelectronics: Implications for Employment, Skills and Wages,* Brighton, Institute of Development Studies, June, pages 12-13.

16 OECD *op cit,* reference 11, page 41.

17 Khamis, C., Lawson, G. and McGuire, S. (1985) *The Engineering Industry: Trends in its Manpower and Training,* Watford, Engineering Industry Training Board, page 10.

18 Spenner, K.I. (1985) 'The upgrading and downgrading of occupations: issue, evidence, and implications for education', *Review of Education Research,* 55, pages 125-154.

20 Buchanan, D.A. and Boddy, D. (1983) *Organizations* in *the Computer Age,* Aldershot, Gower, page 246.

21 Wolfe, D.A. (1989) 'Educational implications of the new techno-economic paradigm', University of Toronto, Department of Political Science, mimeo, page 24.

22 Wagner, K. (1991) 'Training efforts and industrial efficiency in West Germany', in J. Stevens and R. Mackay (eds), *Training and Competitiveness,* London, Kogan Page.

23 Ducatel, K. and Miles, I. (1991) *New Information Technologies and Working Conditions in the European Community,* Brussels, EEC Report M-BR 11, October.

24 £7 million computer "slowed issue of passports"', *The Guardian,* 5 August 1989; D. Hencke, 'Computer passports are halted', *The Guardian,* 16 August 1989; 'PM's expert blamed for passport chaos', *The Guardian,* 17 August 1989.

25 Department of Employment (1988) *Employment for the 1990s,* London, HMSO, Cm 540, December, page 8.

26 Henwood, F. (1990) 'Gender and occupation: discourses on gender, work and equal opportunities in a College of Technology' (University of Sussex, unpublished doctoral thesis.

27 Eggleston, J., Dunn, D. and Anjali, M. (1986) *Education for Some: The Educational and Vocational Experiences of 15-18 year-old Members of Minority Ethnic Groups,* Stoke-on-Trent, Trentham Books, pages 279-284.

TECHNOLOGICAL CHANGE AT WORK

Ian McLoughlin and Jon Clark

MANAGEMENT OBJECTIVES IN INTRODUCING NEW TECHNOLOGY

Why do organisations adopt new technology? Is it, as 'innovation theorists' imply, simply a rational commercial calculation in response to technological imperatives or are managerial decisions, as many labour process writers argue, part of an overall strategy aimed at increasing management control by deskilling labour?

One of the more extensive pieces of case study research on the introduction of computing and information technology has been conducted by Buchanan and Boddy (1983). They carried out research in seven organisations in Scotland covering a variety of different industries, types of firm, and technology (see Figure 1). Their findings reveal that the management objectives behind change are the product of complex processes of strategic choice within organisations. The availability of new computing and information technology was a 'trigger' to, rather than determinant of, processes of managerial decision-making. Thus, decisions were not purely a matter of commercial calculation in response to technological imperatives but rather a product of political processes within organisations. Moreover, a mix of objectives was involved in decisions over how to use the new technology, and labour control objectives were not the decisive consideration in the strategic decisions made by senior managers when deciding to invest.

Case	Technology	Company
1	NC machine tools	Caterpillar Tractors
2	Computer co-ordinated measuring machines	Caterpillar Tractors
3	Computer-aided lofting	Govan Shipbuilders
4	Computer-aided lofting	Reach & Hall Architects
5	Word processors	Y-ARD marine engineering consultants
6	Computerised equipment controls	United Biscuits
7	Computerised process controls	Ciba-Geigy chemicals

Figure 1 Buchanan and Boddy's Scottish Case Studies

In each case studied the decision to adopt and choice of technology were 'championed' by key individuals or small groups who promoted the need to change, often in the context of opposition, scepticism and inertia on the part of other managers. The arguments of these 'promoters of change' were not only based on objective commercial analysis but were also designed to mobilise support, create coalitions with influential managers, and manage the flow of information to back their case. For example, in one instance – a study of the introduction of numerically controlled machine tools at a tractor plant in Glasgow – it was found that the idea of change had been initiated by middle managers in manufacturing-support functions who justified the investment in terms of productivity and cost benefits. They secured the agreement of senior manufacturing managers, who were concerned at the age of the existing plant, but had their proposals resisted by the plant accountants on the basis of a separate investment analysis and by factory managers who felt they would lose their control over the workflow (1983, pp. 47-51). This points to the variety of management interests and objectives that may be involved in the process of technological change.

The various management objectives identified by Buchanan and Boddy in their case studies were classified into three main categories. These were:

1 *Strategic objectives* concerned with external, market and customer-oriented goals such as improved product quality, expanding market share and maintaining market lead over competitors.

2 *Operating objectives* concerned with internal technical and performance-oriented goals such as improvements to product flexibility and reductions in plant running and labour costs.

3 *Control objectives* concerned with reducing uncertainty caused by reliance on informed human intervention in the control of work operations, for example by replacing humans with machines, improving management control over workflow, increasing the amount and speed at which performance information was made available to managers (Buchanan and Boddy, 1983, pp. 243-4; also Buchanan 1983, pp. 75-6).

The pursuit of these objectives varied between management levels and functions. Senior managers tended to have strategic objectives. These goals were closely linked to the 'operating' objectives of middle line and financial managers. Control objectives did not figure significantly in either senior or middle managers' decisions to introduce new technology. There appeared, therefore, to be no overriding objective to introduce new technology in order to control labour. However, control objectives were to the fore in middle and junior line managers' thinking about how the new technology should be used once it was introduced (1983, pp. 241-4). This point will be taken up below.

Buchanan and Boddy's findings are supported by a wide range of case study evidence (see for example, Francis *et al.*, 1982; Jones, 1982; McLoughlin, 1983b; McLoughlin, 1987; Wilkinson, 1983; Willman and Winch, 1985; Batstone and Gourlay, 1986; Batstone *et al.*, 1987; Clark *et al.*, 1988). These studies also suggest that labour control objectives are, if they even figure at all, far from being the only factor in managers' decisions to adopt new technology, although this is not to deny that in some cases – in national newspapers for example – such considerations can exert a significant influence (see Martin, 1984). Wilkinson in four case studies of the introduction of electronics-based technologies in batch engineering firms in the West Midlands' concluded that:

> Owners may sanction capital investment proposals which come from within organisations, and they may demand that certain levels of profitability are maintained; but this research provided no evidence that deskilling manpower policies were connected in any immediate sense to these demands. (1983, pp. 97)

Similarly, Jones studied the introduction of NC machines (a technology cited as the 'classic case' of managements introducing new technology with the objective of deskilling labour by Braverman) in five batch engineering plants in south-west England and Wales. He found that labour costs were rarely, if at all, the decisive factor in decisions to invest in NC machines, while savings in operating costs and improvements in product quality were the principal determinants of managerial choices. He concluded:

> ...the evidence presented here further contradicts even modified theses about general and inherent tendencies to deskill because of 'laws' of capitalist exploitation and accumulation... This is not to deny that such motivations exist among manufacturing management. It merely reasserts that management calculation cannot be concerned solely with labour costs and utilisation. (Jones, 1985, pp. 198-9)

Available survey evidence appears to confirm this picture suggesting that a range of motives exists within the management function as a whole for the introduction of new technology, and that decision-making is distributed through different levels and functions. Surveys covering manufacturing firms and offices conducted for the Policy Studies Institute identified a variety of motivations for adopting new technology among the managerial respondents questioned (see Northcott et al., 1982; Bessant, 1982; Steffens, 1983).

More recent and comprehensive survey data confirms the manner in which managerial decision-making tends to be distributed through the different levels and functions according to the particular stage in the process of change concerned. For example, the WIRS found although there were significant variations between sectors. The general pattern in establishments forming part of larger organisations (eighty-four per cent of the sample), was for decisions to introduce change to be taken at higher levels in the enterprise. However, decisions over how change was to be introduced tended to be taken at establishment level (Daniel, 1987, pp. 86-7; see also Martin, 1988).

To summarise: it appears that ideas that the introduction of new technology can be explained either in terms of 'rational' responses to commercial and technological imperatives or an overall management strategy aimed at increasing management control, are too simplistic. Case-study research on the reasons why new computing and information technologies have been introduced reveals that decisions are the outcomes of processes of strategic choice within organisations and that a variety of objectives may be involved. Moreover, the nature of the objectives pursued by managers varies according to level and function. Senior managers tend to be concerned with using new technology to improve the position of the organisation in the 'external' environment, middle managers with improving the 'internal' operating performance of the organisation, and lower-level line managers with the use of new technology to reduce informed human intervention and thereby increase managerial control of the work process. Motivations to use new technology to deskill labour and increase management control have rarely been decisive in senior managers' decisions to introduce new technology.

THE REGULATION OF LABOUR AND TECHNOLOGICAL CHANGE

The relationship between senior managers' decisions to introduce new technology and policies concerned with the regulation of labour would appear to be more complex than implied in some versions of labour process theory. For example, while there is little evidence to suggest that issues such as labour costs and labour control are always decisive, it is important to recognise that the objectives behind decisions to adopt new technology do set parameters within which decisions over industrial relations and labour control policies are likely to be made. Thus, while such issues may not be an explicit component of overall business strategy, policy assumptions on such matters as labour costs can be implicit in senior managers' decision-making (Batstone *et al.*, 1984; Child, 1985).

This point appears to be borne out by the findings of a survey conducted by the Industrial Relations Research Unit at the University of Warwick which was concerned with the general impact of higher levels of management on workplace industrial relations (see Marginson *et al.* 1988). Part of the survey, which focused on the corporate and divisional levels of seventy-six firms, concerned the industrial relations aspects of decisions over technological change. The findings revealed that the great majority of corporate level managers did take industrial relations issues into account when deciding to introduce new technology, in particular the issues of levels of employment and work organisation (Martin, 1988).

One of the difficulties with much existing case study and survey research is that, whilst pointing to the diversity and complexity surrounding decision-making over technological change, little is said about the way economic circumstances of the firm, or the type of innovations involved, might affect or constrain managerial aims and objectives with regard to the regulation of labour. Paul Willman (1986, pp. 76-80; 1987) suggests a possible categorisation of the various factors which may set the parameters for managerial decision-making in this respect. The key factors are whether a firm's competitive position depends on maximising the performance, maximising the sales, or minimising the production costs of its products. Organisations operating in a relatively young product market are likely to seek to improve competitiveness by applying new technology to maximise the performance of their products, rather than seek to reduce the costs of production. These firms might be expected to introduce policies which aim to develop the skills and expertise of their workforce in order to improve quality and develop new products and services. This description would fit the science-based firms that – according to long wave theory were the first to adopt microelectronics in new technology products.

In contrast, senior managers in firms in maturing product markets are likely to seek to maximise sales by using new technology to improve the efficiency and continuity of production. The implication for management policies for labour regulation here is that these might be directed at securing greater control over work, while at the same time attempting to secure employee acceptance of continuous technological change. Finally, senior managers in firms in mature product markets are likely to seek to maintain their competitive position by using new technology to reduce production costs. Where labour costs are the principal concern, they might be expected to develop policies which aim to improve labour productivity and utilisation, possibly involving a reduction and/or wholesale restructuring of the labour force. Significantly, suggests Willman, it is in mature industries concerned with cost minimisation that new process innovations based on microelectronics may have their greatest impact. This is supported by the current pattern of innovation, which reveals that microelectronics-based innovations are now diffusing more generally into production processes across industry (Willman, 1986, pp. 168-79).

Clearly, then, there are likely to be variations in the implications of decisions to adopt new technology for managerial approaches to labour regulation, depending upon the nature of an organisation's product market, whether the change concerned is a product or process innovation and, if a process innovation, whether this is aimed at improving the quality of output or reducing costs. However, Willman cautions that it is not automatic that organisations introducing new technology in any of these circumstances will necessarily develop the 'appropriate' business strategy or approach to labour regulation. Rather, processes of 'strategic choice' may well be important mediators (1986, pp. 77). Similarly, Batstone et al. (1984) point to the importance of strategic choices in mediating the link between overall business strategy and labour regulation. In this sense the overall business strategy developed by an organisation in response to changes in the commercial and technical environment might best be seen as a 'corporate steering device' (Child, 1985) which sets the parameters within which sub-groups of managers develop policies and approaches to implementing technological change.

Child (1984; 1985) has provisionally identified four choices or 'policy directions' with respect to labour regulation which may be applicable to organisations introducing new computing and information technologies into their production processes. These are:

1 Elimination of direct labour by substituting new technology for human involvement in production to provide completely automated continuous production processes .

2 Sub-contracting of work outside the organisation by using new technology to enable professional and managerial staff to work on a contract basis from home using computer workstations linked to company headquarters. Similar developments may be possible where the high reliability of equipment allows maintenance work to be sub-contracted.

3 Improved labour flexibility ('polyvalence') by breaking down existing horizontal and vertical skill demarcations between workers, thus increasing the range of tasks that they can perform and/or the amount of discretion that they can exercise over task-performance.

4 Degradation of jobs by using new technology to deskill tasks and increase direct management control over work in line with the Taylorist practices identified by Braverman.

In practice, the appropriate balance between these options, suggests Child, is likely to vary according to the circumstances of particular organisations, such as product and labour market conditions and the nature of the production task.

As Child also notes, such policies have immediate implications for what labour economists refer to as an organisation's 'internal labour market'. Researchers at the Institute of Manpower Studies at Sussex University have described the possibilities for the restructuring of internal labour markets in terms of a model of the 'flexible firm' (see Figure 2) (Atkinson, 1984; Atkinson and Meager, 1986; Preece, 1986). This theoretical model distinguishes between the 'core', 'peripheral' and 'external' components of the organisation's. workforce. 'Core' workers are those whose skills are most essential to the conduct of the main activities of the firm. They enjoy primary labour market status which is reflected in relatively high job security, pay and status. They are required to accept 'functional flexibility', so that changes to their jobs (for example the erosion of horizontal and vertical demarcations with other skill groups) can easily be made when required. 'Peripheral workers' conduct less critical activities and are hired on employment contracts (temporary, part-time, flexible working hours, etc.) which allow for 'numerical flexibility' by the easy adjustment of their numbers as the scale of operations changes. 'External workers' are those whose activities are 'distanced' from the firm in the sense that they are no longer employed by it, their employment contract in effect being substituted by a commercial contract with another employer (for a critique of this model see Pollert, 1987).

The 'policy directions' identified by Child suggest that new technology may enable managers to bring about reductions in overall employment levels and increase 'numerical flexibility' among peripheral workers by eliminating and deskilling jobs. It may also facilitate reductions in employment levels and increases in the 'external' workforce by allowing some 'core' and 'peripheral' work to be sub-contracted. Finally, the erosion of skill demarcations when new technology is introduced suggests an increase in 'functional flexibility' amongst 'core workers'. In short, the introduction of new computing and information technology may enable managers to develop labour regulation policies which result in a radical restructuring of an organisation's labour force and be one factor contributing to more flexible forms of work and employment. To what extent though have managers adopted such innovations in their approach to regulating labour when new technology has been introduced?

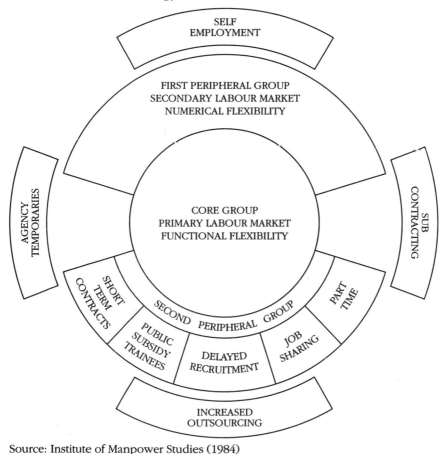

Source: Institute of Manpower Studies (1984)

Figure 2   The flexible firm

INNOVATIONS IN LABOUR REGULATION AND THE ROLE OF PERSONNEL MANAGEMENT

Some commentators have argued that during the recession the introduction of new technology has occasioned the emergence of a 'new management strategy' for handling the industrial relations issues raised by change. This strategy involves a firmer line being taken with trade unions and a willingness to consult and involve employees only within tightly defined limits (see Northcott and Rogers, 1985, pp. 36-8). However, it may be misleading to see such strategies as 'innovative' approaches to labour regulation in the context of the introduction of new computing and information technologies. On the one hand, there is evidence from industries such as automobiles and national newspapers, that some managers have taken a tougher line with trade unions, and have seen direct communication with the workforce as a means of gaining the acceptance of change in situations where the labour market position of unions is weak (see for examples, Willman and Winch, 1985; Martin, 1984). On the other hand, it is by no means clear that such 'new strategies' represent anything more than an attempt to reassert managerial prerogatives based on traditional assumptions and values. For example, Davies concluded from a study of technological change in the brewing industry that managers viewed the weak position of unions as an advantage and an opportunity to avoid bargaining over change or disclosing detailed information on management plans. The assumption was that unions would react negatively and that the superiority of management expertise meant that the shop floor had little to contribute (1986, pp. 181-3).

Sheila Rothwell (1984) studied twenty-one firms engaged in introducing new technology drawn from both manufacturing and service sectors (see Figure 3). According to Rothwell, an organisation's 'employment policies' are likely to vary along five dimensions: relationship to business strategy; extent of a long-term future planning orientation; the significance of the role of the personnel function; the extent to which an employee-centred philosophy exists; and the degree of consistency between various aspects of employment policy (manpower planning, industrial relations, pay) and overall business strategy.

To the extent that the introduction of new technology is being accompanied by innovations in an organisation's approach to labour regulation – for example, along the lines suggested by notions of the 'flexible firm' – it might be expected that a 'high' score would be achieved on some if not all of Rothwell's five dimensions. In fact her case studies revealed that:

1 Employment policies tended to be a 'lower-order' consideration in overall business strategies. Decisions to adopt new technology tended to overlook issues such as the need for training courses to be completed if the technology was to be used effectively.

2 There was a general absence of long-term planning to take account of the effects of adopting new technology on manpower requirements.

3 The personnel function was not usually involved in investment decisions and played a reactive rather than proactive role in implementing new technology.

4 There was little evidence of an employee-centred approach, in particular in the area of work design around the new technology.

5 Various aspects of employment policy did show some changes in approach towards internal labour market structure in a few organisations.

Rothwell concluded that the general lack of change in employment policies at a strategic level probably reflected managerial preferences 'to pour new wine into old bottles' in order to reduce uncertainty, in particular by avoiding linking technological change to wholesale changes in the approach to employment and industrial relations. As one manager commented: 'If I can get away with changing three things, rather than six, I'll do that, because people can't take too much' (1984, pp. 111).

The typicality of these findings can be explored further by looking at more detailed evidence on the role of personnel and industrial specialists in the process of technological change. Preece and Harrison (1986) argue that the major implications of new technology for work and organisation might enhance the role of personnel and industrial relations managers as 'would-be change agents' in developing new approaches to labour regulation. In other words, personnel and industrial relations specialists might be expected to be called upon, in what Thomason (1981) refers to as their 'organisational consultant' role as change increasingly involves dealing with 'human problems' requiring specialist expertise. On the other hand. it can he argued that the historical development of personnel and industrial relations management in Britain has tended to emphasise a reactive rather than proactive approach (see Watson, 1977; 1986, pp. 172-209) concentrating on 'fire fighting' and *ad hoc* decision-making rather than strategic thinking (Purcell and Sisson, 1983). This suggests that personnel specialists are marginal to managerial decisions and planning over technological change. This rather than being involved in the initial stages of change, personnel and industrial relations managers will be called upon only at subsequent stages to deal with employment and control problems once they arise.

Figure 3 Summary of Rothwell's case studies

Industry/case	Application of new technology	Employees in case unit	Trade unions recognised
Engineering			
Electronics	Trade unions recognised	590	x
Heaters	Manufacturing	450	√
Print	Manufacturing	200	√
Engines (2)	Assembly working	1200	√
	Manufacturing	670	√
Power tools	Materials and production control	1400	x
Food, drink and tobacco			
Confections (2)	Chocolate bar manufacturing	1800	√
Packet food	Automated warehousing and packing	75	√
Liquid food (2)	Quality control	330	√
	Accounting	70	√
Chemicals and Pharmaceuticals			
Photo products (2)	Materials and production control	250	√
	Ordering process	160	√
Tablets	Quality control	300	√
Infusions	Materials and production control	900	x
Allergens	Materials and production control	450	√
Drugs	Materials and production control	2800	√
Wholesale distribution			
Agent	Stock control and order processing	111	√
Wholesaler	Order processing	300	√
Own distributor	Stock control	3500	√
Mail order	Automated warehousing	1200	√
Stationer	Order processing	3500	√
Finance & banking			
Insurance	Order processing/accounting	500	√
Computing	Sales & service of computers	60	x
Public utility			
Utility	Customer service/order processing	4000	√

Source Rothwell (1984)

The role played by personnel specialists in seven manufacturing firms in the Midlands and North of England was studied by Preece and Harrison (1986). The cases illustrated the varied nature of the personnel involvement in technology-related changes and the widely varying contribution that they could make. These ranged from cases where personnel managers played an important and influential role supporting line-management decision-making, to situations where there was no personnel involvement at all and where expert involvement might have avoided costly mistakes being made by line-managers.

For example, in the case of an American-owned engineering company, the plant of around 500 employees had a well-developed personnel function. The plant was first occupied in 1972 as a 'greenfield' site and had subsequently introduced a range of CAD and CAM technologies. This created an atmosphere in which technological change was viewed as a 'way of life' and established structures and procedures were developed to handle the introduction and operation of new systems. The role of personnel in the process of change itself was deliberately 'low profile' in order to retain an air of normality when new technology was introduced. However, personnel had an important background influence in advising line managers and attending to any employment and control issues that arose – for example, pay, grading and training.

This situation can be contrasted to that in the plant of a specialist truck body builder with 220 employees. The personnel function in this plant consisted of one personnel manager nearing retirement whose role was essentially administrative. One consequence was that the company had little idea of the skills and knowledge profile of its workforce. When the company installed its first new technology in the form of NC and CNC machine tools the personnel manager had no involvement whatsoever. One consequence was that the absence among the workforce of electronic and programming skills to operate the machines was not realised by line managers until after the machines were installed. Even at this stage there was no attempt to involve personnel. Instead the machines stood idle until an external consultant could be employed to produce the required computer programs.

Rothwell's studies, cited above, point to more involvement on the part of personnel than in this latter case. She found that although it was rare for senior personnel directors to have any major involvement in feasibility studies initiating change or leading to the decision to adopt a particular technology, the personnel function was more involved at subsequent stages of change (1984, pp. 44).

This finding is supported by Clegg and Kemp (1986). They studied the introduction of a 'state of the art' FMS system in a large plant of a UK-based manufacturing company, the planning process for which lasted several years. They describe this process as illustrative of the 'sequential method' of introducing new technology where system design decisions are taken first, after which the human implications of these decisions are considered. In the case concerned, personnel managers were excluded from the system design stage and were subsequently required to react to the technical decisions that had already been made. The effect was that personnel and industrial relations issues were 'squeezed out' at the design stage, subsequent choices over human aspects were constrained by prior technical decisions, and no coherent strategic plan concerning the human aspects of the new system was developed. As a result of the lack of input from personnel, not only were the human aspects of operating the system considered only at a late stage in the process of change, but when they were considered decisions were fragmented and did not constitute a coherent policy (1986, p. 9).

How typical though are these case-study findings? Is the general pattern for personnel to be highly influential at all stages of change, involved only after major decisions have been taken, or simply not involved at all? The Workplace Industrial Relations Survey (WIRS) provides more wide-ranging evidence from organisations in manufacturing which allows a more general picture to be constructed. This tends to suggest that the lack of involvement of the personnel manager in the truck plant studied by Preece and Harrison may well be the most typical. First, it was found that only twenty per cent of manufacturing establishments had personnel managers, although these tended to be the largest workplaces in terms of numbers of employees. Second, as Table 1 indicates, in forty-six per cent of cases personnel managers were not involved at all in the introduction of new microelectronics technologies (denoted in the table as 'advanced technical change'). Third, where personnel was involved, in only fifteen per cent of cases was this in the initial decision to adopt new technology, in most cases involvement coming in the later stages of change – in other words as part of a process of 'sequential' decision-making as described by Clegg and Kemp.

These findings are supported by those of the Warwick survey referred to above. Here no evidence was found to suggest that the introduction of new technology was directly related to an increase in the role of the personnel function, although there was a tendency for the influence of personnel to have grown where managers had engaged in discussions over the introduction of new technology with union representatives (Martin, 1988).

Table 1 Works managers' accounts of the role of the personnel department in manufacturing establishments in the introduction of major change [2]. Column percentages.

	Total	Advanced technical change	Conventional technical change	Organi-sational change
Personnel department involved	46	50	(13)	(80)
Personnel not involved	52	46	(87)	(20)
Not stated	2	4	(1)	-
Stage of involvement				
Decision to change	14	15	(1)	(30)
Immediately after decision to change	20	19	(2)	(50)
After decision to tell workers	6	9	(2)	-
Later stage	6	7	(8)	-
Base: works managers who reported a major change in the previous three years				
Unweighted	*241*	*176*	*40*	*25*
Weighted	*56*	*37*	*12*	*7*

Source: Daniel (1987)

The lack of involvement of personnel managers is made even more striking when compared to their role in organisational changes without a technological content (see Table 1). The WIRS found that in manufacturing personnel was involved in eighty per cent of such cases, and that this involvement was nearly always from the decision to change or immediately after (Daniel 1987: 107-9). Comparing these findings with those of earlier studies of technological change Daniel concludes: 'it appears that very little has altered since the early 1960s, and that technical change is still largely seen as a technical matter within which there is no established role or function for personnel management' (1987: 110). What is surprising, as Daniel notes, is that there is clear evidence that the full and early involvement of personnel in technological change, where it does occur, helps to promote worker acceptance of change. Indeed, the survey found a strong and consistent relationship between the early involvement of personnel managers and favourable worker reactions to advanced technological change (1987, pp. 110).

To summarise so far. It appears that policies for the management of labour do not flow unproblematically from overall business strategies as suggested by many labour process writers. Although business strategies may set the parameters within which such policies may be developed when new technology is introduced, for example by specifying a general requirement to reduce labour costs, they do not necessarily specify the policies to be pursued. To this extent there is strategic choice within any organisation over the precise kind of labour management policy to accompany technological change.

What is significant about the findings of recent research is the lack of innovation in approaches to the regulation of labour when new technology is introduced. In other words, although strategic choices may exist which suggest possibilities for a radical restructuring of work and employment within organisations, there is little evidence that managements have in general actively sought to take such decisions and develop 'new strategies' for labour regulation. Perhaps the clearest indication of this is the marginal role played by personnel specialists who might have been expected to play a leading role as 'organisational consultants' if new policies were to be developed at a strategic level. However, if anything, evidence confirms that they tend to become involved only after decisions to adopt new technology have been taken and in response to discussions with trade unions. In other words, their role is marginal and reactive rather than central and proactive. This brings us to the choices faced by managers with regard to the implementation of new technology – in particular the issues of how far a participatory approach should be adopted and the form of management organisation that should be used to manage the change.

MANAGEMENT CHOICE AND IMPLEMENTING NEW TECHNOLOGY

It was suggested above that business strategies leading to decisions to adopt new technology set the parameters within which lower-level managers responsible for working out detailed policies have to operate. This raises the important question of how far decisions at a senior level are actually carried through in the choices made by managers at the workplace during subsequent stages in the process of change. This is referred to by Child (1985) as the extent of 'attenuation' or the 'tightness of coupling' between corporate strategy and the actions, or as we have termed them elsewhere 'sub-strategies' (see McLoughlin *et al.*, 1985), of lower-level managers.

Whilst the 'sub-strategies' behind the choices made by lower-level managers may fulfil the role of 'plugging gaps' left by corporate decisions to introduce new technology, it is equally possible that managerial actions, or a lack of them, at subsequent stages of change may lead to consequences not anticipated or intended at senior levels in the organisation. In this sense, the actions of middle and junior managers can in certain circumstances be regarded as a 'subversive activity' to the extent that they may actually frustrate corporate objectives (Buchanan, 1986, p. 77). This section will explore the significance of the actions of middle and junior managers at the implementation stage of change. The following section examines management sub-strategies in using new equipment or systems once they are operational .

MANAGEMENT SUB-STRATEGIES FOR IMPLEMENTING NEW TECHNOLOGY

It has already been noted that decisions to adopt new technology open up or trigger further management choices at subsequent stages in the process of change. Having decided to adopt new technology and selected or designed the required equipment, managers then face decisions as to how to implement the new equipment and systems at workplace level. In principle, choices range along two dimensions (see Francis, 1986, pp. 171-96; Davies 1986, pp. 66-72; Child, 1984, pp. 268-93 for discussion). Firstly, there is a question of how far a participatory or non-participatory approach is taken in relation to the workforce. At one extreme managers might take the view that all decisions regarding the introduction of new technology are a managerial prerogative and that a minimum of information should be made available to employees. Alternatively, they may seek to communicate and consult fully with employees about their decision to introduce new technology. Finally, in unionised environments managers have a choice as to whether technological change should be an issue for joint consultation and/or collective bargaining. Obviously, [...] trade unions may well have views of their own on the extent to which managerial decisions should be subject to joint regulation.

Secondly, there is a question of how managers should organise themselves to manage the change, whether decisions should be made from the 'top-down ' or whether a 'bottom-up' approach should be adopted. The 'top-down' approach implies that change is managed centrally by a project team, task force or individual manager. One advantage of this approach is that it enables a high degree of senior management control and maintains continuity of management responsibility throughout the process of change. A disadvantage is that the middle and junior line-managers who will be the 'end-users' of the technology may have little influence over the way change is implemented. A 'bottom-up' approach involves delegating responsibility for managing change to the line-managers in the individual plants, areas of operation, or functional departments who will ultimately be responsible for using the new technology. One obvious advantage is that the requirements of the end-users are more likely to be met since they will be responsible for making decisions at critical junctures during implementation. A disadvantage is that senior managers will have less direct control over the precise way change is managed, and continuity may be more difficult to maintain, especially where line-managers give a higher priority to their day-to-day responsibilities than to the management of change. The range of choices open to managers in developing sub-strategies is summarised in Figure 4.

Organisation theorists who have adopted a contingency approach suggest that there is no 'one best way' to manage change, although nearly all academic commentators point to the advantages of adopting some form of participatory approach towards the workforce. 'Situational factors' which may influence management choices include the timescale of the project; the nature and strength of possible sources of resistance; the identity and influence of 'promoters of change'; existing collective bargaining arrangements; and the nature of trade union reactions. The more a technological change is important to organisational performance and commercial survival the more managers are likely to adopt a top-down approach. The more strong resistance is anticipated from a trade union within an established collective bargaining framework, the more likely a bottom-up approach may be adopted (see Davies, 1986, p. 70).

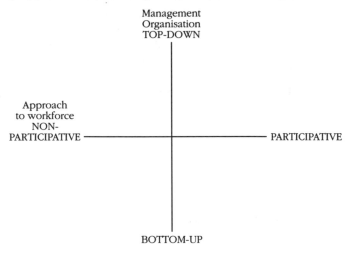

Figure 4 Management choices in implementing new technology

An important point is that the 'sub-strategy' adopted by managers in implementing new technology is likely to be the outcome of choice and negotiation rather than merely, as contingency theory implies, a rational selection from alternatives within a given situation (see also Davies, 1986, pp. 71). Some of these points will now be illustrated by reference to three case studies from research in which the authors have been involved. Each case involves a different implementation sub-strategy which emerged as a result of choice and negotiation within the organisation. As will be seen, the choices made had profound implications for the successful achievement of corporate objectives, in some cases acting to facilitate and in others to frustrate.

THREE CASES OF IMPLEMENTATION

The first example is provided by British Rail and their attempt to introduce a computer-based freight information system ('TOPS') into the rail network during the 1970s (see McLoughlin *et al.*, 1983; 1985). The case provides an excellent illustration of an implementation sub-strategy involving a combination of top-down decision-making and a mixture of a participatory and authoritarian approach at different levels within the organisation. It was designed to overcome potential management and trade union resistance to change by securing a 'tight coupling' between corporate objectives and the manner in which they were implemented at workplace level.

The decision to invest in new technology was based on 'strategic objectives', concerned with arresting the severe economic difficulties of the freight business in the face of declining traffic, 'operating objectives', concerned with improving the efficiency of freight operations, and 'control objectives', aimed at improving the utilisation of freight rolling stock and locomotives. The sum invested was in the region of £13 million (1971 prices) and was British Rail's first venture into large-scale, on-line computer information systems in the control of rolling stock and train movements. The nature of the innovation, and the economic circumstances of its introduction, made the change fraught with risks of failure, especially as a particularly short timescale for implementation was approved as part of the investment justification.

The TOPS project had been 'championed' by British Rail's Chief Executive who acted as a 'promoter of change'. Nevertheless, there had also been considerable trepidation among other Board members and senior managers that implementation would be frustrated and delayed by either failings in the technology or a combination of management and trade union resistance to change – a fate which had befallen attempts at innovation and change in the organisation in the past. In particular there was concern over potential resistance to the new technology on the part of middle and junior line-managers in the operating regions. In the past much of their autonomy and authority had rested on their ability to manipulate and control the flow of information to senior management. The TOPS system, among other things, promised to provide senior managers with rapid access to up-to-date and accurate information which would make the performance of line-managers far more 'visible' […].

In response, the Chief Executive developed a 'top-down' approach to managing implementation. This involved the creation of a specialist multi-disciplinary 'task force' reporting direct to him and autonomous from both headquarters functions and the regional management. The task force was responsible for handling all aspects of implementation, in particular the installation of equipment and the training of staff in a 'rolling' programme across the network. Complete authority was invested in the task force's Project Manager, which not only allowed the task force to override any local management resistance, but also meant he played a leading role in discussions with the railway trade unions. Significantly, the task force did not seek to bypass the existing national industrial relations framework, but made a deliberate and conscious effort to provide national union leaders with information on their plans from the earliest stage. However, while adopting this participatory approach, managers were also adamant that the change should not spark off national claims for increased payments to use the technology.

Discussions with the unions at national level were kept within the industry's procedures for joint consultation and were not allowed by senior managers to become the subject of national negotiations. In the event, national trade union leaders gave the system positive backing: first, because unless something was done to arrest the decline of the freight business then large job losses would have been inevitable; second, because the TOPS system did not involve job losses in manual grades and actually created new jobs for white-collar grades; third, the changes in working practices required provided possibility for negotiating extra payments for their members, at least at local level; fourth, there were no plans to use TOPS to monitor the productivity of train crews, a 'Big Brother' connotation of the system which worried the train drivers' union, ASLEF.

From management's viewpoint the success of the approach was illustrated by the fact that the TOPS system was installed on time and within budget, previously almost unheard of within the industry, and improvements in operational efficiency were achieved almost immediately. Middle and lower management resistance to change was either ignored or challenged by the project task force, and willingness to consult with the unions from the earliest stages was repaid by the active involvement of national leaders in quickly resolving local disputes which arose during implementation. However, despite this the task force approach itself was not considered a success by senior managers at headquarters or in the regions. Considerable animosity had been created by the 'top-down' authoritarian way change had been imposed on middle and junior line-managers, and it was considered politically expedient to disband the task force once implementation was complete, although several enhancements to the system were planned and changes to both supervisory and management organisation still had to be accomplished. It is interesting to note that subsequent technological changes within BR, including the Advanced Passenger Train, have not employed the task force approach, resulting in the latter case in the development of management resistance which ultimately became a key factor in the failure of the project (see Potter, 1987).

The second example is drawn from British Telecom and their introduction of a semi-electronic telephone exchange (TXE4) to replace the electromechanical 'Strowger' system during the late 1970s and early

1980s (see Clark *et al.*, 1988). This case provides an excellent illustration of an approach to implementation, involving a mixture of top-down and bottom-up sub-strategies, which resulted in the 'attenuation' of corporate objectives. The decision to introduce the TXE4 exchanges had been taken in the early 1970s by the Post Office, at that time responsible for the public telephone service as well as the postal service. The decision was based on 'strategic objectives', aimed at meeting the growing demand for telecommunications services and improving the quality of the service but these were linked to 'operating objectives', directed at reducing exchange maintenance costs, and 'control objectives' aimed at cutting staff levels and improving the productivity of maintenance technicians.

The corporate strategy behind modernisation also reflected the problematic nature of the relationship between business strategy and approaches to labour regulation in the post and telecommunications businesses at the time (see Batstone *et al.*, 1984 for discussion). For example, the industrial relations policy developed by senior management provided the basis for an agreed national industrial relations framework to govern the introduction of new technology with the trade unions. However, this framework and the agreements which underpinned it (covering job security and minimum staffing levels) were based on traditional patterns of labour relations in the industry that did not correspond with the new commercial emphasis in overall business strategy. Moreover, the agreements themselves also left open to question and interpretation how their provisions were to be implemented at workplace level. For example, whilst laying down an apparently precise formula by which new staffing levels could be decided, in practice the 'small print' of the agreement concerned left considerable room – or 'design space' – for further interpretation and negotiation at local level (see Clark *et al.*, 1988, pp. 71-5). In similar fashion, senior management's 'control objectives' initially provided little more than national policy and performance guidelines which left open the question of how they were to be achieved in practice, in particular how maintenance work was to be organised and supervised at local level (*ibid.*, pp. 41-50).

While the selection of exchanges for modernisation was planned centrally, the approach taken by British Telecom was to delegate responsibility for actual implementation to middle line-management in each telephone area. Other than the policy guidelines and national agreements already mentioned, area managements had little further guidance on how to set about their task. In other words, they had considerable 'design space' within which 'sub-strategies' to implement the new technology could be developed. This can be illustrated by looking at the substrategies developed by three separate area managements (*ibid.*, pp. 50-4, 76-81). For example, responsibility for implementing the new technology was given different priorities in each of the three areas, and in only one case was one manager given overall responsibility. Similarly, local managers usually interpreted the national agreement on staffing levels generously in order to keep staffing in individual exchanges high enough to cope with absences through training, unexpected maintenance problems, and staffing requirements in the area as a whole.

Finally, on issues such as selection of staff and the organisation and supervision of work, where no national policy or guidelines existed, area managers had the opportunity to develop their own solutions. On the issue of staff selection, two area managements negotiated an informal agreement with local union representatives on the criteria to be employed, while the other decided this unilaterally. One effect of these actions in all three cases was to contribute to the exclusion of junior technicians from selection for retraining – something never expressly intended by senior managers. [...]. Suffice it to say that variations in middle and junior line-managers' responses again led to outcomes not anticipated or intended at corporate level.

The final case concerns the introduction of a new microelectronics-based light-weight TV camera, developed in the United States for electronic news gathering (ENG) and adopted in Britain in the early 1980s by a regional independent TV company (see Jacobs, 1983; Clark *et al.*, 1984; McLoughlin *et al.*, 1985). This case is similar to the BR example in so far as senior management delegated responsibility for managing implementation to a single authority. However, whilst a 'top-down' approach was evident in this sense, the ultimate solution to the principal problem which management confronted during implementation came in the form of an almost purely 'bottom-up' approach. This occurred because management were prepared to go beyond the requirements of the national industrial relations framework covering the industry to allow the development of joint procedures which ensured a high degree of involvement in the decision-making process on the part of the union concerned (the Association of Cinematograph and Television Technicians, ACTT) and the technician workforce. In this sense the case differs from both the BR and BT examples.

The company concerned had recently been awarded the franchise for a local broadcasting region by the Independent Broadcasting Authority. The Company's proposal for the franchise included a strategic commitment to introduce ENG technology as part of its plans for a new style local news programme. Traditionally news pictures and features had been single-camera productions shot and recorded on film by specialist technicians. Unlike film, ENG cameras use video recording technology which eliminates the need for film processing and speeds up the time it takes to bring pictures from the scene to the viewer. With the aid of appropriate telecommunications links it is possible to beam 'live' pictures directly onto the screen. The news programme 'product' proposed by the company was intended to be sharp, immediate and full of 'hard news' items. This style of programme could be produced only by taking advantage of operational improvements enabled by the technical capabilities of ENG technology. In similar fashion to BR, the Company's corporate strategy involved tight time and cost constraints for the introduction of the technology. In particular, since the news programme was regarded as the regional TV station's 'flagship' product, it was particularly keen to have ENG equipment implemented in time for the commencement of broadcasting. This meant ENG had to be introduced within a twelve-month period.

The principal implementation problems facing the Company were industrial relations issues. Since the job-satisfaction of TV camera staff as an occupational group was derived in part from working with the latest technology, the problem was not one of workforce resistance to change as such. Rather, difficulties arose in relation to who would use the ENG cameras since two separate groups of television technicians – 'video' (concerned with directed multi-camera work in the studio and outside broadcasts) and 'film' (concerned with news pictures and other single-camera location work) – laid claim to the new work. On the one hand, there were management control advantages in allocating the new work to video technicians in terms of the lower cost and greater flexibility of their labour. On the other hand, allocating the work to the film technicians carried benefits in terms of their traditional skills and experience. Moreover, the Company was also bound by a nationally agreed code of practice with the ITV industry trade unions on the introduction of new technology, which included a procedural commitment to the fullest local consultation and negotiation. In addition, the employers and the ACTT had made a national commitment to the speedy introduction of ENG.

The approach taken by senior managers was in fact to demonstrate a clear commitment to participation, but under the control of a well-defined central management authority. At the start of the process of change, information on corporate strategy was given directly by senior board members to a meeting of the whole workforce. This was followed up by regular joint consultation with local ACTT representatives as well as direct consultation with members of the workforce concerned, and also feedback with the workforce through the preparation and wide distribution of discussion papers on management strategy. Senior board members delegated responsibility for introducing ENG to the general manager of the site concerned. He was well known to the workforce but was not identified with either the video or film department. In particular his personal style as a quick-talking, astute, and hard negotiator meant he enjoyed the trust of union officials.

The extent of management's commitment to participation is evidenced by the fact that over a five-month period the general manager was involved in over sixty formal and informal meetings with the trade union and the departments likely to be affected. In this way management kept in touch with the views of the union and the workforce and also kept the workforce and union directly informed of management's thinking. Given this participative approach it is also relevant to consider the union's response. In an attempt to overcome the problem of potential divisions among its own members an internal union sub-committee charged with developing a positive and united union strategy towards ENG was formed. At the same time, in order to prioritise the issues raised by the new technology, the union persuaded management to free its two main lay officers from normal duties for the duration of the negotiations. Finally, in order to maximise their expertise and experience, a group of past shop stewards were co-opted on to the executive committee of the local union branch.

Subsequent negotiations were dominated by the question of which group of technicians should be allocated the new ENG work. Management's initial proposals were presented to the workforce in a series of discussion papers which suggested that ENG work would normally be allocated to film technicians. These proposals were unacceptable to the video technicians. In the meantime the special union subcommittee proposed the creation of a new integrated grade of 'television technician' drawing on members of both film and video departments. This proposal was unacceptable to the film technicians. However, rather than exacerbating divisions within the workforce, the rehearsal of these proposals within a participative framework actually paved the way for agreement. This encouraged the union sub-committee and the camera technicians to continue seeking solutions to the of 'good industrial relations', made it clear that a solution devised by the union which had the backing of both groups of technicians, and was not excessively costly, would be accepted.

In the event this is exactly what happened. A detailed solution was worked out and, after discussion with the affected groups of technicians, was put by the union to management who accepted the proposal. This involved a 50/50 split of ENG work between the film and video departments. Ironically, there was then a considerable delay before the technology was actually used. Once negotiations had been successfully concluded a change in the financial position of the company meant that they were no longer able to purchase the equipment as quickly as they had intended.

In sum, these three cases illustrate different approaches to the problems of implementing technological change. In the BR case this involved a top-down/ authoritarian approach based around a project task force and at the same time a participatory commitment to consult with the trade unions within the existing industrial relations framework of the industry. The BT case involved a mixture of top-down and bottom-up approaches with a commitment to a participatory approach with the trade unions at national level and where many aspects of managing implementation were delegated to local operating areas. A negotiated framework for implementing the technology was agreed with the unions at national level but this still left considerable room for further interpretation and negotiation at local level. The ENG case involved a top-down/participatory approach where management responsibility was delegated to a single manager rather than task force. In this case the extent of participation was far more extensive than in the BT and BR cases, going beyond an already participative framework established at national level to develop additional mechanisms for involvement within the company itself. Participation and involvement in this case did not mean simply consulting with trade unions, but also regular meetings with individuals and groups of employees likely to be affected directly by the change.

The British Telecom case provides an example of an approach to implementation which resulted in a very 'loose coupling' between corporate objectives and the way the strategy to introduce new technology was implemented at workplace level. It contrasts with the British Rail and ENG cases in that more 'design space' was left for middle- and lower-level managers by senior management's strategy towards introducing the technology, especially in relation to industrial relations. Whilst the BR and ENG cases illustrated 'top-down' solutions applied at all critical junctures during implementation, the BT approach tended to result in 'bottom-up' solutions which varied from area to area.

All three approaches involved benefits and costs. The BR approach had the benefit of ensuring high-level management control and continuity, but with the cost that change was to a large extent imposed on middle and junior managers. The TV Company's approach also ensured high levels of management control and continuity, but the commitment to participation meant that a compromise solution to the work allocation problem had to be accepted in the interests of 'good industrial relations'. The BT approach had the benefit of allowing managers ultimately responsible for using the new technology to develop their own solutions to problems and issues, but with the cost that lower-level management's responses might be variable in their effectiveness, thereby increasing the risk of unintended consequences arising from their actions. All three cases illustrate the importance of managerial decision-making at critical junctures in the implementation stage of change if new technology is to be introduced successfully.

MANAGEMENT CHOICE AND THE OPERATION OF NEW TECHNOLOGY

Decisions to adopt new technology not only trigger choices with regard to implementation but also raise organisational issues of how the technology is to be used once operational. In particular, questions are raised about the nature of job content, the pattern of work organisation, and how work is to be supervised and controlled. According to Buchanan, when new technology is introduced, 'the key decisions that affect organisational performance are those concerning the reorganisation of work that accompanies technical change' (1986, p. 78). [...] Management choice has a critical bearing on these 'key decisions'.

A predominant view in academic writing in recent years – in particular that influenced by labour process theory – has been that the assumptions underlying management decision-making over the organisation and control of work have been dominated by a relatively narrow set of criteria. These, it is claimed, are based on the theories of scientific management, in particular as influenced at the turn of the century by its most well-known exponent, F. W. Taylor.

For Braverman, 'Taylorism' was synonymous with the theory and practice of capitalist management in *toto* [...]. However, other writers influenced by labour process theory have attempted to provide a more differentiated and sophisticated analysis of the influence of Taylorist ideas on management practice. For example, Littler (1982; 1985; Littler and Salaman, 1984) distinguishes three different areas in which management practices based on these ideas can be implemented: work design; management control structures; and the employment relationship. Taylorist practices in work design seek to deskill jobs through a process of task fragmentation. According to Littler, this fragmentation process involves a progressive reduction in the task range of individual jobs, a reduction in the discretionary components of each job, and a reduction in the skill requirements of any task in order to minimise job-learning times (1985, p. 11). Taylorist practices in the design of management structures seek to reduce worker autonomy by increasing management control and supervision of work performance, to break workgroup solidarity, and to motivate employees through individual incentives (1982, p. 52-5). Finally, implicit in these changes is a fundamental transformation of the employment relationship within the enterprise which seeks to maximise employee substitutability and to minimise the organisation's dependence on individuals' skills and motivation. Littler does note, however, that such 'hire-and-fire' employment relations can give way to more paternalistic relationships (Littler, 1982, pp. 55-7).

Littler also argues that Taylor's ideas have had a varied influence in different national contexts, both in terms of the extent, timing, and nature of their diffusion and the degree to which they have become established as an ideology of management practice. The predominance of Taylor's ideas has also been affected by the extent to which other versions of 'scientific management', such as Henry Ford's ideas on continuous-flow assembly-lines, have been influential (see Littler 1982; 1985; Littler and Salaman 1984). In the case of Britain, Littler has argued that, whilst Taylor's ideas have never been widely accepted as an ideology by senior managers, they – or rather a derivative version of 'scientific management' known as the Bedaux system [3] – have had a significant effect on management practice at workplace level. This, according to Littler, has meant that 'in general the direct and indirect influence of Taylorism on factory jobs has been extensive', such that work-design and technology-design have become 'imbued with a neo-Taylorism' (Littler, 1985, p. 13).

However, other writers have argued that there are serious grounds for doubting Littler's albeit qualified assertions regarding the widespread influence of neoTaylorism on management practices. For example, Batstone *et al.* (1987) argue that the Bedaux system's introduction in Britain was hardly as decisive a development in labour control as Littler appears to believe. They point out that his case rests on the fact that at some point in the period between the two world wars 245 firms adopted this system. As they argue:

This is a minute proportion of all firms, and he provides no evidence that they employed a significant proportion of the labour force. Furthermore, it is clear that the application of the system rarely involved major job redesign, particularly for key groups such as craftsmen, and was frequently manipulated at shop floor level. (Batstone *et al.*, 1987, p. 9)

Thus, as far as Britain is concerned at least, it would seem the idea that the traditional approach by management to the organisation and control of work can be characterised exclusively in terms of Taylorist practices needs to be treated with some caution.

Caution is also needed in interpreting more recent management approaches to the introduction and operation of new technology in terms of a 'Taylorist' or even 'neo-Taylorist' strategy to increase managerial control by deskilling work. For example, Wilkinson (1983; 1985) talks of managers in one of his case-study firms 'openly adopting a deskilling strategy' in their choice of equipment with the intention of increasing management control. In another he describes a debate within line-management and engineering functions over whether new technology should be used to retain or remove skill from the shop floor (1983, pp. 89-90). This and other evidence leads him to suggest that managers often feel that 'current custom and practice represents a lack of control on their own part and try to remedy this by taking advantage of the opportunities lent by the new technology' (1985, pp. 25). Similarly, a number of other commentators have suggested that despite there being alternative choices, new technology is generally seen by managers as a means of wresting control away from the shopfloor along what are in essence Taylorist lines (see for example, Child, 1984, pp. 252-7; Gill, 1985; Baldry and Connolly, 1986; Smith and Wield, 1987).

We would argue that such observations may run the risk of misinterpreting the nature of managerial intentions when they seek to use new technology to increase control. This can be illustrated by looking at Buchanan and Boddy's conclusion, drawn from their Scottish case studies, that middle and junior line-managers were preoccupied with using new technology to satisfy what they term 'control objectives'. These objectives were a 'persuasive theme in discussions with middle and lower managers'. They were expressed as a 'desire for increased predictability, consistency, orderliness and reliability' in work operations and for a reduction in uncertainty in management control. Management expectations were that this could be achieved by increased reliance on computer controls and reduced dependence on what was regarded as the 'undesirable' control exercised by humans (1983, p. 244). If one assumes that Taylorism is an extensive feature of British management practice, then it is a short step to interpret the pursuit of 'control objectives' as a direct expression of 'neo-Taylorist' ideas. However, if one questions such an assumption then the nature of the intentions behind the pursuit of control objectives requires further investigation and explanation.

The nub of our dissatisfaction with Buchanan and Boddy's use of the term 'control objectives' is that it fails to distinguish between what might be termed 'labour control objectives' – aimed specifically at improving human performance and productivity – and 'operational control objectives' – aimed at the overall improvement of the performance of the production process itself (McLoughlin, 1983). Whilst the pursuit of 'operational control objectives' may involve attempts to reduce the need for skilled or informed human intervention, managerial intentions cannot be reduced exclusively to a desire to deskill labour. In fact, other concerns may be more significant and in certain circumstances require a 're-skilling' or 'up-skilling' of labour.

This is illustrated particularly well in four recently published case studies by the late Eric Batstone and his colleagues [4]. Their findings suggest clearly that labour control was not a decisive factor in the decision to introduce new technology. The reasons for its introduction did, nevertheless, have implications for the process of labour regulation in so far as new technology was seen as a means for increasing managerial 'control'. The key point is that management attempts to increase its control were not driven by a concern to deskill labour *per se,* but rather a desire to improve the performance of the production process. For example, in the case of a chemical plant the key factor in management's attempts to reduce its dependence on human labour was their concern with quality, rather than a fear of any reliance upon workers directly. Similarly, in an insurance company the fact that new technology enabled the substitution of labour and reduced worker autonomy was not the sole criterion guiding managerial decisions but followed from the more central concern for reduction of administrative costs' (see Balstone *et al.*, 1987).

We would offer similar interpretations of the nature and significance of control objectives in the cases of technological change studied by ourselves and discussed in the previous section (see McLoughlin, 1983; Clark *et al.*, 1988). For example, in the British Rail case the control objectives behind the introduction of the new technology were concerned primarily with increasing management control over physical resources – wagons and locomotives – rather than human resources. Moreover, control objectives were linked strongly to operating objectives aimed at improving the efficiency of freight operations and strategic objectives aimed at arresting the decline of the freight business. Similarly, in the case of British Telecom's exchange modernisation programme, although labour control objectives in the form of improved labour productivity and staff reductions were intended, these concerns were derived from, and were secondary to, operating objectives aimed at reducing costs and strategic objectives aimed at improving the range and quality of telecommunications services that could be offered to satisfy increasing customer demand.

The implications of the pursuit of control objectives by managers will be returned to in subsequent chapters. For the present it is sufficient to note that the general lack of a consideration at a strategic level of how work should be organised and controlled (what we have termed the 'control issues' highlighted by the introduction of new technology [...]) can result in a further 'attenuation' of corporate objectives. In particular, where lower-level managers have no guidelines to the contrary, the decisions – or nondecisions – they make in relation to such things as job content, work organisation and supervision may in some circumstances frustrate the achievement of the overall objectives behind the introduction of new technology.

CONCLUSION

The empirical evidence reviewed in this chapter suggests that policies concerned with the regulation of labour do not flow unproblematically from overall business strategies. Such decisions involve political processes of strategic choice within organisations, which cannot be explained exclusively in terms of technical or commercial imperatives, or the logic of the historical development of forms of capitalist control over labour. It is apparent that managers pursue a diverse range of objectives when new technology is introduced. These reflect hierarchical and functional divisions and cannot be expressed in terms of a unitary strategy. Moreover, available evidence suggests that the introduction of new technology has not been accompanied by significant innovations in policies for the regulation of labour and that, in general, personnel specialists play a marginal and reactive role. In consequence, decisions to introduce new technology may leave considerable room for manoeuvre – or 'design space' – for lower-level managers at subsequent stages of change. 'Sub-strategies' developed by such managers in implementing and operating new technology can therefore have a critical bearing on the outcomes of change. The cases of technological change in British Rail, British Telecom and the independent television company illustrate different approaches to implementation that can emerge and the ways in which these may facilitate or frustrate the achievement of senior managers' objectives. It was also noted that middle and junior line-managers are often preoccupied with the pursuit of 'control objectives' when new technology is introduced, but that these cannot be reduced to a concern to deskill labour along Taylorist lines as many labour process writers argue. [...].

NOTES

1   Wilkinson's case studies were concerned with the introduction of microelectronics-based controls in a plating company, an optical company, a rubber moulding company and a machine tool manufacturer.

2   For further explanation of notes in tables from the WIRS see Daniel 1987, pp. xv-xvi.

3   The Bedaux system combined Taylorist principles with elements of industrial psychology and the fatigue studies conducted during the First World War aimed at improving industrial productivity (see Littler, 1982; Rose, 1978).

4   Batstone *et al.* studied four cases in all. These were drawn from brewing (automated process controls), small-batch engineering (CNC machine tools), chemicals (automated process-sequence controls) and the insurance sector of finance (on-line processing).

REFERENCES

Atkinson, J. (1984) 'Manpower strategies for flexible organisations', *Personnel Management,* August, pp. 28-9.

Atkinson, J. and Meager, N. (1986) 'Flexibility – just a flash in the pan?', *Personnel Management,* September, pp. 26-7.

Baldry, C. and Connolly, A. (1986) 'Drawing the line: computer aided design and the organisation of the drawing office', *New Technology, Work and Employment,* 1, (1), pp. 59-66.

Batstone, E. and Gourlay, S. (1986) *Unions, Unemployment and Innovation,* Oxford, Basil Blackwell.

Batstone, E. *et al.* (1987) *New Technology and The Process of Labour Regulation,* Oxford, Clarendon Press.

Batstone, E., Ferner, A. and Terry, M. (1984) *Consent and Efficiency: Labour Relations and Management Strategv in a State Enterprise,* Oxford, Basil Blackwell.

Bessant, J. (1982) *Microprocessors in Manufacturing Processes,* London, PSI.

Buchanan, D. (1986) 'Management objectives in technical change', in Knights, D. and Willmott, H. (eds) *Managing the Labour Process,* Aldershot, Gower, pp. 67-84.

Buchanan, D. and Boddy, D. (1983) *Organisations in the Computer Age: Technological Imperatives and Strategic Choice* Aldershot, Gower.

Child, J. (1984) *Organisation: A Guide to Problems and Practice,* 2nd edn, London, Harper and Row.

Child, J. (1985) 'Managerial strategies, new technology and the labour process', in Knights, D., Willmott, H. and Collinson, D. (eds) *Job Redesign: Critical Perspectives on the Labour Process,* Aldershot, Gower, pp. 107-11.

Clark, J. *et al.* (1984) 'New technology, industrial relations and divisions within the workforce', *Industrial Relations Journal,* 15, (3), pp. 36-44.

Clark, J. *et al.* (1988) *The Process of Technological Change New Technology and Social Choice in the Workplace,* Cambridge, Cambridge University Press.

Clegg, C. and Kemp, N. (1986) 'Information technology: Personnel where are you?', *Personnel Review,* 15, (1), pp. 8-15.

Daniel, W. (1987) *Workplace Industrial Relations and Technical Change,* London, Frances Pinter.

Davies, A. (1986) *Industrial Relations and New Technology,* London, Croom Helm.

Francis, A. (1986) *New Technology at Work,* Oxford, Oxford University Press.

Francis, A. *et al.* (1982) 'The impact of information technology at work: the case of CAD/CAM and MIS in engineering plants', in Bannon, L., Barry, U. and Holst, 0. (eds) *Information Technology: Impact on a Way of Life,* Dublin, Tycooly, pp. 182-96.

Gill, C. (1985) *Work, Unemployment and New Technology,* Cambridge, Polity Press.

Institute of Manpower Studies (1984) 'Flexible manning – the way ahead', IMSO report No. 88, Sussex University, IMS and Manpower Ltd.

Jacobs, A. (1983) *Film and Electronic Technologies in the Production of Television News,* PhD Thesis, University of Southampton.

Jones, B. (1982) 'Distribution or redistribution of engineering skills? The case of numerical control', in Wood, S. (ed.) *The Degradation of Work?: Skill, Deskilling and the Labour Process* London, Hutchinson, pp. 179-200.

Jones, B. (1985) 'Technical, organisational and political constraints on system re-design for machinist programming of NC machine tools', Paper presented at IFIP Conference on 'System Design for the Users', Italy, September.

Littler, C. R. (1982) *The Development of the Labour Process in Capitalist Societies,* London, Heinemann.

Littler, C. R. (1985) 'Taylorism, Fordism and job design', in Knights, D., Willmott, H., and Collinson, D. (eds) *Yob Redesign: Critical Perspectives on the Labour Process,* Aldershot, Gower, pp. 10-29.

Littler, C. R. and Salaman, G. (1984) *Class at Work,* London, Batsford.

Martin, R. (1984) 'New technology and industrial relations in Fleet Street', in Warner, M. (ed.) (1984) *Microprocessors, Manpower and Society,* Aldershot, Gower, pp. 240-52.

Martin, R. (1988) 'The management of industrial relations and new technology', in Marginson, P. *et al.* (eds.) *Beyond the Workplace,* Oxford, Basil Blackwell.

McLoughlin, I. P. (1983) 'Problems of management control and the introduction of new technology',.Working Paper, New Technology Research Group, University of Southampton.

McLoughlin, I. P. (1987) 'The Taylorisation of intellectual work?: the case of CAD', Paper presented at British Sociological Association Annual Conference, University of Leeds, April.

McLoughlin, I. P., Rose, H. and Clark, J. (1985) 'Managing the introduction of new technology', *Omega,* 13, (4), pp. 251-62.

McLoughlin, I. P., Smith, J. H. and Dawson, P. M. B. (1983) *The Introduction of a Computerised Freight Information System in British Rail- TOPS,* Research Report, New Technology Research Group, University of Southampton.

Northcott, J. and Rogers, P. (1985) *Chips and jobs,* London, Policy Studies Institute.

Northcott, J. and Rogers, P. with Zeilinger, A. (1982) *Microelectronics in Industry: Survey Statistics,* London, Policy Studies Institute.

Pollert, A. (1987) *The Flexible Firm: a Model in Search of Reality or a Policy in Search of a Practice?,* Warwich Papers in Industrial Relations.

Potter, S. (1987) *On the Right Lines? The Limits to Technological Innovation,* London, Frances Pinter.

Preece, D. A. (1986) 'Organisations, flexibility and new technology', in Voss, C. A. (ed.), *Managing Advanced Manufacturing Technology,* Berlin, Springer-Verlag.

Preece, D. A. and Harrison, M. R. (1986) 'The contribution of personnel specialists to technology related organisational change', Unpublished paper.

Purcell, J. and Sisson, K. (1983) 'Strategies and practice in the management of industrial relations', in Bain, G. (ed.), *Industrial Relations in Britain,* Oxford, Basil Blackwell, pp. 95-120.

Rose, M. (1978) *Industrial Behaviour: Theoretical Development since Taylor,* London, Penguin.

Rothwell, S. (1984) 'Company employment policies and new technology in manufacturing and service sectors', in Warner, M. (ed.), *Microelectronics, Manpower and Society,* Aldershot, Gower.

Smith, S. L. and Wield, D. (1987) 'New technology and bank work: banking on I.T. as an lorganisational technology', in Harris, L. (ed.), *New Perspectives on the Financial System,* London, Croom Helm.

Steffens, J. (1983) *The Electronic Office.- Progress and Problems,* London, Policy Studies Institute.

Thomason, G. (1981) *A Textbook of Personnel Management,* fourth edn., London, Institute of Personnel Management.

Watson, T. J. (1977) *The Personnel Managers,* London, Routledge and Kegan Paul.

Watson, T. J. (1986) *Management Organisation and Employment Strategy,* London, Routledge and Kegan Paul.

Wilkinson, B. (1983) *The Shop F7oor Politics of New Technology,* London, Heinemann.

Wilkinson, B. (1985) 'The politics of technical change', in Forester, T. (ed.) *The Information Technology Revolution,* Oxford, Basil Blackwell, pp. 439-53.

Willman, P. (1986) *Technological Change, Collective Bargaining and Industrial Efficiency,* Oxford, Oxford University Press.

Willman, P. and Winch, G. (1985) *Innovation and Management Control,* Cambridge, Cambridge University Press.

PART 3 IT AND LEARNING

Robin Mason, Institute of Educational Technology, The Open University

INTRODUCTION

The papers chosen for Part 3, *IT and Learning* all give particular answers to the question: 'Why use Information Technology in education and training?' Of course we no longer consider education to be an activity which finishes with adolescence, and training is rarely a once in a lifetime undertaking. One of the reasons why we need to consider learning to be a continual process is that IT is making profound changes to the world around us, for example the social effects stemming from the IT facilities available in the home, and the fundamental re-organisation of the work-place into an information-dependent system.

In addition to the need to include IT in the curriculum of education and training, computers and telecommunications also provide the tools for designing, delivering and accessing education and training. In the following papers, therefore, we discuss IT both as the subject and as the means of learning. The curriculum of education and training is slowly but perceptibly being altered by IT, whilst the use of IT as tools in the learning process is a more dramatic and more publicized occurrence.

The advantages which IT brings to education and training are well ennunciated in these papers and they provide the themes for Part 3:

- resource-based learning – its potential and facilitation with IT,
- collaboration and interactivity – learning through communication,
- effectiveness of using IT – motivation of users, standardization of training,
- increased flexibility of access to education – for the disabled, for remote learners, decentralisation of training.

The dangers of using IT in teaching and training are more subtle and complex. However, the fears of many early critics about the use of IT in education have not been realised:

- massive replacement of teachers by machines,
- impersonalisation of learning through a break-down in human-to-human communication,
- the civilizing role of the arts and humanistic approaches to learning overshadowed by the scientific, right-wrong, computational areas of thought which are capable of binary configuration demanded by computers.

While rumblings of these fears are still heard, the direction in which IT is being exploited in education and training gives very little evidence to support such claims. The teacher's role in education and training certainly changes with the use of IT, as many of these papers show, but it certainly has not been superceded. The explosion of telecommunications capability has increased human-to-human contact particularly in distance education, and collaborations around the computer have increased the opportunities for peer learning. Although arts-based uses of IT lag behind those in the scientific fields, there are many innovative uses of computers and telecommunications in non-scientific areas of the curriculum. The priority given to science, maths and technology in terms of funding and prestige accounts for a good deal of their pre-eminence in using IT.

Some of the well-known drawbacks of the introduction of IT into education stem from the attraction which the computer commands. This has led to an obsession with computer games, to hacking into computer systems and to ownership of the latest technology as status symbols. These are more correctly social rather than educational problems.

APPROACHES TO LEARNING

To consider the real dangers of using IT in learning, we need to have a view about how humans learn, and how they should be educated or trained. A number of papers in this selection address these questions explicitly or implicitly. Perhaps one of the biggest dangers of IT in educational organisations is that after initial enthusiasm and investment, the technology is relegated to the cupboard and teachers return to traditional methods. This is a serious danger because it perpetuates a lack of concern about the teaching/learning process. Most evaluation studies of IT applications show that it is the learning context which determines the success of a particular technology innovation, not the technology itself: for example, the integration of the new medium into the rest of the course, the support provided by the institution in terms of study resources, and the opportunities available for interaction, reflection and feedback from the teacher. One of the most positive outcomes of many educational uses of IT is often cited as the opportunity it creates for improving this teaching/learning process: computer conferencing has been shown to provide better opportunities for interaction and reflection than traditional methods; computer-based training material can release the trainer from the role of content generator to that of facilitator and supporter of learning; resource-based IT material can be used to promote responsibility in the learner and an active role in the educational process. When IT is not used to produce these benefits, the problem in most cases lies in the implementation – failure to provide for the full range of students' learning needs, lack of institutional support, experimental trials peripheral to the main focus of the course.

Several of the papers in this collection suggest the advent of new educational situations which IT is on the way to providing: collaborative, multimedia conferencing both synchronously and asynchronously, accessing resources all over the world from the desktop. The role of the teacher or trainer in this context is clearly quite different from the traditional lecturer standing up in front of a class. Yet the role of the student is also quite different, demanding different skills and attitudes to the learning process. Current technologies provide the vehicle for both teachers and students to develop this expertise. Educational and training organisations will also have to undergo a transformation as supporting their staff and students in this new environment will demand significant changes in libraries, administrative procedures, accommodation requirements and network capabilities.

The real question, then, for the use of IT in education and training is not 'why', but rather how to use it wisely so that it promotes learning and engages learners' interest in the content not the delivery mechanism.

DO COMPANIES NEED TECHNOLOGY-BASED TRAINING?

David Hawkridge

Institute of Educational Technology, The Open University

INTRODUCTION

This paper analyses company training needs and why many companies spend huge sums on training. It discusses what advantages they see in using technology-based training (TBT), and how they find out about TBT before making a decision to adopt it. It identifies attitudes that hinder as well as those that favour adoption of TBT.

COMPANY TRAINING NEEDS

In industrialized countries, companies spend huge sums of money on training. In the late 1980s, American Telephone and Telegraph was said to spend $1 billion a year in the US alone. Such figures may well be underestimates, because the full cost of training is seldom accounted for. UK companies sometimes have an image of not training enough, but they too commit large amounts to training: Employment Department estimates were £16 billion in 1987, growing to £20 billion in 1993. Without doubt, there is investment in human resources on a grand scale, and much of it through on-the-job training and special off-the-job courses.

Why are companies spending so much on training? What needs are being met? First, companies want employees whose training has given them the skills, knowledge and attitudes required to do their jobs well and safely. This is true whether these employees are managers, accountants, clerks or technicians, and whether their jobs are on the factory floor, in the office or the store. New employees often need training before they can be reasonably effective within a company. Existing employees require retraining because companies and jobs are changing and new technology is being installed: many workers now find their knowledge is out-of-date within a year or two. New and existing employees may suddenly require training in how to use technology not accessible to universities and colleges, nor perhaps to other competitor companies. Appraisal, career development and promotion cannot go ahead well without training.

Many companies know that training can lead to increased sales. Training of a company's own employees leads to better quality products and services to customers, improving the image of the company with these customers. In some fields, such as computer manufacture, a company that provides good training to its customers, so that they can use its products efficiently (and sooner), improves its relationship with these customers and boosts its future chances of sales.

Consider, for example, a company operating a large continuous processing plant, such as a nuclear power station or a petrochemical plant producing ammonia. Such a plant is still being designed while it is being built, to incorporate the latest technical developments, yet employees must be fully trained to operate each plant efficiently and safely the moment it starts up. Once started, it cannot be stopped without the company incurring very heavy expense, therefore any employees who leave must be replaced immediately by fully-trained newcomers. Employees must be trained to deal with modifications to the plant, such as the introduction of computerized controls aimed at saving energy or improving output. They must quickly acquire any new knowledge that comes to light about the plant's operation as a result of research or even as a consequence of disasters. Safe operation of the plant is vital, yet employees must be trained in complex emergency procedures without these actually being triggered, and without danger to other employees or expensive equipment. These employees can seldom be trained on the plant itself, however, because the risks are too great.

Or consider a company, such as a bank or building society, with many branches offering computerized financial services to thousands of clients. A bank must train its employees because it sells services that incorporate new procedures, often based on the technology, and aimed at providing greater benefit to the client and greater profit to the bank. Mistakes can mar the bank's reputation as a responsible financial institution; they are costly to rectify, and damage profits. Training is needed.

Retraining is needed to deal with change. In the machine-shops of manufacturing companies, there have been drastic technological changes. Simple numerical control (automation) of the 1950s gave way to computer numerical control in the 1970s, which was then displaced by direct numerical control and flexible manufacturing systems, all computer-based and largely outside the immediate control of operators on the shop floor. Such companies need to retrain operators for other jobs or in using their old craft skills in programming the new systems.

Companies manufacturing electronic and other hi-tech products must cope with even more drastic changes, as their technology is upgraded each year. Apple Computer, Digital Equipment Corporation, Hewlett Packard, Texas Instruments, Wang and Xerox all find that they must retrain a large percentage of their employees. They do so to keep pace with products of their own scientific research and development and to retain employees who have acquired knowledge, experience and expertise that would be valuable to competitors. These companies have an extra training task, too: they must provide training to employees of their customer companies, who will manage and use the hi-tech products.

Retail or distributive companies, with great changes in storage and distribution methods, are not exempt from the need to train and retrain employees. For example, B&Q Retail has special training needs because its retail stores are scattered all over the country. There is a high employee turnover, and new employees must be quickly trained in the operation of each store, including such aspects as safety. Or take another example from the retail sector: Boots was a company that originally manufactured and marketed pharmaceutical products only. Boots has diversified its range of products sold through its chain of high street stores. The company has large numbers of retail employees, scattered in many branches, who must be trained in systems and procedures. The training needs include customer service, cash register training, health and safety, stockbooks, despatch and delivery. Many of these areas were computerized in the late 1980s, therefore there was a heavy demand for retraining. Electronic point of sale (EPOS) and electronic funds transfer (EFT) technologies raise new training needs.

Very large transportation companies, such as British Airways, have training needs arising from the vast geographical spread of their systems and the rapid introduction of new and more complex technology. Safety is at a premium, and the cost of operational delays is high. Training must often fit within their employees' abnormal working hours.

Training is not simply for large companies: small companies, too, should train their employees, to enable them to cope with changing processes, procedures, technologies and markets. Small and medium-sized companies often think of training as an added cost, not an investment, however, and these companies know very little about the latest training methods. Many small companies have no training policy at all and provide the minimum training. Even medium-sized companies (with 100-1000 employees) often do not employ a training officer or manager. A common problem mentioned by these companies is that they cannot spare employees from everyday work, for training. Regrettably, if these small and medium-sized companies fail to train, they lose their competitive edge, unless they can poach trained workers from larger companies. They particularly need training in such areas as management, interpersonal skills, safety, dealing with legislation and introduction of new technology.

NEED FOR COST-EFFECTIVE TRAINING

Company training needs seem set to expand, in large, medium and small companies. The search is on to find more cost-effective training. Training costs will rise at least as fast as training expands, unless techniques are used that either cost less for the same degree of effectiveness, or achieve greater effectiveness for the same cost. Techniques that cost more must yield greater returns.

More cost-effective training brings a variety of benefits, not simply increased company profits. Ineffectual training is rightly despised by employees and rejected by managers, and damages company morale. Expensive training may seem prestigious at the time, but is only worthwhile when it is highly effective. What employees want is training, and retraining, that enables them to do the job well and safely. Only then can they gain greater job satisfaction. Of greatest value to the company is training that makes employees well-motivated and more competent.

Company policy-makers and decision-takers, not least the training managers, need more cost-effective training techniques. Instructor-led or 'stand up' training is very widespread, accounting for more than 80 per cent of the training time, but training based on high technology is attracting attention, too.

NEED FOR TECHNOLOGY-BASED TRAINING

What is 'technology-based training' (commonly labelled TBT)? It could be called IT-based training. On the software side, the term encompasses a range of authoring tools that offer trainer-authors the chance to bring the hardware to bear on specific training needs. TBT also includes ready-made, off-the-shelf programs offering training in commonly-used skills and procedures not specific to one company. TBT encompasses the hardware, too: trainers can draw on computers and telecommunication systems, videodisk or videocassette players, CD-ROMs, and so on, as means of 'delivering' the training.

Can company training needs be met cost-effectively by TBT? This kind of training is different from conventional training through lectures or printed manuals, but is it more effective? Companies look at training effectiveness in several different ways. In general, they want training that is appropriate to the individual, but they also need it to produce more or less the same standard of performance in all employees doing a particular job. They are interested in any system that seems likely to control training by standardizing it. They may also want to set about decentralizing training. Because time costs money, and because it is seldom convenient to have their employees training off-the-job, they want to reduce the time required for training. This may well lead to regular savings on training costs. In a few cases, companies may judge training effectiveness in terms of its success in meeting sudden large-scale training needs. Overall, companies want training to result in improved job performance. It is worth looking at how TBT may satisfy these broad needs.

Standardizing training: In training, increased standardization is often equated with increased effectiveness. Instructor-led training is notoriously unstandardized, varying with the trainer and training centre. TBT appears to offer standardization, therefore companies are likely to view it with interest. Eastman Kodak, for example, decided to use computers to standardize its training of field service engineers. The trainees were widely scattered, worldwide, yet the training had to be done quickly and in standardized form. Texaco Tankerships' trainees are even more widely scattered, on board ships moving across the oceans. Yet tanker crews need standardized and frequent training in safety and emergency procedures. TBT is providing this.

Yet TBT cannot guarantee standardization of performance, as opposed to standardization of training, because ultimately on-the-job performance depends on the individual as well the training. It can increase the chances of performance being up to a particular standard, giving companies more control over training. Some say that with printed manuals, branch offices use the material differently or neglect it altogether, with very uneven results. Unstandardized training can be very expensive in leading to errors in company systems that demand uniformity (e.g., banks and insurance companies). Standardized training can be introduced through TBT because it can include frequent testing and recording of trainees' progress in mastering skills and procedures.

Decentralizing training: Many companies are interested in TBT because they think it will help them to decentralize training. Centralized training is expensive and difficult to organize, particularly in companies with far-flung branches, yet is necessary for conventional training. It can also be untimely. Training is always likely to be seen as more effective if it is available where and when needed. General Motors decided to put the training right on its car assembly system. Jaguar trains its dealers through TBT. TBT may result in reduced demand for central training facilities and personnel, with consequent savings.

Reducing training time: All companies want to reduce the time employees need to become properly trained, as this will reduce overall labour costs and increase profits. Some cannot afford to have employees away from the job or their staff turnover is so high that they need to reduce the ratio of training time to actual working time. Others have many part-time employees who need to be trained just as much as the full-timers. TBT can sometimes yield remarkable savings: Rover and Barclaycard are often-quoted examples of TBT reducing training time.

Saving on training costs: Companies hope that TBT will produce savings. This is particularly true in large companies, which seek to reap economies of scale by training many employees using the same software. They can set off the high initial cost of TBT against large numbers of trainees. British Telecom reckons to have saved £1.4 million through providing TBT for managers to learn appraisal and counselling.

Meeting sudden large-scale training needs: Some companies face dramatically increased training needs because their structure, functions or operations have changed, sometimes due to deregulation. In Britain, the building societies suddenly came into this category in 1986. Abbey National turned to TBT to retrain large numbers of staff scattered in many branches. Allied Carpets, with about 25 new stores opening each year in the 1980s, needed TBT to provide standardized training to hundreds of branch staff.

Improving job performance: Overall, companies are looking to training for improving job performance. If TBT can train people to do their jobs better, then almost any company is likely to become interested in it. Eastman Kodak knew that graphics and simulations would be valuable in training field service technicians. Motivating training was needed that would not simply sit on the shelf. The company chose TBT.

TBT PIGGY-BACKED ON BUSINESS IT

The 1980s new wave of TBT was speeded up by companies installing computers and communications for purposes other than training. For example, most banks already had terminals linked to a mainframe computer for accounting and administrative purposes. To use the terminals for training as well seemed to some managers and trainers to be an obvious step. Training built into the hardware and software used for other purposes is called 'embedded' TBT. Early TBT projects, such as British Airways' seat reservation system, were often of this kind. Insurance agents, airline reservation clerks and many others using IT can expect some embedded training now. The IT systems offer them a range of job aids, at the very least, and often TBT is available too.

Companies have responded very differently, however, to opportunities for introducing embedded training. Computer manufacturers are a specially interesting category in this respect. Confidently, IBM took the lead, years ago, with its own mainframe computers. The company regarded proper training of its employees as essential if it were to sell its hardware. In 1979, about 10,000 IBM employees were using 400 terminals for training in IBM's US offices. Companies operating IBM mainframe computers could, until 1987, purchase an IBM authoring system with which to prepare their own in-company embedded TBT. IBM later adopted the same policy in marketing its personal computers (PCs). Field engineers, dealers and users of IBM products were trained partly through TBT. Other US computer manufacturers followed IBM, offering embedded TBT to help buyers to learn to use their hardware and software. As for job aids, software companies such as MicroSoft and T/Maker started to include Help that explained how to use their programs.

Companies outside the computer industry, however, were (and are) much less certain about embedded TBT. In a famous British retail company, a feasibility study revealed confusion and scepticism. One manager pointed out that computer-time for embedded retail training would get a low priority, because training was seen as less urgent than, say, inventory control or budgeting for salaries. Another argued that the single terminal to be provided in each store would be quite inadequate for training purposes. A third questioned whether the company knew how to produce programs for training its employees. Yet another wanted to be told the advantages of embedded TBT, when employees in stores were already ignoring the printed training manuals and videos put out by his department!

Or take the case of a British bank that had terminals in every one of its hundreds of branches, all linked to mainframe computers. The bank experimented with a system that delivered embedded TBT to over 100 of these terminals. Within five years, it labelled the system a 'zero-stretch' training technology, outside the mainstream of the bank's general IT development, therefore not a long-term proposition.

It is a fact that embedded TBT is often anathema to data processing departments, the staff of which do not want to support training within the service they provide to their companies. Even where a mainframe computer has plenty of spare capacity, these staff may find the training system intrusive. They see training sessions as difficult and expensive to schedule and possibly dangerous to data held in the computer. Training consequently receives low priority and where there is business expansion may be pushed off the computer altogether.

Some other reasons why embedded training is not for everyone may seem trivial, like 'Where shall we put the terminals?', but they are very real to company staff, and stand in the way of adopting this form of TBT. Fortunately, dedicated stand-alone systems offer an alternative. Many companies have rejected the idea of embedded TBT and prefer to use stand-alone systems that are dedicated solely to training.

STRATEGIES IN ADOPTING TBT

Companies can obtain the information required for corporate decision-making about adopting TBT from several sources. Vendors advertise products and services ranging from ready-made software packages and complete systems to consultancy on the needs of a particular company. Conferences and exhibitions bring vendors into contact with trainers. Some vendors maintain their own demonstration centres. Meetings of trainers offer opportunities to exchange views. Books, trade journals and magazines convey information to managers as well as trainers. Contacts with other companies, at manager and trainer level, can be very important. Companies actually using TBT may be willing to talk about their experience. Those that have not yet adopted it can certainly learn from others in the same situation. Informal networks are vitally important.

Companies are faced with a fairly bewildering array of information, once they find it. For example, there are numerous authoring systems on the market, mostly for use in creating stand-alone TBT. Even if the choice has been narrowed down because the buying company is already committed to a particular hardware manufacturer, many options probably remain. Vendors frequently update and adapt their already proven systems.

Four basic strategies are available to companies that want to find out about TBT in a systematic way: they can ask consultants for advice; invite several vendors to provide details of what they sell; visit other companies; and/or use the companies' own resources.

Asking consultants: Many companies ask one or more 'independent' consultants for advice. What a consultant can do for the client is to analyse the training needs, in consultation with the managers and trainers, and propose at least one solution, which may well include training hardware and software from a particular provider with whom the consultant has worked satisfactorily before. The consultant will also provide cost estimates, founded on his or her knowledge and experience, but forecasts in this field are notoriously inaccurate.

Exceptionally, consultants may be asked for a comprehensive report containing (a) training needs analysis, (b) design specification, including objectives, (c) schedule for development of TBT in the company, (d) staffing and resources plan, (e) costing, (f) cost-benefit analysis comparing at least two alternatives, based on predicted throughput of trainees, (g) advice on maintenance and support of the system, once installed, and (h) names of possible vendors.

Asking several vendors: Another strategy is to ask several vendors to provide details and demonstrations of their products and services. Before a company can adopt this strategy, it must know its needs. If it has not drawn up a training needs analysis and possibly a design specification, then the vendors are likely to press for one. Up to a point, they may be willing to assist the company without charge in arriving at a written statement, but they can reasonably ask for consulting fees if the assessment of training needs really has not been done by the company.

Visiting other companies: A third strategy is to visit other companies using TBT and those considering it. There is much to be learned from their successes and failures. Companies using older systems may be able to warn about problems that have arisen, as well as exhibiting their success. Of course, if these companies are competitors, they may be unwilling to talk much. Or they may have proprietary products which they are unwilling to demonstrate. Even vendors have to be careful about saying too much about TBT in the companies they sell to, particularly if something very new is being tried out. Visiting conferences, trade shows and exhibitions, where other user companies are present together with vendors, is an excellent way to collect information. In Britain and on the Continent, there are several annual gatherings focusing on TBT. Vendors demonstrate their products and offer seminars, and so do some user companies.

Using the company's own resources: A fourth strategy is to use the internal services of the company. Companies that have large data processing and training departments may well have employees who are qualified to assess vendors' products. Instead of buying in services, a company may decide to establish a team across departments, taking into account inter-departmental politics, and charge it with the task of advising management on the options. As always, using the company's own resources has important pay-offs in terms of motivation and involvement of employees. There is less danger of a TBT solution being foisted onto trainees. If the company lacks particular skills in its team, it may be possible to second one or two employees for specialized crash training. Ultimately, the team may become an in-house TBT development group.

COMBINING STRATEGIES AND REDUCING RISKS

These strategies are seldom used singly. Most companies decide to use two or three, in parallel or in sequence, before deciding whether to invest money in TBT. Some companies want to start with a small, cheap system over which they feel they have a good deal of control. In other words, they want to minimize the risks. For example, back in the early 1980s, Rank Xerox trainers found it easy to convince the managers to invest in a low-cost £3,000 system, 'Take Five', based on well-known hardware (the

BBC-B microcomputer and a videotape recorder). This was partly because Rank Xerox already had its own video studio and favoured having its own employees, rather than actors, on the tapes. It was also because the trainers themselves could produce, test and revise the packages in a reasonably short time, without calling in an outside team.

Other companies reduce risks by first conducting a pilot, perhaps making use of an existing mainframe system with terminals. For example, British Gas South East (SEGAS) set up in 1979 quite a large two-year pilot during which about 25 basic training packages were developed and tested through some 200 terminals. The company decided to try TBT because it needed increased training efficiency and because reduced manning levels were making it difficult for units to release employees for training at a specified time. Standardized but individualized and highly effective training was required. Many of the SEGAS prototypes had to be shelved or modified, but eventually over 100 packages were introduced, available through some 2000 terminals. Whereas TBT was at first seen to be mainly for employees at lower levels, later it was used by managerial staff as well.

Another British company, the Abbey National, carried out a pilot project using microcomputers in just 13 of its many branches. At these, 84 per cent of the trainees who used TBT felt positive about it, and the company expanded its TBT. Similarly, the Midland Bank commissioned development of a pilot interactive videodisk, using existing training materials, to explore the feasibility of this training medium. In each case, the pilot was a way of deferring, until more evidence became available, the big 'up-front' investment required for TBT.

ATTITUDES CAN HINDER ADOPTION OF TBT

Why do some companies reject TBT? TBT is a high-risk training strategy, usually requiring substantial 'up-front' investment. The single factor that most often leads companies to turn away from this technology after a period of interest in it is the loss of a board member or manager who was enthusiastic about it and willing to shoulder the risk. When the drive from the board or management suddenly stops, company strategy falters, pilot projects die unnoticed and trainers can seldom follow up successfully the initiative the board member or manager took.

Vendors and consultants must sometimes take the blame. Even with a strong training department that includes experienced trainer-authors, a company may decide against adopting TBT for reasons related more to a provider's approach than to inherent qualities of the technology. Vendors, in their enthusiasm for their product and driven by the need to make a profit in a highly competitive market, may occasionally sell to a company an inappropriate authoring system, say. Nothing is so damning to TBT as hardware and software merely gathering dust.

Companies that have already invested large sums in TBT may decide, with the passage of time, that they cannot sustain the effort required to maintain the system. There are certainly cases where a mainframe system had spare capacity, available for training purposes, that was gradually used up. After a few years, training was low on the priority list, employees were frustrated at having to wait for a convenient time for training and the programs were used less and less.

To introduce TBT into a company also needs a strong training department, with staff who are willing to be innovative. If there is no such commitment, then the company is likely to turn away from the technology. For example, one trainer said glumly:

> We are not very keen on computer-assisted learning because it is too impersonal. I am afraid the whole phrase 'Training Technologies' is too much like a new-fangled buzz word. We believe in Training but not in gimmicks. The best training results from the personal inspiration of a good trainer, from his or her ability to communicate with the trainee and whet the appetite for further knowledge and the ways to use that knowledge to good effect on the shop floor, in everyday ways.

Finally, the attitude of trainees is paramount. If they do not like TBT, it must be withdrawn. Strangely enough, their attitude is often more positive than the trainers'!

CONCLUSION

Fundamental to companies' adoption of TBT is the analysis of their training needs. They also need information about TBT systems. Only then should companies decide whether to invest in TBT some of their large annual expenditure on training. Successful adoption depends heavily on attitudes of all concerned.

ACKNOWLEDGEMENT

This paper is based on a study, funded by the Leverhulme Trust and directed by David Hawkridge, of technology-based training in the United Kingdom and the United States.

Computer Supported Collaborative Learning

Anthony Kaye

Institute of Educational Technology, The Open University

Introduction: The Social and Technological Context

This paper tries to define a relatively new and promising field in the use of computers and telecommunications in education and training: computer-supported collaborative learning (CSCL). The emphasis is on the ways in which information technology can be used to mediate and support communication between members of groups engaged in a learning activity, regardless of space or time constraints. Although CSCL can take place in the school or college classroom, its greatest potential is probably in the context of open and distance learning programmes for post-secondary and adult education and training.

Several factors underlie the interest in technology support for collaborative learning. The emphasis on learning as a social process, involving the active construction of new knowledge and understandings through group interaction and peer discussion, can be interpreted as a reaction against a behaviourist perspective, where learning is seen very much as an individual activity. Collaborative and peer learning methods are being tried in the school system, as a basis for structured group activities in the classroom, as well as in adult education and professional training and updating (an obvious example being syndicate work and group role-playing exercises in management training). Dede (1990) attributes the effectiveness of cooperative (or collaborative) learning approaches to the fact that students simultaneously experience:

- the active construction of knowledge;
- peer teaching, and the chance to develop oral explanation skills;
- peer learning, with exposure to different models for problem-solving and interaction;
- the motivating feedback from others.

He also points out that the use of computers and information technology in classrooms has led to an increase in the use of collaborative learning methods and group work, around the computer.

There are socio-economic pressures which favour the development of flexible education, training, and re-training programmes. One way of introducing flexibility is to provide environments in which experts can be brought in through networking. The trend away from from hierarchical to lateral, cellular, and networked structures in many large organisations, and the increasing emphasis on the importance of team work, provide a positive climate in which collaborative learning methods can develop.

Technological influences on the methods, systems, and software which can be used for education and training include:

- The growing availability of low-cost and more powerful personal computers at home and in the workplace.

- The arrival on the market of multimedia 'teleputers' which can be used for all the traditional PC applications, for reception of TV and video signals, and as personal communications centres, with audio and video-telephony, as well as asynchronous communication (fax, email, computer conferencing, remote database access, etc.).

- Increasing miniaturisation of components, and a resultant increase in portability of personal computers.

- The development of interfaces for voice and handwritten inputs.

In parallel with the above trends, several developments in public and private telecommunications networks will have an impact on distance learning and training:

- The progressive installation of ISDN networks and of broadband fibre optic 'highways' by many telecoms operators.

- The globalisation and exponential growth in academic and other networks: for example, the total number of users of the Internet grew from under 2 million in January 1991 to an estimated 20 million three years later.

- The expansion of personal 'wire-less' communications from telephony to data transfer (satellite communications, packet radio etc).

At the same time we are seeing corporate mergers and widescale jockeying for position as telecoms operators, cable TV companies, entertainment and media corporations, and consumer electronics manufacturers try to identify profitable commercial opportunities. Distance learning is seen as a potentially fruitful market by telecom companies and network operators. In Europe, both British Telecom and France Telecom are targeting education and training organisations as customers for ISDN services. In North America, US West sees distance education as a key growth area for various network services. As the technologies for video-conferencing and audio-conferencing have improved and become less costly, their increasing use for organisational purposes is already spilling over into training and corporate staff development. In parallel, there has been a steady growth in the use of computer conferencing for education and training. Multimedia desktop conferencing systems are now available and are soon likely to be standard features on many organisations' networked computer systems: one analyst predicts a growth in sales of desktop video-conferencing systems (which include other features such as whiteboards, screen-sharing etc) from 10,000 in 1994 to nearly 800,000 in 1997 (Reinhardt, 1993).

COLLABORATIVE LEARNING

The thing that distinguishes collaborative communities from most other communities is [this] desire to construct new meanings about the world through interaction with others. The collaborative community becomes a medium for both self-knowledge and self-expression. (Schrage, 1990, p. 48)

...Computers can provide a conversational environment in which the learner can apply knowledge to problems and consider their actions as reusable events. Learners can control their learning, learn from others and develop reflection on actions as metacognitive skills. ... We believe that learning environments should support collaborative construction of knowledge involving both teachers and students. [...] Collaborative knowledge construction environments enable all members of a class or learning group the opportunity to contribute their interpretation. It is important for advanced knowledge acquisition that learners realise that there exist multiple interpretations for every event or object. Those interpretations may be dissonant or consonant, but they reflect the natural complexity that define most advanced knowledge domains. Collaborative environments enable learners to identify and reconcile those multiple perspectives in order to solve problems. (Jonassen *et al.*, 1993)

GROUPS, COLLABORATION, AND COOPERATION

It is easier to describe what does not count as collaborative learning, than it is to produce a universally acceptable definition. Learning based on a transmissive or information-processing model of education, where the main learning activity is the individual study and organisation of information from books, lectures, videos or computer-based training materials, is not collaborative. On the other hand, learners constituted into groups (e.g. a school class or a training group) are not necessarily learning collaboratively when engaged in group discussion and communication. For effective collaboration and cooperation to occur, there needs to be real interdependence between group members in accomplishing a task, a commitment to mutual help, a sense of responsibility for the group and its goals, and attention given to social and interpersonal skills in the development of group processes.

It is important to distinguish collaboration from communication. Clear communication, and effective communication tools and channels, may be necessary pre-requisites for effective collaboration, but they are not sufficient. A good teacher, or an effective meeting chair or manager, equipped with flip charts, slides, and transparencies, may well be an excellent communicator, but will not necessarily know how to create and promote an effective collaborative environment. A lecture or a meeting may be an effective way of transmitting and sharing information, but it would be a mistake for the participants to believe that they are – in any real sense – 'collaborating' with each other in the process.

> Most people kid themselves into thinking that they're collaborating when, in reality, they're just saying words. Traditional modes of discourse in no way capture the subtleties, the bandwidth, the power, and the degrees of interaction necessary for effective collaboration. Presentations and the usual modes of organizational communication are to collaboration what smoke signals are to movie epics; puffs of smoke in the wind just aren't as colorful or compelling as *Gone With the Wind*. The practical reality of collaboration is that it requires a higher order of involvement, as well as a different approach to sharing and creating information. (Schrage, 1990, p. 29)

To collaborate (*co-labore*) means to work together, which implies a concept of shared goals, and an explicit intention to 'add value' – to create something new or different through a deliberate and structured collaborative process, as opposed to simply exchanging information or passing on instructions. A broad definition of collaborative learning would be *the acquisition by individuals of knowledge, skills, or attitudes occurring as the result of group interaction*, or put more tersely, *individual learning as a result of group process* (Kaye, 1992). Successful collaboration assumes some agreement on common goals and values, the pooling of individual competencies for the benefit of the group as a whole, the autonomy of the learners in choosing with whom they want to work, and flexibility in the organisation of the group. The factors identified by Schrage (Schrage, 1990, ch. 11) which determine the likely success of any form of collaboration are undoubtedly relevant to collaborative learning activities. They include: competence amongst group members; a shared and understood goal; mutual respect and trust; the creation and manipulation of shared spaces; multiple forms of representation; continuous – but not continual – communication; formal and informal environments; clear lines of responsibility, but no restrictive boundaries; the acceptance that decisions do not have to be based on consensus, and that physical presence is not necessary; the selective use of outsiders; and the realisation that the collaboration ends when its goal has been achieved.

In an educational context, successful collaborative learning depends on a number of important factors, not least of which is the structure within which group processes occur, and the management of these processes. The role of the tutor as facilitator and organiser is crucial, in forming the groups, in structuring the activities, and in supporting the work of the group through observation and the provision of feedback and guidance concerning the success or failure of group processes and individual contributions to them. One important aspect of the group process which needs to be addressed by the teacher, for example, is whether the group members work in parallel on each task, helping each other as they do it, or whether different tasks are given to different members (task specialisation), and the results brought together at the end. Some researchers (e.g. Hooper, 1992) would call the task specialisation approach 'cooperative learning', and reserve the term 'collaborative learning' for cases in which each member works in parallel on the same tasks, at the same time sharing their understandings and difficulties with the other group members.

THEORY AND RESEARCH ISSUES

The interest in collaborative learning, and in its technological support, seems to be associated with a number of positively loaded assumptions, which can be linked to various theoretical perspectives. Some of the strongest of these assumptions include the following:

- Much significant learning and deep-level understanding arises from conversation, argument, debate, and discussion (often unplanned, sometimes structured) amongst and between learners, peers, colleagues, experts, and teachers; learning is essentially a communal activity (Bruner, 1984) involving the social construction of knowledge.

- Peer collaboration in learning can directly help to develop general problem-solving skills and strategies through the internalisation of the cognitive processes implicit in interaction and communication (Damon, 1984; Vygotsky, 1978).

- The strengths of collaborative learning through discussion and conversation include the sharing of different perspectives, the obligation to make explicit and communicate one's own knowledge and understandings to others through verbalisation or writing (Vygotsky, 1962), and the motivational value of being a member of a healthy group (Rogers, 1970).

- Many jobs involves working in teams and groups, and job achievements often rely heavily on successful collaboration with colleagues; formal education should prepare people to work together healthily in groups.

- Groups of adults following educational or training programmes, especially in-service training programmes, often have a valuable repertoire of personal knowledge and experience to contribute (Knowles, 1970).

- Outside formal education (in society at large, in organisations), much individual learning results from informal group interactions and the help and support provided by peers and colleagues, through what Illich (1971), many years ago, called 'learning webs'.

However, it is not always easy to design learning environments based on these assumptions:

- Much educational practice assumes a transmissive model, with all authority and knowledge invested in the teacher; as a result, it can often be difficult to use constructive group discussion as a learning medium (Beard and Hartley, 1984).

- The experience of working or learning in groups can be associated with 'process loss' (Steiner, 1972) and be frustrating, time-consuming, and conflict-ridden.
- Research findings on educational achievement and collaborative learning methods are inconsistent, some reviews suggesting that individual competition produces better results than group conditions, others show no significant difference, others show an opposite trend (Webb, 1982); in the classroom situation, it seems that cooperative learning methods only result in improved achievement levels if they incorporate both group goals and individual accountability (Slavin, 1990).
- The widening of possibilities for group collaboration into an existing system can lead to rejection, because the new opportunities may run counter to traditional working practices, assessment methods, or hierarchies.

In summary, the following seven elements are amongst the most important in trying to encapsulate the field of collaborative learning:

- Learning is inherently an individual, not a collective, process, which is influenced by a variety of external factors, including group and inter-personal interactions
- Group and inter-personal interactions involve the use of language (a social process) in the re-organisation and modification of personal understandings and knowledge structures, so learning is simultaneously a private and a social phenomenon.
- Learning collaboratively implies peer exchange, interaction amongst equals, successful negotiation of power relationships in the group, and interchangeability of roles.
- Collaboration involves synergy, and assumes that, in some way, 'the whole is greater than the individual parts', so that learning collaboratively has the potential to produce gains superior to learning alone.
- Not all attempts at collaborative learning will succeed: in some cases, collaboration can lead to conformity, process loss, lack of initiative, conflict, misunderstandings, and compromise, and the potential benefits are not always realised.
- Collaborative learning does not *always* imply learning in an organised group, but does mean being able to rely on other people to support one's own learning and to give feedback, as and when necessary, within a non-competitive environment.
- Any collaborative task or process has a finite time span, a start and a finish, and the nature of the group interactions, and group support needs, will change and evolve during this time span.

The last point is worth developing, as it has a bearing on the technologies and systems used to support and mediate collaboration. A group is a socially constituted entity, brought together for a given period of time for a specific purpose. A group's activities (McGrath, 1990) can be seen in terms of:

- projects or overall goals;
- tasks, which are carried out over time to realise the project;
- activities or steps which make up individual tasks.

During the period of a group project, attention needs to be paid at all times to the varying balance of production, wellbeing, and support functions. The nature of the tasks, their component steps, and the type of support tools and systems needed, will vary during each of the classical four stages of group process ('forming, storming, norming, performing'), depending on the relative balance of functions at each stage. For example, in the first stage, a rich inter-personal and social communication environment (e.g. a series of face-to-face meetings and social events) would generally be needed; whereas in the last two stages, technology support may have a much more important role to play.

TECHNOLOGIES FOR COMPUTER-SUPPORTED COLLABORATIVE LEARNING

There are three classes of technology which, combined, can provide groupware environments suitable for collaborative learning (van Eijkelenburg *et al.*, 1992):

- *communication systems* (synchronous text, audio, audio-graphics, and video communication; asynchronous electronic mail, computer conferencing, voicemail, and fax).

- *resource sharing systems* (synchronous screen-sharing and electronic whiteboards, concept mapping tools; asynchronous access to file systems and databases).

- *group process support systems* (project management systems, shared calendars, co-authoring tools, voting tools, ideas generation and brainstorming tools).

Previously, these systems tended to be used independently, and the classic audio, audiographic, and video-conferencing systems, of course, were in use long before the advent of multimedia personal computers. However, it is the bringing together of these three classes of technology into one computer-supported environment, on the desktop, or in educational resource centres, that will make a major qualitative difference in the educational potential of computer support for collaborative learning and group work. This claim is supported by evidence from trials of technology-supported collaborative environments in the workplace: for example, the experiments carried out at Xerox PARC from 1985 – 87, when a 'media space' based on video links was used for coordination of groupwork between members of a laboratory split between two sites: Palo Alto, California, and Portland, Oregon (Bly *et al.*, 1993). Although the system was judged excellent for maintaining group contact through informal communication as well as formal meetings, one of the problems encountered was the lack of shared tools (such as a shared drawing surface) for collaborative work – pointing the camera at a whiteboard on the wall is a poor substitute for a shared computer-based resource in this respect. Approaching the issue from a different angle, through adding audio and video links to shared computer-based whiteboard on a LAN, work at Hewlett-Packard has demonstrated the value of video in maintaining (often unconscious) communication during performance of a group task, and for social communication (Gale, 1991)

As Vallée (1992) has pointed out, the possible number of multimedia groupware configurations of these various technologies is vast: the challenge for designers of systems lies in putting together specific combinations into integrated systems which will provide appropriate support for the social, educational, and group processes involved in CSCL activities. In this respect, many useful concepts and software ideas can be derived from earlier research on computer-supported collaborative work.

COMMUNICATIONS SYSTEMS

REAL TIME

Synchronous or real time communications technologies have a long and respectable history of educational use. For example, the Iowa School District started using telephones for teaching to children ill at home or in hospital in 1939 (Olgren and Parker, 1983). Nowadays, audio-teleconferencing is routinely used in many universities and organisations. Audiographic systems add to the audio channel various forms of low-bandwidth graphics, such as text, diagrams, telewriting, or still pictures. The addition of graphics overcomes the obvious pictorial limitations of 'pure' audio teleconferencing, and some research has indicated that even in subjects with no obvious pictorial content, the use of graphics assists the teaching process, probably because the screen provides a focus of attention for the students. Early systems (such as the Electrowriter and early electronic blackboards), were fairly primitive, with low resolution black and white images, slow transmission speeds, and no graphic feedback from reception sites. At the University of Wisconsin, the systems that had been used for some time were abandoned in 1987 because of such problems, and use of audio-graphics has only re-emerged as a success story since the introduction of a high-resolution PC-based system using 9600 baud modems and twin telephone lines (Smith, 1992).

For both audio and audiographic conferencing, a number of points come out time and again from evaluation studies. Advance preparation by the teacher or animateur is of even more importance than it is in the classroom: sessions need to be carefully structured, and preferably divided into 15-20 minute blocks, with a variety of different types of activity; pre-prepared visuals should be of a high quality, and printed material needs to be prepared and sent out in advance if it cannot be delivered by the system. It is important to ensure that participants are questioned regularly, and invited to contribute and exchange their own views. On the technical side, sound quality and good support for turn-taking are of extreme importance. The social aspects of the group process need particular attention because of the lack of visual cues and body language signals, with time allocated for introductions of participants, for informal communication, and for appropriate ending (particularly in systems which use audiobridges booked for set periods of time).

Traditional video-conferencing requires relatively expensive fixed delivery and reception installations, and involves high transmission costs over full bandwidth analogue video channels or high capacity digital channels. High grade services allow full two-way audio and video communication between several locations; a more common configuration is for real time one-way video with two-way audio. The costs, and the inflexibility associated with fixed installations, have limited the educational uses of video-conferencing in the past, although a number of well-known examples exist (e.g. the Irvine Interactive Television System, the Alaska Instructional Communications Consortium, the National University Teleconferencing Network, IBM's interactive satellite education network, and the Livenet system at the University of London). Recently, the development of video compression and codec technology is leading to an increased use of video-conferencing applications over relatively low-bandwidth ISDN circuits, using a variety of display formats such as videoprojectors, large monitors, videotelephones, or video windows on personal computers (Mason and Bacsich, 1994).

It is naive to believe that the addition of a realtime video channel to a remote conferencing situation means that an 'ideal' face-to-face classroom situation can be realised at a distance. The ability to see the remote tutor, or for the tutor to see a group of participants at a remote site, does not *per se* lead to increased levels of interaction (i.e. spontaneous interruptions and questions which support and develop the communication process). Many studies have shown that two-way video-conferencing cannot serve as a direct replacement for face-to-face meetings (e.g. Edigo, 1988); Gensollen and Curien (1985), in reviewing research findings on interactions in video (and audio) conferences, point out that the technological communication channels in use inevitably filter out and distort many of the (often unconscious) signals which, in a face-to-face setting, regulate the management, maintenance, and progression of verbal interactions in a co-located group. Paradoxically, the existence of a visual channel may encourage lecturers using a video-conferencing system to be far less attentive to eliciting questions and responses than they might be under an audio-only situation, precisely because they can see the remote participants, and can verify that they are still there without interrupting their own discourse. The high cost and communication limitations of traditional video-conferencing suggest that its most appropriate use is for well-structured lectures to large remote groups where visual information (e.g. for scientific or medical demonstrations) is of crucial importance to the content of the lecture.

In small group situations, where inter-personal collaboration is needed to solve, say, a problem-solving task, the existence of a video channel for provision of eye contact between remote participants, over and above a voice-only channel, may lead to smoother collaboration and more efficient performance (Taylor *et al.*, 1991). However, it is not possible to generalise about the relative importance of real-time audio and video communication in group learning/teaching situations without clearly defining the educational scenario, the group size, and the role of the tutor.

DEFERRED TIME

Increased access to personal computers and to networking facilities has led to growing use of deferred time, or asynchronous, computer conferencing for education and training. Conferencing supports many-to-many communication (whereas electronic mail is essentially for one-to-one or one-to-many messaging), and conferencing software includes features specifically designed to help in the organisation, structuring, and retrieval of messages. Several recent publications review educational applications (see, for example: Mason and Kaye, 1989; Harasim, 1990; Waggoner, 1992; Kaye, 1992). These show that computer conferencing is a communication medium in its own right, although sharing some of the features of spoken discourse (such as group interaction, and the possibility of rapid, spontaneous exchanges) and of written discourse (text-mediated, asynchronous, revisable). It has the potential to be an excellent medium for group work and collaborative learning, as all utterances are stored, retrievable and editable, participants can contribute at their own pace, at times convenient to them, and the asynchronous nature of the medium allows time for reflection and careful composition of contributions. Several types of group activity can be supported through computer conferencing, including seminars, small group discussion, dyads, team presentations, debates, peer learning groups, and so on.

RESOURCE SHARING SYSTEMS

Software for use in real-time contexts include remote screen sharing facilities and intelligent whiteboards based on the principle of a 'public workspace' visible and accessible to all participants, on a WYSIWIS (what you see is what I see) basis. Each participant has access to a variety of tools (for writing, drawing, pointing, highlighting, erasing ...), with input via a mouse, a trackball, a graphics pad, or a touch-sensitive screen. One problem in learning to use these features successfully for group work is one of turn-taking, and the avoidance of 'mouse wars' and 'window wars' (Morris *et al.*, 1992) Some systems assign different colours of drawing and writing tools to each participant, to aid in identifying who is doing what. Synchronous audio and/or video allows for discussion and communication about the task in hand. Some systems provide private workspaces (a window on each user's screen only visible to that user) which allow for drafting and preparation of material before it is transferred to the public window; another, semi-private, facility, is a realtime 'chatter' tool which enables participants to compose and send text messages to one or more other participants, in parallel to verbal discussion with the whole group (rather like passing a scribbled note to another participant in a face-to-face meeting). An example of such an environment specifically tailored for learning in groups, is the real-time multimedia conferencing facility in the Co-Learn system (Derycke and Kaye, 1993; Kaye, 1994). So-called 'intelligent' whiteboard systems will extend these types of capability with version control, hypertext, collating, reorganising, and printing functions (Wilson, 1991).

Shared resources that are accessible asynchronously are stored on databases located on one or more servers: these resources may either be 'read only' (e.g. graphics, sound files, reference texts used as core material for group discussion), or files that can be interactively edited or modified by any user. Somewhere between these two poles is the concept of the 'evolving knowledge base', where contributions made by participants (e.g. in a computer conferencing discussion) are analysed, sorted, and selected, and then transferred into a growing file of material which reflects the accumulated wisdom and experience of the group as a whole (Boder, 1994).

Various software tools are available for asynchronous interactive work on text and graphics documents, including both linear and hypertext systems. For many collaborative learning situations, concept mapping software which allows participants to jointly prepare representations of a body of knowledge by linking related concepts visually, is particularly interesting (Heeren and Collis, 1993). The main issues to be resolved in using such systems concern control of access to a file (to prevent two or more users trying to modify a document simultaneously), version control (which is the current version and when was it last modified?), and attribution of modifications to individual group members. The role of the group moderator or tutor becomes crucial in the effective use of such software.

GROUP PROCESS SUPPORT SYSTEMS

Some of the software tools that have been developed for office use as part of CSCW environments can usefully be integrated into CSCL systems. These include project management tools (for listing group and individual tasks to be done and deadlines for their completion), shared diaries and calendars with automatic reminder features, tools for generating and prioritising ideas, tools for structuring specific types of discussion format, and 'browsers' for helping users to navigate inside complex virtual environments, providing information at all times on the three essential navigational questions (*Where am I? Where have I been? Where can I go?*). In education and training contexts, with different members of a group taking on different roles at different times (tutor, learner, resource person, animateur, expert, etc.), software which can provide support for specialist roles, giving differential access to resources, tools, and activities, could play an important role in supporting the group process.

Finally, it is very important to build into any system tools and resources for informal communication, socialisation, and group bonding. In the campus or office environment, informal and chance discussions in the corridor, the canteen, around the coffee machine, in the library, provide the 'social glue' for interpersonal collaboration. Effective virtual environments for group learning need to provide similar opportunities for serendipitous encounters. Examples include the 'cafe' areas in most computer conferencing environments, the 'electronic hallway' (Johansen, 1988), the video 'media spaces' at Xerox PARC (Bly *et al.*, 1993), or the 'cruise', and 'glance' tools which provide opportunities for 'lightweight social interaction' in the Cruiser videotelephony system developed at Bellcore Labs (Fish *et al.*, 1993).

THE EFFECTS AND IMPLICATIONS OF TECHNOLOGY MEDIATION

The dynamics of educational and interpersonal interaction are changed, more or less profoundly, when mediated by technological communication channels. This is the case for audio and audiographic teleconferencing, where one would expect the lack of a visual channel to be compensated for by more frequent verbal exchanges than in a face-to-face class:

> It's precisely because I was frightened of silences that we tried to define a pedagogy of action [...] I avoid silences by posing very targeted questions [...] I need to maintain a frequent verbal contact with my students [...] I vary the exercises, and I go round each student continually, to compensate for the lack of gesture...It's a more personal and intimate form of teaching, and the effort of concentration prevents us from being distracted [...] Hearing others talk is good for noticing one's own mistakes, and the use of the telephone makes us more attentive to what the others say [...] the telephone forces us to speak. (translated from Kaye and Kerbrat, 1992)

> The long-term impact is a pedagogy centred on the interactions in the group, where the teacher is a facilitator and regulator of discussions; this calls into question traditional teaching methods (where the teacher dominates and the students are passive) and replaces them with an active pedagogy. (translated from Laure, 1993)

But it is also clear from evaluations of video-conferencing that tutors and learners cannot expect to replicate the communication patterns and styles of a face-to-face class, even though they have some visual contact:

> ... compressed digital video-conferencing technology requires a different teaching methodology from any that lecturers have used previously. It necessitates different ways of interacting, different ways of moving, different ways of presenting information, and different ways of judging the meaning of messages going in both directions. (Schiller and Mitchell, 1992)

In typical audio and video-conferencing situations, the teacher or tutor has to manage one co-present group, and one or more remote groups: this completely changes the communication patterns found in a conventional classroom situation, and raises issues over which group the teacher should address as a priority, as well as the additional complexity caused by the (often very limited) communication channels between members of the groups in the different sites. These factors, again, lead to the need for changes in teaching and interaction styles.

In the case of asynchronous, text-only group communication, there is an even greater divergence from conventional classroom-based approaches: a history professor who uses computer conferencing for off-campus students says:

> ... speaking personally, when I began using CMC a dozen years ago, I planned to use it to replicate classroom interactions for people off campus. I had no idea of using it to change what I do or how I do it. In spite of myself, that is in fact what has happened. (Coombs, 1992)

> In normal academic life (primary, secondary,tertiary and beyond) dialogue in speech usually leads to writing for assessment or publication, whereas in CMC it is dialogue in writing (I've been calling it ("say-writing") that leads to writing for assessment or publication. It is this "say-writing" that hopefully exhibits slow thrownness – fast and spontaneous enough to motivate people to stay involved and to take risks with ideas, slow enough (and this is the extra dimension that computer-mediated communication offers) to allow people to reflect during (and especially after) the exchange on the nature of the exchange and how it makes meaning. (McMahon and O'Neill, 1993)

The new multimedia desktop conferencing systems, and those systems under development which combine both realtime and store-and-forward communication in one environment, will require even greater adaptations in teaching and learning styles, and will further develop the potential for innovative and conceptually advanced pedagogies. It could be argued that a well designed groupware system can provide a richer environment for conversation, interaction, and discussion of multiple interpretations than a face-to-face situation, because of the possibilities for parallel activities, for storage, organisation, and retrieval of communications, and for the integration of realtime and deferred time interactions. The potentially communication-rich features of such environments will provide major challenges both to groupware developers and to educators.

GROUPWARE DEVELOPMENT

Perhaps the greatest challenge lies in the development of environments for the effective communication of 'telepresence', for monitoring group presence and activity, and for 'de-attenuating' meta-communicative and control cues. In the face-to-face situation, the progress of a discussion depends on a host of acts, gestures, phatic utterances (Watzlawick *et al*.., 1972) and underlying control signals, emitted by participants, which are quite separate from the actual content of the discussion. In a mediated communication environment, which depends on audio and screen communication, possibly supported with a video window, many of these meta-communicative and control signals will be lost or attenuated. CSCL environments designed around a paradigm of conversation or discussion will need to provide active telepresence indicators to compensate for the cues that we use to regulate face-to-face conversations. Video contact will not be sufficient or appropriate to provide good levels of telepresence, especially when a situation involves more than a handful of participants. There is perhaps a useful role here for virtual reality simulations of engagement (Benford and Fahlén, 1993). It should also be stressed that sound, which has been treated very much as a poor relation in traditional CSCW applications, has an important role to play in supporting telepresence. Now that high quality sound is becoming a feature of personal computer systems, attention must be paid to handling spatialisation of sound, the functions of different types of auditory cues, and the psychological role that auditory imagery might play in CSCL environments (Derycke and Barme, 1993).

A second area where more thought is needed concerns the choice of appropriate metaphors for collaborative learning environments, to aid participants in navigating through the different discussion and work spaces, and to help them exploit the full potential of the virtual environment. Some groupware systems (e.g. Co-Learn, Co-Op Lab, ShareMe...) use a rooms metaphor, but such a metaphor risks limiting the communication possibilities to those found in a physical building (seminar room, private study, lecture room, library, etc.). This 'horseless carriage' approach may hinder the development of modes of activity and communication which are special to a virtual environment. Support for different roles and actions appropriate to collaborative learning needs to be designed in such a way that groups and users can tailor the environment to the tasks they wish to undertake, to the different stages of the group process, and to the relationships and privileges which they feel are appropriate for their project.

Finally, there are several ergonomic and interface design issues which need more attention. The organisation, handling, and filtering of the stored record of messages and utterances is one of these: it is now potentially feasible to store realtime as well as deferred time communications, including audio and video messages as well as the more familiar electronic mail and conferencing messages. These possibilities raise major navigation and information overload issues. Interfaces are needed which can transparently handle a variety of input devices (cameras, microphones, keyboards, graphics tablets, scanners, CD-ROM etc), and display the necessary information about the status and communication flows of remote sites, in both real time and deferred time modes.

THE CHALLENGES FOR EDUCATORS

It has taken nearly two decades for guidelines and scenarios for good practice in the educational use of audio-conferencing, video-conferencing, and computer conferencing to develop. It is not yet clear whether the accumulated experience in these areas can be integrated and applied to the use of new multimedia and 'multi-temporal' systems. Educators will need to exercise much ingenuity in devising scenarios for the effective use of CSCL.

One obvious issue is the management of communication flows amongst participants in up to five or six remote sites, as well as a co-present group: a situation in which groups or individuals at different sites can only communicate with the tutor is quite different from one in which there are open and transparent communications between participants at all connected sites. The nature of the activities to be undertaken will also depend on the number of participants at each remote site – the learning situation is very different if each remote site is represented by one learner at a workstation, or a room with 20 or 30 people watching a video display or electronic whiteboard. And if intermediaries, assistants, or animateurs are present at remote sites, their roles vis-à-vis their group and the tutor will need to be carefully defined.

The specific features of groupware environments should be exploited in developing educational scenarios. One example is the potential for 'parallel processing' (e.g. two or more participants making screen inputs at the same time; co-located participants talking amongst themselves while simultaneously taking part in an electronic discussion with remote learners; activities in private windows, or private messaging, going on at the same time as group discussion). Another is the creative use of the different group support and resource sharing tools, and the most effective ways of integrating them into the different stages in the work of a group engaged in a collaborative learning task. A third challenge is the assignment of appropriate roles and collaborative tasks to realtime and deferred time modes: the quality of 'slow thrownness' of computer conferencing or 'bubble dialogue' discussions (McMahon and O'Neill, 1993), contrasts with the rapid-fire cut and thrust of realtime discussion – pedagogical scenarios should exploit the relative benefits of each mode.

Educators will need to learn new skills for the management of social control: it is easier to leave an electronic room than it is to walk out of a face-to-face class; relatively anonymous contributions might be possible; turn-taking and monitoring of individual presence may need to be more rigorously structured than in a face-to-face discussion; the blending of group interaction and individual activity on the same workstation needs to be effectively coordinated.

Finally, the integration into networked learning environments of the information and human resources available over national, regional, and global electronic networks presents both an enormous potential for education, as well as serious risks of information overload and wasted ime.

CONCLUSION

The educationally effective use of technology-mediated communication and computer support for collaborative learning will require much ingenuity on the part of teachers and course designers. Traditional teaching / learning situations (whether in the classroom or the distance education context) do not seem to provide the most appropriate models: looking to the past because we may not have the imagination to see the future is not a fruitful approach to adopt. How many of us use our telephones to listen to sermons or operas? Yet these were foreseen by Alexander Graham Bell as being two of the main potential applications of telephony. It will be necessary to invent new scenarios for group activity and collaborative learning, and new modes of educational interaction, if the full potential of integrated groupware systems are to be exploited for education and training. If software and systems are to be accepted and used effectively, and if the educational world is to benefit from the lessons learned from the successes and failures of groupware implementations in office environments (Grudin, 1994), educators and groupware developers will need to work closely together, evaluating different uses and going back to the drawing board as often as is necessary.

REFERENCES

Beard, R. and Hartley, J. (1984) *Teaching and Learning in Higher Education,* London, Harper and Row.

Benford, S. and Fahlén, L. (1993) 'A spatial model of interaction in large virtual environments' in *Proceedings of the Third European Conference on Computer Supported Cooperative Work,* Milan, Sept 1993, Amsterdam, Kluwer Academic Publishers.

Bly, S.A., Harrison, S.R., and Irwin, S. (1993) 'Media spaces: bringing people together in a video, audio, and computing environment', *Communications of the ACM,* vol. 36 , no. 1, pp. 28-47.

Boder, A (1994) 'Building an evolving knowledge base from computer teleconferencing,' in Verdejo, F. (ed) *Collaborative Dialogue Technologies in Distance Learning,* Springer-Verlag (in press).

Bruner, J. S. (1984) *Actual Minds, Possible Worlds*, London, Harvard University Press.

Coombs, N. (1992) 'How does CMC impact the teaching and learning process?' *Edutel*, February 18, 1992.

Damon, W. (1984) 'Peer education: the untapped potential'. *Journal of Applied Developmental Psychology*, vol. 5, pp. 331-343.

Dede, C.J. (1990) 'The evolution of distance learning: technology-mediated interactive learning' *Journal of Research on Computing in Education*, vol. 22, pp. 247-264.

Derycke, A.C. and Barme, L. B. (1993) *Some Issues on Sound in CSCW: An Often Neglected Factor.* Lille: Université de Lille 1, Laboratoire Trigone, CUEEP (mimeo).

Derycke, A.C. and Kaye, A.R. (1993) 'Participative modelling and the design of collaborative distance learning tools in the Co-Learn project', in Davies, G. and Samways, B. (eds) *Teleteaching, Proceedings of the IFIP TC3 Third teleteaching Conference*, Trondheim, Norway, 20-25 August, 1993. Amsterdam, North-Holland, pp. 191-200.

Edigo, C. (1988) 'Videoconferecing as a technology to support group work: a review of its failure'. In *Proceedings of the Conference on CSCW*, Portland, OR, September 26-28, 1988, pp. 13-24.

Van Eijkelenberg, K., Heeren, E., and Vermeulen, L. (1992) *ECOLE as a Computer-Supported Cooperative Learning Service*, Eindhoven, PTT Research.

Fish, R.S., Kraut, R.E. Root, R.W., and Rice, R.E. (1993) 'Video as a technology for informal communication', *Communications of the ACM*, vol. 36, no.1, pp. 48-61.

Gale, S. (1991) 'Adding audio and video to an office environment', *ECSCW'91 Proceedings*, pp. 121- 130.

Gensollen, M. and Curien, N. (1985) 'De l'analyse du fonctionnment interactif à lévaluation des marchés des téléconférences', *Annales des Télécommunications*, vol. 40, no 1-2, Jan/Feb 1985.

Grudin, J. (1994) 'Groupware and social dynamics: Eight challenges for developers', *Communications of the ACM*, vol. 37, no. 1, pp. 93-105.

Harasim, L. (ed) (1990) *Online Education: Perspectives on a New Environment,* New York, Praeger.

Heeren, E. and Collis, B. (1993) 'Design considerations for tele-communications-supported cooperative learning environments: concept mapping as a "telecooperation support tool", *Journal of Educational Media and Hypermedia*, vol. 4, no. 2, pp. 107-127.

Hooper, S. (1992) 'Cooperative learning and computer-based instruction' *Educational Technology Research and Development*, vol. 40, no. 3.

Illich, I. D. (1971) *Deschooling Society*, London, Calder and Boyars.

Johansen , R. (1988) *Groupware: Computer Support for Business Teams*, New York, The Free Press.

Jonassen, D., Mayes, T. and McAleese, R. (1993) 'A manifesto for a constructivist approach to uses of technology in higher education' in Duffy, T.M., Lowyck, J., Jonassen, D. (eds) *Designing Environments for Constructive Learning* NATO ASI series, F105, Heidelberg, Springer-Verlag, pp. 231-247.

Kaye, A.R. (1992) 'Learning together apart,' in A.R.Kaye (ed.) *Collaborative Learning Through Computer Conferencing: The Najaden Papers* NATO ASI Series,Vol F90, Heidelberg, Springer-Verlag, pp. 1-24.

Kaye, A.R. (1994) 'Co-Learn: an ISDN-based multimedia environment for collaborative learning', in Mason, R.D. and Bacsich, P.D. (eds) *ISDN Applications in education and training,* London, The Institution of Electrical Engineers, pp. 179-200.

Kaye, A.R. and Kerbrat, C. (1992) *Télécours d'anglais du tourisme: rapport d'évaluation,* Montpellier, ATENA.

Knowles, M.S. (1970) *The Modern Practice of Adult Education: From Pedagogy to Andragogy,* New York, Association Press.

Laure, L. (1993) *Rapport d'évaluation: la Télé-Présentation via Numéris,* Montpellier, Conservatoire National des Arts et Métiers.

Mason, R.D. and Bacsich, P.D. (eds) (1994) *ISDN Applications in Education and Training,* London, The Institution of Electrical Engineers.

Mason, R.D. and Kaye A.R. (eds) (1989) *Mindweave: Communication, Computers, and Distance Education,* Oxford, Pergamon Press.

McGrath, J.E. (1990) 'Time matters in groups', in Galegher J. *et al.* (eds) *Intellectual Teamwork: Social and Technological Foundations of Cooperative Work,* Hillsdale, N.J., Lawrence Erlbaum.

McMahon, H. and O'Neill, W. (1993) 'Computer-mediated zones of engagement in learning', in Duffy, T.M., Lowyck, J., Jonassen, D. (eds) *Designing Environments for Constructive Learning* NATO ASI series, F105, Heidelberg, Springer-Verlag, pp. 37-57.

Morris, M.E., Plant, T.A., and Hughes, P.T. (1992) 'CoOpLab: Practical experiences with evaluating a multi-user system' in Monk, A. *et al.* (eds) (1992) *People and Computers VII: proceedings of the HCI'92 Conference,* Cambridge University Press, pp. 355 – 368.

Olgren, C. and Parker, L. (1983) *Teleconferencing Technology and Applications,* Artech House.

Reinhardt, A. (1993) 'Video conquers the desktop', *Byte Magazine,* September 1993.

Rogers, C. (1970) *Encounter Groups,* London, Allen Lane, The Penguin Press.

Schrage, M. (1990) *Shared Minds: The New Technologies of Collaboration,* New York, Random House.

Schiller, J. and Mitchell, J. (1992) *Interacting at a distance: staff and student perceptions of teaching and learning via video-conferencing,* AARE/NZARE Joint Conference Educational Research, Deakin University, Geelong, Victoria.

Slavin, R.E. (1990) *Co-Operative Learning: Theory, Research, and Practice,* Englewood Cliffs, N.J., Prentice Hall.

Smith, T.W. (1992) 'The evolution of audio-graphics teleconferencing for continuing education at the University of Wisconsin-Madison', *International Journal for Continuing Engineering Education.*

Steiner, I.D. (1972) *Group Process and Productivity,* New York, Academic Press.

Taylor, J. *et al.* (1991) 'Discourse and harmony: preliminary findings in a case-study of multimedia collaborative problem solving', in Glanville, R. and de Zeeuw, G. (eds) *Interactive Interfaces and Human Networks,* Amsterdam, Thesis Publishers.

Vallée, O. (1992) *Group Multimedia Communications* (mimeo).

Vygotsky, L.S. (1962) *Thought and Language,* Cambridge, MA., MIT Press.

Vygotsky, L.S. (1978) *Mind in Society,* Cambridge, MA, Harvard University Press.

Waggoner, M. (ed) (1992) *Empowering Networks: Computer Conferencing in Education,* Englewood Cliffs, N.J., Educational Technology Publications.

Watzlawick, P., Helmick-Beavan, and Jackson, P.(1972) *Une logique de la communication,* Paris, Seuil.

Webb, N.M. (1982) 'Student interaction and learning in small groups', *Review of Educational Research.*vol. 52, no. 3, pp. 421-445.

Wilson, P. (1991) *Computer-Supported Cooperative Work: An Introduction,* Oxford, Intellect.

THE EDUCATIONAL VALUE OF ISDN

Robin Mason
Institute of Educational Technology, The Open University

INTRODUCTION

The road show advertising the wonders of yet another educational revolution has set off to the usual tune of brass band, hawkers and slick sales pitches: ISDN is the mega-medium which is going to transform education, turning boring books and lectures into cost-effective, multi-media, convenient choices, easily adapted to the demands of life-long learning, busy schedules and specialist requests. Above all else, ISDN will be interactive.

Can the educationalist rev up any enthusiasm for this latest offering? Will 'technology' really deliver this time? And what is wrong with education that it needs saving by ISDN anyway? This article will look closely at these questions and aim to provide those involved in education and training with a 'learners guide' to ISDN.

The article will survey the current applications running over ISDN, commenting on the range of teaching/learning strategies possible, and looking forward to developmental trends in software. A critical analysis will be made of the vogue for interaction in education and training, including a review of the kind of interaction which actually takes place through typical ISDN applications. Finally, the article will put ISDN in the context of other educational technologies and indicate those areas in which its implementation is most appropriate.

INSTITUTIONAL CONTEXT

Current pressures in educational and training institutions which have relevance to the use of ISDN can be summarised as follows:

- financial constraints as well as a need to increase student numbers
- a dispersed population requiring specialist, up-to-date training;
- a perceived demand for interactive teaching strategies;
- regulations requiring equal access to educational facilities;
- increasing time constraints and other commitments operating against fixed location, face-to-face education and training.

These pressures have been building for some time and have led to a world-wide expansion in various forms of distance education. Technological developments have undoubtedly made this expansion feasible: twenty years ago, distance education turned to broadcast television and radio, then to video and audio cassettes, then to computers and satellites. Whether driven by educational demand, or pulled by communications technology, we are now very strongly in the grip of an 'interaction paradigm' of the learning experience. Technologies which offer some form of interaction are, of course, already available on analogue telephone lines and are being used: audio conferencing is an example of a real time application, and computer conferencing and electronic mail are examples of asynchronous uses. What ISDN promises is better, cheaper, faster video interaction.

The pronounced divide between face-to-face teaching and distance teaching is simply disappearing with the host of educational technologies and institutional strategies for responding to the pressures listed earlier. Examples include:

- students at traditional campuses taking some courses via conferencing, using equipment on site to access teaching at a linked institution (video conferencing) or even from the same institution, but in their own time (computer conferencing);
- professionals taking a course (e.g. MBA) in the workplace delivered by print, video or audio-graphics from a distant university, but with a local facilitator or tutor from their own organisation;
- courses which combine face-to-face seminars, residential weekends or lectures with computer conferencing as the delivery medium 'in between';
- groups of students at several sites linked by audio-graphics with the teacher taking turns at each site to run the session.

Where once distance education and training were criticised for being over-packaged, isolating and uniform, the new interactive, technology-based learning (the concept of distance has faded away) is much vaunted for offering consumer choice, convenience and contact. As the advertising slogans present it: 'better than being there'! Some predictors say that ISDN will make distance learning the norm (Rajasingham, 1990) and face-to-face contact will have to be justified as a special case (Romiszowski, 1990).

ISDN APPLICATIONS

In educational terms, ISDN is a set of international standards for computer and communications technologies, which support video, audio and computer data on a telephone line. In theory, therefore, it means that multi-media material can be accessed, processed and stored through the telephone network we already have in our homes and offices. Although there are a number of companies offering this 'desk-top multi-media conferencing', there are very few uses being made of these facilities for education and training as yet. This is due to the cost of the equipment/software/phone charges, the lack of penetration of ISDN, and the inevitable lag time in educational circles to develop innovative programmes. In fact, current applications are primarily modifications and enhancements of technologies which run over analogue lines or other means: audio-graphics, video-conferencing and various forms of remote database access and file exchange.

AUDIO-GRAPHICS

The term audio-graphics applies to a small range of technologies which combine a live voice link with a shared screen for graphics, real-time drawing or pre-prepared material. It is a technology in transition, partly due to ISDN capabilities, but almost certainly destined to be subsumed by multi-media desk-top conferencing. For example, most of the vendors of audio-graphics systems are adding video windows, integration with other facilities resident on the local machine, and of course, ability to run over ISDN. Another 'add-on' is a projector screen, which enables audio-graphics to be used in lecture mode to large groups of students. The remote lecturer's slides, graphics or drawings appear on the projector, accompanied by voice and live pointer on the screen. The CoLearn software is a clear example of audio-graphics evolving towards desk-top conferencing. CoLearn combines three forms of audio-graphic interchange (lecture, small group and one-to-one) with the facilities of an asynchronous messaging system.

In this interim period, audio-graphics applications are particularly exploited in the primary/secondary sector, and to a lesser extent in tertiary and vocational education. Its cost effectiveness has been proven in a number of studies (Chute *et al.*, 1990; Smith, 1992). Its main niche seems to be in extending the course choices of urban students to small, isolated communities. Students who would otherwise have to move to larger centres to receive more specialised courses, can now be accommodated in their own environment. Although certain subject areas like mathematics, technology, engineering, etc., would seem to be most appropriate for use of audio-graphics, in fact, there are applications across all curriculum areas. Examples abound in North America, Australia, the UK and Finland. Not all of audio-graphics use is over ISDN, but many of the sites are planning to upgrade soon.

The simplest configuration of the system is linking two sites – for example, the expert teacher with the remote classroom. More complex arrangements involving an audio bridge can connect several sites – usually not more than five, and hence the possibilities for student-to-student exchanges, peer learning and live discussion can be exploited. The systems are relatively simple to learn and to operate, and most allow any participating site to receive and transmit.

Strictly speaking, the term audio-graphics should be reserved for systems which include proprietary hardware and software. However, the facility to share a screen across several sites can now be accomplished without buying in a specific audio-graphics package, for instance, by adding software which allows one machine to take-over the working of another machine. Combined with facilities already resident on a typical machine, such as a drawing package, word processor, etc., or purchased independently, such as a graphics pad, all of the aspects of an audio-graphics system can be put together. One issue which arises with drawing packages rather than a graphics pad, is that it is much easier for new users to work with a graphics pen and tablet than to learn how to manipulate a drawing package. Users who are already familiar with their own drawing package, would find a 'put together' system quite acceptable. In fact, such a system is another step towards multi-media desktop conferencing.

Whether current systems do, or do not, have a video window (showing the person at the opposite end), there is one main factor which distinguishes audio-graphics from desk-top video-conferencing. Audio-graphics equipment is typically accessed from a school, a training room or a community centre, where a group of students sit around a table and share the graphics pad. Desk-top conferencing is a 'one person per machine' concept, where each machine may be in a different building, city or country. The difference is significant pedagogically, but both have benefits and limitations. Some audio-graphics courses capitalise on the presence of the group by assigning group tasks, providing 'down-time' during a session for the group to break the connection and work together, or simply by encouraging a social environment for learning. Some teachers take care to identify each student, and call on them by name with specific questions. Interactions amongst the group before and after the audio-graphics session are also part of the whole educational experience for each person. Despite lack of evaluation evidence from desk-top conferencing applications, it is obvious that individuals working at their own machine have the tremendous advantage of control: over their participation, access, input and all the facilities on their machine. Their contact with all other students, however, is mediated by the technology, and any group work, such as shared report writing, consists of individuals working together, rather than groups interacting with other groups.

The limitations of audio-graphics systems are two-fold. First of all, lesson planning (creating computer visuals) can be considerably time-consuming for the teacher.

> Audio-graphics slides must be well designed and properly sequenced. Instructors should 'story board' or carefully plan each visual for a lesson before actually creating the slide/visual on the computer. Principles of effective visual communication (balance, harmony, contrasts, lettering, etc.) should be incorporated when creating slides. (Barker and Goodwin, 1992)

Secondly, audio-bridge systems are notoriously prone to technical hitches. Losses in transmission connection, extraneous noise or interference on the telephone lines can cause havoc in speaker telephones, and acoustic echo can be difficult to control. ISDN promises to end these technical problems – we await confirmation.

VIDEO-CONFERENCING

Video-conferencing is a confusing term in that it encompasses, on the one hand, live video-lecturing to large audiences, and on the other, desk-top conferencing point-to-point. The majority of large-scale educational use is currently satellite based – one-way video, two-way audio. Students at a remote site, or sites, see and hear the lecturer on several monitors positioned around the room. Using a telephone, they can call in questions live to the remote lecturer. ISDN promises to make two way video equally as cost-effective but more interactive. With two way video, every site can hear and see and speak to any other site. ISDN also facilitates smaller scale, multi-site video-conferencing, which lends itself to seminars, peer interaction, demonstrations of equipment or procedures, or round-robin discussions and training sessions. Like audio-graphics, video-conferencing with ISDN shades into desk-top multi-media conferencing, and the major suppliers of video equipment all offer room-based systems for large scale applications, 'rollabouts' for medium size flexibility and desk-top versions for personalised interaction. One manufacturer even markets its desk-top video-conferencing system much like audio-graphics, with electronic pens in six different colours for marking documents from each site.

If the demarcations between the actual technologies are shifting, the terminology used to describe them creates the ultimate confusion. Almost without exception, manufacturers (and their promotions departments) and to some extent users in different countries choose the same words for different facilities and technologies (e.g. 'teleconferencing' means different things on either side of the Atlantic, 'multi-media' can mean enhanced computer-based training, multiple media, or networked desk-top conferencing, and the term, 'virtual classroom' can be based on video lectures or computer conferencing). Equally, different words are frequently used for the same facility (e.g. candid classroom, video lectures, television, teleconferencing, video-conferencing are all used for the same activity).

The diversity of ways of using video-conferencing also contributes to the confusion about what it is and how to use it for education and training. Although referring to satellite-based video-conferencing, a report written by the Audio Visual Centre at University College Dublin, lays out the range of pedagogic scenarios for using video in education most comprehensively (Phelan, 1992). A brief summary will help to clarify the options :

- A lecturer (usually an expert) delivers a lecture from a studio – with graphic or other illustrative material – to students at a remote site or sites. This scenario may die completely with the two-way video-conferencing on ISDN.

- Candid classroom, where some students are present with the lecturer and some are remote. This is the most popular option with the advent of ISDN.

- Mediated presentation – often used in training applications where various experts are used to explain and present material, and a range of artefacts, pre-prepared graphics or complex procedures are demonstrated. Inserted video clips made beforehand or selected from video banks, can be used. This kind of video-conferencing usually requires considerable planning and is closer to what we are familiar with as live television programmes.

There are many ISDN training applications of video lecturing and small-scale video-conferencing around the world – in Australia and the US and, increasingly, in Europe. The benefits are obvious: maximisation of lecturing time and expertise, travel savings for teachers and/or students, extended course choice for students at smaller institutions, in some cases, better vision of equipment, procedures, computer graphics, artefacts, and more timely access to information. Lecturers can do what they have always done, which is lecture (at least in the first two types), and organisations claim it reduces costs. Finally, reports, evaluations and research on applications invariably show that students are positive about learning in this medium. It is no wonder that the literature abounds with predictions that this kind of application will grow and grow (Gunawardena, 1991; Stone, 1990).

If the model one begins with is the face-to-face lecture, then video-conferencing has few disadvantages. With two-way video now more affordable with ISDN, it is almost as good as being there (for spontaneity, feeling of presence and sense of a group) and, in some cases, better than being there (for ease of access and a better view of certain procedures or equipment). The limitations are inherent in the nature of lectures and the transmissive model of education. With the continuing pressure to increase student numbers without increasing costs, it is unlikely that smaller teacher/student ratios, discussion groups and other encouragements towards deep-level learning will find much financial support. There are indications, however, that one of the most positive outcomes of technology-mediated education and training is that teachers are improving their standard lecturing techniques: preparation of visual aids for audio-graphics and video-conferencing leads to better lectures and the interactive potential of these technologies has kept lecturers 'on their toes'.

REMOTE ACCESS TO INFORMATION

This third category of applications is admittedly amorphous, but is intended to encompass a range of unique uses of ISDN. Access to data banks of pictures is one example of a facility which can be woven into any number of educational applications. Faster access to textual databases and much speedier file transfer afforded by ISDN mean that a whole range of activities can be used educationally, which were otherwise too slow or too expensive. Researchers at museums or hospitals can access and work on banks of image stores at remote sites, for example; similarly, trainees in the workplace can download technical drawings to their workstation. ISDN links are also used in combination with satellite, as the return channel from receive sites, or as the access route to an image bank during live video-conferences.

Resource-based learning, in which students choose their own path through a range of resources under the guidance of a tutor, is a pedagogical approach ideally suited to ISDN. Institutions can build up a bank of material, still images, lecture notes, databases and audio tapes etc. to make available to students to access in their own time.

> Integrated systems put a plethora of telecomputing capabilities at the fingertips of teacher and learner. Both can access multiple programs simultaneously, and use different application software as they may need. These systems are also capable of driving other digital media, such as CD-ROM players and videodisc players. There are virtually no limits to databases, conceivably worldwide, and multimedia libraries of digital sound, text and image (Saba, 1990)

With careful planning, resource-based learning could resolve the conflicting pressure to increase student numbers while providing personalised, student-led learning and convenient access to education and training. It also has the major advantage of traditional distance education: the learning material can be accessed at times of the students' choosing. Video-conferencing and audio-graphics courses may be, to some extent, place independent, but they are not time independent. For dedicated distance teaching universities, which have built up a student body used to fitting their studies around a competing range of work, domestic responsibilities, and leisure activities, course components based on attendance at a particular place and time, are not generally welcomed (Bowser and Shepherd, 1991).

As the market grows, ISDN will undoubtedly be exploited in a variety of novel and unique ways to carry parts of education and training courses. In the meantime, this area of innovation is the most exciting aspect of the advent of ISDN, in that it is being used to provide new educational situations. It is slow to develop because it is not based on standard models, but on a real exploitation of what ISDN uniquely provides to the education and training market.

LEARNING THROUGH INTERACTION

Interaction is not just 'in vogue' in educational circles; it sometimes threatens to become synonymous with the term learning! Without interaction, the teacher cannot know who actually understands the material, and cannot resolve misunderstandings. Without interaction, there is no way of answering unanticipated questions. Without interaction, students cannot express their learning difficulties. These concerns are in fact, only the beginning of the story. Interaction at the question/answer level is a first order use of communication. It does not disrupt the 'transmissive model' of education, which emphasises mastery of a body of pre-structured material. In some learning situations (e.g. skills training), this model may be appropriate. However, much more challenging for teacher and learner is the kind of interactive model of learning in which understanding is achieved through dialogue, commenting on ideas, reformulating ideas, and building on group energy and synergy. The technology which best supports this model of interaction is computer conferencing, because it is asynchronous and users can reflect on their interactions through written communications. Multi-media desk-top conferencing may well follow this path, as it provides messaging facilities in addition to real-time interaction. Small group teaching situations, whether technology-mediated or face-to-face, also have potential for real interaction – for active involvement of all participants, for peer commenting and group synergy. Lectures are a different educational activity altogether, and the kind of interaction which typically takes place is question and answer. Interestingly, one researcher reports that students rated feedback on their written assignments more highly than the ability to ask questions in video lectures (Barnard, 1992).

Interaction between student and teacher or amongst students is, in fact, quite a small element in the process of learning. In most sustained education or training courses, whether face-to-face or mediated by technology at a distance, the student will spend more time and put most attention into the isolated activity of 'interacting' with the learning material.

> There is an even greater myth that students in conventional institutions are engaged for the greater part of their time in meaningful, face-to-face interaction. The fact is that for both conventional and distance education students, by far the largest part of their studying is done alone, interacting with textbooks or other learning media. (Bates, 1991)

Lectures, textbooks, and other printed material are tried and true 'media' for presenting the stuff of knowledge. Just as some lecturers can present information in a vivid or thought-provoking way, so textbooks can use self-assessment questions, activities and model answers to encourage analysis and integration of new material with existing knowledge. This stimulates a form of interaction in the listener/reader, which is no less valid or important than human to human communication. Some forms of CBT and most Interactive Video Disks are also called interactive by their promoters, meaning that students can make choices, carry out exercises and procedures to test their understanding and work through material in their own way.

Theories of learning suggest that it is through interaction with ideas and with other people, that the student develops understanding. Opportunities for both types of interaction are increasingly considered essential for the best quality provision. Not surprisingly, therefore, most of the applications of ISDN facilitate and support interaction: between teacher and student, amongst students themselves, and with ideas. Access to vast stores of text and images via ISDN, is certainly the least exploited form of interaction at the moment by teachers and trainers, although this is probably due to the cost of equipping individual students. Student to student interaction is another under-developed resource which ISDN should be facilitating. Audio-graphics applications are leading the way here. Interaction between teacher and student is by far the most common interpretation of the concept, and it is not coincidental that this model directly reproduces the non-technology-mediated version – the lecture followed by a question and answer session.

A further development of the 'interaction debate' considers that active participation by each student in discussions and group work, should be the norm where technology permits. In the educational use of computer conferencing, for instance, pressure is often put on all students to comment regularly and contribute to exercises and discussions. 'Lurking' is the term used to describe users who just read the inputs of the tutor and other students, and some consider it unacceptable and unfair to the other participants. At the very least, it is thought to be more beneficial educationally to engage in debate, than merely to observe it.

Integrated systems have added a new dimension to the interactivity issue: virtual contiguity. Beyond the kind of interaction that takes place face-to-face, there is the interaction around shared resources which need not be synchronous.

> Sharing and multitasking intensify voice and sight dialog beyond face-to-face communication. This intensification is a significant feature of integrated systems. Its significance does not lie in its comparative value of face-to-face communication. Its importance is that it enables the teacher to respond to the needs of the learner by accessing a variety of information sources and making it expeditiously available to the learner (Saba, 1990).

With the multi-tasking potential of desktop multi-media conferencing, interaction may take an entirely new direction.

Nevertheless, as most teachers, trainers and tutors who have tried to facilitate interaction know well, there is a difference between providing the opportunity for discussion (whether after lectures or in technology-based courses) and students making use of the opportunity. Equally, there is a difference between the first order use of the opportunity for interaction (factual queries, clarifying misunderstandings and 'clever' questions), and a significant discussion (where ideas are formulated and expressed, and comments on the substance of the ideas are heard and considered). Setting up an educational environment which fosters this kind of interaction is a skilled undertaking, in which the use of any technological media is a minor part of the whole enterprise. Much of what passes for interaction in educational settings may be beneficial, but it does not amount to much more than clarification and information exchange. The educational literature abounds with articles on the new interactive technologies (primarily video-conferencing); however, although interactivity is clearly the major selling point, there is almost never any mention of the nature, quality or even quantity of use made of this facility.

> Interaction does not simply happen with a two-way interactive medium. It is also important for designers and instructors to think

219

of interaction in a broader sense rather than as telephoned-in questions from the sites during class time, and to provide for interactive activities before, after and between class sessions. (Gunawardena, 1993)

Experienced audio-graphics instructors give the same advice:

One has to adopt a much stronger approach with students in a telematics link in order to engage them effectively. This 'dialectical encounter' is necessary to keep students involved in worthwhile interaction. It is too simplistic a view to assume that opening a telematics link once a week necessarily engages students in effective dialogue, particularly given the lack of experience of many students with the technology. (Smith *et al.*, 1993)

The current vogue for interaction has put non-interactive technologies, such as broadcast TV, radio, video cassettes, and to some extent, CBT, into the developmental shade. Yet, a recent American survey shows that non-interactive technologies are still by far the most common in distance education. What it also shows is the range of student support services used by institutions, which may be as effective as most interactive technologies: telephone office-hours for faculty teaching the course, study guides, individualised feedback from faculty, student access to public or college libraries, pre-broadcast notes and follow-up exercises (Gunawardena, 1991).

It is much too simple to divide courses into those which are interactive and those which are not (and implicitly to regard those which offer human to human interaction as best). When the word interactive is applied not only to video lectures with hundreds of students but also to small groups in an audio-graphics sessions, as well as to CD-I (compact disk interactive), it is time to find a new word – in fact, at least three words!

It is perhaps also worth referring to the negative aspect of interaction – heretical as that may be in the current climate. Working in groups can lead to group transference, to the 'lowest common denominator' solution to problems, and to time consuming process discussions:

Collaborative learning is not a pure good. One cost of working in groups is that some resources must be invested in group coordination. For instance, planning as a group takes time and effort, and may have psychological costs. When a group member is listening to others, he or she is not writing. When a group member is talking to others, he or she is not listening. Social psychologists who study small groups have called the transaction costs of being in a group 'process losses'. (Kiesler, 1992)

If group coordination activities take time face-to-face, they invariably take longer when mediated by technology, especially asynchronous messaging media.

ISDN AND EDUCATIONAL TECHNOLOGY

Anyone who has been involved in education or training for very long, has seen many technologies come and go, but each was proclaimed to be revolutionary during its ascendance. The revolutionary picture conjured up by ISDN enthusiasts involves instructors and students using the ordinary telephone in an office, classroom or workplace, to connect up their desktop workstations. Students can go through an interactive video lesson, work through a multi-media, computer-based package, watch a video segment, take a test and communicate in classes with the instructor and other students about course issues. Dismissing questions of cost, this is all possible now.

Much of the visionary literature about teaching machines, educational television and satellite was also true, and technically feasible. Some of the benefits were even achieved, but the overall prediction of revolutionary changes in education and training have not happened. It is unlikely that ISDN will affect education or training profoundly either. This has more to do with the conservative core of the massive education and training activity world-wide, than it does with educational technologies.

If lack of knowledge about ISDN and how it can be used educationally is a current deterrent to its spread, over-selling of its potential is equally dangerous to its successful spread. This is the main lesson to be learned from the history of previous technologies. ISDN will be superseded (Kirvan, 1993; Warwick, 1993); it will not totally transform education and training, but what it will do is integrate voice, text and video onto the students' and teachers' desktop. It does provide a very broad base on which to build education and training applications: large scale video-conferencing, small group co-operative learning, computer-based packages, multi-media interactive sessions, and very fast file exchange and access to learning resources.

Should trainers and educationalists invest in ISDN? The answer is yes, under the following conditions:

- if there is a need for relatively high bandwidth at relatively low cost;
- if two institutions want to cooperate on course delivery;
- if there are several sites in remote locations all wanting to access courses;
- if expertise must be shared amongst distant locations.

In short, ISDN offers two facilities: bandwidth and connectivity. For those practitioners who are realistic about innovation, there is another reason to look to ISDN:

- because it is easier to attract financial support for technologies at the leading edge.

Why not stick with POTS technologies (Plain Old Telephone Service) and lie in wait for the next educational 'revolution'? This question can be generalised to any technology, and the general answer is that it is harder to maintain a state of 'innovative readiness' than it is to go ahead and innovate. Those who are best placed to capitalise on the next educational technology are not those who have sat back and watched this one go by. What is important to look at with ISDN is the nature of interactivity required – whether surface or deep. Secondly, programmes which are balanced and 'fit for purpose' should be designed such that expensive, high contact (video and face-to-face) sessions are interspersed with reflective interaction (computer conferencing and print). Finally, it must be remembered that the educational objectives of the implementation are the first priority; the technology is but the servant.

REFERENCES

Barnard, J. (1992) 'Video-based instruction: issues of effectiveness, interaction, and learner control', *Journal of Educational Technology Systems*, **21**, 1, pp. 45-50.

Bates, A. W. (1991) 'Interactivity as a criterion for media selection in distance education', *Never Too Far*, **16**, pp. 5-9.

Barker, B., and R. Goodwin (1992) 'Audio-graphics: linking remote classrooms', *The Computing Teacher*, April 1992, pp. 11-15.

Bowser, D. and Shepherd, D. (1991) 'Student perceptions of the role of technology in enhancing the quality of management education at a distance', in *Quality in Distance Education: ASPESA Forum* , R. Atkinson, C. McBeath and D. Meacham (eds), Australian and South Pacific External Studies Association, Lismore Heights, NSW.

Chute, A., Balthazar, L., and Poston, C. (1990) 'Learning from Teletraining: What AT&T research says', in *Contemporary Issues in American Distance Education* , M. Moore (ed.) Pergamon Press.

Gunawardena, C. (1991) 'Current trends in the use of communications technologies for delivering distance education', *International Journal of Instructional Media*, **13**, 3, pp. 201-213.

Gunawardena, C. (1993) 'Review of Video-conferencing and the Adult Learner' *Open Learning*, **8**, 2, pp. 66-7.

Kiesler, S. (1992) 'Talking, teaching, and learning in network groups', in *Collaborative Learning Through Computer Conferencing* , A. R. Kaye (ed.) Springer Verlag, Berlin.

Kirvan, P. (1993) 'ISDN in the US?' *Communications Networks*, January 1993, pp. 17-20.

Phelan, A. (1992) 'DBS pedagogical scenarios: the use of direct broadcast satellite in the multimedia teleschool for European personnel development', Delta Deliverable 5, Project MTS D2021, Brussels.

Rajasingham, L. (1990) 'Integrated services digital networks and distance education', *ETTI*, **27**, 3, pp. 301-304.

Romiszowski, A. (1990) 'Shifting paradigms in education and training: what is the connection with telecommunications?' *ETTI*, **27**, 3, pp. 233-237.

Saba, F. (1990) 'Integrated telecommunications systems and instructional transaction', In: *Contemporary Issues in American Distance Education,* M. Moore (ed.) Pergamon Press.

Smith, K., C. Fyffe and L. Lyons (1993) Telematics: the 'language of possibility', *Open Learning,* 8, 2, pp. 45-49.

Smith, T. (1992) 'The evolution of audio-graphics teleconferencing for continuing engineering education at the University of Wisconsin – Madison', *International Journal for Continuing Engineering Education,* **2**, 2/3/4, pp. 155-160.

Stone, H. (1990) 'Economic development and technology transfer: implications for video-based distance education', in *Contemporary Issues in American Distance Education* , M. Moore (ed.) Pergamon Press.

Warwick, M. (1993) 'A technology still in the wilderness?' *Communications International,* **20**, 4, pp. 55-57.

Access to Books for Visually Impaired Learners – An Investigation into the use of Compact Disc Technology (CD-ROM)

Tom Vincent and Mary Taylor
Institute of Educational Technology, The Open University

Barriers to Learning for Visually Impaired People

In educational terms, the most difficult problems for blind and partially sighted learners are associated with reading and writing (Hawkridge and Vincent, 1992). They cannot depend on speech and hearing for all educational activities, and there have been numerous developments to overcome communication problems caused by loss of sight.

Learners must have access to printed material. In addition to the printed word, diagrams, pictures and models are used in many subjects to convey information in a concise and often interesting form. For example, a simple graph can replace a paragraph or more of words. A blind person is denied access to printed material, and must use the tactile and auditory senses. Many blind learners depend on braille to convey information. An important facility for many visually impaired learners is the 'talking book' with text being transcribed on to audio cassettes which are played back through conventional or adapted (variable speed) cassette players.

Most visually impaired learners have some residual vision, and this applies to many of those who are registered blind. For people with poor central vision, some form of magnification is often appropriate. For those with a restricted field of view, magnification does not help with reading. Indeed, it can make the situation worse. As the major problem with tunnel vision is orientation within text, aids which assist in maintaining or changing position are often used.

In an educational context there are two activities where there is a fundamental need to produce written material: note-taking and essay writing. Clearly the use of pen and paper by a blind person is very difficult, and other methods have emerged to suit individual needs.

Preparing essays or similar written material throws up another common problem that is often experienced: the need to communicate with a sighted person. In some cases, an essay in braille may be the appropriate medium for the learner but a totally inappropriate one if the essay has to be read by a sighted person with no knowledge of braille.

Using Computers to Overcome Barriers to Learning

With the widespread availability of computers in education, the question arises as to whether computers can help learners with a visual impairment.

Before computers came on the educational scene, a few technological solutions to the problems of visually-impaired learners already existed. Among these were large print displays, often through closed circuit television. Computers can provide a range of magnifications of text and graphics, in colour or not, via cheap software compatible with commercially available software. In addition to a conventional-sized display, they offer a smooth, fast display of enlarged text and graphics, with automatic, adjustable scrolling, movement of the viewing window to any part of the screen and automatic return to the cursor location.

For blind learners with good hearing, the greatest advance has been the development of screen readers, which can provide a spoken (synthetic speech) equivalent to the visual screen display for computer software that functions in a text mode. When speech synthesisers were first added to computers in the 1970s, the interface was often simple and crude. Typically, text would be spoken at the time that it was displayed on a computer screen. This was adequate for many applications as text was written to the screen sequentially (like a teletype terminal or printer) rather than to single screen displays where characters can appear anywhere at any time as with most current computer applications. If large amounts of text were involved then significant delays would result as all of the text was spoken. For a sighted person the display of large amounts of text is not a problem as the eye can quickly scan the screen for information that could lead to the next action.

Development of screen readers in the 1980s significantly improved access for a blind person to computer applications. A screen reader usually works in two different modes: review, and live or application. In the review mode, the screen output from an application (word processor, spreadsheet, database) is 'frozen' and the text on the screen can be interrogated with a set of functions through the computer keyboard or a separate keypad. These functions are associated with a speech cursor that can be moved anywhere on the screen and characters, words or lines of text can be spoken. There are usually additional facilities to assist with 'navigation' around the screen such as the speaking of the x and y coordinates of the speech cursor, or directional and positional tones as the cursor is moved. Information about the attributes of a character can be reported, such as the colour or brightness. These review facilities provide detailed access to text or other ASCII characters on a screen but slowly because of the amount of navigation around the screen. Review mode is likely to be used by blind learners unfamiliar with a screen layout or by programmers. For effective access to computer applications, the live mode is better.

In live mode, the screen reader is programmed to match the display of a particular application to various speech windows and event markers. Speech windows define areas of the screen which can be read using a sequence of keystrokes, or automatically. These windows are used in conjunction with an event marker which is programmed to monitor changes in pre-defined locations on a screen. For complex screen displays there may be numerous speech windows and event markers that combine to provide a spoken output when appropriate. Skilful programming of screen readers minimises the amount of speech and maximises the amount of information required for the next action. This action should be as obvious as when a sighted person has a screen display. The output from the application at any one time is a single line of speech compared with a screen that might have 25 rows of 80 characters to convey information.

Speech windows, event markers, speech rates, and other features, together make up a speech environment which can be customised both for a computer application and an individual user. Good design of these environments can make all the difference between efficient and frustrating access for learners to a computer application.

Current software often uses a graphical user interface. Conventional screen reading techniques only give access to text on screens. Hence the heralding of these interfaces as a major step forward in user friendliness can only be described as a step backwards for blind people as the techniques associated with these interfaces are so visually dependent. Adaptation of graphical user interfaces is discussed more fully by Edwards (1991), and in a special edition of the *Journal of Human-Computer Interaction* (1989).

Screen readers have fostered widespread use of wordprocessors by blind learners, who can thereby produce printed text, perhaps for essays or examinations, even though handwriting is impossible or very difficult for them. For someone who prefers to retain copies in braille, computers can provide braille as well as print output.

ACCESS TO PRINTED TEXT FOR BLIND LEARNERS

Complementary to the needs of a learner to have a means of writing for essays, note taking and examinations, is the need to be able to access printed text such as books. Currently, the most popular way that blind people have access to books is by audiotape recordings made by sighted readers. These are commonly known as 'talking books'. A disadvantage of this method is that audiotape is a linear medium: reading reference material is particularly awkward, and frequent cross referencing, often essential for study purposes, is impossible.

Access to printed text through computers with speech output is not well developed. Hypertext software for personal computers offers new opportunities if it can be integrated with speech environments. In turn, this requires the development of new learning strategies. Hypertext systems contain features which, combined with speech output, offer blind learners new means of accessing, retrieving and interrogating information. Many publications are now produced electronically using word processors or desktop publishing: the complete text can be transferred easily to browsing and retrieval software such as a hypertext program.

AN EXPERIMENT WITH HYPERBOOK

During 1991, two students at the Open University received all of their course material on floppy disk in a form that could be read with hypertext software. *Hyperbook* was used as it is compatible with screen reading techniques. One student used speech output; the other used a refreshable braille display. In both cases they had detailed and non-linear access to the text, and extracts were taken for notes or essays. Neither of these techniques was available to them in the past when they used audio recordings. This development has been extended by the use of compact disc technology (CD-ROM) so that an *entire* course can be provided on one disc.

COMPACT DISC TECHNOLOGY

An established technology, electronic publishing, together with CD-ROM as the delivery medium provide new opportunities to make books accessible to people with a visual impairment. Many books are already available in an electronic form and can be readily transferred to a delivery medium such as CD-ROM. For those books only in print, optical character recognition systems can greatly assist in the transfer process. The re-keying of text is also an option. Numerous CD-ROMs are being produced by publishers that take advantage of the high storage capacity of the discs. With approximately 250,000 pages of A4 text per disc, the complete works of Shakespeare go on one disc. Encyclopedias and dictionaries have been transferred to this medium. By adding a speech interface such as a screen reader, blind people can access books that were difficult or impossible to access by any other means. This is particularly true of dictionaries which have often been produced in a shortened form to overcome the problem of the large amount of space taken up by a complete braille version.

A number of existing CD-ROMs have been made accessible to blind people using speech output. Examples include the Microsoft Bookshelf and the Times/Sunday Times CD-ROM. One of the advantages of this approach is that a speech synthesiser and memory resident speech software are the only additional items needed to be added to a conventional computer/CD-ROM system. The CD-ROM disc does not have to be adapted.

For people who are partially sighted, memory resident software can be added which provides magnification of text. A search facility on the computer can help considerably in locating text which may not be as easy with a printed book.

Having a wide range of books available on CD-ROM with speech/large character compatible retrieval software is an exciting prospect for learners with a visual impairment as it offers new opportunities to access the curriculum. It was significant for a UK Department for Education funded project at the Open University (in conjunction with the Royal National Institute for the Blind and the National Council for Educational Technology) which sought new ways of providing alternative access to the conventional library for visually impaired learners. The findings from this project follow.

OPENING UP THE LIBRARY FOR VISUALLY IMPAIRED LEARNERS PROJECT (NCET, 1993)

The aim of the project was to bring together existing CD-ROM technology and enabling technology (providing speech output and magnification) in a system suitable for use in an educational resource area which could be used independently by a visually impaired learner to improve access to resource material for the National Curriculum (Taylor, 1993).

The project involved four schools and one college. The age of learners involved varied from 7 to 17 years, and they had a wide range of visual impairments which ranged from inability to difficulty in reading printed text.

At the beginning of the project, three major problem areas affecting access to material for course work by visually impaired learners were identified. These areas were:

- the lack of learner control over selection of material from print resources,
- the difficulty and expense of providing resource material in large print, braille or audiotape format,
- the additional time required by visually impaired people to carry out some tasks.

The computer/CD-ROM workstation used in the project was straightforward enough for young children and less able older learners to use it at a simple level, with variable amounts of help. Additional features allowed more able and older learners to explore further and to use it independently.

OUTCOMES OF THE PROJECT

The project showed that putting together CD-ROM technology and enabling technology could make it possible for visually impaired learners to have:

- independent control of the search of, and retrieval from, huge amounts of information,
- immediate and low cost provision of resource material in large print or braille,
- the time previously spent searching for and manipulating information to be spent addressing the content.

The teaching staff were overwhelmingly positive about the benefits of independent access to resource material, finding it stimulating and a challenge, both to themselves and to their students. Where children are integrated into a mainstream secondary school, there is no longer any need for them to be excused homework because they can't use the library.

PROBLEMS AND SOLUTIONS

The issues of access to print based resources are difficult to separate under distinct headings, Figure 1 (Taylor, 1993) shows the three main areas and the overlap of issues.

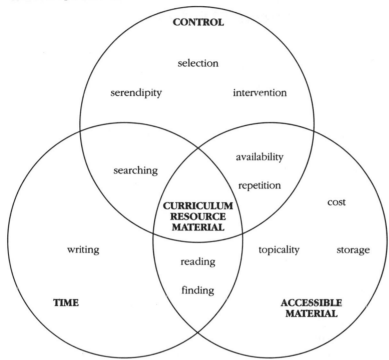

Figure 1

CONTROL – SELECTION AND INTERVENTION

Conventional methods of providing reference material for visually impaired learners rely on someone selecting material from available print resources and deciding which parts are appropriate. A section of material is then either brailled, enlarged or read aloud, directly or taped. This bypasses two stages of the search process, selecting a book from a shelf and selecting an extract from the book. The person who decides which material and how much of it, may be a teacher, a classroom assistant, a library assistant or a volunteer personal reader.

A pupil commented:

> It's nicer to sit down and listen without bothering anybody, not badgering someone to do tapes.

In a library, *locating* material often causes more problems than reading it once it has been correctly identified.

Whenever a person acts as an intermediary, there is a danger that they will unconsciously edit the material to save time, interpreting it according to their own understanding of what they are reading. They may get bored if asked to repeat something several times or the learner may feel that they are being judged adversely if they don't understand something the first time.

> It's embarrassing if you get behind with your work, they know where you've got to all the time.

The CD-ROM system gives the control back to the learner. It gives access to *all* of the original resource. The learner can decide which disc to use and the search strategy to adopt. The system will read out only what is there, as many times as necessary, leaving the learner to interpret it. Having found relevant material, they can decide what to to with it, save all or part for editing later, print it in large print or record selected spoken output onto tape for future reference.

Visually impaired children like using computers, they have been using them, often without any enabling technology, since they have been available in schools.

> Let's go and do it on the computer, we won't have to do any work then. [overheard by teacher]

CONTROL – SEARCHING FOR PLEASURE AND SERENDIPITY

An interesting phenomenon is the use of the CD-ROM to browse the encyclopedia discs for hobby information, an activity that is not possible with any other medium. One child's family had recently bought a pet garter snake, the pet shop was unable to supply much information, but both encyclopedias had articles about them and the Grolier Encyclopedia had a picture. Other 'hobby' topics found were radio wave bands, wind power, science fiction films and musical instrument sounds.

One of the exciting features of searching computer databases is finding information which is unexpected. Sighted people are surrounded by printed information which they can choose to ignore, including advertising hoardings, road signs, street names, book covers, food labels and posters; all make them aware of information which is available if it is needed. Blind people have to seek out information and may not be aware of how much material there is and what to ask for.

A teacher commented:

> It's no use asking a blind child if she would like access to a newspaper if she doesn't know what's in one.

Computer searches often give a list of article titles that relate to a word or phrase. Only one may be strictly relevant, but listening to this list may alert the learner to possibilities for exploring further.

> She has just lost what remaining sight she had for reading print and described the new CD-ROM system as 'brilliant – really good',

spending many a lunch hour browsing through the Grolier as well as working for her A-levels.

ACCESSIBLE MATERIAL

Educational material is accessible if it is in a medium which can be used by a visually impaired person. It may be braille, large or enhanced print, audiotape, tactile diagram or output from a computer with enabling technology. *The most effective medium for a particular task depends on the functional skills of the learner and the reason for needing access to the material.* For example, a science student needs a reference copy of values of fundamental constants, an English student needs a reference copy of a poem to be analysed, but both can make notes from audiotape versions of descriptive text.

AVAILABILITY AND TOPICALITY

Most resource centres have a limited stock of braille and large print. Much braille information is out of date, as it was produced before the introduction of the National Curriculum and topic-based learning. Teachers are constrained by what material is available, restricting their choice of topics.

Provision of new material depends on a person being available to key it in, photocopy it, braille it or make a tactile copy. It may take up to a year to fulfil a request to a braille transcription service for a new title. There are a limited number of people with the skills to produce braille and demand is high.

CD-ROM encyclopedias are available in recent editions and can often be updated at a reasonable cost. CD-ROM newspaper collections are available which are at most only 3 months old.

Electronic text is machine readable, once it has been created, computer based programs can be used to translate it into braille or large print. CD-ROM discs are a huge source of up-to-date information for translation into accessible media. This was recognised by some schools before the possibility of individual access to books was explored. One teacher reported:

> We wanted a class of braille and large print users to read a scene from Romeo and Juliet, it would have taken several months to get new copies of the complete play from the RNIB service. We just dumped the text of the scene from the CD-ROM and had five braille copies and three large print copies in time for the lesson the next day.

COST

Because of the high degree of manual processing and the small number of copies required, the cost per copy for braille is much higher than with conventional print. Once text extracted from a CD-ROM has been prepared for computer embossing and stored on disk, any number of copies can be made. The braille copies can be treated as disposable.

STORAGE

CD-ROM discs are small and light. They can be stored in caddies which can have a large print or braille label. A single disc can hold many volumes of a print encyclopedia or the complete works of an author, Shakespeare or Jane Austen for example. Up to 2,000 average sized books can be stored on one disc.

TIME – READING

If a learner can find a book, they can use an electronic reading machine (scanner) or closed circuit television (CCTV) to scan the text and read it out. A scanner is a slow and sometimes inaccurate tool, both are more appropriate for reading whole pages sequentially as in a novel, rather than for searching reference material. Reading braille, large print or reading with a low vision aid is slow.

> Some of our partially sighted pupils have a reading speed of about 40 words per minute which affects their concentration.

> We don't encourage all braille users to learn to use the braille dictionary and encyclopedia, it proved so difficult for some that they were very negative about it.

For some learners the physical act of reading is so slow and difficult that very little of what is read is absorbed. One pupil commented:

> You have to remember the [braille code] signs and then remember the words.

Although some additional skills are required to use a personal computer with enabling technology, *young learners or those with less ability can use the equipment at a simple level, and still get useful information*. By combining a simple menu access facility with with single word searches, the number of keystrokes and decisions can be significantly reduced.

By using the CD-ROM with appropriate enabling technology, the skills needed for reading braille, or reading with low vision aids, can be detached from the skills of understanding information presented as text.

TIME – SEARCHING

Finding specific information within a book or on a page can be time consuming for learners who do not have sufficient vision to scan for keywords.

Visually impaired learners can use the powerful searching features often available with CD-ROM applications to access information as fast as, and often faster than, sighted peers using a standard print library. This is breaking down a barrier to independence and equality of access. They still need to read more of the text sequentially to confirm that it is relevant, but the speed of narrowing down to a manageable amount of information provides the time for attending to the content.

EXAMPLE

Catherine, aged 15 years, is totally blind and integrated into a mainstream class for most lessons. Her class was beginning a project on Brazil. She came to the resource room for a session to look up information for herself. She was able to switch on the system and find the Information Finder disc from the stack of braille labelled discs on the desk. She also plugged in and switched on her portable computer (which has the same wordprocessing package as the main system). A single braille sheet of instructions had been prepared to remind her of the task and the instructions for using the Information Finder disc.

She found the article on Brazil, making no mistakes in the keypresses needed and was able to begin listening within a few minutes of sitting down at the computer.

She spent some time listening to the first page of the article before starting making notes. She listened to a few lines then made notes on her portable, in a similar way to a sighted child reading a textbook and making notes on paper. She demonstrated that she could also use Information Finder's outline feature to check the structure of the article.

The Information Finder interface is not very efficient for reading single lines, Catherine had to use screenreader to read single lines and to spell out words. She is beginning to learn about the more advanced features as she gains confidence. There is usually a member of the resource team in the room to help out if she gets stuck, but she spent most of the session getting on by herself.

Children supported by the Visual Impairment Unit who need to produce print can use one of a range of portable devices for wordprocessing which can be connected to a standard printer. Catherine is able to produce print copy for sighted teachers and group activities.

Children like Catherine are getting significantly better grades for their work since the CD-ROM system was installed.

SUPPORT MATERIAL AND TRAINING

Support material was provided at intervals during the project. Technical information was provided as appendices to more general instructions and advice for users of the workstation, the menu system and for each of the CD-ROM discs which could be used with speech output or magnification.

Staff have not made much systematic use of the material, preferring to use the system at the simplest level. As their use and confidence has grown, they are beginning to turn to the support material for information about additional features.

It was clear from the series of visits made by both project workers that *support for staff and learners is needed in small amounts over a period of time.* In a single session it is possible to show the straightforward features and overall strategies, but the use of more sophisticated features depends on what kind of task is being carried out. This is particularly true for the speech output and magnification programs which provide for individual needs and preferences and offer more than one route to the same information. Unless a teacher is aware of all the features of each program, they cannot introduce a new feature to a learner when it is needed.

ISSUES FOR TEACHERS

The CD-ROM workstation is another device for giving visually impaired learners the same opportunities as sighted peers. Its strength is in information processing, a task which can be very tedious using more traditional methods. The skill and experience of a teacher is required to analyse the reasons for setting a particular task and to determine which tool is most appropriate for each learner.

Topic work can be used to reinforce conventional communication methods, reading and handwriting using low vision aids or braille. However, for those who are so slow that they cannot yet process useful amounts of information, the CD-ROM workstation frees them from the need to read or write and enables them to concentrate on the content of the topic material.

For some specialist schools for visually impaired children, time and resource constraints have lead to teaching styles which rely heavily on 'pre-digested' material. The CD-ROM system offers an opportunity to develop new methods which are closer to those used to teach the National Curriculum in mainstream schools.

The computer workstation used for the project has been designed to give simple access to information as it appears on the screen and learners are already using it to carry out tasks which they could not do without the technology. It is still not possible for learners dependent on speech output to scan text in the same way as a print reader does. There are features within the screen reader program which speed up reading, increasing the speed of the speech or ignoring words such as 'and' and 'the'.

As they progress, learners need to be able to use these tools to enhance their basic use and to develop strategies for dealing with reference material. Schools which are using enabling technology need to consider where in their school is the most appropriate setting for teaching the use of speech output and screen magnification, in the same way as they take responsibility for teaching braille and mobility training.

INFORMATION TECHNOLOGY (IT) SKILLS AND NATIONAL CURRICULUM

The National Curriculum expects learners at all levels to have opportunities to use a computer to process information. Most of the CD-ROM programs are very large databases, some have very powerful searching features. They can be used to teach all aspects of the search process, as well as to retrieve and process information. The wordprocessor can be used to amend information, organise it, prepare it for presentation and store it in an appropriate format.

The workstation could also be used for other aspects of IT, the same enabling technologies can be used effectively with communication, database creation and spreadsheet programs.

SKILLS FOR FURTHER EDUCATION AND EMPLOYMENT

The use of the same or similar enabling technology as that used within the project is becoming standard in further education and employment. Visually impaired people can use industry standard computer programs, enhancing integration and equality.

KEY FINDINGS FROM THE PROJECT

- Independent access to books can be achieved for blind and partially sighted learners.

- Using CD-ROM as the delivery medium, electronic books can be accessed with current enabling technologies (speech output, screen magnification and braille).

- Experiences of pupils and students suggest that accessing books through the CD-ROM system can be both informative and enjoyable.

- A key feature of using CD-ROM to access text is the facility to find information quickly. This contrasts with other media, such as braille, where the reading of text is improved but information is more difficult to find.

- Searching for words and phrases often leads to them being found in an unexpected context, thereby broadening a learners understanding of the words and phrases and how they are used. This is an enriching experience which is particularly relevant to this way of accessing text.

- Teachers require training and support for the most effective use of a CD-ROM workstation. In particular, the integration of this resource into a school or college means that teaching methods may need to change.

- The findings of the project confirm the view that the information technology content of most training courses for teachers of visually impaired pupils should be more extensive.

- The current range of materials on CD-ROM is limited both in content and suitability for all age ranges. This is an issue which may be resolved with the increase in the number of publishers becoming involved in producing CD-ROM titles.

- There is a need to influence publishers of CD-ROM titles to ensure that the potential for access for learners with disabilities is maximised. (CD-ROM technology is advantageous to many learners who have difficulty accessing conventional print.)

- If publishers can provide unformatted text files on a CD-ROM disc, it is feasible to create braille and large print copies as required.

REFERENCES

Hawkridge, D. and Vincent, T. (1992) *Learning Difficulties and Computers: Access to the Curriculum*, London, Jessica Kingsley.

Edwards, A.D.N. (1991) *Speech Synthesis: Technology and Disabled People*, London, Chapman.

Edwards, A.D.N. (1989) *Journal of Human-Computer Interaction.*

NCET (1993) *Opening up the Library for Visually Impaired Learners*, Coventry, NCET.

Taylor, M.E. (1993) *CD-ROM for Blind and Partially Sighted Learners: Accessing the Curriculum (Report 4 – Evaluation)*, Internal Report.

SUPPORTING RESOURCE BASED LEARNING

Josie Taylor and Diana Laurillard

Institute of Educational Technology, The Open University

1 INTRODUCTION

1.1 WHAT IS RESOURCE BASED LEARNING?

Resource based learning (RBL) means open access, self-directed learning from a large information source. Imagine a student going into a large library armed with a note-pad, pens and a couple of questions. The library represents the resource in various formats – books are the first obvious one, but there may also be journals, magazines and newspapers; reference items such as telephone directories, catalogues, dictionaries. There may also be other facilities in the form of video tapes, audio-cassettes, computer databases and so on. These can be accessed in a variety of ways – by walking along looking at shelves, by consulting an on-line service, using microfiches and so on. At the end of the day the student hopes to emerge with answers to the questions, or at least clutching an armful of books or papers and notes from which the answers can be derived. These are the fundamentals of resource based learning – or independent learning – question formulation, searching, finding and integrating information.

Resource-based learning has been used in education for many years. The value of RBL is that the learner's active involvement in every stage of the learning process puts them in the position of being able to negotiate knowledge, not merely receive it. They have to develop the argument from the basis of evidence collected, and integrate different aspects of the subject matter together in a coherent argument, not merely reiterate someone else's construction. Its value is recognised throughout the educational system. At primary level this is reflected in tasks where pupils gather information about a topic and record what they have found in a topic folder, right through to post-graduate level where students use the resources at their disposal to create new knowledge articulated in a thesis.

The recent rapid growth and development in new technologies has affected resource based learning in several ways. First, by providing easy access to much larger and more diverse information sources than ever before, it is easier for all of us to find and use information which previously was only available to a relatively small number of scholars. Second, the ability to combine, in one application, not only text and pictures, but also video and audio, challenges accepted ways of presenting information, and augments our perception of the role of different modalities for learning. We can search across several types of data sources, audio-visual as well as text – e.g. an interactive videodisc of pictures in the Louvre, a CD-ROM of annotated slides of mammals, a musical piece linked to a graphical display of its score, etc. Third, we can do things with new technologies which previously were impossible, or would have taken a very long time. For example, John Diamond in his article in *The Guardian* (4 October 1993) explains how, using his CD-ROM version of the Oxford English Dictionary he can find

> ... all the words in the English language which have come from the Algonquin Indians or from the Hindi or the Yiddish .. And which were also used by Jane Austen .. And which disappeared after 1900. To carry out searches like that on the paper OED would take literally years: on CD it takes perhaps 40 seconds.

The value to the student is that they can enter into some academic debates in a way that would only have been available to scholars with months to spend on library searches. The student can now be equipped not only to make a claim such as 'Algonquin words began entering the English language after 1800...' but could also challenge another scholar's claim that 'Jane Austen never used Yiddish', by judicious juggling of the appropriate databases. Whether such fragments are worthwhile, of course, is a separate, though important, issue.

Supporters of RBL would argue that it is an extremely satisfying and rewarding way of learning. Students can follow a line of enquiry which they find interesting, each new discovery being their own. Control of the learning process is in their hands and they feel free to approach the task proceeding at their own pace in a way which suits them, rather than one imposed by someone else. This sense of personal engagement with information, knowledge and learning can be motivating for adults and children alike.

Sceptics of developments in resource-based learning have argued that the mere existence of, what is in effect, an electronic library is no guarantee that learning will take place. Without teaching, learning does not occur spontaneously, they would argue. One of the most difficult aspects of RBL (or learning of any sort in fact) is knowing how to ask the right question and how to recognise an appropriate answer. Empowering the learner is all very well, but sensibly taking control of one's own learning process carries with it the responsibility for understanding how to specify attainable goals, realising the overall aims of the study programme and knowing how to assess and evaluate one's progress. These things normally fall to the teacher who is specially trained to accomplish them. Removing control from the teacher complicates the process of assessment and evaluation of learning, and learners are at risk of becoming adrift in a sea of unmarshalled data from which the disempowered teacher cannot rescue them. So what is the teacher to teach? What are the roles of teacher and pupil in this new environment? How can we be sure that self-directed learners will cover the curriculum? How can student progress be examined if everyone is doing something different?

RBL, mediated by technology, therefore presents quite a challenge to accepted views of how to teach, what to teach, and the politics of control and assessment in schools and classrooms. Capitalising on the opportunities offered by new technologies in the areas of resource based learning could involve major shifts from traditional styles of pedagogy, rethinking education from the politics of the role of education in society, through to the organisation of educational institutions, right down to the function of the teacher and the minutiae of classroom organisation.

In what follows, we outline the sets of skills needed to accomplish RBL and discuss these in relation to studies of new technologies in the classroom. From this analysis, it should be possible to form a judgement about the use of RBL as an educational method. The discussion is framed in the classroom context (primary and secondary) because this is where change is happening fastest at present.

2 ANALYSING RESOURCE BASED LEARNING

We shall focus on two aspects of resource based learning in the classroom. The first is concerned with looking at the user in relation to the system. How do learners perceive the system, how do they interact with it and what do they need to know? The second is concerned with the overall task in hand, and looks at how children need to be able to cope with the information which such systems deliver.

2.1 LEARNERS USING THE SYSTEM

There are various ways of delivering the resources to be used in RBL, through multimedia systems, interactive video-disc, CD-ROMs and so on. For our discussion, the physical apparatus is not a matter of major concern because we are interested in how learners interact with systems, how activities are organised around systems, and what effect this has on learning.

It suffices to describe the sort of scenario in the classroom in which RBL might take place. Imagine a small group of children sitting in front of a computer screen which is presenting various kinds of information in different windows. The children select what to do next, or input a response to a question by typing at a keyboard, clicking with a mouse, swiping with a bar-code reader on a sheet of paper, or perhaps using a touch sensitive screen to indicate responses. The information resource is typically contained on a disc whose contents may or may not be mediated by a computer. There will always be an electronic 'environment' which the learner moves around. Typically a series of menus is offered for the learner to select where to go and what to do next. Calling up different applications or packages may mean that the environment changes as that application begins to run.

Consider the task these children are engaged in – they need to get on to the machine, checking that it is loaded with appropriate discs, and then to run whatever application they need. They have to consider what to do, where to go and how to get there, perhaps by reference to a worksheet. Having arrived, they need to engage with the task they intended to accomplish, negotiating with the environment to find the information they want. At one level it seems simple enough and, you might argue, children's video games make all these demands, so we might expect the majority of children to find these activities routine, perhaps even trivial.

2.2 LEARNERS AND INFORMATION

But there are difficulties and to understand them we need to bear in mind that, in general, knowing what questions to ask, and how to ask them is a very important skill. Most of us are not very good at asking the right questions at the right level of detail to get intelligent answers first time round. We tend to iterate, or go round several times, refining our questions and developing a sense of what we want to know. Sometimes we find that we have had an answer all along, but that we hadn't spotted it. These skills of understanding how to ask questions and how to recognise answers need developing. This is especially true for children, who have a natural propensity to enjoy themselves, and given a stimulating interface with entertaining video-clips and moving graphics, will keep themselves happy for a surprisingly long time. Whether or not they are learning anything useful is heavily dependent on how well-developed their information handling skills are. In order to support the development of these skills, we need to analyse their component parts.

2.3 INFORMATION HANDLING SKILLS FOR RBL

Like any complex learning task, RBL can be examined from several perspectives. Each perspective highlights different types of activity or skill required to accomplish goals at that level. These are not phases in learning, or stages in the process of RBL. They are views of the process, each one associated with a task, and each one having a set of skills or knowledge needed to accomplish that task. Each level shades into the next, and divisions between task areas are not always clean. However, a learner must recognise or master all of them to some degree of proficiency, in order to succeed.

- **Operation** – run the physical system (e.g. what buttons to press, how to switch things on, protocols for what gets loaded first, how to log on, interactions between peripherals, what runs under what system).

- **Navigation** – run the software (e.g. how applications run, how different packages interface with one another, how to respond to the system when it asks questions, how to keep track of places visited, and how to get back, how to retrace steps; how to jump from one place to another; how/where to make notes).

- **Investigation** – do the appropriate question framing/search/find (e.g. how to ask a sensible question in the context; identify suitable goals; recognise what kind of information is actually relevant versus what is interesting but irrelevant; interpret information to spot concordance, dissonance, variation; analyse information to recognise potential answers).

- **Reflection** – satisfactorily integrate the information thus found into project work or final write-up (e.g. go back to original task, evaluate whether enough information has been gathered, analyse and evaluate the material, integrate and compose).

Whilst working, a pupil will need to do all these things at different times, iterating between them, doing a bit of each here and there. Thus, we can see that supporting RBL involves looking both at what the learner is doing at all these levels, and ensuring that the hardware/software helps and does not hinder them.

Of course, it is crucial to bear in mind that learners do not learn in a vacuum. Other factors will influence performance, such as whether pupils are working alone, in pairs, in small groups or as a whole class, and the general ethos of the classroom. But having outlined what learners need to know to do RBL, we now examine some views from the literature about how such systems should be integrated in the educational sector, and what effect this might have on schools.

2.4 VIEWS ON THE USES OF NEW TECHNOLOGIES FOR RBL

Romiszowski (1993) draws a distinction between instructional systems and information dissemination systems. In an instructional system the teaching component presents information, evaluates the student's performance and feeds that back into the interaction to improve the quality of learning. Information dissemination systems, however, do not address the issue of whether or not the student has learned. Instead they focus on content, organisation, structure and presentation. In resource based learning, using information dissemination systems, the role of the machine is to provide the vast resource of subject matter for pupils to use. Romiszowski suggests that students' motivation for studying subjects is not enhanced through this type of use in the classroom because it is associated with a curriculum of standard content which all students have to work through. He claims this does not elicit emotional involvement with the subject area – instead

> ... we are seeking to empower each student to select areas of interest and follow them up by accessing relevant information. However, unless students have some goals, what will they choose to follow up? Surely there is still a great need for the creation of motivation through engagement of the student's interest and passion for learning in the topic. (p. 68)

He suggests that topic work ought to be conducted on a series of small multimedia machines, where the activity is prefaced by 'passionate front-end introductions' to sub-sets of content area. These presentations could exploit the affective elements of the media component, which, after all, are used to excite the emotions in entertainment. Whether or not we agree with Romiszowski's conclusions, students certainly need support to clearly articulate the goals which they are working towards – whether those are determined by the teacher, by the curriculum, or by students themselves.

In terms of our framework, this would mean support for both investigative and reflective activities. There may well be a very wide spread of goals associated with reflection ranging from high level motivation or emotional engagement with the subject of study, through to the relatively pragmatic. For example: 'I want to study mathematics because it holds the key to so many other subject areas' is much more general than: 'I want to get my maths A-level because I need it to get the job I want'. This in turn is very different from: 'What do I need to do to get this project finished today so I can go on a trip tomorrow?' However, it is possible to help students generate achievable objectives from very high level goals without destroying inspiration in the process, and to take them through the process of linking these to investigation – what you actually need to do to search the material to find what you want.

Heppell (1993) presents a view of the way new technologies should be integrated into schools. After an introduction to the developing use of computers in school and how pedagogy might respond to accommodate new technologies, he offers a developmental taxonomy of the modes of interaction that integrated media should support. He suggests that, first, integrated media can be used as a *narrative* form (much in the style of current television and film) which leaves the user in a passive role of exerting only 'stop, start, watch, listen' choices. This may be fine for introductory materials, or for providing overviews. Second, it can be used in *interactive* mode, where users do much more in the way of browsing and searching, which is important to support the development of information handling skills. Third, in the *participative* mode, users can construct their own multimedia products as well as use ready-made ones. These various functions are not 'pure' – multimedia is often delivered using combinations of modes, though Heppel would like to see more development in participative software.

But what is it like using RBL in the classroom? How do systems interface with existing classroom practice? Plowman (1988) provides a teacher's perspective on the nature of, in this case, interactive video in classrooms. She contrasts the common understanding amongst teachers of the benefits of 'active learning' with the forms of interactivity which the IV system allows. Active learning, as practised in primary schools already, normally engages not only the minds, but also the bodies of young children, who are expected to move around and outside of the classroom to find evidence, answers and information from a variety of sources. Teachers plan lessons carefully to make sure that children engage with many different tasks and learning situations. IV systems, on the other hand, often engage the child in a series of multiple choice questions which can often be answered in stock ways. Knowledge is presented in 'frame-sized' bites, is segmented, fragmented and often interrupted by text insertions. This can present difficulties to children as they try to integrate and consolidate the material. In our analytic framework, therefore, children are practising navigation skills but are not spontaneously developing the higher-order skills associated with investigation and reflection.

The importance of looking at real learners using a system cannot be over-emphasised. Laurillard (1987) discusses the nature of meaningful and constructive 'decision' activity, and the complex analysis of both student behaviour and domain information which it requires. Understanding the learner's experience with a system is often extremely revealing in terms of uncovering hidden difficulties with software. Laurillard discusses the pedagogical design of interactive media, and articulates a basic law of interactive design that 'quality of interaction determines quality of thinking'. She illustrates through a worked example the kinds of analysis which an instructional designer needs to go through to produce interaction events which result in meaningful learning for students. This analysis depends upon proper evaluation of the system in use with real learners, so that observations can be analysed and the findings fed back into the design process. Unfortunately, most applications have yet to be evaluated at all, let alone in a way which improves design.

Nevertheless, it is important when discussing the impact of new technologies to look at real users in real settings in order to assess effectiveness and usability, rather than describe potential. To this end we look to the various evaluation studies which have been carried out in schools.

3 SUPPORTING RESOURCE BASED LEARNING IN SCHOOLS

Disc-based materials for RBL are proliferating fast, and lessons in usability are being learned. Recent evaluations of interactive technologies for RBL, have all shown how important it is to provide adequate support for the learner (Watson et al., 1993; Steadman et al., 1992; Laurillard et al., 1994). This does not mean 'instructing' them, but making sure that the learning session is conducted in a way that is conducive to genuine learning benefits. We discuss how this might be done in terms of: *access, objectives, the teacher's role, and group work.*

All the following points are drawn from these evaluation studies.

3.1 ACCESS

Any amount of information is limited in its usefulness if the learner, or user of the system does not know how or where to find relevant material. It would seem obvious and essential to have comprehensive and effective documentation for the contents of discs or databases, but unfortunately, this is not always the case. Manufacturers have not always produced adequate routine documentation, but this situation is bound to change as users express their frustration. A comprehensive set of documents ought to include at the very least an index and some amount of cataloguing of items. Really useful documentation would also cover cross-referencing and perhaps hypertext or use of hot words to make searching for related items easier.

It is interesting to note that in a recent national evaluation of the use of IV in schools, teachers spent a good deal of time familiarising themselves with materials on interactive videodiscs, and some schools benefited by undertaking the detailed cataloguing of items themselves. This allowed profitable cross-curricular links to be made – e.g. use of a video clip of birds landing on a lake, found on the maths disc, in a poetry class. Similarly, some of the sequences of track athletes used primarily for maths tasks were found to have great value in sports sessions. What this means is that the material is not just a vast resource for learners to access, but that teachers can be proactive in searching out material which will enhance their teaching. This kind of flexible use ensures that new technologies are incorporated into teachers' planning, and form part of the bedrock of good teaching in a school.

But these kinds of uses depend on deployment of staff time and energy within school, or on happy accidents – not all schools or users have the time to browse through vast information sources, and manufacturers should not expect this.

3.2 DEVELOPING SUITABLE AIMS AND OBJECTIVES

In traditional teaching, the aims and objectives of courses of study are givens. Typically, teachers derive classroom work from a plan which is based on agreed curriculum goals. Activities are developed which enable pupils to engage in the work gradually and in stepwise fashion, making assessment and evaluation a reasonably straightforward enterprise. Students are informed about what they are to do, how they are to do it, what the expected outcomes are and when the exercise should be completed. There is often some degree of flexibility, and opportunities are provided for pupils to make choices within this framework, but there is rarely a point at which a pupil can decide (albeit temporarily) to reject the teacher's aims and objectives in order to pursue an interesting line of thought on their own.

It is equally true that, although RBL is usually project based, students are expected to take a more active role in drawing up their own aims and objectives: they cannot simply pursue whatever course of study takes their fancy. Students are expected to work from a general description of what needs to be covered and usually some examples of questions they ought to be able to answer or discuss when they have completed their project. They are also normally aware of the format submitted work should take. Students will need to understand how to take this information and convert it into a list of manageable aims and achievable objectives which the teacher accepts as reasonable. The process needs careful support and, if children are to reap the benefit of 'appropriating' their learning, and taking more control, then teachers need to consider carefully how they will intervene and, perhaps more importantly, how they will withdraw without leaving their pupils floundering.

Control of learning was raised as an issue earlier in the discussion, and we suggested that it is helpful for learners to feel that they are in charge of their learning. It helps to cultivate a sense of ownership, and foster a mature, scholarly and reflective approach to learning which will be valuable throughout life, not just in school. The only pitfall to avoid is noted by Plowman (op. cit.) who highlights problems associated with the illusion of control that systems sometimes engender.

In the classroom the reality is that control shifts from teacher to learner, but in a way which the teacher determines. By designing worksheets and carefully setting up tasks, teachers can carefully engineer situations in which children feel that decision making is in their hands and that they are in control, but which the teacher is directing. This makes it a safe environment for children to be exuberant and engage in exploration. The teacher may decide that in order to promote operational and navigational skills, free access to the system is appropriate. The subject-specific learning involved in investigation and reflection needs a closer involvement on the part of the teacher.

3.3 ROLE OF TEACHER AND MATERIALS

Helping learners acquire information handling skills can be a demanding task for the teacher. Instead of focusing on the content of learning, the teacher needs to focus on the process of learning, and, paradoxically, this may mean that learners apparently learn less for a while. For example, it is important that learners make mistakes at some level, for this is often a very effective way of developing strategies. The temptation to intervene as a learner heads off into probable disaster is overwhelming, though an absolute – or, worse, repeated – failure is unlikely to stimulate even the most dogged pupil. So it is a matter of degree. The teacher needs to develop a sense of when to intervene to help avoid catastrophe, but otherwise to allow productive mistakes to occur in order for pupils to develop strategies for coping. A balance needs to be struck with the type of intervention that is most appropriate. Snatching the keyboard away and typing arcane formulae into the machine to retrieve a situation may save time, but is unlikely to help learners if they are confronted with such a situation again, and may only encourage dependency.

Teachers may find themselves acting more as therapists than instructors. The teacher helps pupils to debug their strategies and techniques for accessing information, offering advice and useful hints, but allowing students to develop their own way of handling their learning. When things have gone wrong, teachers may find themselves conducting quasi-therapeutic sessions with pupils: 'Why did you think it was important to do that? What did you think was going to happen? What were your expectations? Where's your plan and list of goals? What were you doing just before the machine crashed? How would you like to interpret that experience?' and so on. This kind of interaction is much more personal than formal chalk and talk teaching, and in a classroom centred around RBL, tutoring to individuals or small groups is liable to become commonplace. Indeed some schools already operate this kind of classroom procedure based around project work even when new technologies are not driving the process.

Teachers can play an important supporting role as intermediary between student and information. Worksheets developed by the teacher are an important prop for students to use which can usefully provide examples of achievable goals. Some forms of worksheet can be used by the teacher not only to structure the task in which pupils are engaged, but also to limit access to other parts of the resource or to help as navigational guides. Worksheets which demand little more than a ticked box in response to multiple choice questions will not help learners draw the best out of the resource. Whatever the overall purpose of the worksheet, teachers need to ensure that they provide a suitable context, and clear aims for students to work to, and that they engage children with the material on the disc. A well-designed worksheet can also provide an effective transition between off-line and on-line work.

3.4 COLLABORATION AND GROUP WORK

Learners can also help each other. One of the claims for use of new technologies in the classrooms has always been that they facilitate groupwork and foster collaborative working practices in children. Whether or not groups of pupils work better together using new technology in the classroom depends on how the task has been set up by the teacher, and the general classroom ethos. If children are used to group work, then technology can enhance it. If not, then children may end up working co-operatively, but basically independently. New technology will not bring about a spontaneous change of working patterns unless positive action is taken to stimulate it.

However, it is sometimes the case that children know as much, or even more, about how to set up and run the equipment than the teacher does. And of course children are often at their most enthusiastic when they perceive their own effectiveness in such matters. Capitalising on this situation is an opportunity not to be missed, and a form of cascade training is frequently used in classrooms, where a slightly more expert pupil trains another in various methods or techniques. This approach can work very well, provided that the teacher monitors what is being taught. For example, when the teaching child is giving procedural instruction on how to set up the system, load discs and access materials, there is unlikely to be a problem. However, one child instructing another about conceptual matters – e.g. on how to do maths problems presented by the discs – may not be so reliable. Some procedural training might also be simply undesirable – such as how to sidestep having to answer a question posed by the system, or how to corrupt information. In terms of our analysis of RBL, peer support for operation and navigation would easily be taught using cascade training. Learning investigation and reflection might need much closer supervision. Collaborating in pairs or small groups may be very productive for these higher-order activities, but children need to understand what exactly the task is, and what responsibility they have in the group.

4 CONCLUSION

In our discussion we have established that new technologies may offer all kinds of opportunities and pitfalls for learners, and resource based learning inherits most of them. The reported case studies show that children need support and help in order to reap the benefits of RBL, and that the best learning takes place in an environment which has been well-structured by the teacher, however that structure manifests itself. It might be in preparatory work, it might be through worksheets, or it might be through working with peers, or a combination of all these. So the role of the teacher turns out to be a crucial determinant of success for children engaged in RBL. This nicely contradicts expectations that teachers would find themselves redundant as new technology becomes incorporated in the classroom.

It seems inevitable that developments in new technology will change our view of learning throughout society. New technologies are enabling many educational establishments to make good use of distance learning techniques, and schools are no exception in encouraging independent learning. But teaching learners not only *what* to learn, but *how* to learn (Plowman, *op.cit.*) is the key to real empowerment for children and adults alike. It will become increasingly important for everyone to develop effective information handling skills, and to engage in resource based learning in order to take advantage of our information-rich environment, otherwise we will just find ourselves overwhelmed. Children are not frightened by the technology in a way that their parents might have been. We must make sure that this confidence is carried forward productively so that children can make their own judgements about the relative values of different kinds of information which they wish to access on demand, rather than receive anything which the commercial sector pushes towards them.

REFERENCES

Diamond, J. (1993) 'Small and perfectly informed', *The Guardian*, 4 October 1993.

Heppel, S. (1993) 'Eyes on the horizon, feet on the ground?', in C. Latchem, J. Williamson and L. Henderson-Lancett, *Interactive Multimedia: Practice and promise,* London, Kogan Page, pp. 97-114.

Laurillard, D. (1987) 'Pedagogical design for interactive video' in D M Laurillard (ed) *Interactive Media: Working Methods and Practical Applications,* Ellis Horwood Ltd.

Laurillard, D., Baric, L., Chambers, P., Easting G., Kirkwood, A., Plowman, L., Russell, P. and Taylor, J., (1993/4) *Interactive Video and Associated Technology in the School Curriculum, Evaluation Report,* The Open University/National Council for Educational Technology, NCET, Coventry.

Plowman, L. (1988) 'Active learning and interactive video: a contradiction in terms?'*Programmed Learning and Educational Technology*, 25, (4), pp. 289-293.

Romiszowski, A. (1993) 'Developing interactive multimedia courseware and networks: Some current issues', in C. Latchem, J. Williamson & L. Henderson-Lancett, *Interactive Multimedia: Practice and promise,* London, Kogan Page, pp. 57-78.

Steadman, S., Nash, C. and Eraut, M. (1992) *CD-ROM in Schools Scheme, Evaluation Report,* University of Sussex/National Council for Educational Technology, NCET, Coventry.

Watson, D., Cox, M. and Johnson, D. (1993) *The ImpacT Report: An evaluation of the impact of information technology on children's achievements in primary and secondary schools,* Dept. for Education and King's College London.

Constructivist Learning Theories and IT

Ann Jones
Institute of Educational Technology, The Open University

Introduction

This article is concerned with constructivist theories of learning and how they relate to the design and use of IT in education. Not surprisingly, much of the work on learning theories comes from developmental psychology, and it is mainly this that I shall draw on. Changes in the way that cognitive development has been viewed and accounted for during the past thirty years have been paralleled to some extent in changes in views and theories of *adult* learning, but less so in theories of teaching. Theories of teaching and instructional design often bear little resemblance to ideas about learning and I shall argue that it is accounts of cognition, of learning, that will be most helpful in analysing what is happening when learners engage with information technology of all kinds, rather than accounts of teaching.

Why should we be concerned with theories of learning if we are interested in using IT for learning? The most obvious possibility is that knowledge about how people learn can help us think about how to teach them, so learning theories might lead or underpin the design of IT tools, e.g. software. However when educational IT is examined there is often little evidence of it being grounded in any learning theory: the exception being LOGO and other microworlds and particular pieces of software such as Bubble Dialogue which will be discussed later. Instructional theories, though, which have been influential in American educational software design, have in the main drawn on behaviourist ideas which are not discussed in this article. Another possibility is that although software designers are not consciously basing their design on a particular theory of learning, they will of course make assumptions about learning, and particular assumptions may make effective learning more or less likely to happen. I believe that the strongest argument for looking at learning theories, however, is that theories help us to account for how people learn and use IT: they help to suggest what to look for ways of analysing and making sense of what's already there. For example, many educational uses of IT, currently, are collaborative or co-operative. Rather than a program being designed for an individual user, the idea is that two or more people are engaged in the exercise - and although some of the reasons for having machines shared between users may be pragmatic (such as saving money) I shall look at how this resonates with changes in learning theories and claims for the benefits of learning in groups. But we begin in the next section by looking at two theories from developmental psychology.

THE INFLUENCE OF DEVELOPMENTAL THEORIES OF LEARNING

PIAGET: A COGNITIVE APPROACH

The theories discussed in this section are part of developmental psychology, which, like any field, has a particular set of terms which are used with precise meaning. It is often such specialised language that is described as 'jargon' either because it is unfamiliar, or because it is felt that such specialised or technical language is unnecessary. As far as possible the use of such terms will be avoided, and explanations will be given when they do have to be used.

There are three ideas in Piaget's work which are important when we look at how it can help us to analyse learning with IT. These are the idea of *active construction*, of *structuring knowledge* and of *stages of development*. In Piaget's theory children are seen as active in their learning: through interacting with the world around them, they develop and refine their ideas about the world.

Piaget emphasised the way in which knowledge is structured and organised, the way in which these knowledge structures are changed in order for new information to be added to them, and how children's perceptions of their experiences are themselves modified to fit into these structures. He also emphasised that children are qualitatively different in the way they think from adults: they are not just smaller versions with less knowledge, but view the world in quite a different way, and the way they think is determined by their stage of development. In Piaget's stage theory he describes development as involving a progression through three main stages of thinking, each of which is characterised by increasingly logical underlying structures and increasing organisation. He saw children's thinking developing from early sensorimotor beginnings, through concrete reasoning in early school years to abstract reasoning in adolescence and beyond.

The three developmental stages that are relevant to school age children are the pre-operational stage (approximately ages two to seven); concrete operational (age seven to age eleven) and formal operational (from approximately age 12). Piaget's *pre-operational* thinkers cannot yet deal with thinking in a formal or abstract way: they need to be able to think about real or concrete objects, thus they are helped by having concrete objects to count with, for example. When they are older, they will be able to internalise some of the actions that they have carried out on the world, and solve problems without recourse to the physical world. Piaget's most famous experiments, of course, in terms of his stage theory, are those of conservation, where, for example, he showed how pre-operational children could pour liquid from one container to another thinner but taller container, and not realize that the amount stayed the same. Much of the focus of his work was on mathematical thinking and so he investigated how children dealt with essentially mathematical ideas such as grouping, adding, combining, etc. Concrete operational children who are aged about seven to eleven are able to carry on actions on the world, such as combining and ordering things, and they can carry out such actions in their minds, that is symbolic actions. They know that some actions are reversible and they understand conservation. In the final stage, children, like adults, can manipulate ideas rather than things:

> The formal operational thinker can entertain hypotheses, deduce consequences and use these deductions to put hypotheses to the test.' (Donaldson, p. 139)

These three ideas *active construction, structuring knowledge* and *stages of development,* have been drawn on extensively in education and in using computers in education in particular. For example Davis remarks how:

> The stress on the stage-like nature of cognition has given support to the notions of readiness-children will only learn effectively if their educational experiences are suitably matched to their current level of understanding. (Davis, 1991, p19)

Schools have ensured that young children have many opportunities to interact with their environment, and have been given plenty of concrete materials to help develop their mathematical understanding. In using computers in education, Seymour Papert, who worked with Jean Piaget in Geneva, has been particularly influenced by Piaget's ideas and has argued that we should design educational software which will help to develop children's thinking. In particular he applied these arguments to the use of the programming language LOGO, which he claims can benefit children in their mathematical thinking. Papert lays out his philosophy of learning in Mindstorms (Papert, 1980). Essentially, he claims that LOGO provides a culture which helps to make abstract mathematical concepts simple and concrete so that the child can relate them to his or her existing knowledge and fit them into his or her knowledge structures.

One metaphor which has been a strong influence on Papert's work is how children learn to talk, a process which happens without any formal, organised learning, and which is fostered by the environment. Papert used this analogy in describing 'Mathland' - 'a context which is to learning Maths what living in France is to learning French.' Another model in Papert's mind was the way his own concrete experience of gears as a child helped to foster and develop mathematical thinking. From the time he was very young, he had been intensely interested in cars, and in particular the gearbox and especially the differential. Once he understood how gears worked, playing with gears became a favourite occupation, and led him into working out exactly how such systems as the differential gear worked. Later, gears served as a model for abstract mathematical ideas:

> I saw multiplication tables as gears, and my first brush with equations in two variables (e.g., $3x + 4y = 10$) immediately evoked the differential. By the time I had made a mental gear model of the relation between x and y, figuring how many teeth each gear

needed, the equation had become a comfortable friend. (Papert, 1980, pp vi-vii)

The gears themselves were therefore be used to think about formal systems: they served as 'objects to think with'. LOGO provides learners with a 'turtle', as part of its turtle graphics. When younger children use LOGO they often use a floor turtle. This is a small device on wheels into which a pen is fitted, and it is placed on paper, so that when it is moved (via LOGO commands), it leaves a trace of its movements. LOGO instructions direct the turtle's movements; for example RIGHT 90 turns the turtle 90 degrees to the right (clockwise) and FORWARD 50 moves it forward by 50 units. Such instructions can be combined into a program. For older children and adults, the turtle becomes the pointer on the screen: an arrowhead whose direction and movements are again directed by LOGO instructions. Papert sees the turtle in the programming language LOGO as being equivalent to the gears he became so fond of: an object to think with, to help make the formal concrete. The idea is that through using the turtle children can explore mathematical shapes, and ideas. The need for the turtle, and LOGO itself arises because, in Papert's view, although our culture is very rich in material which helps the child to develop certain aspects of mathematical and logical thinking (counting, conservation, reversibility) it is poor in providing materials to help the child develop other aspects of mathematics such as the ideas involved in geometry.

Papert's claims for LOGO being helpful in the development of high level thinking skills and abstract thought have been extensively evaluated and Littleton (1993) summarises the main three points as being first that programming in LOGO does not necessarily lead to better problem solving capabilities; second, any cognitive gains are more likely to be found when LOGO activities are carefully structured by the teacher and third, that the experience of working with LOGO has a profound effect on children's social interaction. This last finding about the social effects of LOGO was one of the early findings that has been supported by later research. A more recent use of Piagetian theory in education, therefore, is to see how it can explain the seeming benefits of some kinds of group use of the computer.

WORKING IN GROUPS WITH COMPUTERS

One issue raised by Papert's approach to computers in education was that of resource. His notion of the computer as an everyday tool like the pencil, meant that each child needed easy access to one and he does acknowledge the requirement for a vast number of computers and for children to have a lot of exposure. This has not been a possibility for most schools and a pattern has therefore evolved of children working on computers in small groups. This also fits in with the practice and ethos of group work in primary schools in the UK. However, as a result of this partly pragmatic way of working, it seems that group work with computers offers particular benefits that other kinds of group work do not. There is some evidence (Bennett, 1987 and Galton, 1989) that when children are working together with a computer, they are collaborating rather than just working alongside each other, which is often the case in typical British primary school work. Such collaboration has been called for in numerous government reports-and the lack of it has caused some concern. There is also some evidence that when a computer is used the interaction is related to the task, and children ask each other for help instead of relying on the teacher. Not surprisingly, the success of a session depends on how it has been set up by the teacher, and on who is working together and what the task is. There has recently therefore been much research on children working with the computers in pairs or small groups to try and investigate the factors that contribute or hinder such success, to see if, when and why learning is more effective.

One line of research has been investigating the role of conflicts in children who are engaged in a learning task. The kind of conflict focused on here is *cognitive* conflict and stems from Piaget's work on stage development. The argument is that when a child fails to see that when liquid is poured from one glass container into a differently shaped one the amount stays the same, it is because she is focusing on only one relevant dimension - perhaps the second glass is taller, although thinner, and she says there is more liquid in it because the level is higher. However, if it is pointed out that the second glass is thinner she may now focus on the width and reverse her decision. Conservation is achieved when she can take both attributes into account.

> Development results from her integrating these two centrations into one single organised scheme which can deal with the compensation of opposing equal differences. (Joiner, 1993)

When two or more children work together there is the opportunity for *socio-cognitive* conflict. The idea is that when one child works with another who holds a different theory, or model, it can point up discrepancies in the first child's ideas in the same way that when the non conserving child pours the liquid back into the original container, he notices that it does indeed now appear to be the same quantity as ever. It is argued, however, that discrepancies between children (socio-cognitive conflict) are more powerful than the impact of discrepant models within the same child. By encouraging collaboration, computers can provide a good medium where such conflicts can be provoked in order to facilitate learning.

Research on collaborative learning with computers need not involve the idea of such socio-cognitive conflict. For example Mevarech, Silber and Fine (1987) investigated whether children learn more when they work together, and concluded that they did. Other studies have focused on the dialogue between children when they use computers, such as the work of Hoyles and her colleagues (e.g. Hoyles, Sutherland and Healy, 1990). In their work on learning mathematics they discuss how learning collaboratively helps children to produce and articulate hypotheses about patterns and regularities and helps them, through discussion, to eventually make appropriate generalisations. Some researchers who have focused in particular on the kinds of language that children use when working with computers believe that a more satisfactory theoretical base for looking at collaborative work is provided by Vygotsky who emphasised the role of language much more than Piaget, and so it is to Vygotsky that we turn in the next section.

THE SOCIAL CONTEXT OF LEARNING AND VYGOTSKY

Piaget believed that language was important, but it was tied into the general course of cognitive growth: language does not in itself create thought, although language acquisition is dependent on certain intellectual structures. However, it has been argued that Piaget very much under emphasised the role of language: the work summarised by Donaldson for example (Donaldson, op. cit.) shows that language and children's understanding of the task has a crucial role to play in the classic conservation experiments. There is also evidence that children are nowhere near so egocentric as Piaget suggests, and that in fact the tendency to 'centre' on one aspect of a problem is shared by adults too (Wason and Johnson-Laird, 1972.)

Vygotsky was a Russian psychologist who was writing at the same time as Piaget, and even before him, but his publications were banned by the Soviet state and so had little impact on European developmental psychology until the 1980s, although a translation of one book, *Thought and Language,* had appeared in 1962. For Vygotsky, language plays a special role in learning and development. By acquiring language, a child is enabled to think in new ways and gains a new cognitive tool for making sense of the world:

> Children solve practical tasks with the help of their speech, as well as their eyes and hands. (Vygotsky, 1978, p. 26)

Language is used by children as an additional tool in solving problems, to overcome impulsive action, to plan a solution before trying it out and to control their own behaviour. However, the main function of language for children is social. They also use speech to enlist another person's help to solve a problem and, unlike Piaget, Vygotsky places the origins of learning firmly in a social context:

> ..in the process of development the child begins to practice with respect to himself the same forms of behaviour that others formerly practised with respect to him. (Vygotsky, 1966, p. 36)

The important point here is that the meaning of such behaviour is *only* understood in a social context: indeed the behaviour only takes on meaning by being used as a social gesture. The whole thrust of Vygotsky's argument is that cognitive development is socially located, and that individual learning *follows* social learning. The significance of symbols is first understood socially, and then may be individually applied. He examines the history of pointing as an example.

> ...in the beginning the pointing gesture' (for an infant) 'is merely an unsuccessful grasping movement aimed at an object and signifying forthcoming action. (*Ibid.* p. 38)

The child cannot reach the object and so his fingers make grasping movements:

> When the mother comes to the aid of the child and comprehends his movement as a pointing gesture the situation essentially changes. The pointing gesture becomes a gesture for others. (*Ibid.*, pp. 38-39)

Although this is still a constructivist view, the thrust is quite different from Piaget's. Now the social context is seen as crucial, and language is also seen as crucial and interrelated with action (for children); providing them with an additional tool used both to reflect on and direct behaviour. Vygotsky's work is therefore viewed as particularly relevant for those who are concerned with the use of language. For example, Mercer (1991) gives the starting question for the SLANT project (Spoken Language and New Technology) as being: 'what kinds of opportunities for talk are provided by computer-mediated activities?'. Here the educational process is viewed as 'a communicative process whereby Knowledge is constructed, shared, interpreted and misinterpreted as teachers talk with children and ...children talk with children'. (Mercer, *op. cit.*, pp. 195-196)

The *social* nature of learning as constantly emphasised by Vygotsky is currently accepted as a very important aspect of learning. A related idea which has recently been very influential, but this time from rather different fields such as cognitive psychology and instructional design is that all learning takes place in a particular context and likewise knowledge is also embedded in a context and neither can be viewed as separate from that context. This is often referred to as 'situated cognition'. Although some of the work covered here does concern school learning, this is not essentially a developmental perspective, though it does, as Brown, Collins and Duguid (1989) acknowledge, owe much of its ideas to theorists such as Vygotsky.

FROM LEARNING THEORIES TO USING IT

In looking briefly at the two constructivist theories of Piaget and Vygotsky I have moved from the more individualistic approach of Piaget to the more communicative theory of Vygotsky. This move reflects a shift in the dominant theories in the field of cognitive development and learning, where individualist theories of development and learning have given way to more socially and culturally sensitive views of cognition. Butterworth (1992) goes further to describe three phases of the study of cognitive development: from a focus on the intellectual processes of the individual child (à la Piaget) through social cognition (influenced by Vygotsky) and recently into a third phase

> ...in which theorists are beginning to stress an inextricable link between contextual constrains and the acquisition of knowledge. Moreover the physical context is being united with the social, with the thought process. The contemporary view tends to be that cognition is typically situated in a social and physical context and is rarely, if ever, decontextualised. (Butterworth, *op. cit.*, p. 1).

In terms of the broader study of *cognition*, however, which also embraces the study of learning, but not from a developmental perspective, there is no such contemporary view. As in the field of cognitive development there is an increasing acceptance of the importance of environmental and social issues, though the language (here it is termed situated cognition or situated action) and emphasis are different. Often the focus is on the extent to which 'knowledge' can be abstracted from the context in which it is acquired. Brown, Collins and Duguid (*op. cit.*) focus on the separation between 'formal' knowledge and its use in context, in their discussion of situated cognition:

> Many methods of didactic education assume a separation between knowing and doing, treating knowledge as integral, self-sufficient substance, theoretically independent of the situations in which it is learned and used. The primary concern of schools often seems to be the transfer of this substance, which comprises abstract, decontextualised formal concepts. (Brown *et al.*, *op. cit.*, p. 32).

They argue that knowledge must be viewed as part of a context; that is 'situated'. The debate, however, is still continuing. In an introduction to an issue of *Cognitive Science* containing articles from proponents of both approaches, Don Norman (1993) offers a caricature of each. He caricatures the focus of traditional studies of cognition as being (entirely) 'upon the processing structures of the brain and the symbolic representations of mind. All the action is inside the head, yielding a natural distinction between the stuff out there and the processes taking place inside here.' (Norman, *op. cit.*, p. 3). The situated cognition advocates, on the other hand, 'tend to emphasise the importance of historical influences, social interaction, culture, and the environment, and to minimize the importance of internal cognition'. (*ibid.*, p. 3). The debate is important to the use of IT in education, because the extent to which educators and instructional designers believe cognition is situated will affect their conception of how IT may best be utilised for learning.

So far, we have only briefly touched on the applications of such theories in using IT in education Interestingly, in parallel with the changes in the emphasis in theories of learning, changes have occurred in the kinds of learning activities that students are engaged in when interacting with IT. As noted earlier, in schools there has been a move from individual to collaborative working, both when using software which has not been designed for group use, such as using computers for problem-solving activities and in making use of computer networks and computer conferencing. Such collaborative use of computers has also increased in higher and distance education, for example in the use of computer conferencing, and this is consistent with the increasing emphasis on social interaction which is occurring in adult as well as children's learning, and an increasing recognition of the situated nature of learning.

In the next section I want to look at two examples of how the learning theories considered have influenced IT in education. The first is an example of educational software designed from a constructivist perspective; the second is a project on investigating conceptual changes in Science.

TWO EXAMPLES

BUBBLE DIALOGUE: A CONSTRUCTIVIST TOOL

McMahon and O'Neill (1992) view their Bubble Dialogue tool as compatible with constructivist views of learning and in particular as reflecting a Vygotskian view of learning in which the context is particularly important. It provides a comic-script environment (within the Hypercard application) where there will be typically two characters. It is probably best illustrated through an example. At the beginning of a session the learners are presented with a particular scenario given in the 'prologue' on the first screen. This is shown in Figure 1 which shows the first screen which displays the prologue. The characters (in this case Debbie and Bobbie) are also introduced here. Clicking on the dialogue icon (the hand) takes the learner to the next screen which is the beginning of the dialogue. From this point on the learner is invited to create the characters' dialogue and thus produce a script. Each character has both speech and thought bubbles, and the characters take it in turn to speak, think, or speak and think. In Figure 2, the opening dialogue is shown, where Bobby is speaking. Typically this will already be provided by the teacher, although this need not be the case. At this point, there are two options; Bobby can also be given a thought bubble, or Debbie can take up the dialogue. In this example, the next move is Debbie's and in Figure 3 Debbie's thought bubble is shown, followed by her speech bubble in Figure 4. From this point on, the dialogue continues, until the learners decide they have finished.

Figure 1

Figure 2

Figure 3

Figure 4

There are two modes: creation (illustrated above) and review. Whereas in creation mode the only movement forward to the next think or speech bubble, in review mode users can move backwards or forwards and add notes, speech or thought. The authors note that: 'use of the tool in review mode has proven to be very powerful, encouraging reflexivity in the users'

(p. 42). Bubble Dialogue has now been used in a number of very diverse situations and its power and potential lie (I believe) in two features: the ability to operate in both public and private domains through the speech and thought bubbles and also in its versatility. One particular way of using Bubble Dialogue was illustrated earlier, but it is a flexible tool which can be used in a number of different ways. McMahon and Neill give several examples of how Bubble Dialogue can be used in education. The first type of use is where the teacher works with one particular pupil and each takes a role.

> For example, a pupil thought to be misunderstanding a key concept could be asked to pay the role of an expert on the screen and the teacher could play the role of a novice interrogating the expert at an appropriate level of cognitive demand. Evidence of the pupils' learning deficit accumulates on the screen and in the off the screen dialogue about what is happening on the screen.

Alternatively, each of a pair of pupils can be allocated one of the two characters. Pupils can also be asked to collaborate in creating the dialogue for one of the roles whilst the teacher plays the other. Pupils could collaboratively analyse a previously 'canned' dialogue.

In the case of designing Bubble Dialogue, the designers had a particular theory of learning in mind: 'One of the most fundamental assumptions that has guided our work is the view of Vygotsky that the mind is continually engaged in a process of social formation.' (p. 46) As we saw earlier, Vygotsky's view was that social communication is essential for learning to take place: we learn from each other in social contexts, and especially from dialogue between each other.

McMahon and O'Neill argue that the language used and the context shared by the participants are vital in making the best instructional use of conversation, both between pupils and pupils and between pupils and their teacher: 'it is part of the teachers' art to find the common purpose and shared conceptual ground with each and every child' (p. 47)

The importance of such a shared context or culture has been stressed by many other constructivist theorists. For example Bruner (1987) comments on the relationship between particular cultures and the experience of privacy: 'The nature of the untold and the untellable are deeply cultural in character...How a culture defines privacy plays an enormous part in what people feel private about and when and how' (p. 47). Donaldson (*op. cit.*) also emphasises the importance of trying to understand how language is used and understood by each party. McMahon and Neill comment on their theoretical position thus:

> In summary our theoretical position is that it is in and through our interactions with others that we make meaning. However, as much of languageing remains hidden from us, contextualised or privatised to a degree which makes it invisible to either or both parties in the exchange, teachers must find a way to make children see and hear

their own dialogue so that they can engage in the reflective, decontextualizing process of using language to understand dialogue. Our goal should be to develop forms of instruction, forms of scaffolding, which foster this process and so maximise internalization....We would like to suggest that bubble dialogue...is an example of an instructional system which promotes reflection, reconstruction and decontexualization within.... that region of sensitivity in which the transition from social to personal takes place.

Evidence from research on Bubble Dialogue, points to a number of factors influencing its use and how it is viewed. Two particularly salient issues are identification and distancing. Many children tend to identify with a character but at the same time they can create the character's dialogue without 'becoming' the character:

The character can be made to say and think things that the user would not want to say or have the courage to say in real life...things which would normally like outside the perceived norms of acceptable convention in a particular context. (p. 50).

This in itself can be powerful and it can provide both the teacher and other learners with 'windows' into what are normally private areas:

More often than not, ...the use of the tool can bring out issues for discussion and examination, encourage seeing more than one side of a question, and promote a dialogue aimed at adopting a publicly held position. These outcomes lie at the heart of constructivism. (Cunningham, McMahon and O'Neill, 1992) .

CONCEPTUAL CHANGE IN SCIENCE
The starting point for the Conceptual Change in Science project (CCIS) was the difficulties that school pupils have in understanding certain theories in the physical sciences, and its aims were to:

Understand this process of conceptual change better, and to devise and test ways in which such a change can be promoted in classroom teaching programmes. Particular attention will be paid to the role that computer software can play in promoting such a change. (Driver, R. and Scanlon, E., 1988)

Here, then, the computer is seen as a tool for addressing a particular problem. Essentially, conceptual change refers to the ways in which informal theories that children have already developed prior to being taught science in school are modified (or not) by the science teaching in schools so that science learning has come to be seen as a process of conceptual change. One of the models proposed to explain how the process occurs is a Piagetian one:

> This model proposes that learners, when confronted with discrepant information will attempt to adjust their conception in order to resolve the conflict. (Driver, R.and Scanlon, E. *op. cit.,* p. 28)

Driver and Scanlon argue that computers should be appropriate for helping children change towards accepted scientific conceptions from alternative conceptions because:

> They require children to make their implicit reasoning explicit (through, for example, simulations of object motion or collisions); they enable children to visualise the consequences of their reasoning and provide an object for reflection and communication with others; they provide pictorial representations and dynamic displays of models of phenomena which could form useful bridging analogies data logging and display facilities can provide rapid numerical or graphic representations of how variables are interrelated in ongoing situations. (Driver, R.and Scanlon, E. *op. cit.,* p. 30)

Two software systems were designed and developed for use in this project. The first, DM3, is a simulation environment for exploring some of the rules of physics. It simulates the motion of objects under applied forces, gravity and friction, and users can directly manipulate these objects and forces via mouse-activated buttons and sliders. Learners could use a second program, VARILAB, to express their explanations of the events they explored and manipulated by building qualitative models. Output from the models (e.g. graphs) could be matched against those of DM3 to allow students and their teachers to check out the models, to discuss them and make any refinements that they needed to. The software systems were used as parts of lessons designed to promote conceptual change, and an evaluation of the teaching/learning system indicated that such change did indeed occur: the children who used the materials 'displayed more sophisticated reasoning in immediate and delayed post-tests than did their counterparts in companion classes'. (Draper *et al.*, 1992).

Cognitive conflict was also the focus for Joiner's work (Joiner, 1993). Here the aim is as much to increase understanding of learning and development as to develop software, and this work, like the case studies discussed above, is underpinned by the belief that the design and development of software must be informed by research into learning which develops the theories of learning that we already have:

> ...unless we understand more about the nature of conflicts and how they are resolved and how their resolution leads to learning, then we will not be in a position to support learning through the development of appropriate software in collaborative problem solving. (p. 33).

Both Bubble Dialogue and the CCIS project are examples of how the design of particular educational software was motivated and underpinned by particular theories of learning. Producing and trying out such software should therefore be beneficial to the learners involved and will also test out the theories to some extent. In reviewing the relationship between theories of learning and the use of IT to support learning we find that not only do the designers and users of IT in education look towards learning theories from developmental psychology, but also that educationalists and psychologists, especially those interested in collaborative learning, view children's use of computers as a rich domain for developing their theories.

CONCLUSIONS

Two theoretical positions have been considered in some detail here: those of Piaget and Vygotsky, although the situated learning camp can also be viewed as related to Vygotsky's work. Both Piaget's views of the structuring of knowledge and of stage development were central to the argument about how one line of development in software, LOGO, could be educationally beneficial by bridging for the child, the abstract and concrete. This way of thinking was entirely consistent with the child-centred ideology of the time. It has been argued that this individualist position has been supplanted by a more social approach with an emphasis on both children and adults learning together, and that this move has happened both at a theoretical level (where it is the social aspects of learning theories that are currently emphasised) and at a practical level where many educational uses of IT, currently, are collaborative or co-operative. Although it is unlikely that learners using LOGO benefited to the extent that Papert claimed, we do know that LOGO can lead to particular social benefits when used in groups, and that the benefit of groups using computers goes beyond LOGO. To try and understand and capitalise on such benefits it is necessary, I argue, to consider some theoretically based analysis of what's going on. Whilst one line of argument and research has looked to the more social aspects of Piaget's theory (e.g. conflict resolution) to understand the benefits of group work, another line has looked at Vygotsky's work for the cultural and linguistic emphases.

The current emphasis on the benefits of working together goes beyond the classroom and adult education to considerations of how other communities (e.g. Kaye's article in this book, p. 192) can benefit from working collaboratively. Some of these other issues will be picked up in forthcoming chapters. However in order to make sense of such events we need to analyse the process: the theoretical work described here can give us a framework for starting to do this.

REFERENCES

Bennett, N. (1987) 'Cooperative learning: children do it in small groups - or do they?', *Educational and Child psychology*, 4, pp. 7-18.

Brown, J.S., Collins, A. and Duguid, P. (1989) 'Situated cognition and the culture of learning', *Educational Researcher,* 18, (1), pp. 32-42.

Butterworth, G. (1992) 'Context and cognition in models of cognitive growth', in *Context and Cognition: Ways of Learning and Knowing,* Paul Light and George Butterworth (eds), Harvester Wheatsheaf.

Crook, C. (1992) 'Cultural artefacts in social development: the case of computers, in H. McGurk, *Childhood Social Development: Contemporary Perspectives,* Lawrence Erlbaum.

Cunningham, D., McMahon, H. F. and O'Neill, W. (1992) 'Bubble dialogue: a new tool for instruction and assessment', *Educational Technology Research and Development,* 40, (2), pp. 59-65.

Davis, A. (1991) 'Piaget, teachers and education: into the 1990s', in *Learning to Think,* P. Light, S. Sheldon and M. Woodhead (eds), Routledge.

Donaldson, M. (1987) *Children's Minds,* Fontana Press.

Driver, R. and Scanlon, E. (1989) 'Conceptual change in Science', *JCAL,* 5, 1, pp. 25-35.

Driver, R., Guesne, E. and Tiberghien,A. (1985) *Children's Ideas in Science,* Open University Press, Milton Keynes

Galton, M. (1989) *Teaching in the Primary School,* London, David Fulton Publishers.

Hoyles, C., Sutherland R. and Healy, L. (1991) 'Children talking in computer environments: new insights on the role of dicussion in mathematics learning', in Durkin, K. and Shire, B (eds) *Language in Mathematical Education: research and practice,* Milton Keynes, Open University Press.

Joiner, R. (1993) A dialogue model of the resolution of inter-individual conflicts: Implications for computer based collaborative Learning. Unpublished PhD thesis, Open University.

Jonassen, D. (1991) 'Hypertext as instructional design', *Educational Technology Research and Development,* 7, (1) pp. 210-228.

Littleton, K. (1994) 'Children and computer technology', in *Influencing Children's Development,* Book 4 of the Open University second level course ED209, *Child Development,* Open University.

McMahon, H. and O'Neill, B. (1992) 'Computer-mediated zones of engagement in learning', in *Designing Environments for Constructivist Learning,* Springer-Verlag.

Mercer, D., Phillips, T. and Somekh, B. (1991) 'Research note: Spoken language and new technology', *Journal of Computer-Assisted Learning,* Vol. 7, pp. 195-202.

Mevarech, Z., Silber, O. and Fine, D. (1987) 'Learning with computers in small groups: cognitive and affective outcomes', *Journal of Educational Computing Research,* 7, (2), pp. 233-43.

Norman, D. (1993) 'Cognition in the head and in the world: An introduction to the Special Issue on Situated Action', *Cognitive Science,* 17, pp. 1-6.

Papert, S. (1980) *Mindstorms: Children, Computers and Powerful Ideas,* Brighton, Harvester Press.

Vygotsky, L. S. (1978) *Mind in Society: the Development of Higher Psychological Processes,* Cambridge (Mass.), Havard University Press.

Vygotsky, L.S. (1991) 'Genesis of the higher mental functions', Reprinted in *Learning to Think,* P. Light, S. Sheldon and M. Woodhead (eds), Routledge.

Wason, P. C. and Johnson-Laird, P. N. (1972) *Psychology of Reasoning: Structure and Content,* London, Batsford.

PART 4 IT AND THE HOME

Hughie Mackay, The Open University in Wales

INTRODUCTION

The domestic has been the subject of renewed interest in recent years. Rather than being seen as the site of trivia and inconsequence, and secondary to the 'real' world of paid work, the home is increasingly seen as an important arena. This shift is manifest in debates about the value and importance of housework and of consumption, but applies also to IT. Far from being a marginal arena, the home is a key location for our experience of IT, and for the success (or otherwise) of specific IT products. Whilst some of the forecasts of IT controls in the home have proved fanciful, in relation to leisure activities IT is becoming increasingly significant. Domestic leisure as we now know it is inconceivable without an extensive range of IT devices. Rather than being marginal, or 'not real IT', these devices are absolutely central to IT markets, IT developments and our daily experience of IT.

The paper by Murdock *et al.* introduces a range of issues and debates about IT in the home which have been developed in cultural and media studies. Although concerned with a past era – that of the early home computer, 'one of the most conspicuous consumer products of the 1980s' – the arguments and concepts which they deploy are entirely relevant to making sense of the arrival of contemporary and future domestic IT devices. Computing activities, they argue, are structured by available resources – of a material, social and symbolic order. Drawing on three longitudinal interviews in over a thousand households, Murdock *et al.* argue that income is but one determinant of home computer ownership; but that income shapes not just ownership patterns but also how home computers are *used*. Murdock *et al.*'s evidence supports the 'diffusion of innovations' perspective's emphasis on social networks, in that they found that other users who can offer advice, encouragement and practical support encouraged more sophisticated and extensive ownership and use. They argue, however, that there are other resources, too, on which users draw: *discursive resources*. The home computer, they argue, is enmeshed in a web of competing definitions of uses and users. Specifically, they identify: the utilitarian emphasis of hard and software manufacturers; the computer literacy arguments of government discourses, in the form of the Department of Education and Science and the BBC's computer literacy project; the hobbyist notion of the 'self referential' machine, in which the use of a computer is an *end in itself*, as opposed to it being something with which one can achieve some other purpose; games playing, which soon came to dominate usage; and, finally, the moral panic that followed this, the concern about games content and, crucially, the amount of time youths spent playing computer games. Murdock *et al.*'s argument is that such discourses constitute resources for owners (and potential owners) to make sense of – and actively construct – the IT.

Moyal's concern is with women rather than men, and with the telephone – which, despite its far-reaching influence on our daily lives, has been all but ignored by scholars. She reports the findings of a qualitative survey of 200 women in Australia. Her concern is to explore the feminine culture of the telephone, to gather the experience, attitudes and voices of women. From the outset, telephone companies saw (women's) gossip as *misuse* of the technology. Moyal asked interviewees to distinguish between 'instrumental' and 'intrinsic' telephone calls. Instrumental calls are defined as appointment and arrangement making, purchasing and seeking information; whilst intrinsic calls are for personal exchange and communication. She found that women make an average of four instrumental calls a week, and twenty-four intrinsic, which were longer in duration and many of them long distance. Moyal then relates this pattern of telephone usage to key elements of Australian culture. Families, she argues, are deep-rooted, and family relationships are sustained by telephone contact between female family members. The other main form of intrinsic call constituted networking with close friends. Here, again, the telephone was seen as central to maintaining relationships, providing support and care and, in some cases, alleviating boredom and loneliness. Interestingly, her interviewees reported that they talk *more* freely and intimately on the telephone than face-to-face. Her argument is that – in contrast with the common and pejorative view of women's telephone usage – the telephone is a crucial technology in holding together families and communities.

The final paper, by Mackay, was written for this volume. It presents some quantitative data on ownership and usage levels and patterns of a number of key IT devices in the home. Drawing largely on marketing and government data, Mackay quantifies the significance – in terms of unit sales and their value, and the time devoted by householders to their usage – of these devices. He argues that the six devices with which he is concerned – the telephone, the television, video cassette recorder (VCR), home computer, computer games console and compact disc (CD) player – constitute the heart of a revolution in leisure in the home: already the synergy of these devices is changing fundamentally traditional patterns of domestic IT usage and leisure. Particularly, the phenomenal success of computer games, which has coincided with a decline in television viewing, can be seen as an expression of consumer demand for interactivity, for greater participation and control. Increasingly these IT devices are components of integrated systems which both bridge a range of leisure and work activities, but which also redefine these, offering new possibilities. Ownership and usage levels of these six devices are discussed in terms of income, social class, occupation, sex, age, household composition, housing tenure and geographical variables. Whilst the data available for each device varies, the detailed quantification complements the qualitative approaches of the other papers in this section.

CONTEXTUALIZING HOME COMPUTING: RESOURCES AND PRACTICES

Graham Murdock, Paul Hartmann and Peggy Gray

Along with the video cassette recorder, the Walkman and the compact disc player, home computers were one of the most conspicuous consumer products of the 1980s. From their first appearance at the beginning of the decade, they attracted an increasing amount of research aimed at finding out who was entering the domestic micro market and who wasn't, identifying barriers to adoption and how they might be overcome, and exploring what people were actually doing with their machines. This work, which began in the United States but spread rapidly to other advanced economies, employed a variety of methods, ranging from nationwide surveys (e.g. Danko and MacLachlan, 1983) to studies of early adopters and computer enthusiasts (e.g. Dickerson and Gentry, 1983; Hall *et al.*, 1985) and ethnographies of computer households (e.g. Tinnell, 1985). But beneath the differences of approach, virtually all these studies were united in viewing home computing activity in a radically decontextualized way. They shared this myopia with much of the new reception analysis that was emerging within mass media research over the same period (see Murdock, 1989). Both currents of work focused on the practical activities of audiences and users but took little account of the way these activities were structured by the resources that consumers could draw upon, or were excluded from.

These resources are material, social and symbolic. Home computers are not just commodities that are traded for a price in the market. They are also the site of a continual cultural struggle over the meaning of the machine and its appropriate uses. In Britain, this has taken the form of a contest between offical discourses stressing home computing's educational and instrumental potentials, and commercial discourses promoting its entertaining, playful and expressive uses. Each discourse offers particular user identities, which intersect with the material resources and social relations inside and outside the household to produce specific patterns of use or disuse.

This article sets out to explore the relations between practices and resources, drawing on material gathered in the course of a longitudinal study of domestic communication technologies based on samples of just over one thousand households, drawn from four contrasted locations in the English Midlands [1]. All respondents were interviewed at three points in time about their use of media and new technology, including home computers. These indexical data were supplemented by focused interviews with computer users, drawn from the main samples. Because the detailed material presented here is not properly ethnographic, in the sense that it did not involve periods of observation outside the interview visits, it is necessarily limited in the issues it can raise about the relation of computing to household structures. At the same time, the fact that the interviewees were located through a large cross-sectional survey, provided access to a wider range of experiences than is usually the case with qualitative studies.

The period covered by the research, 1983 to 1987, coincided with the British home computer market's takeoff to growth. At the end of 1981 (when the first cheap, easy-to-use machines were launched) less than a quarter of a million households had a micro. By the spring of 1986, this figure had climbed to 3.06 million (*Marketing Week*, 1986). Because the Midlands interviews were conducted over this crucial period, they provided clues to the complex interplay between the user careers of individuals and households and the general development of the home computer industry as a whole.

Most research on home computing has either ignored the diachronic dimension, and settled for a snapshot at a particular moment, or approached it from the point of view of the computer industry's interest in devising more effective marketing strategies (e.g. Venkatesh and Vitalari, 1986). Work on the diffusion of innovations is a partial exception, however. This is centrally concerned with the social dynamics of adoption and use over time but until recently has paid little attention to material constraints, and no attention at all to the role of public discourse in organizing use.

MATERIAL RESOURCES: FROM DIFFUSION TO DIFFERENTIAL ACCESS

Writers in the 'diffusion of innovations' tradition are concerned with the processes whereby a novel object or practice comes to be adopted by the members of a society or social group and incorporated into everyday routines and practices (Rogers, 1983). Diffusion models were orginally developed in relation to studies of agricultural innovations in rural America in the 1940s, in an attempt to explain why some farmers were more willing to adopt new techniques. After World War II they became one of the major theoretical linchpins of US-sponsored 'modernization' strategies in the Third World.

In the early 1980s, one of the key figures in developing the diffusion perspective. Everett Rogers, began to apply it to the spread of home computers in the United States. As a resident of southern California, living close to Silicon Valley, one of the major sites of commercial activity concerned with microcomputing, he was particularly well placed to observe its development as both an industry (see Rogers and Larsen, 1984) and a market (e.g. Dutton *et al.*, 1987). In seeking to explain patterns of adoption and use, Rogers and his co-workers originally focused on the interplay between the capacities and characteristics of the available machines – what they could do and how easy they were to use – and the personal needs and dispositions of users and potential users – what they wanted a machine for, whether they had any relevant skills or experience, and whether their attitude towards technology in general was positive or hostile. They paid comparatively little attention to the role of material resources in regulating market entry.

This was largely because their model took it for granted that everybody was a potential computer owner and that the diffusion curve would follow other major innovations in consumer electronics, such as the television set, with adoption trickling steadily down the income scale. This ignored the widening income gap and rising levels of unemployment produced by Reaganomics. As the decade wore on, however, research showed quite clearly that, despite a massive promotional effort, home computer ownership remained concentrated within the professional and managerial strata. The diffusionists accordingly modified their position, and accepted that 'differential access seems to be primarily based on income differentials across socio-economic status groups' (Dutton *et al.*, 1988, p.14). This pattern was repeated in other advanced capitalist societies (e.g. Jouet, 1988). It was particularly marked in Britain, where the Family Expenditure Surveys revealed a clear linear relation between income and computer ownership. In 1986, for example, only 7.6 per cent of households with a weekly income of under £125 had a home computer, compared to 26.6 per cent of households in the income band £325-75 (see Murdock and Golding, 1989).

The Midlands study confirms and extends this point. Economic capacity not only played a central role in determining whether or not a household entered the home computer market, it also shaped subsequent patterns of use in significant ways. A number of applications, such as word processing, are either made much more difficult or ruled out altogether if the machine owned is one of the cheaper models without a dedicated monitor or a printer. The last wave of the panel study, conducted in 1987, revealed that, despite the rapid growth of the Amstrad PCW range and the proliferation of relatively cheap IBM PC 'clones', the majority of computer households in the study still only had the machine they had first bought, more than half of which were basic Sinclair or Commodore models. Only one in four had traded up and acquired a more sophisticated model.

Behind these figures lay experiences of disillusion, particularly among those who had bought into 'the home computer revolution' in its first phase.

The limits of these early cheap machines were not obvious at first. On the contrary, as one teenager recounted, in 1983 when sales first boomed, they seemed exciting and full of possibility.

> I don't know really why, because it suddenly started didn't it, computers everywhere. The first one I ever saw was the [Sinclair] ZX81, which I thought was really good when I first saw it. It's nothing really is it? Because it can only print the name on the screen.

This restriction was a source of considerable disappointment to users who bought one thinking it could do more than it could.

> I wanted it as a word processor, but of course it's no good for that at all. I didn't appreciate it at the time. You can't get enough words on the screen, unless you get one that's about four or five times the price.... With this one you can only read four or five words across and you've had it. I just went round a bit and I thought, well this was the best for the price you know. I wanted it for a word processor and they said, 'Oh yes they can do this' and 'Oh yes they do that', you know. And of course it does, but not satisfactorily for proper use.

Programming also proved to be a problem, with naive users often finding that it took far longer than they anticipated to master the skills they needed to pursue their own projects. As one young teacher explained: 'I quite enjoyed the programming side of it, but found that it was a lot of work to achieve very, very simple results. Although it was quite a challenge.'

Often initial enthusiasm dwindled rapidly, as in this account by a woman who had seen her husband and son lose interest:

> I think they thought they were going to do great things with it, and make programmes and use it in all sorts of ways. But then they realized what a long time it was going to be to learn to do this, and a long time putting the programme in. They haven't had the time.

The problems of using the basic models to produce self-generated material were often compounded by two other material limitations.

One of the attractions of the early Sinclair and Commodore machines, besides their relatively low price, was the fact that they did not need a disc drive or dedicated monitor. They could be operated using a standard black-and-white television set as a display screen and a portable audio cassette recorder to load and store software. But both these selling points imposed important limitations on use. Whilst tape technology was cheap and convenient, it was not particularly robust in use and took a considerable time both to load programmes into the machine and retrieve stored material. Even in 1987, however, when the third wave of the Midlands survey was conducted, three-quarters of computer households still relied entirely on tape technology. An even higher proportion, 80 per cent, had computers without their own screens, and were still using a domestic television set for visual display facilities.

This was less of a problem where the machine was connected to a set reserved for the purpose and placed in a permanent location. As the survey results showed, however, this was a luxury that poorer households could not always afford. Because they were less likely to own a second or third television set, the home computer became a literal extension of the main set, competing with broadcast programming and video cassette recorder use for access to the screen. This meant that computing activity was restricted both spatially and temporally, with the keyboard and television set having to be connected and disconnected each time the machine was used. Not having an integral computer screen will become even more of a disadvantage if and when Britain's fifth terrestrial television channel comes on stream. This will employ the same frequency as home computers currently using a television set as a monitor and, though these machines could be re-tuned, the industry consensus is that most owners will not bother.

To sum up: the available evidence reveals a consistent relationship between patterns of home computer ownership and use and a household's income and class position. The more affluent the household the more likely it is to own a home computer and the more likely that this will be one of the more expensive and versatile machines with a built-in screen, a disc drive and a printer, capable of supporting a wide range of uses and applications.

The material resources at a household's disposal – in the form of discretionary income, domestic space and related technologies – can be said to be determinant in 'the first instance', in the sense that they establish the basic conditions of access to and exclusion from the various configurations of computing equipment (see Murdock, 1989). To explain why this equipment is used in particular ways, however, or why it falls into disuse, we need to go on to explore the social resources at the user's disposal.

SOCIAL RESOURCES: NETWORKS AND DISCONNECTIONS

One of the strengths of the 'diffusion of innovations' perspective is its emphasis on the role of social networks in fostering and sustaining new practices. According to this argument, the maintenance of particular forms of computer use will depend in large part on access to other users who can offer advice, encouragement and practical support. Conversely, users who are isolated from or marginal to such networks may find it difficult to acquire competences and sustain interest over time. The centrality of networks emerged strongly from the Midlands data. As the following interview account makes clear, contacts can play an important role in providing back-up support at key moments.

> My friend down round the estate, who's got the same machine, which is useful because he has a lot of system software that I don't have. He's into computers as a job. It's useful. The other day when I was using the word processor, l was trying to save it. I had spent all morning keying it in. It's only an extract from a magazine. Started at 8 o'clock and finished about lunch. You make one mistake and it's rubbish. Terrifies you. Oh it's a swine to type in, and I wanted to make sure I'd save it. So, I saved a load of tape without turning the machine off. I then carried my tape recorder round to his machine to see if it would load on his machine. If it would then I was alright. So I was lucky, because if I'd turned it off I'd have wasted eight hours of work.

Contacts also help to legitimate particular patterns of use through the swopping of information and anecdotes and exchanging software. Almost 60 per cent of the computer users interviewed in the Midlands study said that they often talked about computing to friends and acquaintances, and around half claimed to borrow and exchange software on a regular basis. Significantly, those with little or no contact with other users were more likely to have stopped using their machines once the initial novelty had worn off. They tended to live in households where no one had a job that involved using computers or gave them access to relevant expertise and contacts, and in neighbourhoods with relatively few other users. These patterns of social and spatial segregation interacted with the differential distribution of material resources described earlier to reinforce the disadvantaged position of users and would-be users in low-income households.

At the same time, we must be careful not to overstate the importance of class location. Computer use is also very strongly inflected by generation and gender. Among the Midlands sample, domestic micros were overwhelmingly concentrated in households with children and adolescents. By 1985, when the second wave of interviews was conducted, over a third (35 per cent) of 'nuclear families' had acquired one, as against 5 per cent of couples without children and 6 per cent of people living alone. When households with computers were asked to say who the main user was, only one in seven nominated a female. In fact, apart from a small number of adults in professional and managerial jobs, who mainly used their machines for work-related tasks, and a scattering of hobbyists, home computing was the province of children and teenagers and of boys rather than girls, a pattern confirmed by Jane Wheelock's recent research on Wearside (Wheelock, 1990; 1992). To explain these age and gender biases we need to go beyond the differential distribution of material and social resources, and explore the way the promotional discourses around home computing have drawn on activities and identities associated with youth and masculinity.

DISCURSIVE RESOURCES: THE MULTIPLE MEANINGS OF THE HOME MICRO

From its first entry into the British market, the home computer has been enmeshed in a web of competing definitions of uses and users, as the promotional discourses of the hardware and software industries (see Haddon, 1988a) jostled for public attention with governmental discourses about information technology and education. By defining the micro's potentialities and pleasures in different ways, these discourses played an important role in structuring the ways it was used.

The push to market a micro for home use came initially from firms selling kits that purchasers assembled themselves. These began to appear in the late 1970s and were aimed firmly at committed hobbyists who wanted to explore the possibilities of the technology and had the competence to cope with the machines' far from user-friendly' characteristics, including the complete lack of pre-written software. They were, in Leslie Haddon's useful phrase, 'self-referring', in the sense that the pleasures they offered derived not from particular applications but from the possession of the technology itself and from solving the problems involved in getting it to perform.

This notion of the 'self-referring' machine was generalized by the British entrepreneur, Clive Sinclair, whose consumer electronics company had grown out of his own interest in inventing and brainstorming. He launched his first model, the ZX 80, in 1980, as a machine for learning to program on. Since there was no supporting software, this was more of a necessity than an invitation. Not surprisingly, it found its main market among enthusiasts with computer skills. They were also among the first to buy his second and more powerful model, the ZX 81, launched the following year. This extract from an interview captures the computer hobbyist's pleasure in possession particularly well.

> I caught the bug over ten years ago at college on the mainframe there. I was so keen that one summer holiday period I conned this company that I was just a little guy with a couple of 'O' levels and I wanted to be an operator, and they trained me up. It was 8K. So, an expanded ZX 81 is more powerful. And this was a mainframe. This took up a whole room. I always thought one day I would have my own, you know. I just can't believe it now, I still haven't got over the shock.

At the same time, the ZX 81 began to pick up sales in the general consumer market among households with little or no previous computer experience. Within twelve months of its launch, 400,000 had been sold, establishing it as the brand leader in the British home computer market. Its nearest rival was the VIC 20, produced by the American company, Commodore, which, like the Sinclair, used an ordinary domestic television as a display screen and a portable audio cassette recorder in place of a disc drive.

1981 also saw the launch of the government's scheme to put a microcomputer into every secondary school as part of its plan to help 'prepare children for life in a society in which devices and systems based on microelectronics are commonplace and pervasive' (Department of Education and Science, 1981, p.1). In line with the diffuse 'Buy British' policy in information technology, schools were directed to the machines manufactured by two domestic companies, Acorn and Research Machines. Acorn had a distinct advantage in this competition since the BBC's well-publicized computer literacy course, launched at the beginning of 1982, was built around their model. In October 1982, the Micros in Schools scheme was extended to primary schools, and once again Acorn was on the list of approved suppliers. This double seal of official approval, from the government and the BBC, gave a considerable fillip to Acorn's push into the general consumer market, and by the end of 1983 their machines had achieved sales of around 250,000.

Their marketing strategy resonated strongly with official discourse about the coming 'information age', and played on parents' hopes and fears about their children's future employment prospects. The advertisement for the second generation of Acorn machines is a good example. Headed 'Think of it as a downpayment on your child's future uniform', it featured a girl in her graduation robes, bathed in sunlight, standing in the cloisters of one of the country's ancient universities. The accompanying copy was addressed directly to parental worries.

> Your child's degree ceremony might seem a long way off. But the BBC Master Compact is equipment to help at every step of the way. Our new micro can provide your child with constant support throughout education, eventually graduating into business and professional use. Put it on your Christmas list. It should help to put a few letters after your child's name.

A contemporaneous advertisement, for the colour monitors aproved for use with BBC micros in schools, underlined this message, arguing that:

> This year, no less than 20,000 schools rely on the high resolution of Cub monitors to make computer-related education more clearly understood… Now Microvite have made this same range available for home use… It has never been more vital to ensure that your child has the benefit of the finest teaching aids… The Microvite Cub is the colour monitor which your child will expect and is unlikely to out-grow.

These promotional appeals presented home computing as a form of rational recreation, in which domestic space becomes an extension of the classroom and the office, and the user practises 'useful' skills, gradually moving on to more complex tasks and becoming a fully functioning member of the computerized society.

This vision of the micro as an essential aid to educational and career advancement played a key role in encouraging parents to invest in one. Altogether, three-quarters of all the households in the Midlands survey that had a computer claimed to have purchased a machine with children and teenagers in mind. Many had gone out and bought one in much the same spirit as they might earlier have bought a set of encyclopedias. Its acquisition often coincided with the development of computer studies in school. Sometimes the push came from the children, as in this teenager's account of using his BBC micro:

> It was the time when everybody was getting a computer really, and I wanted one for school. So I thought I'd get one like the stuff I used at school, so I used it to get through my 'O' level… We did a project in the Fifth Form, which was handy, 'cause I could do it at at home you see.

He also experimented with uses linked to his interests: 'what I used to like writing was sound programmes. Doing, you know, making? 'cause I used to have a music book and I used to type in. That's what I used to do a lot of.'

This form of micro use as rational recreation was the exception rather than the rule, however. With the prices of basic models starting at around £300, comparatively few families in the Midlands sample could afford an Acorn/BBC machine, and most therefore settled for one of the cheaper machines, in the belief that simply having one in the house would be beneficial. The following account is typical.

Son (14) We didn't have anything to do with it. It was him over there [indicating the father]. We got in from school one day and he said, 'Right we're going to go and get a computer'.

Father We'd obviously got a bit of spare cash like. I'd got some money coming at the end of the summer, and I said we'd go out and buy it at the beginning of the summer, didn't I?

Son Yes.

Father They were just about to start learning it at school when we got it, and I thought it wouldn't be fair if they got left behind .... I thought I could try it anyway, and then I found that I couldn't drive it at all [laughs] .

In common with many parents with little or no knowledge of computers, this father hadn't realized that the cheaper machines were not well suited to educational applications. Their primary uses were being constructed by a quite different discourse.

The initial wave of parental decisions to buy a basic Sinclair or Commodore coincided with the point in time when the cheap micro was beginning to emerge as a games-playing machine. The major push in this direction came from the software companies rather than the hardware producers, several of whom feared that too close an identification with games would undermine the micro's status as a general-purpose machine. As the executive who handled Commodore's advertising campaign in the early 1980s put it: 'We wanted always to see our product as a proper piece of technology: but fun technology. We didn't want to see it as a toy' (quoted in Haddon, 1988b, p.71). By 1983, however, this precarious balance between 'proper' and playful uses had been tipped in favour of games-playing by the promotional activities of the entertainment entrepreneurs who were entering the software market. They saw home computer games as a logical extension of two other screen-based entertainment systems: the video games console that plugged into a domestic television set, and the coin-operated video games machines installed in amusement arcades.

In the United States, higher levels of disposable income combined with tax breaks encouraged households to invest in relatively powerful domestic computers, leaving a definable market niche for dedicated games consoles. Sales took off in 1975, when Atari launched its tennis game, 'Pong' and grew substantially after 1976, when reprogrammable cartridges were introduced. In contrast, the British console market started a little later and was undercut by cheap computers before it had a chance to establish itself. As a result, only 2 per cent of households had acquired a video games console by the end of 1982, compared to 15 per cent in the United States. Price was again a significant factor. In 1983, reprogrammable video consoles cost between £70 and £140, with games cartridges selling for between £20 and £30. By that time, consumers could purchase a basic Sinclair machine for less than £70, and select games from a rapidly expanding catalogue of titles for around £5 each. Moreover, the ubiquity of cassette recorders meant that games borrowed from other users could be copied for the price of a blank tape, despite the software manufacturers' best efforts to protect their sales with anti-piracy devices. Breaking these security systems became a popular pastime among computer hobbyists. For some, the main pleasure was in beating the system. Actually playing the game was secondary. As one teenager recounted: 'I must admit, I do have great fun trying to crack protection systems. But that's more to do with the fun of it, rather than anything to do with the programme once you've got it on tape.'

Other hobbyists, like this 21-year-old unemployed male, experimented with altering standard software and writing their own games. As he explained in interview:

> Games are nice to play, but I always have a go. I say, 'I wonder if I could make that game', and then I try it myself. Sometimes people come and say 'That's a nice programme. Did you buy it?' and I say 'No, I made it' My talent seems to lie in making it look better... For a start, I look for a different presentation, the title screen, etcetera, adding all little items like that... One of me greatest achievements was writing me own adventure programmes, where I could slot in any adventure I wanted.

Most users, however, were content to buy commercially produced games tapes. These drew on a range of sources, including the genres that had proved popular in the arcades.

Video games began to replace pinball machines in the arcades in the late 1970s. Their iconography was overwhelmingly masculine. Most were either simulations of glamorized male activities, such as flying a fighter aircraft or driving a Grand Prix racing car, or variants on the scenario where the player defended territory against enemy attack. The most famous of these games, 'Space Invaders', was introduced in 1979, to be followed by hosts of others. According to one American study, by the mid-1980s, women appeared in only 8 per cent of arcade games, and then mostly in passive roles (Toles, 1985). The more polymorphous games such as 'Pac-Man', were less obviously gendered, but overall, the imaginary world of arcade games was overwhelmingly masculine. This bias was reinforced by the social organization of the arcades themselves and the fact that they had mostly been commandeered by adolescent male peer groups as arenas for competitive display.

This masculine orientation carried over into the home computer market when the most popular arcade games were adapted for domestic use. It was also evident in the other major games genres: sports and adventure games. Although some adventures drew on sources popular with girls as well as boys, such as J.R.R. Tolkien's fantasy, *The Hobbit*, many relied on predominantly masculine genres such as horror and science fiction (Skirrow, 1986). A recent survey of Midlands teenagers, conducted in 1989, confirms the continuing gender bias of games-playing, with boys being twice as likely as girls to play once or twice a week and six times as likely to play three or more times a week [2]. Arcade games were still far and away the most popular genre followed some way behind by simulations, sports and adventure games. There was also a strong age pattern, with games-playing falling away sharply by the age of 15, when activities outside the home become more central in peer group life. Nevertheless, it remains easily the most common use of micros by young people.

Despite its centrality, games-playing has never quite shaken off the connotations of addiction that surrounded the early arcade games. In 1981, the Labour MP George Foulkes narrowly failed to push through his 'Control of Space Invaders (and Other Electronic Games) Bill' in the House of Commons. Concern continued through the decade, but in 1988 a Home Office study concluded that there was no need for further legislation, and placed the responsibility for controlling adolescent use of arcades firmly on the shoulders of parents and managers (Graham, 1988). Early worries about harmful 'effects' had already carried over into the domestic market, however, and home computer games were included in the terms of the 1985 Video Recording Act, which was introduced to regulate pre-recorded video tapes and eradicate the so-called 'video nasties'. Beneath these debates lay the familiar Victorian concern with the 'proper' use of leisure, and the continual clashes between contrasted definitions of rational recreation, trivial pursuits and dangerous pleasures.

By mid-decade, then, there were at least four major discourses around home computing, offering competing definitions of its potentialities and pleasures: the discourse of self-referring practice in which the machines appeared as a space for creative activity and problem-solving; the discourse of 'serious' applications related to the schoolroom and workplace; the discourse of games-playing and fun which presented the micro as another screen-based entertainment facility; and the discourse of righteous concern for the welfare of the young. These discourses provided the symbolic context within which the parents and children in the Midlands study negotiated and struggled over the uses of their machines.

MICROS AND MORAL ECONOMIES

The outcomes depended on the way households were organized as economic and cultural units, their moral economies (Silverstone, 1991, p.139; 1992) and, in particular, on the structure of authority and the distribution of computing expertise among family members.

Parents familiar with computers sometimes made a determined effort to encourage 'serious' use, as in this mother s account of activities with her 10-year-old son and 12-year-old daughter:

> The first computer came when we had the children, even though my husband used to be a computer engineer and I use a computer at school with the children I work with. It is for educational purposes. We have always encouraged them. It is not just for playing games. Even when we had the Spectrum, before this Atari, we had a word processing package. They would write little stories, and we had a comprehension package, and a maths package, even when they were little. We all use the Atari.... We play games together. We have chess and so on.

Other parents, even those used to working with computers, had given up an unequal struggle and accepted that the machine would be mainly used for games, though some rationed computer use in an effort to encourage their children to spend more time on 'improving' activities. As one mother (who taught computing in a secondary school) explained:

> On the whole they use it mainly for games, and therefore I do restrict how long they use it, because a lot of games I consider as not very worth while, and, like television, I believe in restricting what they do in some way.

Other families resorted to more stringent measures, such as packing the computer away. As another mother related:

> We don't like to get it out too often because it's a temptation to them to give up their swotting. 'Cause once they start playing games, it's difficult to stop, we found that.... They are quite good and disciplined about it. They know that they've got work to do at the moment. So I say, 'Right, we'll put it away'.

In all three of these cases, the parents attempted to exercise control over use, either positively or negatively. But, as the Midlands interviews revealed, this was much more difficult with older teenagers, particularly where the parents had little or no computer competence themselves. In these situations children could use their time on the micro to win space and privacy within the household and assert their separation and independence from their parents. This was particularly important in the case of fathers and sons, as in this account by a an unemployed man in his early twenties living at home. His father, a skilled tradesman, had never attempted to master the computer but valued practical expertise.

It's a programme that's very simple to make. It just keeps jiggling through all the numbers. It's a system a lot have used to crack telephone numbers. 'Cause this place is ex-directory, and me dad said 'You can't do it in a week', and I said, 'Yes, I can'. And using the number plan and the telephone book and a bit of guesswork as well, I located the number. And he says, 'I backed you twenty pound that you can't do it in a week', he says. And I got my sister involved in as well, and we ended up taking forty pounds off him. Served him right.

CONCLUSION

These tales from the field afford fleeting glimpses of complex processes, deeply embedded in the sedimented structures of families' interior lives. To tell these tales in the detail they deserve, we will certainly need better and deeper ethnographies of everyday consumption. But, as we have also argued, if we are interested in explanation as well as description, we will also need to look for better ways of linking these micro processes to the wider economic, social and symbolic formations that surround and shape them. We need more sensitive explorations of the continual traffic between public and private, interiors and exteriors, and of connections between user careers and the general trajectory of the computer industry, between biographies and history.

As we have argued, the British home computer market was divided, almost from the outset, into a 'serious' sector based around relatively powerful machines of the type being introduced into schools and offices, and a games-playing sector in which cheap computers became another extension of screen-based entertainment, often literally, since many families used a television set as a monitor. There is every sign that this bifurcation will continue. The recent *rapprochement* between the two leading personal computer companies, Apple and IBM, looks likely to consolidate their control over the market for 'serious' machines, whilst the Japanese companies, Nintendo and Sega, have revivified the market for dedicated games consoles, selling half a million units by the middle of 1991.

The Midlands data suggest that this industrial segmentation will be mapped onto social divisions, and that self-determined computing will remain concentrated in the relatively affluent and well-educated households of the professional and managerial strata, whilst the rest of the population are largely confined to participating in professionally crafted fantasies. They will have interactivity without power. The consequences of this situation for democratic participation, in a society increasingly organized around screen-based systems, deserves more extended discussion than it has so far received.

NOTES

1 The research was made possible by grants from Central Independent Television, the Economic and Social Research Council and the Research Board of Leicester University. We are grateful to all three organizations for their support.

2 This study, based on a survey of 460 11 to 15-year-olds in six schools in a Midlands town, was conducted by Mr Robert Cromwell in 1989 as part of his research for his doctoral thesis at the University of Loughborough.

REFERENCES

Danko, W. D. and MacLachlan J. M. (1983) 'Research to accelerate the diffusion of a new invention: the case of personal computers', *Journal of Advertising Research,* 23, (3), pp. 39-43.

Department of Education and Science (1981) *Microelectronics Education Programme: The Strategy,* London, Department of Education and Science.

Dickerson, M. and Gentry, J. (1983) 'Characteristics of adopters and non-adopters of home computers', *Journal of Consumer Research,* 10, pp. 225-34.

Dutton, W. H., Rogers, E. M and Jun, Suk-Ho (1987) 'The diffusion and impacts of information technology in households', *Oxford Surveys in Information Technology,* 4, pp. 133-93.

Dutton, W. H., Sweet, P. L. and Rogers, E. M. (1988) 'Socio-economic status and the diffusion of personal computing in the United States', paper presented to the conference of the International Association for Mass Communication Research, Barcelona, 24-8 July.

Graham, J. (1988) *Amusement Machines: Dependency and Delinquency,* Home Office Research Study no. 101, London, HMSO.

Haddon, L. (1988a) The home computer: the making of a consumer electronic', *Science as Culture,* 2, pp. 7-51.

Haddon, L. (1988b) 'Electronic and computer games: the history of an interactive medium', *Screen* 29, (2), pp. 52-73.

Hall, P.H., Nightingale, J.J. and MacAulay, T.G. (1985) 'A survey of micro-computer ownership and usage', *Prometheus* 3, (1), pp. 156-73.

Jouet, J. (1988) 'Social uses of micro-computers in France', paper presented to the conference of the International Association of Mass Communication Research, Barcelona, 24-8 July.

Marketing Week (1986) 'Mediabank: videographics', 17 October.

Murdock, G. (1989) 'Critical inquiry and audience activity', in B. Dervin, L. Grossberg, B. J. O'Keefe and E. Wartella (eds) *Rethinking Communication vol.* 2: *Paradigm Exemplars,* London, Sage 226-49.

Murdock, G. and Golding, P. (1989) 'Information, poverty and political inequality: citizenship in the age of privatized communications', *Journal of Communication,* 39, (3), pp. 180-95.

Rogers, E. M. (1983) *Diffusion of Innovations,* 3rd edn, New York: Free Press.

Rogers, E. and Larsen, J.K. (1984) *Silicon Valley Fever: Growth of High-Technology Culture,* New York, Basic Books.

Silverstone, R. (1991) 'From audiences to consumers: the household and the consumption of communication and information technologies', *European Journal of Communication,* 6, pp. 135-54.

Silverstone, R., Hirsch, E. and Morley, D. (1992) 'Information and communication technologies and the moral economy of the household', in R. Silverstone and E. Hirsch (1992) *Consuming Technologies: Media and Information in Domestic Spaces,* London, Routledge.

Skirrow, G. (1986) 'Hellivision: an anaysis of video games', in Colin McCabe (ed.) *High Theory/Low Culture: Analysing Popular Television and Film,* Manchester: Manchester University Press, pp. 115-42.

Tinnell, C. S. (1985) 'An ethnographic look at personal computers in the family setting', *Marriage and Family Review,* 8, (1-2), pp. 59-69.

Toles, T. (1985) Video games and American military ideology', in Vincent Mosco and Janet Wasko (eds) *The Critical Communications Review, vol.* 3: *Popular Culture and Media Events,* Norwood N. J., Ablex, pp. 207-23.

Venkatesh, A. and Vitalari, N. P. (1986) 'Computing technology for the home: product strategies for the next generation', *Journal of Product Innovation and Management,* 3, (3), pp. 171-86.

Wheelock, J. (1990) 'Personal computers, gender and an institutional model of the household', paper presented to the ESRC/PICT workshop on Domestic Consumption and Information Technologies, Brunel University, May.

THE FEMININE CULTURE OF THE TELEPHONE: PEOPLE, PATTERNS AND POLICY

Ann Moyal

INTRODUCTION

This study has [...] been prompted in part by a perception that, as Australian telecommunications organizational change and deregulatory measures are being framed, important social data should be added to the equation. Significantly, to date, no systematic examination has been made by either carriers or scholars of telephone use in Australia [1]. Broad international generalizations, and a few case specific studies, can be found [2]. But while a flow of books and papers both at home and abroad examine broadcasting, television, video, cable, satellite communication, the information society, and the organization and politicization of telecommunications, that ubiquitous, taken-for-granted medium for two-way human communication, the telephone, remains largely invisible to scholars despite its central, and far-reaching influence on our daily lives. 'While extensively used,' comments Noble, 'the telephone has been all but conceptually ignored.'[3] This omission is the more critical in the light of major changes that have overtaken society in the past two decades. Rising divorce rates, single parenthood, disturbance of the nuclear family, the ageing of our population, the impact of feminism, problems of public transport, migration, youth unemployment, the diversification of home work sites, mature age re-entry into education, the impact of rural crisis, the development of the Northern Territory and the Aboriginal outstation movements, all have combined to change many of the old contours of Australian society and to pose questions about our social systems of communication.

In addition, then, to the well canvassed pressures from business and industry for telecommunications deregulation, more competitive tariffs, and the principle of 'user pays' [4], we need to know how the Australian people *use* the telephone; how historical conditioning has influenced our telephone use, and what input may be made from the Australian community to the critical debate of reframing a national telecommunications policy. 'Society,' wrote a founder of the computer society, Norbert Wiener, 'can only be understood through a study of the messages and communications facilities which belong to it.' [5] This survey represents one piece of the evidence. It focuses on an important component of telephone users, Australian women. As such, it is the first survey of women's telephone use to be conducted in Australia and the first such national survey to be made in any country. It is presented in the hope that its findings may offer useful insights to Australian, and other national policy-makers, regulators, carriers and administrators, and provide pertinent data for sociologists, social policy, communication, gender and other disciplinary scholars and researchers.

RESEARCH STRATEGY

The concept for the study arose early in 1988 when Telecom's projection of the introduction of timed local calls (TLCs) raised a highly critical response in the Australian community. From a background of telecommunications research, I initiated a pilot study of older women and the telephone conducted by questionnaire in four States on attitudes to, and usage of, the telephone. The questionnaire drew a distinction between (a) 'instrumental' and (b) 'intrinsic' calls, calls made (a) for making appointments, shopping, seeking information, timetables, entertainments, making business arrangements, dealing with emergencies, accidents, household crises and (b) personal communication with relatives, friends, volunteer work, counselling, and initmate discussion and exchange [6]. The data returned from 50 respondents (aged 55 and over) was striking in its conformity. It revealed that the women in this sample made from 4-6 instrumental telephone calls per week lasting 2-6 minutes, and some 28-40 intrinsic telephone calls (extending across day and evening) to relatives, children, grandchildren, inlaws and friends, occupying from 10-15 minutes, quite often 20-25 minutes and, at times, from 45 minutes to one hour; that the telephone played a key, and continuing, role in building kin and friend relationships; fortified a sense of security and self-worth; created a 'psychological neighbourhood' that substituted for face-to-face contact, and that the familiar, 'invisible', telephone had assumed a distinctive significance for older Australian women as an essential part of their culture and as a central factor in the conduct of their lives.

The pilot study led to an approach to Telecom to commission a national study of women's telephone usage that would embrace women of all ages from teenagers to nonogenarians; women at home and in the workforce; single, married, divorced and widowed women; single mothers; the aged; students and unemployed women; migrants; Aborigines; urban, rural and remote region women, and women without access to a private telephone – 'the telephone poor'. The survey, directed at respondents in metropolitan and country sites in all States, was launched in July 1988 [7]. Two hundred women were included in the survey (exclusive of the original pilot group). Since the object of the survey was to gather the experience, attitudes, and voices of women, the method selected was qualitative rather than quantitative, and based on a 40 question questionnaire distributed in person to respondents followed by in-depth interviews. The research design took as its model the ethnographic, 'deep slice' methodology mounted by anthropologist, Diane Bell, in her Bicentennial study, *Generations. Grandmothers, Mothers and Daughters* [8]. Bell's study derived from in-depth interviewing by herself and a team of ten research assistants of one hundred women across the nation and focused on the material and emotional culture of Australian women. Her aim was to retrieve direct and reflective material on the 'enduring dynamic culture' of Australian women and to discern how women construct and transmit a 'sense of self' in a rapidly changing world. She saw a pertinent extension of her methodology in a study of the feminine culture of the telephone, and several of her research assistants were co-opted for the study.

The research strategy for a qualitative study of how women of a wide spectrum of life experience, location, age, and education, use the telephone was based on the involvement of fifteen research assistants scattered across Australia, themselves recruited from different backgrounds, professional and personal experience, and with access to different aspects of Australian society. Each assistant was equipped with the research protocol and questionnaire and required to provide 7-10 respondents of different ages from their network of contacts, and to record, tape, transcribe interviews and present written reports. Questions covered demographic data, occupation, living situation, telephone use (including local, STD and international), its instrumental or intrinsic character, timing and duration, last call, the respondent's network of contacts, her access to transport, volunteer work, hobbies and interests, attitudes to the telephone both positive and negative, views on charging (including timed local calls, STD, zonal and community access charging), historical conditioning, and, where relevant, responses to public phone use. Respondents were issued with time sheets and asked to monitor a week's incoming and outgoing calls. Importantly, privacy and confidentiality was assured and strictly protected by the uniform use of a pseudonym or first name. A further series of interviews, with additional questions to cover aspects of 'acculturation' were conducted by multilingual interviewers to bring a sample of Greek, Lebanese, Italian, Vietnamese, Polish and Spanish women within the survey. As chief investigator, I conducted interviews with surburban, rural and remote area women and some Aboriginal women, and classified and analysed the collected data. Significantly, in a survey of telephone personal use, the telephone itself served as a most valuable instrument in gathering direct and detailed information, in recruiting very isolated women, and in ensuring a representative geographical and demographic diversity.

No methodology is free from problems. Some researchers drew richer material; some tended, for efficiency, to compress and stereotype some attitudinal responses; one half of the respondents failed to complete the weekly time sheet of calls on the grounds that, because of the atypicality of the 'check week', they preferred to furnish an 'observed average' of their weekly pattern of calls [9]. The sample does not claim to cover 'everywoman'. With a female population of just over 8 million in Australia, such expectation would be unreal, and no attempt was made to look for occupational or social categories. It is, nonetheless, indicative of the validity of the survey approach that it closely reflected the Australian demographic profile. While 200 was selected as an acceptable national sample (and almost *de rigeur* in Bicentennial year), respondent inputs on attitudes and telephone usage reached a degree of repetition before data collection was complete. Even so, the women ran the gamut from straightforward, pragmatic countrywomen, migrants of complex – and restricted – experience, Aborigines in the Centre and in academic employment, home-based mothers of wide diversity, women working in an 'electronic cottage' situation, through students, teenagers, sporty and intellectual women, the 'aged', through primary, secondary, tertiary and postgraduate education, and on to high profile women in the workforce. Their frank participation, reflective viewpoints, and a sense that their evidence was of interest and relevance, yielded data that a statistically larger, but impersonal, quantitative methodology would not retrieve.

Demographically, the sample of 134 women from capital cities, and 66 from rural areas and country towns [10], corresponded with Telecom's regional partition of customer responsibilities into 67 per cent 'Metropolitan', and 33 per cent 'Country'. Age distribution of respondents conformed broadly with national percentages. There were 10 women aged 15-19; 70 aged 20-39; 52 aged 40-54; 32 aged 55-64; 24 aged 65-74, and 12 over 75 [11]. One in every five Australians is a migrant and 47 migrants featured in the survey, a representation of 22 per cent. 15 respondents were interviewed belonging to the category 'without private phones'. There are recognizable gaps: the sample, for example, produced no women from remote mining towns or from distant defence service locations, both areas that offer a fruitful scene for further research. While the study, however, does not purport to assert 'universality' of experience, it has *cut* a swathe through a diverse spectrum of Australia's female population – the 50.07 per cent that make up half of Telecom Australia's constituency.

SURVEY FINDINGS

USAGE

The survey threw into strong relief feminine patterns of telephone calling.

A demarcation was drawn between 'instrumental' (appointment and arrangement making, purchasing or information seeking) and 'intrinsic' (personal exchange and communication) calls, though the point was made by several respondents that instrumental calls – relating to making arrangements for children's outings, volunteer acitivites, or in pursuit of information – could lead to friendship and intrinsic communication. Consistent with evidence from sources overseas, the great proportion of telephone calling pertained to local calls. Women surveyed in all States made, on average, from 2-6 local instrumental calls per week, with the exception of women who work at home and use the telephone for workrelated or business matters, home-based women temporarily involved in renovation, health crises involving children, or irregular charity commitments, and phone-dependent physically disadvantaged women [12]. In the latter category (6 in the sample), instrumental calls could rise to 10-12 per week.

Instrumental calls were made across the day (tending only to emergency calls at night) and occupied from 1-3 minutes (a uniform 2 minutes was most frequently cited), except when the call involved Commonwealth or State government departments and utilities where the now broadly established 'queueing mechanism' for handling callers pushed the telephone call up to 10, 15 or 20 minutes and elicited widespread and trenchant criticism from respondents.

Evidence on women's personal instrumental use of the telephone in Australia thus suggested that users conducted these calls with despatch; that, in this context, the telephone was a valued substitute for personal contact – many used the telephone 'to let their fingers do the walking' (paying bills, enquiring about potential purchases, seeking quotes) – but that the concept of teleshopping had not taken root among the sample (young, middle-aged and even older women like to get out to do their shopping) [13], and that the telephone was used rather as a constructive aid for the efficient, time-saving, control and handling of their personal concerns. Migrant women tended to contribute to the top range of instrumental calls (often using language-skilled kin to make the transaction) for the purpose of obtaining information from government departments and ethnic agencies and organizations to help them in the process of acculturation.

The respondents' pattern was very different for intrinsic calls. A high proportion of calls made were local calls though rural women showed a concentration of STD (trunk) intrinsic calls, while findings revealed a rising trend in STD intrinsic calling as the geographical spread of adult children to other States and cities, exposed a marked mobility among Australian families. In summary terms, women in the sample made from 14-42 personal communication calls per week, the average settling around 20-28. A small contingent – young mothers living close to parents and kin, women of British origin, and a small number of women over 75 – contributed to the low end of the user curve, while the highest number – from 25-48 each week – attached to women who worked at home, some older women aged 65-75, and women from different ethnic groups. Women without access to a private telephone – 15 in the sample dispersed in Sydney, Melbourne, Adelaide, Wollongong, Albury-Wodonga (NSW), in rural Queensland and South Australia – made a comparatively low number (5-18) of intrinsic calls, while some rural, and Aboriginal women, registered high intrinsic calling rates of 25-35-41-45 calls a week [14].

Significant evidence related to the duration of intrinsic calls. Only 38 (19 per cent) of the 200 women attested that their intrinsic calls occupied less than 5 minutes; 20 per cent (40 respondents) averaged these calls at from 10-15 minutes, and the remaining 61 per cent of the sample affirmed that their intrinsic calls commonly centred around 15-20 minutes, not infrequently reaching 30-45 minutes, and, on occasion, extended over an hour. Intrinsic calls were made by the sample from 7 a.m. across the day, commonly 9 a.m. to midmorning (after husbands had departed for work), at lunchtime, notably from 5-7 p.m., and in the evening. The aged (over

75) and the physically disadvantaged tended to make intrinsic calls at all times of the day and early evening. Other patterns emerged. Women in the full-time workforce – 40 – concentrated their calling after 6 p.m., occasionally early morning and at weekends, although almost half the sample, also had access for personal calling to a work phone. Teenagers specialized in late afternoon and evening calls, while women 'homeworkers' made their intrinsic calls at lunchtime, from 5-7 p.m., and in the evening, developing a pattern of structured personal communication to break up the isolation of their working day. Rural women scattered their local intrinsic calls across the day but concentrated personal STD calling to coincide with cheaper evening and Sunday calling rates. The geographical location of respondents produced some minor differences. Queensland women appeared to use the telephone for some local intrinsic contact before 7 a.m.; Northern Territory and Western Australian women, experiencing significant time differences with southern and eastern States, were often unable to take advantage of the after 10 p.m. cheaper STD calling rate, to reach relatives in other towns and cities.

The sample's evidence on intrinsic calls, thus, clearly confirmed that while the number of weekly calls made by individual women was not large, their duration rarely fell within the time span characterized by telecommunications carriers as 'average' local calls [15]. Moreover, the call's duration, and the sense of unpressured communication it contained, was perceived as a key component of the purpose and satisfaction of the call. The viewpoint was endorsed by 192 members of the sample, an attitude unaffected by the education, occupation or age of the respondent [16].

WOMEN'S TELEPHONE NETWORKS

In his broad and critical overview of *The Sociology of the Telephone,* republished in 1986, American sociologist, Sidney Aronson, pertinently observes that 'that which we take for granted usually needs to be most closely examined.' The questions concerning telephone use yet to be answered, he sums up, are, in brief, 'who talks to whom, for how long, and for what reasons and with what results.'

The evidence from this survey suggests that Australians are a deeply familial people and enjoy a society in which ongoing telephone communication between female family members (both geographically proximate and remote) constitutes an important part of their support structure and contributes significantly to their sense of well-being, security, stability, and self-esteem. A total of 184 respondents confirmed that the prime importance of the telephone in their daily life related to 'sustaining family relationships' and to their contact with children, parents, and, to a less regular extent, with siblings, grandchildren and other members of the family. Conspicuously, 'kinkeeping' floods the lines. A singular proportion of these calls and time, is devoted to communication between mothers and daughters, who establish telephone contact daily or regularly throughout the week, and maintain an intimate and caring telephone relationship across their lives. The communication link appears at its most concentrated when the daughters have moved away from home, are in their childbearing/childrearing period, work in the same town or city, and live within an area of local call. Costs clearly govern the shorter duration calls between more geographically distant mothers and daughters (their regret at the constraint emerges in their replies), but the importance of the connection – regular, caring, and detailed in its content – was undiminished by geography.

Women's voices from the survey illustrate the gratification of the communication and the individual character of the response. A retired resident of a Queensland country town, attests: 'Each night my daughter and I talk for half an hour by phone. We discuss the routine of the day, things we want to do when we meet. It helps my life entirely. It helps my daughter too. We get very depressed and lonely otherwise.' A Melbourne woman, in her sixties rang her daughters and sisters frequently and, they in turn, kept in regular telephone touch with her. 'Family contact is very important with one's children scattered and hard at work,' she confirmed. 'I need the phone for ongoing contact. My brother has a terminal illness and needs constant reassurance, as does my sister-in-law. Some days, with illness, I seem never to be off the phone.' The mother emerged as 'the nexus in the family of what's going on'. 'You offer a forum on the telephone,' one said, 'for listening to your children's problems.' A younger Sydney woman, 33, defining the telephone as 'crucial to the quality of my life,' noted that she kept in constant touch with her mother and 'in times of family crisis, Mum rings me constantly. The process of talking it out can go on for a long time, but it's vital to us and helps us work out the worry.' Similarly, a mother in the Canberra workforce began each day, for a 4 month period, with a half hour phone call to a son who, devastated by marital breakdown, needed her call 'to get him going'. 'It was the support he needed,' she said, 'just to speak to someone first thing in the morning.'

Conversely, young mothers raising new babies and young children, made daily phone calls to their mothers and, at times, sisters to report on their child's progress, make baby-minding arrangements, and to gain confirmation and reassurance from the exchange. Two Victorian sisters interviewed, both young mothers, found that the daily phone call to each other 'certainly helped with the baby.' 'To know that she is having the same problems with her baby, when I'm a new time mother,' said one, 'does help the self-esteem. We find it easier to talk more intimately about things over the phone particularly relating to the baby.' A young Perth mother attached particular importance to telephone contact in the major change of circumstances which withdrawal from the workforce and solitary days at home with a baby implied. 'My mother calls daily,' she reported, 'to enquire about my son. I'd used the telephone extensively at work, and it's very important as a connection to the outside world. Going from being at work where you are surrounded by people and activity to just being you and the baby at home without a car – you need these phone conversations to survive!' It was a reiterative theme. Distance raised problems, but the tenor of fortifying mother-daughter communication did not change. One older Canberra mother recounted that when her young married daughter moved to a city setting where other young wives were out at work, she would ring her with the plaintive cry, 'Mum, I've put the egg-timer on, talk to me for 3 minutes!' Even when family members cohabit, interviews reveal how a 10-minute telephone call daily could break the isolation and bleakness experienced by a frail, elderly mother as the evidence of an 83-year old Greek respondent confirmed: 'My daughter rings daily from work,' she recorded, 'for 10 minutes and sometimes more depending on her circumstance. Just the contact with my daughter's voice is a comfort to me and I look forward to her call as my loneliness grows.'

The telephone relationship between grandmother and grandchild was also highlighted in the transcripts. Several older women recalled how grandchildren could command lengthy telephone calls, taking over a call to a parent with 'Grandma I want to tell you something' and recounting a story that goes on for 45 minutes. Another emphasized the value of this kind of communication in a society where distance prevented frequent face-to-face contact with grandchildren and where a grandchild engaged in a close transgeneration relationship could enjoy ongoing, and uninterrupted converse with the grandmother. A Brisbane woman noted that:

> ...calls to and from her grandchildren in another suburb could last for 30 minutes and often longer. A great deal of my contact with my grandchildren is by phone. It is extremely important that they feel free to phone me often and hold these detailed conversations when they don't have to compete for my attention as they would if our contact was limited to face-to-face contact when other family members are present.

An Albury grandmother recorded that her toddler grandchild:

> ...expects to speak to me on the phone at least every second day. The telephone is now an element in the lives of very small children.

In Nambour, Queensland, an Aboriginal grandmother who raised three grandchildren now at boarding school had the telephone connected for the first time when her grandchildren left for school. 'I find the phone a wonderful thing,' she summed up,

> because it keeps me in contact with the 'children' all the time. They've travelled around a lot in their sport, one to every State in Australia. I get a big bill, but if they only say 'we're safe and enjoying ourselves and we've still got some money left', then I don't worry and it's worth it. I find this contraption a very handy thing!

Clearly, the filial connection and its impetus to the process of ongoing discourse between women in the nuclear family feeds a major strand of telephone traffic in Australia. Contact breeds more contact, frequency gives continuity to the talk, and the very detail of the communication – a point stressed independently by many women – gave particular value to the calls. There were some negative images – the demanding mother who, when feeling lonely, 'would not let her daughter off the phone', or the interfering mother who phoned to 'overadvise' on child care. But, in the sample of 200, the 'cons' came down to three. Significantly, the last call made registered by many respondents was 'to my daughter', or 'to Mum'.

Beyond the inner family, the second most important scene of telephone networking was between close women friends, an area of communication which, in both range and kind, has extended significantly in the past two decades. Not only do more women live alone, undergo marital break-up or separation, and assume responsibilities as single parents, but, in a period of rising feminist influence and ideas, they find increasing support and emotional and intellectual stimulus from women friends. In this, evidence from the sample appeared undifferentiated by education, social environment, or age. The sociological importance of confidants, girlfriends, and women's enduring friendships is well understood. What emerged conspicuously from this study was the high importance of the telephone in maintaining and enhancing these key feminine relationships. Most women interviewed gave their close friendship calls a high priority, 'top' for women without parents or children, and very important for married women of all ages, widows, the retired, elderly, those distant from relatives overseas, and those 'in relationships' with men. The exceptions in terms of volume of use were students or single women living in communal situations, a small cluster of married women in exclusively close relationships, and the telephone poor.

'Talking by phone to a close friend,' said one young, home-bound Adelaide mother, 'is a life-saver. When you're feeling lonely, these calls can transform your view.' 'My calls to close friends are the longest calls I make,' a young Perth mother summed up for many women. 'It's difficult to get to see them and I need frequent contact to exchange ideas about our kids and what we're all doing. After my last child's birth I was depressed and these phone calls helped me to get back to normal.' Another Perth mother, married to a busy professional husband, maintained, 'The telephone is very important to me because suburban home life is lonely and the phone is a link with colour and variety and with people one loves. There's a need to communicate feeling and caring: the telephone is more personal than letters. What I want to know is how my friends 'feel' and I can hear this on the telephone.'

Despite Noble's evidence to the contrary that instrinsic calls were in his study 'used more for making arrangements and the organization of personal contacts in which feelings were expressed, rather than to unload one's heart through the telephone' [17], this survey's reiterative finding was that women talk more freely and intimately on the phone with close friends that they do face-to-face, that the telephone highlights warmth and sympathy in the voice, that (as one respondent put it) 'you can convey 'I know you're worried' even if you don't say it', and that women can reach 'greater depth in conversation on the telephone'. An older postgraduate student, studying to re-enter the workforce, pinpointed a salient trend in society when she said:

When I was younger and in the workforce and sharing accommodation I was much more gregarious, and there was no great need to use the telephone as a lifeline. Now the telephone is the 'frontline' when it comes to giving or receiving news, good or bad. With friends, it's grabbed instantly and in all sorts of situations – in response to mail, another telephone call, about something I'm reading or heard on the radio, to air a grievance, share a success seek support for an injustice or unlucky break, share news about health or holidays. It contributes to my sense of direction and participation, particularly if I need to discuss professional ideas I'm turning over.

Another mature-age student confirmed:

With the phone it's instant gratification. If you are lucky, and if there's something preying on your mind, you can solve it speedily. The phone creates this psychological neighbourhood for women. Women are not doing all the same thing now, not all staying at home in the family, they're moving about and talking to people. Professional women working at home may not have anything in common with their immediate neighbours, but they've created a close-knit phone neighbourhood. It alleviates loneliness which is very important. My phone calls now are a lot deeper. I need people and I'm more attentive to the needs of my women friends. Feminism has made us not feel ashamed of being close to women; we encourage and support each other.

'The telephone,' reflected a young Aboriginal woman counsellor in a rural university, 'that's what friendship is all about.'

Women with secondary education brought other perspectives to this view. Older women with children scattered interstate, sometimes widowed, some retired, carried on regular telephone networking with their circle of close friends, at times making daily contacts in late afternoon or evening to enquire how each fared. Such networking was essential to women who have moved through their share of life crises, and, through telephone contact, they found, and gave, important mutual support and care. Many respondents testified to long call durations from '30 to 45 to 60 minutes or more' with friends who, for example, had been widowed and who found telephone discussion often the only accessible communication for their grief. Women of all ages readily engaged in 'reflective listening' with friends in stress or personal need. Even women who avoided personal telephone initiatives appeared responsive in this listening art [18], accepting long calls, often disruptive to their own programmes, from distressed or traumatically involved friends. A 41-year-old Sydney woman identified the trend.

> Friends telephone me with their troubles. My 'last call' was from a friend who was very depressed; it lasted 2 hours which is normal for such calls. People seem to be feeling more stress these days and need to talk without getting their kids out of bed to go and visit. The telephone relieves a lot of tension.

'Telephoning is a form of care-giving,' Rakow concludes in her study of women and the telephone in Prospect, USA. 'It is gendered work and gender work.' [19] The point is amply illustrated by the experience of women across Australia. On interview evidence, women in country towns, cities and suburbs, engaged widely in the process of maintaining phone contact with elderly relatives, aunts, in-laws, extended family members, the father living alone, and with frail older friends or members of the community living alone or in nursing homes who were isolated or without family. Volunteer work also ranked high. In a 'nation of joiners', women's voluntary work ranged extensively from Brownie helper to aged care, from conservation to neighbourhood centres, disturbed and handicapped children, women's refuges and counselling, regional, local and national sport, rural groups and networks, church and school activities, to medical causes, Red Cross, palliative care, and ethnic community and cultural organizations. Twenty-three per cent of women surveyed contributed to these activities. 'The purpose of volunteer work,' said a Darwin woman, 'is to get the best out of our lives.' But it also conferred a substantial contribution of time, saved costs, and personal effort on the nation. For volunteer workers, 'the telephone,' said one, 'is the tool.' For women from the ethnic communities, community volunteer work figured prominently. Language fluent members of these communities were heavily committed to assisting parents, relatives, and community members in their telephone affairs, and several gave time to community projects. One respondent noted that 50 per cent of her 48 intrinsic calls a week were linked with community assistance. While many friendships grew from volunteer involvement, this part of women's 'telephone care' remained a largely hidden and taken-for-granted activity. As one respondent affirmed, 'If every volunteer totted up her telephone calls, the sum would amaze you. We're contributing this as well as our time and enterprise, and everything else as well.'

Across the broad community patterns of telephone contact, reflecting altered social conditions emerged. Children of divorced homes frequently took initiatives to sustain a close telephone relationship with a non-custodial parent. One 16-year old teenager, in her father's custody for several years, telephoned her mother after school daily for long sessions of talk. A single mother reported that her three children initiated regular calls to their 'non-supporting' father in an effort to arrange outings or 'merely to talk', and quite young children felt it their right to have telephone access to key adults [20]. The single mother's evidence added potent testimony on the telephone's parenting and supportive role. Single mothers were heavy telephone users, dependent on extended local calls with family and friends, commonly constrained by cost factors in STD use, and keen adapters of this communication form for difficult instrumental or other dealings with a former husband. One working single mother summed up the value of the telephone for this growing, and vulnerable, group in these terms:

> Without this form of parenting check to ring my daughter when she comes home from school, I would be unable to work. The telephone allows me to earn an income and sustain some social contact. As a single parent, there's little margin for the optional 'extras' of social life. It's an unrelenting lifestyle, and seldom of one's choice. What sustains me are lengthy late evening phone calls to a small nucleus of friends (often in the same boat). Without this lifeline I would very likely be a candidate for suicide or hospitalisation.

SPECIAL SECTORS: PATTERNS AND NEEDS

The foregoing outlines telephone networks and usage made by women, and the purposes and satisfactions such use imparts. The following looks at particular sectors of the feminine culture of the telephone in Australia that invite special notice for their variations and national relevance, and serve as pointers to future social and communication trends.

THE AGED

There is no group in the Australian community to whom the telephone offers more effective functional communication or a sense of personal participation and well-being than the 'aged'. For the purposes of this survey, the classification is applied to women over 75. While the Australian Bureau of Statistics marks its categorization of 'aged' at 65 [21], there was too great a commonality in the life and telephone patterns of the 24 members of the sample aged 65-74 and those 32 aged 55-64, to group women aged from 65 to 90 as a cohesive division in terms of telephone use or to identify a cohort of predominantly active, part-work/part-volunteer – involved women in the analysis of a long-living, but frailer, senior group. Accordingly, 12 respondents over 75 were allocated to the 'aged' subset, drawn from women living in cities and country towns, living alone, with family members, or in retirement villages, but not living in nursing homes or hostel accommodation. The interest and significance of the experience of this group, however, lies in the fact that women outlive their male contemporaries to a noted degree, and that the longevity of women and the 'greying' of Australia, poses serious questions for social planning and elderly care. 'The growth in the numbers of older people', predict the authors of *Greying Australia: Future Impacts of Population Ageing,* 'is likely to be one of the greatest challenges facing Australia society over the next few decades.' [22]

Yet, despite this, and the research lavished on the physical capacities, needs, environment, health and support arrangements for the aged, there is a dearth of literature on the telephone and the aged, and there has, to date, been no attempt in Australia, or elsewhere, to examine the importance of 'telephone relationships' in the aged's daily or weekly care. Data from this sample does not purport to map a territory but to point the seriousness of the research gap, and to focus the role of the telephone as a major agent in, and option for, the elderly's continuing independence and support [23].

All the women interviewed in this subset gave first priority to the sense of security and safety the telephone conferred and its importance in providing instant connection for their well-being and health. Most kept the telephone beside the bed. Those respondents who lived alone (nine out of twelve), conformed with the national sample in setting the greatest store by contact the telephone gave them to immediate members of their family, most frequently a daughter who kept in daily touch to find out about their health and needs, and to furnish the companionship of a 'chat'. One 83-year old South Australian woman, recently widowed, living alone and crippled with arthritis, was a significant example, being 'heavily telephone dependent', carrying a cordless phone everywhere and charging up the battery at night. For her, the telephone was 'a vital link', enabling her to remain in her own home and function independently. 'If she needs to get something down from a top cupboard,' said the transcript, 'she telephones either her cleaning girl or one of the Support Care systems available. She made 6-7 calls a day, some 42 a week. Many calls were instrumental, banking, shopping, medical, chemists, since everything she does comes by the medium of the phone, and as she cannot use public transport or drive, 'the calls snowball'.' Her daughter in Adelaide made telephone contact each night to help her mother over her mourning and loneliness.

In Perth, a widow of 86 living in a retirement village with daughters nearby made notably fewer phone calls (10-15 a week) but kept in regular touch with daughters to arrange meetings, and discuss her health and the activities of grandchildren and great grandchildren. To an 87-year old respondent living with a daughter in Sydney, the telephone had assumed great importance over the past five years when she was often unwell, could not use public transport easily, and did not wish to obtrude on her daughter's plans. As her intimate circle of friends shrank through death, she depended greatly on incoming calls to bring her connection with a wider world. 'The telephone,' she said, 'is very important to me to maintain contact. I ring less often as so many old friends have gone, but my life is invigorated by the people who phone in.' Similarly, a housebound migrant, 75, enfeebled by a stroke, made all her contacts by telephone in Greek while her daughter was at work, reducing loneliness and connecting herself, as she put it, to the 'multicultural Australian community'.

For the aged group, the telephone emerged as the human connector that brought encouragement and a feeling of adequacy and worth. The process flowed two ways. From Albury-Wodonga a 75-year old pensioner underscored the telephone and transport theme. 'I would not be able to live without a phone,' she said. 'I don't drive a car. There is no transport on Saturday afternoon or Sunday, and you need a telephone to make appointments to work in with the bus. It's an hour and a half between buses!' Intrinsic family, and instrumental calls were very important to her, letter writing was no substitute ('It often takes a week'); and she left her intrinsic calls till evening 'because then I'm lonely.' As a recent widow she had been greatly helped by the telephone. 'People have helped me in my bereavement, talking to me, and it's been wonderful. Now I find that I can help them.' Reflecting on the changed nature of telephone use in her adult life, and on the importance of the communication we have now, she noted that while women used the phone in earlier decades 'for family and friendship purposes, these calls were not the relaxed and long types of calls we are used to today.' 'We can't be a silent people,' she concluded, 'we must communicate.'

Such evidence is significant. All respondents in this age group made their telephone calls across the day; most were not well-off, many calls were long (15-20-45 minutes to one hour) and it is clear that this set of women would especially forfeit much of the comfort and purpose of their calling if they were hemmed in, from any change in national charging policy, to specific, cheaper, local calling times. Evidence from this sample indicated that aged women's instrumental calls were essential to their autonomy and maintenance as their physical strength declined, while their intrinsic calls furnished psychological comfort and support and illustrated the value to the well-being and survival of elderly women of confidants and friends. 'If interaction with friends is an important buffer against the threat that life change presents to self-esteem,' wrote gerontologist Alice Day, 'it is the widowed elderly woman, rather than the married, that has the most ready access to this resource.' [24]

Despite the small sample size of the subset, its sociological findings should be stressed [25]. In an ageing community, with women at its forward edge [26], any resource that can increase the number of non-institutionalised elderly and reduce their occupation of nursing home, hospital and special accomodation offers positive social gain. The role of the telephone as a coping mechanism, a 'lifeline', support system and companion to the community's 'aged', focuses this largely invisible, taken-for-granted technology as a resource that should be fully recognised in future planning for the aged. With the wide introduction to the homes of elderly people of cordless phones, Versatel phones with amplified, no hands communication, and beeper systems to connect those living alone with medical help, the telephone stands as a major option for innovative public and private sector plan for elderly care [27].

MIGRANT WOMEN

A second sector that shows distinctive characteristics of telephone use is that of ethnic communities in Australia. The experience of migrant women's telephone use has received little attention in this country. Yet

Australia is a nation of immigrants. One in five residents was born overseas, and 40 per cent of the population has parents born outside Australia. While Government policy shifted from the firm cultural 'assimilation' of all 'New Australians' in the decades of the fiftes and sixties to that of service to, and recognition of, 'ethnic diversity' in the last seventeen years, the individual experience of transplantation, of a new environment and language exposed migrants to severe psychological and cultural change. Women, housebound, and restricted in their social contact and exchange, often proved especially vulnerable, and were for periods 'hidden' members of the Australian community, underprivileged and 'depressed'. In these circumstances, it is useful to ask did the telephone play a useful part in the acculturation of the migrant woman? Did it help in their settlement and adaptation, did it keep their links with their homeland firm, and did it offer them, in the privacy of their own language, an 'ethnic place'?

These questions and others were added to the survey questionnaire and administered by researchers in several languages. The results show a striking commitment by women of different ethnic communities to telephone use. They also show how women with little or no telephone experience in their own country have become significant telephone users here, and how, in multicultural Australia, there is a daily concourse of many languages in Australia's telecommunications links.

Of the 47 migrant women surveyed 12 were Greek, 8 Italian, 7 Vietnamese, 6 British, 5 Lebanese, 5 Polish, 2 Spanish, one Peruvian, one Indian, while one Portugese and two American women appeared among the sample. As the largest ethnic community, Greeks assumed some prominence in the survey. Several were aged or older women who entered Australia in the 1950s and 1960s, had either no formal or primary education and had had no exposure to telephone communication in their villages before leaving Greece. There, women's 'distance' communication was of the pre-semaphor type. In the Greek village, one recalled, there was no phone, the bell rang out the messages to bring people to the square for discussion, and women separated by small distances, called from hill to valley to get a message through. At first, these migrants made little use of the telephone in Australia, costs of installation were high, they found the technology 'alien', and they could not at that time afford to telephone kin 'at home'. When, after several years, they installed a phone, they 'used the telephone a good deal.' The experience was common to all ethnic groups. For all, instrumental calls loomed large. Migrants of all sectors surveyed make conspicuous use of the telephone for information-seeking from government departments and agencies to ascertain their rights (the Telephone Interpreter Service (TIS) introduced in 1974 had been used by only two women surveyed), and the telephone served consistently as an access route to jobs, community services and medical care. For these calls, older women from all groups with poor language skills, called uniformly on relatives, and later their children, to conduct this instrumental exchange.

On the intrinsic front, however, the telephone developed rapidly as a welcome connector in the migrant's own language, to communicate with immediate and extended family, cultivate friendships within their ethnic groups, and reduce their sense of alienation and 'loss'. 'Speaking my own language by telephone,' said a 45-year old Greek woman, 'is comforting and reassuring, it alleviates tension and loneliness.' Another Greek said that, with language problems, at first she avoided the phone, but now it is 'often her only company, linking her with a supportive family and with close Greek friends.' Italian respondents were also deeply engaged in telephone kinkeeping and 'in helping each other with difficult problems by phone.' For some, participation in the workforce overcame their resistance to unfamiliar telephone use, and migrant women in general testified that using the telephone in their own language encouraged their confidence in moving into the community, and attempting to communicate with Australians. 'Having the security of knowing that I can call my family and friends in my native tongue,' one 75-year old Greek woman summed up, 'has given me confidence to try and communicate face-to-face with my Australian neighbours.'

Some women depended on the telephone entirely for their career. A young Greek woman outworker housebound with children, needed it 'to make arrangements for pick up and delivery and for the progress of her work'; others practised their English in shops and other avenues of work, retreating in the evening to first language telephone calls 'to relax and unwind'. There was wide confirmation from most respondents of the telephone as an 'ethnic place' and evidence revealed that even among those respondents who emigrated to Australia at an early age, they spoke their first language at home. The Lebanese respondents were home-based women whose phone usage was significantly smaller than Greek and Italian groups; most had no phone experience in their homeland, spoke Arabic for their intrinsic calls, carried on lengthy discussion in their family calls, and depended on younger members of the family to conduct their instrumental calls. Such kin and community co-operation was central to all groups. Several Vietnamese women aged 30-44, were high telephone users for whom some 50 per cent of calls were 'directed to family and community helping'. In general, ethnic community volunteerism rated high, while the ongoing role of the younger family 'interpreter' appeared as a thread in the telephone tapestry. Not all, perhaps, would agree with the 30-year old Polish respondent who recalled:

> I always had to make calls for my parents because they couldn't speak English well. Until I left home they never used the phone except to speak in their own language to friends. They used it as a lifeline. It really 'freaked' me because the responsibility was so great. I was too young to deal with bureaucracy.

The experience represents, nonetheless, an important piece of social history.

In addition to local calling, STD calls (facilitated by direct dialling and the replacement of the more difficult operator connected calls) were regularly made by European respondents to immediate and extended family members in a circle of contacts deeply geared to kin. Overseas calls were also increasingly made after settlement as incomes increased. Most calls were made to mothers who could neither read nor write; 'The only way I can communicate with my mother so far away,' said one Greek woman, 'is over the telephone,' and the calls gave emotional support. Italian and Greek women kept up strong lines of communication with the overseas family, the calls expanding at times of ill-health, lasting normally from 15 to 30 minutes, sometimes 45 minutes to an hour, and as one Italian woman put it, 'never declining in value across the years.' These intrinsic calls, said another, were 'vital for catching up on health, to feel close, to learn what is happening in Italy, and to find out if parents need financial help.'

The British proved a significant subset. Unlike the European migrants and those from Asia and the Middle East, they did not adapt to different telephone habits when they reached Australia. British women generally registered the lowest number of intrinsic calling in the sample (from 4-9 a week, with the exception of one postgraduate home worker whose score rated 16 a week), and their call duration at 2-10 minutes (again with one exception) was characteristically brief. Moreover, despite the OTC plea to Britishers flying to Australia on a Qantas ticket to 'ring home', overseas telephone calls figured minimally (with one exception) among British respondents in the survey.

Yet the female migrant experience of the telephone in Australia marks a positive venture in acculturation. For women in the male dominated Greek, Italian and Lebanese cultures, this technology offered an accepted opportunity for building a feminine network of family solidarity, communication and control, and for many women, after initial years of lonelines and deprivation, access to a domestic telephone established their 'telecommunication neighbourhoods', brought language instruction within their reach [28], and, from their own testimony, enriched and enhanced their lives [29].

RURAL WOMEN

While women living in country towns and rural settings share common attitudes with their metropolitan sisters to telephone gratification and use, there is some difference and distinctiveness in patterns of rural use that stem from geography, lifestyle, available technology and costs.

Evidence from these respondents encompassed both gratitude for access to telephone technology and the security and facility such access gives, but also a wide concern for some reassessment of charging policy that will mitigate the cost of distance and spur a new conceptual look at rural problems and needs.

For women living in country towns, intrinsic networking has increased perceptibly in the past five years. The rural crisis of 1987 in the Mallee district of Victoria graphically illustrated this trend. 'We were having a crisis and the men were silent about their difficulties with each other,' one woman reported, 'and we realized that the women could not afford to talk to each other' (zoned calls in country town and rural fringes are metered after the first 3 minutes). Overtures from the women prompted a Felton Bequest donation that enabled rural women of the area to communicate by telephone for the local call charge. 'I found that I could have a good intrinsic chat for 25 minutes,' said one organizer, 'that is the true length of a satisfactory call for someone who – as we were in this crisis – was worried or upset.' Time charging for calls outside a 'community access' radius which links the caller to her nearest commercial centre, provided a different telephone environment from city and suburbs, and acted as a cost brake on personal calls. Country women surveyed believed that, as one put it 'there is a continued underrating of the woman's function in rural society. We are part of the production process, and we work for the community but our labour is taken for granted, and unpaid.' In the critical times in the Mallee, younger women were forced into paid work, and there was a decline in the numbers of women willing to do important community work. 'We're paying quite heavily to do this voluntary work through zonal charging,' another respondent affirmed. 'How are our country communities going to be held together in the future without such volunteers and in a society where the emphasis has swung so strongly to 'user pays'?'

For these and other similarly sited women, the telephone was 'top priority'. 'We would be absolutely lost without it.' For many it was not just a route to family, vital in emergencies and for rapid contact, but also a 'therapeutic place'. At the same time, country women widely felt that community networking, caring and kinkeeping were 'disregarded from the policy point of view' and that women's voices on rural changing 'were not sufficiently heeded.' There was strong evidence of 'telephone neighbourhoods'. The telephone replaced transport in personal affairs. 'People haven't time to visit each other,' said one farmer's wife. 'By the time you've got food in, spent money on petrol, you rely more on the telephone. Face-to-face contact is withering, but this is not a substitute, it's a new kind of neighbourhood of its own.' As in suburbs and city, country women emphasized the telephone's intimate role. 'We pick up the phone when we *need to* talk,' said a Victorian woman, 'hence our dialogue is more open, and deep.' Older women, widowed, staying alone on their farms, use the telephone among confidants 'to recollect their lives'. Neighbourhood networking in new rural development areas was nourished by the telephone.

In the Northern Territory where distance dominated living, women in community and volunteer organizations were innovative in adopting new communications means. The scattered members of the Northern Territory Women's Advisory Council and the N.T. Children's Service, Reform and Advisory Programme, to cite two, conducted much of their business by teleconferencing to obviate the vast journeys and poor connections involved in meeting face-to-face. At the same time STD calling was a vital and booming connection for Top End families to connect them to kin and close friends in the south. From the uranium mining town of Jabiru, one respondent observed:

> This town is very family oriented because of the telephone. Many women come here because their husbands decided to work here for a limited period (an average of 2-2½ years). It's a very fertile population. The town of 1400 is virtually young and childbearing. Very few have relations here, their support networks are in the south; they're tied up looking after kids. The mother-daughter relationship looms large. They often just want to hear a voice from the south.

In the remote outback of Western Australia, South Australia and the Northern Territory, some women are still unconnected, many still rely on the radio telephone (a mantle of communication flung over the inland when the Maralinga rocket development of the fifties required a warning system along its firing line). For these women, climatic fluctuations greatly affect their communication mode; privacy may be non-existent, and conversations restricted in personal matters or transfigured into codes. 'You try and judge what your children distant at school are trying to say to you,' said one remotely settled woman in North Queensland. 'You can tell they're troubled, but you can't get them to repeat this several times!' Most respondents tied to the radio telephone were pragmatic however about this communication form; some would be reluctant to lose the warm link of operator connection, others were frustrated by bad evening connection and whirring, singing, and 'whooshing' on the waves. In remote regions, the Digital Radio Concentrator Scheme (DRCS) now brings direct STD connection to outback stations spreading out from Darwin and Alice Springs south, east, west and to the Gulf of Carpentaria in a widening arc. 'It's transforming, fantastic' was the common cry. No longer the 12 minute maximum of radio telephone connection but, when all calls are STD, costs are high.

For remote Aboriginal women, telephone communication is problematic. 'Aborigines are great talkers on the phone, it's been Aboriginised,' one commentator noted. But men dominate the telephone. Federal Government policy ordains that every outback station will have a radio telephone, but in the words of one prominent Alice Springs Aboriginal woman, the system is 'man-controlled'. 'Women are really disadvantaged in the rural outback. Even in a rural community like Hermannsberg, it's very difficult for women to get access to the office phone. You have to fight the person in charge to get access.' Similar experiences were reported in Kintore and in other outpost settlements. The evidence was illuminating. 'Male domination was not cultural,' one woman affirmed.

Aboriginal men and women are equal, side by side. Each plays their role. But white men have contaminated the Aboriginal man's attitude to women in many parts. It's an 'imposed' inequality now. When we seek to use the outpost telephone, a man will say 'you have to wait, men must go first'.

The solution appeared to several women to be the installation of a second radio telephone connection, a dual system, that would give ongoing access to Aboriginal women for use in domestic or community violence, in health matters, in seeking information, and for social communication with their children away in training or education in Darwin or Alice Springs.

CONCLUSIONS, CHARGING, AND POLICY

Here are the voices of women. They have not hitherto been heard in Australia. Yet, in their diversity and complexity, they reflect a pervasive feminine culture of the telephone in which kinkeeping, nurturing, community support, and the caring culture of women forms a key dynamic of our society and invites the careful attention of policy makers. This paper represents the first report of material gathered in the survey. It focuses on the broad attitudes and views of women on telephone use in a period of projected telecommunications change, and offers evidence that challenges existing mainstream, sociologiocal and carrier interpretations of patterns and purposes of telephone use [30]. As such it represents a preliminary presentation of the evidence which, in the Report [31] and elsewhere, will additionally address such other sociological questions as the historical conditioning of Australian women and their telephone use, teenagers and the telephone, the telephone in the homeworking ('electronic cottage') situation, changing attitudes to telephone communication and contact face-to-face, and women's resistance, or adaptation to, new, value-added telecommunications innovations. While household income was specifically excluded from a survey dependent on interview candour and rapport, material retrieved sheds light on economic and other relationships between transport and telephone use, on Aborigines and the telephone, and the 'feminization of poverty' among the 'telephone poor'.

Centrally in the present study, the evidence opens up an arena of 'private sphere' social organization and activity that has, politically, been overlooked. Since the telephone's invention, the canon of women's particular 'addiction' to the telephone has become entrenched, and, fuelled by Mark Twain's classic story 'The Telephone Conversation' (1880), women's telephone communication has been persistently portrayed in literature and the media as 'gossip' and a trivial pursuit [32]. The point, however, has drawn some pertinent comment from feminist scholars of gender and technology. 'As we have discovered through our 1970s and 1980s studies,' writes the American scholar, Cheris Kramarae, 'the stereotypes and jokes are misleading,' embedded in a masculine mindset and 'malestream communication theorizing' [33]. Most explicitly, Lana

Rakow in her study of 43 women and their telephone use in the midwestern town of Prospect, USA, confirms the care-giving, socially salutary role of women's telephone talk and points up a continuing tendency in western society to demote and undervalue this activity. 'Women's telephone talk fits into the appropriate spheres of activity and interests designated for women,' she observes. 'It is both 'gendered work' and 'gender work', in that it is work that women do to hold together the fabric of the community, build and maintain relationships, and accomplish important care-giving and receiving functions.'

> It is through their care-giving work at home and their jobs that women occupy their place in society…taking responsibility for the emotional and material needs of husbands and children, the elderly, the handicapped, the sick and the unhappy. While this role has been little recognised or valued, the caring work of women over the telephone has been even less noted. [34]

The same holds true for the situation in Australia. Historically, women's telephone communication has moved a long way from its major instrumental uses of some decades ago to a notable concentration on protracted intrinsic calling. The role of the telephone has thus changed from an important facility for expediting daily life and transforming the problem of distance in Australia, to an arena where the claims of feeling are acknowledged and to a key site for the execution of women's care-giving gendered work. As in Prospect, USA, 'the telephone runs like a thread' [35] through the lives of women in Australia. The voices of men, contrastingly, have played little part in this study except as brothers, fathers, and lovers interacting in the women's world. The phenomenon is cultural. While there are, identifiably, men who deploy the telephone as women do, women and men in general inhabit different (if intersecting) economic, and telephone network worlds. Their separation, and the differing values they acknowledge, impact directly on policy making. Technology, notes Kramarae:

> …is designed and developed by people with assumptions about what makes for necessary, desirable, profitable and important human activity; planners, manufacturers, and systems organizers may consider women's labour and efficiency, but seldom is women's communication with other women and with men considered as a necessary part of the planning evaluation. [36]

In the 'new telecommunications environment' in Australia, the claims of industry, competition, rationality and production would appear to overtower the values of human co-operation, nurturing, emotion and mutual care, and, to date, women have had little access to the decision-making.

This survey aims to bring relevant data to the evaluation. It bears on changing charging policy in Australia. Like Canada, Australians have been traditionally conditioned to a telephone service based on spreading universalism, unmetered local calling, and costs to the rural population linked with distance. Upgraded technology has now removed much of the cost factor from distance links, data telephone communication impacts significantly on voice telephone lines, and considerations of timed local calling have altered elements in the telecommunications scene. Women in the survey were highly vocal on the issue of timed local calls [37]. Ninety-two per cent reacted strongly against the prospect. Many attested that their phone use would radically change; many would 'stop using the phone except for emergencies'; several migrant respondents declared that they would 'cancel the telephone'; others indicated that it 'would no longer be easy to reach out for help'; still others felt that it 'would become difficult to manage for calls that involved worry, depression or distress', that volunteerism would 'fall away', and that TLC's would seriously disturb the character of feminine telephone communication built up since domestic phone installation had become commonplace in Australia. Women with recourse only to Public Phones believed that they would be forced further into a poverty trap, and that, while the telephone service was not universal in Australia, timed phone box local calling would seriously penalise the 'have nots'. For the elderly, the single parent, the pensioner, the country woman, the woman who worked at home, the prospect of timed local calls threatened solace and security. 'Lots of people would be in trouble,' said one Albury pensioner – 'all my neighbours would.' An aged Greek migrant, who had worked in Australia for 50 years, saw timing as a poor return on long invested labour. 'If calls were timed,' she said, 'we would be further isolated from our family and friends. My husband and I only have independence as long as we have the phone as it is.' Even among high income and working women who comprehended the downward trend of local call rates over the past decade [38], opposition was firm. Significantly, the words used by respondents to express their response to TLCs were highly charged: 'outrageous, horrendous, devastating to our humanitarian concerns'. Unmetered calls were, indeed, perceived not as a 'utility', but as a 'social good', as vital to national and social progress as economic development. [39].

With Canada, Australia now stands alone among industrial nations in offering untimed calling for local telephone communication. In Canada, the universal service is under threat. 'The thrust to deregulation,' comment social scientists, Pike and Musco, 'threatens to limit the telephone, for those who can still afford the service, to instrumental use. The intrinsic value of the telephone, for the maintenance of contact with family and friends, would be reduced.' They see a shift to 'cost-based pricing' as a backwards historical step, one which could take the Canadian consumer 'from luxury to necessity and back again' and condemn many Canadians to 'an information desert' [40]. Both countries also face challenges, implicit in this survey, of more equitable, rural and remote, distance costs. Planners need wide, and democratic, perspectives. A telecommunications policy that lowers the social equity of its people on industrial and economic grounds may forfeit Australia's reputation as a telecommunications leader widen the political 'gender gap', and impoverish the character of women's communication and its part in our evolving information society.

NOTES AND REFERENCES

1   But see Grant Noble, 'Discriminating between the intrinsic and instrumental domestic telephone user'. *Australian Journal of Communication,* No. 11, pp. 63-85 for a broad examination of 100 people.

2   I. de Sola Pool (ed.), *The Social Impact of the Telephone,* Cambridge, MIT Press, 1977, a collection of essays assembled to mark the centenary of the invention of the telephone in 1976, remains the most seminal source book. In addition broad commentary on telephone use can be found in S. Aronson, 'The sociology of the telephone', in C. Gumpert and R. Carthcart (eds) (1986) *Intermedia. Interpersonal Communication in a Media World,* 3rd ed., New York, Oxford University Press; Guy Fielding and Peter Hartley (1988) 'The telephone: a neglected medium', in A. Cashdan and M. Jordin (eds), *Studies in Communication,* Oxford, Blackwell; Frederick Williams (ed.) (1987) *Technology and Communication Behavior,* Belmont, California, Wadsworth Publishing Co.; and Herbert S. Dordick (1983) 'Reflections on a wired world', *Media & Values,* 26, Winter 1984, pp. 2-3 and *Intermedia.* Place specific studies of suites of telephone users include G. Claisse and F. Rowe (1987) 'The telephone in question: questions on communication', *Computer Networks and ISDN Systems,* International Journal of Computer and Telecommunications Networking, 24, 2-5, pp. 207-219 which examines 663 French telephone callers in 1984; Belinda Brandon (ed.) (1981) *The Effect of the Demographies of Individual Households on their Telephone Usage,* Cambridge, Mass., Ballinger, a detailed analysis of the household characteristics of some 500 telephone users in Chicago, 1972-4; and W. Infosino, 'Relationship between demand for local telephone calls and household characteristics', *Bell Telephone Technical Journal,* 59, 6, July 1980, pp. 31-53, a study of 998 individuals in California and Cincinnati, 1972-3, 1975-6.

3   Noble, *op. cit.,* p. 83.

4   These found full expression in submissions to the Davidson Inquiry, and its *Report of the Committee to inquire into telecommunications services in Australia,* 1981/82, rejected by the Hawke Government.

5   Quoted Suzanne Keller, 'The telephone in new communities and old', Pool, *op. cit.,* p. 289.

6   The 'instrumental/intrinsic' categorisation was first defined by Keller, *op. cit,* p. 284. See also Noble, *op. cit.*

7   From its design stages and as the research grew, it has attracted the interest of a spectrum of women's organizations including the Office of the Status of Women, the Office of Multicultural Affairs, the Australian Institute of Family Studies, the National Council of Women of Australia,

the Rural Womens' Network of the Victorian Department of Agriculture, the Rural Women's Information Service of S.A., Department of Agriculture, the Northern Territory Women's Advisory Council, and the National Women's Consultative Council. I thank them for their encouragement and constructive ideas.

8   Diane Bell (1988) Photographs by Ponch Hawkes, *Generations. Grandmothers, Mothers and Daughters* Bicentennial Landmark Publication for Women, Gribble/Penguin.

9   Telecommunication carriers, including Telecom, suggest that survey respondents relying on memory invariably underestimate their calling patterns when it comes to challenging telephone bills and, conversely, would overestimate the average number and duration of local calls per day. Martin Mayer confirms this in 'The telephone and the uses of time', in Pool, *op. cit.* In the present survey, a comparison of time sheets and recorded calls suggested that interviewees tended rather to *underestimate* both the number, and duration, of calls.

10 Distribution among capital cities was: Sydney 40, Melbourne 25, Canberra 17, Brisbane 14, Adelaide 12, Perth 11, Hobart 9, and Darwin 6. Country distribution included country towns, rural fringe and remote settlements: NSW 14, Victoria 16, Northern Territory 15, Queensland 11, South Australia 5, and Western Australia 5.

11 Australian Bureau of Statistics, 1987. In this source 11 per cent of Australian women were aged 0-14, 8 per cent aged 15-19; 32 per cent 20-39; 16.5 per cent aged 40-54; 9 per cent aged 55-64; 7 per cent aged 65-74 and 5 per cent over 75. The skewing to a higher percentile representation in the survey arises from the absence of any representatives of respondents aged 0-14.

12 The survey did not seek information on work-based calls for either those made in the workforce or from home.

13 A similar resistance to altering established and participatory shopping patterns is also reported from Japan. Tessa Morris-Suzuki (1988) 'The communications revolution and the household: some thoughts from the Japanese experience', *Prometheus,* 6, 2, p. 242.

14 Comparative data on weekly calls made by women in other countries is not available. Neither Brandon's (ed.) 1981 study of telephone use in Chicago households, *op. cit.* or Infosino's 1980 study of Cincinnati and California households, *op. cit.,* or Claisse and Rowe's 1983 study of French urban telephone use, *op. cit.,* offer data breakdown on gender. Mayer, *op. cit.,* demonstrates the pervasiveness of male value judgments on the issue when he alludes to an American 'Statewide' survey where the average length of call of four and a half minutes was 'dragged up by those who hang on the phone' (p. 228). Unfortunately Lana F. Rakow's pioneering gender study, *Gender, Communication and Technology. A Case Study of Women and the Telephone,* University of Illinois at Urbana-Champagne, PhD 1987 (University Microfilm International, copy

held by Macquarie University Library) based on interview data of 43 women and their telephone use and attitudes in the Midwestern rural town of Prospect, USA, furnishes no record of call duration or number of telephone calls made.

15   The concept of three minutes as the basic unit of telephone call 'conversation time' has long been accepted internationally. The calculation is based on recorded call time measured at telephone exchanges at the busiest time of day and encompasses an average over all types of business and residential voice calls. While little independent research has been published on the subject, it is now considered in Sweden, for example, that as unanswered (unsuccessful) calls, wrong numbers, etc. are included in the calculation, the measure of 'conversation time' is artificial.

16   The educational range of the sample encompassed 5 women without formal education, 24 with primary education, 118 with secondary education, 48 with tertiary education and 5 with postgraduate qualifications. No attempt was made in this survey to establish incomes of respondents.

17   Noble (1987), *op. cit.,* p. 81.

18   Feminist scholar, Dale Spender points out that little research has yet been done on listening, a form of interactional work particularly associated with women and 'as complex and important as talk' quoted by Rakow, *op. cit.,* p. 175.

19   Rakow, *op. cit.,* p. 176.

20   Data retrieved on children's telephone use was both random, and small. It points, however, to a revealing area of telephone usage for further research.

21   There were 421,255 women aged 75 + in Australia and 917,056 women aged 65 years and over in June 1987 against a male population of 736,769 aged 65+. Australian Bureau of Statistics (1987). Combined, the total number of Australians aged 65 +, represented 11 per cent of the population.

22   Hal. L. Kendig and John McCallum (1988) *Ageing and the Family Project,* Australian National University, Canberra, Australian Government Publishing Service.

23   It is, for example, worth noting that the questionnaire of the 'Survey of the Aged in Sydney' conducted by the ANU Ageing and the Family Project in 1981, only briefly listed 'phone contact' with enquiries about numbers of children, days seen, letters received, and the broad question 'is there a phone in the home or flat'. More recently the 'Australian Longitudinal Study of Ageing, Initial Survey Questionnaire (1988), of the Centre for Ageing Studies, Flinders University (a WHO Collaborating Centre for research on the epidemiology of ageing), with its many questions on the physical condition, illnesses, available services,

emergencies, relationships, leisure activities of the aged, contains only one question – the strictly functional 'do you need help using the telephone?' for a survey concerned with the biomedical, psychological and social characteristics of ageing.

24 Alice T. Day (1988) 'Family Caregiving and the Elderly: Myths, Realities and Environmental Implications, Seminar in Human Sciences, Australian National University, 11 August.

25 Interestingly, Brandon's American findings, which combine men and women in the sample, sugest that 'the medians of total local and suburban message units display a strong downward trend with increasing age', 1981, *op. cit.,* p. 6.

26 The Australian Bureau of Statistics reports 19 July 1988 that 'only 73 per cent of males, compared to 91 per cent of females, living alone, had the telephone connected'.

27 The Red Cross Telephone Security Service, a voluntary caring service aimed at providing security for aged, frail, sick, disabled or housebound people living alone and medically at risk offers an example for further development. In this scheme, volunteers telephone recipients of the service each morning 7 days a week to check their well-being. If there is no answer after a repeated call, the Red Cross office is advised and an emergency procedure taken to contact the recipient. The service is provided to recipients free of charge *(In Action,* 17, June 1988). In Japan, experiments are currently being conducted with videophones that may enable doctors to offer a service of 'checking up on elderly invalids with no acute health problem' over the phone; Morris-Suzuki, *op. cit.,* p. 242.

28 The Home Tutor Scheme, a Joint Government and Community Service, from 1988 offered telephone instruction in English to homebound migrants.

29 The role of the Women's Information Switchboard in Adelaide, for example, in helping migrant women in difficult home situation via telephone contact is noteworthy, though no such use was recorded in this survey. Cf. Des Storer (ed.) (1985) *Ethnic Family Values in Australia,* Institute of Family Studies. Prentice-Hall of Australia.

30 See Endnote 7. Fielding and Hartley, commenting on the paucity of telephone communication research, *op. cit.,* 1987, summed up: 'we know little and are therefore forced to speculate'.

31 Cf. Ann Moyal, *Women and the Telephone in Australia. A Report to Telecom Australia,* April 1989.

32 Alexander Graham Bell was guilty of the suggestion that the telephone would become a venue 'where Mrs Smith could spend an enjoyable hour with Mrs Brown, pleasantly dissecting Mrs Jones' and the theme resounds through the literature. See John Brooks, 'The first and only century of telephone literature' in Pool, *op. cit.,* 1977, pp. 208-224. In

Australia, a *Sydney Morning Herald* column on telephone use, 15 June, 1988, characteristically proclaimed 'Women Do Love to Chinwag'.

33 Cheris Kramarae (ed.) (1988) *Technology and Women's Voices,* New York, Routledge & Kegan Paul, Preface, pp. 5 and 7.

34 *Gender, Communications, and Technology, op. cit.,* 1987, pp. 1-2, and Lana F. Rakow, 'Women and the telephone: the gendering of a communications technology', in Kramarae (ed.), *Technology and Women's Voices,* pp. 207-228.

35 *Ibid.* See also Lana F. Rakow, 'Rethinking gender research in communications', *Journal of Communications,* Autumn 1986, 36, pp. 11-26; and Lana F. Rakow, 'Looking to the future: five questions for gender research', *Women's Studies in Communication,* Fall 1987, 10, pp. 79-86.

36 *op. cit.,* p. 10.

37 Their opposition was also widely articulated when Telecom Australia opened the debate on timed local calling in late 1987-88, promoting a statement from the Prime Minister in February 1988, that Australia would not introduce timed local calls. The issue, however, remains on the telecommunications policy agenda.

38 Since its inauguration in June 1975, Telecom Australia has kept its telephone charges down. 'Average price increase for the overall range of basic services' have risen by 36 per cent between June 1975 and June 1987, compared with a 167 per cent rise in the Consumer Price Index, 211 per cent rise in Public Transport Fares, a 230 per cent rise in fuel and light, and a 279 per cent rise in petrol prices. Australian Telecommunication Commission *Annual Report,* 1987-88.

39 Telecom, to date, appears short of data relating to length of local calls. Some 'very limited surveys' suggest an average voice business call occupies $2\frac{1}{2}$ to 3 minutes; and an average domestic call under 6 minutes. Telecom Australia.

40 Robert Pike and Vincent Musco, 'Canadian consumers and telephone pricing: from luxury to necessity and back again?', *Telecommunications Policy,* March 1986, 10, 1, pp. 17-32.

ACKNOWLEDGEMENTS

This study has been supported by Telecom Australia and by an Australian Research Council grant on 'The Social Impact of the Telephone in Australia'.

I acknowledge with thanks the generous assistance of Professor Henry Mayer and Professor Diane Bell in indicating, and shaping the model, and of Dr Pauline Newell and Danny Hasofer for helpful methodological discussion.

PATTERNS OF OWNERSHIP OF IT DEVICES IN THE HOME

Hughie Mackay [1]

The aim of this article is to describe, with some precision, the past, present and projected levels and patterns of ownership and uses, of a number of important IT devices in the home. In this, I draw on government survey data, the research and analyses of commentators and market research organisations, and a little data which I have gathered from relevant industries. My focus is on the *quantitative*, in an effort to provide some complement to the burgeoning *qualitative* studies of IT in the home [2]. The aim is to provide some evidential base for the range of claims which are made in relation both to specific devices and to the broader phenomenon of the growth of technology in the home; and to show something of the diversity, or patterning, which lies behind broad trends.

For this I have selected six crucial domestic IT devices: the telephone, television, video cassette recorder (VCR), home computer, computer games console, and compact disc (CD) player. For reasons of space, a number of relevant technologies have been excluded – the camcorder and cable and satellite television, in particular, are interesting and closely linked to those I have selected. My choice is based on the inextricable and developing links between them; together these devices constitute the heart of existing and foreseeable IT devices in the home. Such technological synergy is reflected in shifting patterns of corporate activity: Sony, JVC and Matsushita are now involved in film production, and Sega has bought a Hollywood studio where it will make original movies as well as computer animations for its interactive games. Similarly, the synthesised music which accompanies Super Mario and other computer games has been in the pop music charts. Consumer electronics, computer, communications and entertainment industries are merging. Using the telephone line, a PC can be used to communicate with remote computers, to work at home, or for remote shopping and banking; pilots are underway using the telephone system for video on demand, the interactive transmission of video into the home, and thus the telephone system can be a part of a cable television system; games can be played on a console or a PC; and some CD players can be connected to televisions and PCs, as well as to stereo systems. The mass basis of the television audience is being diluted as more delivery routes and reception devices become available. In short, boundaries are blurred and changing. Activities which traditionally have been associated with one medium are being delivered on another, with profound consequences not just for the fortunes of the corporations involved, but also for the relationship of producer to consumer, the power and control of the consumer, the locales of leisure activity and, indeed, the very nature of leisure.

First, a note of caution. Whilst some forms of data gathering are more suitable to particular circumstances than others, all have their limitations. Much of the data on which I draw is from survey research. Most of the trends and phenomena which I introduce and discuss are supported by alternative data sources. The data varies for each device, because for some it is more readily available, whereas for others the privatised nature of suppliers makes commercial confidentiality more significant.

1 THE TELEPHONE

I shall deal with three forms of telephone: the domestic, the mobile, and the answering machine (TAM).

To get an idea of the number of telephones in use we can look at data on telephone connections, telephone sales and telephone ownership. Data on the number of connections (Table 1) shows a steady though diminishing growth. About 75% of BT connections are residential; and, although growing reasonably fast, the number of Mercury connections is dwarfed by those of BT.

Table 1 BT and Mercury exchange connections (million) (March 31 each year)

	1988	1989	1990	1991	1992	1993
BT Residential	18.11	18.70	19.25	19.57	19.73	20.11
BT Business	4.56	5.04	5.55	5.80	5.87	5.97
BT Total	22.66	23.74	25.80	25.37	25.60	26.08
Mercury		0.13	0.26	0.48	0.76	1.06

Source: BT and Mercury.

There has been a decline in the sale of residential telephones, with an even sharper decline in the value of these sales, as unit costs have fallen (Table 2). Business sales, by contrast, have fluctuated (with economic activity), in terms of both units and their value; business telephones are more complex and unit costs higher.

Table 2 Fixed Telephone sales

	Business		Residential		Total	
	000	*£m*	*000*	*£m*	*000*	*£m*
1986	2422	168	1500	66	3922	234
1987	606	40	1348	47	1954	87
1988	897	54	1348	37	2245	91
1989	578	33	1351	30	1926	63
1990	1234	60	1199	22	2433	82
1991	1786	90	905	14	2691	104
1992	1400	75	700	11	2100	86
1993e	1303	72	735	14	2038	86

Source: Mintel 1994.

The residential telephone market is divided between one- and two-piece telephones. The former are simple and cheap, and aimed primarily at the residential market, whereas the latter are more sophisticated, and include additional features, such as last number redial, number memory, hand free dialling, mute, and displays showing the time, number dialled and units used. Telephones of a novelty or feature nature (e.g. Mickey Mouse) are available, but not sold in large numbers. There has been a clear shift from one-piece to two-piece telephones (Table 3). Sales of both have declined, the former more drastically.

Table 3   Retail Sales of Residential Telephones

	One-piece		Two-piece			One-piece		Two-piece	
	000	*£m*	*000*	*£m*		*000*	*£m*	*000*	*£m*
1986	342	12	1158	54	1990	387	6	812	16
1987	435	13	913	34	1991	329	4	576	10
1988	461	10	887	27	1992	270	4	430	7
1989	450	9	901	21					

Source: Mintel 1994.

Despite these seemingly vast sales, three-quarters of households retain a rental telephone. Although household penetration is about 90%, demand is maintained for telephones with additional features and mobile telephones. It is predicted that in the period 1992-97 one-piece residential telephone sales will fall by 7% and two-piece sales will remain about constant over the same period [3].

Different official statistical sources come up with slightly different levels of telephone ownership. These vary little, and for the sake of clarity I shall refer to one set of such data (Table 4). This shows that telephone ownership more than doubled during the 1970s, from about a third to over two-thirds of households; today about 90% of households have a telephone.

Table 4   Proportions of households with a telephone, GB

1964	22	1974	50	1982	76	1990	87
1969	32	1976	53	1984	78	1992	88
1970	35	1978	62	1986	81		
1972	42	1980	72	1988	85		

Sources: Family Spending 1992.

Many households, of course, own more than one telephone. There is data on levels of multiple telephone ownership (Table 5) and on the patternings which underlie such ownership levels – in terms of region, class, income, occupation, household composition and form of housing tenure (Tables 5-7). Starting with region, the lowest penetration is in the North, the highest in East Anglia and the South East – though regional variations are not great. Ownership is greatest amongst higher income earners and owner occupiers, and lowest in households consisting of one retired adult who is mainly dependent on a state retirement pension.

Evidence suggests that 48% of households have one telephone, 31% have two and 11% three or more (and 10% no telephone) (Target Group Index (TGI), cited by Mintel 1994). Older people are more likely to have just one telephone; whilst the 35-54 age group is where three or more telephones are most heavily concentrated. The number of telephones per household rises with social class, and the non-ownership of a telephone shows the inverse trend (Table 5).

Table 5   Ownership of number of telephones, by social class, 1990.
Sample: 980 adults

Social class [4]	One	Two	Three+	Total with a telephone	None
	%	%	%	%	%
AB	38	40	21	99	1
C1	47	36	13	96	4
C2	51	32	10	93	8
D	53	24	6	83	17
E	52	19	4	75	26

Source: Mintel, 1994.

Telephone ownership shows a similar patterning (Table 6).

Table 6   Households with telephones: by socio-economic group of head, 1992

Professional	98	Unskilled manual	73
Employers and Managers	98	All economically active	91
Other non-manual	93	Economically inactive	86
Skilled manual	87	All heads of households	89

Source: Social Trends 1994, Table 6.7.

Similarly, we can look at the distribution of ownership in terms of income, household composition and tenure of dwelling (Table 7). The higher the income, the more likely a household is to own a telephone. Retired households are more likely than average to have a telephone, though those dependent mainly on state pensions are only at the average level of ownership. Single parents are much less likely to own a telephone, and even less likely to if they have more than one child. There are strong contrasts between households in different forms of housing tenure, for example local authority rented versus owner occupied.

Table 7   Percentage of households with telephone, 1992

All households	88.4
Household weekly income	
Under £60	68.1
£60 and under £80	73.6
£80 and under £100	74.5
£100 and under £130	79.1
£130 and under £160	85.2
£160 and under £200	87.1
£200 and under £240	86.6
£240 and under £280	90.4
£280 and under £320	92.0
£320 and under £370	90.7
£370 and under £420	95.3
£420 and under £470	96.0
£470 and under £540	97.4
£540 and under £640	99.3
£640 and under £800	99.5
£800 and more	99.8

Table 7   Percentage of households with telephone, 1992

Household composition

Households with:

One adult		
	Retired, mainly dependent on state pensions	80.5
	Other retired	94.1
	Non-retired	80.0
One adult, one child		70.8
One adult, two or more children		64.0
One man, one woman		
	Retired, mainly dependent on state pensions	92.1
	Other retired	96.4
	Non-retired	93.5
One man, one woman, one child		88.8
One man, one woman, two children		91.7
One man, one woman, three child		88.9
Two adults, four or more children		77.8
Three adults, one or more children		90.8

Tenure of dwelling

Rented unfurnished		72.0
	Local authority	70.0
	Housing association	73.9
	Other	82.4
Rented furnished		68.5
Rent free		88.6
Owner occupied		96.6

Source: Family Spending 1992, Table 4.

Let us turn from sales and ownership to usage. Telephone usage is inextricably linked to the level of economic activity – indeed, so much so that telephone usage is being considered as an indicator of the level of economic activity. BT's lowering of average charges in real terms also contributes to levels of usage. Telephone usage (business and residential combined) stagnated in 1992-93, while international calls grew (Table 8).

Table 8   Call growth on BT network 1985-93 (March each year)

	Inland	International		Inland	International
	%	%		%	%
1985	8	14	1990	10	13
1986	7	11	1991	4	6
1987	7	11	1992	1	4
1988	8	14	1993	-	6
1989	11	13			

Source: BT.

It would be interesting to know how much different groups *use* the telephone, the proportion of their budget and leisure time which they spend on it, and so on. Some of the papers in the excellent collection on the telephone edited by Pool (1977) contains some pertinent data, but of a historical (and largely North American) nature.

The market for mobile telephones has seen a huge growth. Launched in 1985, predictions were for 450,000 subscribers by 1990; the outcome, in fact, was over double that – with this huge and unanticipated growth in large part responsible for the high level of customer complaints. With the onset of the recession in 1989, sales slowed dramatically and the decision by the Chancellor to tax mobile telephones as a business perk in the 1991 budget has contributed to this decline (Table 9).

Table 9   UK users, cellular mobile telephones

	Installed base 000	Unit sales 000		Installed base 000	Unit sales 000
1985	45	45	1990	1,130	520
1986	122	77	1991	1,220	470
1987	230	8	1992	1,320	510
1988	420	280	1993e	1,550	620
1989	880	390			

Source: Mintel 1994.

Mobile telephone sales are about seven times the figure for fixed telephones. In other words, the market for mobile telephones is huge. Despite the drastic reductions in price, national penetration rates remain very low: 3 cellular telephones per 100 of the population (whilst Sweden has the highest density of mobile telephones with 8.6 units per 100 of the population, the USA is lower than the UK at just over 1%, and Germany has about 4%). There is an overwhelming concentration of owners in the ranks of business and the professions; but these areas are seen as approaching saturation, and we are seeing the mobile telephone move down the social scale (Wood 1993). Only recently has the domestic, private, market been a focus for advertising. Increasingly, however, it is privately owned – perhaps as an extra telephone for the family or by women as a security device. It is unlikely, however, to become a mass technology without a fall in the cost of its use (Williamson 1993).

It is anticipated that the (digital) cellular telephone market will increase by 250% in the period 1992-97. The proportion of this market which is domestic is difficult to judge. Providers of services for mobile telephones target particular groups for particular services: Vodafone has about a third of its subscribers on low user services and two-thirds on business services; Cellnet has the opposite balance, in roughly a 60: 40 ratio. Low user subscribers (customers who want to receive rather than make calls at peak time) however, are not all private subscribers, but will include small business users (and, indeed, some universities!) as well.

Telephone answering machines (TAMs) have been another fast-growing sector of the market (Table 10).

Table 10   Sales of TAMs

	Unit sales 000		Unit sales 000
1985	170	1990	640
1986	252	1991	732
1987	346	1992	800
1988	447	1993e	900
1989	560		

Source: Mintel 1994.

Of this market, retail sales constitute the fastest growing area, and about two-thirds of sales – though retail sales cover more than merely the domestic market; nonetheless, falling prices have led to the technology entering the home. The future of TAMs, however, is uncertain because they could be replaced by voice messaging.

2 THE TELEVISION [5]

Today a television is owned by virtually all households. Ownership levels have grown over the years, slowing down as the market has reached near total saturation (Table 11).

Table 11   Percentage of households with a television 1964-92

1964	80.4	1978	95.6	1988	98.0
1970	91.2	1980	96.9	1990	98.1
1972	93.2	1982	96.8	1992	98.3
1974	94.0	1984	97.2		
1976	95.6	1986	97.1		

Source: Family Spending, 1992.

In addition to a nearly 100% penetration level, there is a growing trend towards multiple ownership, caused by both old sets being kept, and an increasing tendency to install sets in different rooms of the home. Almost as many adults now have three or more sets as have only one set. Single set ownership is now a minority status; it is highest in age groups most likely to have single-person and childless households. There has been a slight growth in the number of televisions in the kitchen, and a quite dramatic growth of sets in the bedroom (Table 12).

Table 12   Household penetration and location of television sets, 1985-93

	1985	1990	1993	% change 1985-93
Adult sample	24,651	25,975	25,832	
	%	%	%	%
Have a TV set	97	98	98	+1
1 set only	50	39	34	-16
2 sets	37	38	39	+2
3 or more sets	11	21	25	+14
Location				
Living room	92	94	93	+1
Breakfast room/ kitchen	9	12	13	+4
Bedroom	29	40	45	+16
Other room	6	8	8	+2

Source: TGI, British Market Research Bureau (BMRB) 1985-93 cited by Mintel 1994.

Multiple set ownership is fairly evenly spread across social groups, except in group E, where it is lower. In other words, those who watch most television (see below) are the least likely to buy or own a new television. Households with more children are more likely to have multiple sets. Ownership is fairly even across the regions, though with Scotland showing a slightly higher level of ownership and likelihood of purchase of a set in the past twelve months. There is little difference between men and women in terms of ownership levels (Table 13).

Table 13   Number of television sets owned, 1993. Base: 25,832 adults

		One set	*Two sets*	*Three or more sets*	*New in last 12 months*
		%	%	%	%
All		31	40	27	17
Men		30	40	28	18
Women		32	41	26	16
Age	15-19	24	50	22	22
	20-24	42	37	17	19
	25-34	32	44	23	21
	35-44	20	36	42	21
	45-54	20	38	40	18
	55-64	30	45	24	15
	65+	46	40	36	11
Class	AB	25	43	31	19
	C1	29	40	29	18
	C2	27	42	30	18
	D	31	42	25	19
	E	50	32	13	12
No children		35	41	22	15
Children <1 year		38	42	19	17
Children 1-4 years		33	43	22	19
Children 5-9 years		22	42	35	21
Children 10-15 yrs		13	33	53	24

Source: TGI, BMRB 1993 cited by Mintel 1994.

The market for monochrome sets has been virtually non existent for some years, except for a few hand held sets. Of colour televisions which are sold, 5% are to first time buyers, 35% are replacement purchases and 60% are additional sets. Low consumer demand in recent years has meant a shift to cheaper sets: the average amount spent on a television in 1988 was £276, and in 1992, at equivalent prices, £249.

Renting televisions has become less popular, and is still falling – 1992 was about 25% down on 1988 (Table 14).

Table 14   Television set rentals

	000	Index		000	Index
1988	555	100	1991	430	77
1989	465	84	1992	415	75
1990	450	81	1993e	400	72

Source: Mintel 1994.

However, it is projected that both rental (as well as sales) will grow – reflecting demand for the latest technical developments, e.g. large screens, Nicam, Dolby, HDTV. What is it that shapes demand for television sets? Given that nearly every household has a television, critical to the market is the number of households. Over the period 1980-90 this has grown by an average of 1.3%, but is forecast to grow less (1.1%) in the period 1990-2000. Demand is influenced, in addition, by the recession and consumer confidence – though television sales have been affected by the recession less than other consumer goods, perhaps because families have economised on leisure pursuits outside the home and focused on in-house entertainment. The increasing popularity of video – and CD-I and games – is likely to add to demand for television sets. Finally, the replacement cycle of televisions sets is getting shorter: in the mid 1980s it was 11 years, but by the early 1990s 8 years. Rather successfully from the designers' and manufacturers' perspective, technical developments (and the demand for such new features) shortens the life of the commodity.

Turning from ownership to use, there is data which suggests that over the period 1987-90 there was a tendency to watch more television. For example, in 1987 33% of the sample watched over 5 hours, and in 1990 40%. By 1993, however, the situation had reversed to something similar to 1987 (Table 15).

Table 15   Time spent watching TV on average weekday, 1987-93

	1987 March	1990 February	1993 September	% change 1987-93
Base: adults	1,026	1,431	1,030	
	%	%	%	
11+ hours	5	7	6	+1
9-10 hours	3	4	3	-
7-8 hours	7	8	7	-
5-6 hours	18	21	16	-2
3-4 hours	36	37	39	+3
1-2 hours	25	19	23	-2
<1 hour	3	4	5	+2

Source: BMRB/Mintel 1994.

Government statistics suggest some fluctuation – of up to an hour a week – in the average time spent watching television between 1986 and 1990, with an increase in the viewing hours of some social classes and a decrease for other social classes (Table 16).

Table 16   Weekly television viewing by social class. Hours: minutes

	1986	1987	1988	1989	1990	1991
AB	19:50	19:18	18:39	18:41	17:52	18:51
C1	23:05	24:05	23:41	23:11	23:12	23:56
C2	26:00	25:29	26:23	26:21	26:17	26:57
DE	33:35	32:15	32:20	32:00	31:51	31:56
All	26:32	26:02	26:08	25:54	25:33	26:04

Source: Social Trends 1993 Table 10.7.

Women are likely to view television for more hours than men. Members of socio-economic groups D and E watch noticeably more hours, and ABs least. The unemployed in particular (who are over-represented in groups D and E) also view television for long hours (Table 17).

Table 17   Time spent watching TV on average weekday, September 1993. Base: 1,030 adults

	11+ hrs %	9-10 hrs %	7-8 hrs %	5-6 hrs %	3-4 hrs %	1-2 hrs %	<1 hr %
All	6	3	7	16	39	23	5
Men	5	3	4	14	40	26	6
Women	7	3	9	19	37	20	5
AB	2	1	2	8	39	36	12
C1	3	3	4	16	40	29	4
C2	6	4	5	19	41	19	6
D	10	2	11	19	39	16	2
E	14	5	14	21	33	10	1
Working	4	2	3	13	41	30	6
Not working	11	4	11	16	36	17	5
Retired	4	6	8	29	37	14	2

Source: BMRB/ Mintel 1994.

Television viewing, as defined for such data, does not, of course, mean that the audience are attentive to the broadcast. Tunstall (1983) distinguishes between primary viewers (who are really focusing on the broadcast), secondary viewers (who are doing something else, such as reading a book, at the same time) and tertiary viewers (who may be in another room while the television is on). Finally, it is worth noting that having more television to watch – cable and satellite channels – has *not* meant that people watch more television.

3 THE VIDEO CASSETTE RECORDER

The VCR is a relatively recent entrant to the home. Since its arrival in the mid 1980s it has found a place in over two thirds of households (Table 18), an enormous penetration rate in such a short time. The VCR is one of the most popular consumer electronic devices. It has exceeded even relatively recent predictions about ownership and penetration levels. By 1991 it had penetrated one in three television households world-wide [6]; the UK has the second highest penetration rate of any country [7].

Table 18 Percentage of households with video recorder

1985	30	1987	43.5	1989	57	1991	65
1986	36	1988	50	1990	61	1992	69

Source: Family Spending 1992.

Most recently, in 1993, it was found that 79% of households owned a VCR (Mintel, 1994a). Further, we have seen the emergence of multiple ownership of VCRs, such that by 1991 10% of households have two or more VCRs (Table 19).

Table 19 VCR Household penetration, 1985-91. Base: 1,000 plus adults

	First machine %	Two or more %		First machine %	Two or more %
1985	30	-	1990	64	8
1987	52	5	1991	69	10
1988	60	7			

Source: BMRB/ Mintel 1994.

If we break these overall ownership levels down in to social classes, it is evident that C2s and those with children are the most likely to have a VCR – the latter perhaps because of the cost of alternative leisure, or the potential clash of television interest being greater. The older the children, the more likely it is that there is a VCR in the household. Members of group E (which includes students, the unemployed and pensioners) remain the lowest purchasers of VCRs – due, presumably, to their poverty, their greater capacity to be available when a programme is broadcast and their lesser familiarity with the technology (Table 20).

Table 20   Household ownership of VCRs

	1985 %	1991 %
All	30	69
AB	33	73
C1	32	71
C2	38	78
D	31	72
E	16	43
Children under 1 year	38	82
1-4 years	42	84
5-9 years	43	87
10-15 years	44	89

Source: TGI, BMRB 1985, 1991 cited by Mintel 1994.

More recent government data shows slightly higher levels of ownership, though with the same patterning (Table 21).

Table 21   Households with video: by socio-economic group of head, 1992

	%
Professional	87
Employers and managers	91
Other non-manual	84
Skilled manual	88
Unskilled manual	73
All economically active	87
Economically inactive	48
All heads of household	72

Source: General Household Survey, cited by Social Trends 1994.

The same pattern is reflected clearly in ownership levels of those with various incomes: the higher the income, the more likely it is that a household owns a VCR. Indeed, the ownership rate more than triples between the lowest and highest income brackets (Table 22).

Table 22   Percentage of households with video recorder, 1992

All households	69.3
Household weekly income	
Under £60	26.7
£60 and under £80	30.4
£80 and under £100	40.7
£100 and under £130	50.7
£130 and under £160	57.6
£160 and under £200	62.9
£200 and under £240	70.4
£240 and under £280	71.7
£280 and under £320	80.3
£320 and under £370	82.2
£370 and under £420	85.6
£420 and under £470	88.0
£470 and under £540	92.0
£540 and under £640	88.7
£640 and under £800	91.8
£800 and more	90.0
Household composition	
Households with:	
One adult	
Retired, mainly dependent on state pensions	15.9
Other retired	25.7
Non-retired	56.9
One adult, one child	74.9
One adult, two or more children	76.1
One man, one woman	
Retired, mainly dependent on state pensions	40.1
Other retired	52.5
Non-retired	83.4
One man, one woman, one child	91.2
One man, one woman, two children	90.6
One man, one woman, three child	91.4
Two adults, four or more children	86.1
Three adults, one or more children	92.1

Table 22   Percentage of households with video recorder, 1992

Tenure of dwelling	
Rented unfurnished	55.2
Local authority	55.4
Housing association	55.9
Other	53.6
Rented furnished	53.0
Rent free	59.7
Owner occupied	76.6

Source: Family Spending 1992, Table 4.

In contrast with television sets, men are more likely than women to own a VCR (Table 23). This is in accord with research which suggests that the higher tech an artefact, the more likely it is to be seen as a male artefact (Cockburn 1985, Gray 1992).

Table 23   VCR ownership by sex, 1985 and 1991

	1985	*1991*
Sample	24,651	25,604
	%	%
All	33	73
Men	35	77
Women	31	70

Source: TGI, BMRB 1985, 1991 cited by Mintel 1994.

The middle age band is more likely to own a VCR, and those over 65 the least likely – perhaps because of unfamiliarity with such technology. The lower age band presumably enjoys access to parents' VCRs, so has no need of ownership (Table 24).

Table 24   **Ownership of VCRs by age, 1985 and 1991**

	1985	1991		1985	1991
Sample	24,651	25,604		24,651	25,604
	%	%		%	%
15-19	20	62	45-54	40	85
20-24	34	74	55-64	24	72
25-34	43	85	65+	12	40
35-44	47	89			

Source: TGI, BMRB 1985, 1991 cited by Mintel 1994.

The growth in the number of television sets in households will have an impact on VCR ownership and sales, especially if the additional televisions are for children. Although new features *are* available on VCRs [8], these are fewer or less significant than with televisions. Most VCRs are functionally similar; this reduces that element of demand which is, precisely, for such new features. The declines of rentals – from 37% in 1985 to 19% in 1991 – in part reflects this. Volume demand until 1988 increased at an average of about 10% per annum, and declined after the peak of the consumer boom of 1988-89. The average price of a VCR has tended to rise in absolute terms, unlike television – from £320 in 1987 to £340 in 1993 (British Radio and Electronic Manufacturers (BREMA) cited by Mintel 1994). It is forecast that sales of VCRs in the UK will grow by 6% over the period 1993-97 (Mintel 1994).

Despite its relatively recent arrival in the home, the use to which the VCR is put has already shifted significantly. Specifically, there is less hiring of pre-recorded tape (Table 25).

Table 25   **Hiring of pre-recorded VCR tapes**

	1986	1989	1990	1991
% of VCR owners hiring tapes during previous 7 days	30	30	26	22

Source: British Videogram Association, cited by Social Trends 1993, 10.8.

Turning to usage, and comparing the data with that on television viewing, it is clear that watching a pre-recorded video is something done by about a quarter of people who watch television; and that about a third of those who watch television watch a recorded television programme (Table 26). In other words, one and a half times as many people watch recorded television as pre-recorded video tapes. Those who watch pre-recorded tapes are slightly more likely to be male and in the younger age groups (15-34). Those watching recorded television programmes are more likely to be aged 20-54 and to be at work, in full time education, or to have a family.

Table 26 Respondents watching over one hour a week of video tape, October 1991

Base: 1,081 adults.

	Watching pre-recorded video	Watching video recorded from television
	%	%
All	21	31
Men	23	34
Women	20	29
15-19	39	29
20-24	42	47
25-34	30	39
35-44	22	37
45-54	15	32
55-64	11	29
65+	5	13
AB	19	29
C1	20	30
C2	26	33
D	24	39
E	18	24

Source: BMRB/ Mintel 1994.

Preference is for films and soap operas, half from ITV and a third from BBC, and this is fairly standard across social class [9]. The average VCR household makes 3.75 recordings a week and plays back 2.5 recordings, mostly pre-recorded the previous week (Levy and Gunter 1988). VCR users in the Middle East and Third World, and Third World nationals living in the developed world watch more pre-recorded tapes and little time-shifted material. Finally, the VCR can be used to play videotape recordings made on home video cameras, owned by a small but growing number.

There is debate about whether video viewing is seen as something different from television viewing – about whether the audience sees it as a unique form of communication or merely as a part of the television set. However, there is little doubt that the capacity to fast forward has altered the nature of the viewing audience, offering greater control to the consumer (Levy and Gunter 1988).

There is also data on owners' ability to operate a VCR. According to this (Table 27) twice as many women as men admitted that they could not use a VCR at all; and respondents without children were less likely to know how to operate the VCR. In addition, younger people are more able to operate a VCR; and the ability to operate it also corresponds to social class, with the ABs most able, and the Es (a group which includes a high proportion of older people) least able.

Table 27   Ability to operate a VCR, December 1991

Base: 1,138 VCR owners.

	All	*Men*	*Women*	*Children*	*No children*
	%	%	%	%	%
I can't use the VCR at all	6	4	9	3	9
I can just play a pre recorded tape	3	1	5	3	3
I can record a programme at the same time as it is playing on TV	11	6	15	11	10
I can set the machine to record one programme at a time	13	8	17	11	14
I can set the machine to record more than one programme	4	3	4	3	4
I can use just about all the facilities on the machine	15	17	14	18	14
I have no problems at all using all the facilities on the machine	47	60	35	50	45
Don't know	1				

Source: BMRB, cited by Mintel 1994.

3 THE HOME COMPUTER

The home computer arrived at about the same time as the VCR; but has subsequently achieved a far lower penetration (Table 28).

Table 28   Sales of home computers, by volume and value, 1987-92

	000 units	*Index*	*£m at current price*	*Index*
1987	850	100	255	100
1988	750	88	262	103
1989	750	88	300	118
1990	900	106	400	157
1991	875	103	360	141
1992e	900	106	390	153

Source: Mintel 1994

The market grew fastest during the period 1985-88, after which sales for educational purposes declined (it became apparent that they were used mainly for games playing) and sales shifted to more upmarket, business style, PCs. Falling prices contributed crucially to this shift, as a business machine became available at a price affordable to most households. The shift of games from general purpose machines to dedicated consoles (Table 29) further slowed the growth, whilst developing use of Midi, for music, has led to an increased demand. The home computer market can be seen in terms of three key segments.

Table 29   Segmentation of home computer market, by volume and value, 1989-91

	1989		1990		1991		% change by volume
	000	£m	000	£m	000	£m	1989-91
Games-based machines	270	28	220	27	181	20	-33
Home computers	362	157	527	226	545	215	+51
Business computers	118	115	153	147	149	125	+26
Total	750	300	900	400	875	360	+17

Source: Mintel 1994.

Together, these lead to an ownership level of 19.1%, or 34%, depending on whose data one is using (Tables 30 and 31).

Table 30   Availability in households of home computer

	%
1985	12.6
1986	15.1
1987	16.6
1988	16.9
1989	16.6
1990	16.8
1991	18.1
1992	19.1

Source: Annual Abstract of Statistics, 1993, Table 15.4; Family Spending 1992.

Mintel (1994) come up with rather higher figures than 'Family Spending'. (Table 31); most recently, Mintel reported a 30% ownership level in 1993 (Mintel 1994a). Mintel's figures also show considerable trading up as a proportion of sales: of 2.5m sales in 1991, 2.4m were replacements or additions, and only 0.2m first purchases.

Table 31   Number of adults with home computer (year ending March), 1985-91

Base: approx 25,000 adults.

	% of adults	Installed base 000	Net addition to base 000
1985	14.7	6,351	-
1988	28.7	12,878	+6,527
1989	29.7	13,400	+522
1990	30.0	13,559	+159
1991	30.4	13,731	+172

Source: TGI, BMRB 1985-91 cited by Mintel 1994.

Behind these overall figures lie sharp distinctions between social classes (Tables 32 and 34) and age groups (Table 33). Whereas the economically inactive have a 7% level of ownership of a home computer, the professional class has a 52% level. Regarding age, ownership is highest in the 15-19 year old age bracket, then the 35-44 bracket, with other age bands roughly the same except for a rapid drop of ownership level in those age 55+. Regarding regional differences, Harlech and TSW television areas have the highest ownership levels and the Granada area the lowest. The differences between men and women are greater than with television or VCR ownership.

Table 32   Households with home computer: by socio-economic group of head, 1992

	%
Professional	52
Employers and managers	41
Other non-manual	33
Skilled manual	27
Unskilled manual	21
All economically active	33
Economically inactive	7
All heads of household	23

Source: General Household Survey, cited in Social Trends, 1994.

Table 33   Home computer owners, demographic detail, April 1992

Base: 1,121 adults.

	Owners *%*
All	32
Men	37
Women	27
15-19	59
20-24	32
25-34	34
35-44	54
45-54	35
55-64	13
65+	6
AB	44
C1	35
C2	30
D	30
E	17
TV areas:	
London/ TVS	33
Anglia/ Central	30
Harlech/ TSW	38
Yorkshire/ Tyne Tees	32
Granada	26
Scotland	30
Children	55
No children	19

Source: BMRB cited by Mintel 1994.

Table 34   Percentage of households with home computer, 1992

All households	19.1
Household weekly income	
Under £60	4.7
£60 and under £80	3.4
£80 and under £100	6.5
£100 and under £130	8.3
£130 and under £160	8.8
£160 and under £200	12.5
£200 and under £240	14.7
£240 and under £280	17.8
£280 and under £320	16.3
£320 and under £370	22.4
£370 and under £420	23.3
£420 and under £470	26.1
£470 and under £540	29.1
£540 and under £640	34.6
£640 and under £800	36.9
£800 and more	43.9
Household composition	
Households with:	
One adult	
Retired, mainly dependent	
on state pensions	0.4
Other retired	1.8
Non-retired	10.8
One adult, one child	16.4
One adult, two or more children	29.7
One man, one woman	
Retired, mainly dependent	
on state pensions	-
Other retired	4.8
Non-retired	16.1
One man, one woman, one child	29.2
One man, one woman, two children	43.7
One man, one woman, three child	45.5
Two adults, four or more children	40.7
Three adults, one or more children	38.4

Table 34   Percentage of households with home computer, 1992

Tenure of dwelling		
Rented unfurnished		10.6
	Local authority	10.0
	Housing association	12.2
	Other	12.4
Rented furnished		19.7
Rent free		15.4
Owner occupied		22.9

Source: Family Spending 1992, Table 4.

The future market depends on a number of factors: first, the recovery from the recession. The home computer is becoming a part of the broader brown (i.e. leisure, as opposed to white, utility) goods industry. Second, it depends on demography: whilst the number of 5-14 year olds will grow up to the end of the millennium, the number of 15-24 year olds will decline. The growth of 'empty nesters' – adults aged 45+ whose children have left home – is likely to be important; they may take up computing for a hobby, or purchase computers for their grandchildren. Third, prices affect levels of consumption – and they have been falling quite dramatically. Apple Computers is reported reckoning that 7m US families can afford to purchase a home computer but have not, so far, done so (Kehoe 1992a). As global sales of computers are falling, the home becomes an increasingly important target market (Kehoe 1992b). Fourth, the market is stimulated by a new generation or model of hardware, new processors, for example, render older machines obsolete. Finally, the uses to which home computers are put will affect the size of the market. For example, the home computer *could* become the focus of the centre of home leisure / entertainment technologies, interfacing with the telephone system (e.g. for working at home, home banking, shopping and film watching), CD players (for holiday snaps as well as interactive multimedia applications – for education and entertainment), infrastructural controls, etc. (Table 35).

Table 35   Market size forecast for home computers at constant 1992 prices, 1992-96

	£m	Index		£m	Index
1992	390	100	1995	474	122
1993	406	104	1996	507	130
1994	441	113			

Source: Mintel 1994.

Turning to use (Table 36), there are three main reasons for ownership: first, to play games, which remains the key to the market, though with declining importance. Second is the business role, which has declined due to the recession; homeworking levels depend on a broad range of external factors. Third is the computer education of children, which parents have become less committed to as the use of computers by children has been shown to be for games.

Table 36   The main use for a home computer, 1985-92

	1985	1987	1990	1992
Base: adults	1,034	983	1,006	986
	%	%	%	%
To play computer games	57	64	16	34
For children to learn computing	31	18	46	31
For business purposes	6	11	21	15
For adults to learn computing	19	10	6	4
For managing family finances	1	4	5	3
Other reasons	8	7	2	3
Don't know	15	2	7	10

Source: BMRB/Mintel. Market Intelligence, August 1992, p21.

Similar data which uses respondents' age in addition shows that the games motive is strongest for the youngest consumers, showing that it is the main motivation of children and young adults to have a home computer. The educational motive is strongest among the 25-44 age group. In other words, parents views' differ from those of children. The main users of computers for business purposes are ABs and those aged 20-24.

4 THE COMPUTER GAMES CONSOLE

Computer games are one of the few toys which can be marketed to children of 11+. The main target for these games is boys aged between 5-14, though they are also played by many girls and adults.

One of the three main growth areas for toys over the next few years is likely to be in electronic games; industry analysts expect the British market for video games to continue growing rapidly throughout the 1990s (Shepherd 1993).

Video and computer games, including electronic games played with a screen, easily head the list of toy sales by type. Most types of toy experienced a decline between 1988-90, whereas the TV games sector experienced a massive (173%) rise. It grew by a further 160% between 1990-91; Nintendo's Game Boy was the best selling toy in 1991. Video games have 'almost certainly been the best selling consumer use product in the UK during the recession' (Shepherd 1993). In March 1992 Sega's TV based video games was the best selling toy (by value, UK), and Bandai's Nintendo the second best (Harvest). The best selling ten toys at Hamleys for Christmas 1993 included only two toys costing over £26: the best selling toy, Sega Mega Drive, at £129.99; and the Nintendo Super NES at £99.99. Despite the massive sales, market penetration is only 15% in the UK (though Appleyard (1993) cites this figure as 25%), compared with 50% in Japan and the USA (Shepherd 1993, though Harvest refers to 33% penetration in USA and Japan). Eight million 5-19 year olds have a console or PC at home, and 87% of these play regularly (Carter 1993). However we measure it, the computer console market is huge, and growing fast (Table 37).

Table 37   Retail sales of video and computer games at current prices, 1988-91

	£m		£m
1988	24.6	1990	67.3
1989	47.6	1991	174.7

Source: Mintel, 1994.

The interactive nature of computer games is clearly central to their enormous popularity. The growth of such media, together with falling television audiences, would suggest consumer demand for interactivity, for a changed relationship between producer and audience. The camcorder and karaoke constitute further evidence to refute the notion that people want to slump in front of the television and *do* nothing. The scale and significance of this shift should not be underestimated: for a whole generation, video games have superseded popular music as the main form of entertainment.

5 THE CD PLAYER

CD-ROM drives have been around since about 1986. Initially they were owned almost exclusively by corporate and institutional users with a requirement for large scale data storage. CD-ROMs with PCs only began to emerge as a consumer technology from 1991, since when the vast majority of sales have been in the USA (Table 38).

Table 38   In home PC + CD-ROM installed base

	USA	Europe	World
1991	62	4	75
1992	801	54	981
1993	4,512	283	5,317
1994	9,230	676	10,886
1995	15,680	1,633	19,100
1996	23,625	3,500	30,225

Source: INECO/ *Screen Digest* May 1994, p105.

PC based CD players, however, are but a part of the market. More common is the CD player used as a part of an audio system. This form of CD player has seen a fast growing level of ownership (Table 39).

Table 39   UK Computer hardware CD ROM and CD player sales

	Computer hardware CD ROM 000	CD player sales 000
1983		19
1984		33
1985		141
1986	0.1	644
1987	0.5	1,042
1988	1.0	1,425
1989	2.8	1,832
1990	10.0	2,085
1991	17.0	2,211
1992		2,370

Source: Philips Consumer Electronics, and BPI, cited by *Screen Digest* June 1993, p134.

Such ownership, predictably, varies with social class (Table 40).

Table 40   CD player by socio-economic group of head of household

	1990	1992\
Professional	35	54
Employers and managers	34	53
Intermediate non-manual	29	45
Skilled manual/ Semi-skilled manual and personal service	26/22	40
Unskilled manual	18	29
Economically inactive	8	15

Source: General Household Survey 1990 and 1992, cited by Social Trends 1993 (Table 10.6) and 1994 (Table 6.7).

At least two other forms of CD can be identified: Kodak's Photo CD, which allows the storage on CD of photographs, and their display (with such features as enlargement) on the television screen, and which also functions as an audio CD; and Philip's CD-I which combines video, photography, graphics, data, animation and sound on a CD which is connected to a television screen.

Increasingly it can be expected that users will be interactive – and not just with material created for CDs, but also with films and music which were produced originally for other purposes.

CONCLUSION

From this highly descriptive account, a number of conclusions can be drawn. First, there are cases where the data contradicts popular myths – for example, that demand is for passive leisure as provided by television broadcasting.

Second, there is no shortage of examples of how people have held exaggerated expectations of technology: whilst many in the 1960s predicted holidays on the moon, so too has it been thought that television would make reading obsolete, that teleshopping would be the norm, and that most households would have a computer (Braid 1992). Notwithstanding such technological optimism or naivety, it is quite clear that the home is an enormous market for IT products, and a key arena for our experience of, or with, IT. Further, this is occurring at a time when both computer sales and television viewing are in decline.

Third, the fluctuations in sales and ownership levels which are discussed constitute evidence to counter at least cruder versions of technological determinism. The sales, or household penetration, of an IT device are often not all regular or linear. Further, although I have been discussing 'successful' ITs, not all technologies *have* been successful.

Fourth, this is not to say that we should ignore the technical in the developments which we are witnessing. The point is that technical developments need to be understood in their social context. The emergence of standards is a clear – and crucial – example of how the technical is important but inseparable from the social.

Fifth, it is quite clear that to understand the pervasiveness, or effect of a technology we have to understand a range of 'non technological' factors. These include broader social processes (the global economic recession, for example), the meta level (of broadcasting, software and hardware organisations – which, in turn, depend on not just the structure and development of these industries, but also on regulatory frameworks) and how people respond to available technologies (for example, the needs which they experience, the meanings which they attach to these needs and their leisure technologies, and the uses to which they put them).

Sixth, if we are to understand patterns of sales and ownership, we have to have an understanding of the relationships between different IT devices, and of the synergy which is occurring. Increasingly these devices are components of integrated systems which span a range of leisure and work activities.

Finally, the broader trends which I have described mask profound differences – in relation to class, sex, age and region. Had I not confined myself to the UK, then I would have demonstrated far greater disparities. It is important to temper any account of the broader picture by considering those to whom this broader picture does *not* apply.

NOTES

1 Thanks to Gareth Gillespie for the library research on which this article is based, and to Tim O'Sullivan for comments on a draft.

2 See Silverstone and Hirsch (1992) for a collection of such material.

3 Mintel 1994.

4 Social classes can be defined in a variety of ways. The following uses the six-category JICNARS scale, probably the most widely recognised marketing classification, of A (upper middle class), B (middle class), C1 (lower middle class, 'white collar' workers), C2 (skilled working class), D (semi-skilled and unskilled working class) and E (those at the lowest levels of subsistence, including pensioners, widows and those dependent on state benefits). Like the Registrar General's numeric classification of social class, this is a model based on segmentation of the population by occupation.

5 For data on television ownership and audiences, see *Spectrum, Screen Digest*, BARB (Broadcasting Audience Research Board) and the *Annual Review of BBC Broadcasting Research Findings.*

6 *Screen Digest* June 1991 p 129.

7 *Screen Digest* June 1992 p 129.

8 VHS is now completely dominant. Remote control is found on 98% of models. 75% of VCRs sold in 1993 had a long play facility. NICAM stereo was available on 19% of VCRs sold in 1992 and 25% of those sold in

1993. PlusCode, which makes programming easier, is a recent new feature.

9   See Alvarado (1988) for other data on VCR usage, for the UK and elsewhere in the world.

REFERENCES

Alvarado, M. (ed) (1988) *Video World-wide*, John Libbey, London.

Appleyard, B. (1993) 'Dr Mario made me an addict: Are the Brooklyn plumbers really draining our children's brains? Or is it all just a game?', *The Independent,* 16 June, p. 23.

Braid, M. (1992) 'Cautious public learns the limits of new technology', *The Independent,* 30 December, p. 2.

Carter, M. (1993) 'Selling through computer games isn't child's play', *The Independent on Sunday,* 5 December 1993, p. 14.

Cockburn, C. (1985) *Machinery of Dominance. Women, Men and Technical Know-How,* Pluto, London.

Gray, A. (1992) *Video Playtime. The Gendering of a Leisure Technology,* Routledge, London.

Kehoe, L. (1992a) 'Technology: computers on the home front – technically speaking', *Financial Times,* 22 September, p. 11.

Kehoe, L. (1992b) International company news: first global decline in sales of computers', *Financial Times,* 21 January, p. 4.

Levy, M. and Gunter, B. (1988) *Home Video and the Changing Nature of the Television Audience,* John Libbey, London.

Mintel (1994) *On Line* (on line marketing database).

Mintel (1994a) 'British lifestyles', reported in *The Guardian,* 1 February 1994.

de Sola Pool, I. (ed) (1977) *The Social Impact of the Telephone,* MIT Press, Cambridge, MA.

Shepherd, S. (1993) 'Rhino set to buy video game shop from Virgin', *The Independent,* 3 November, p. 36.

Silverstone, R. and Hirsch, E. (eds) (1992) *Consuming Technology: Media and Information in Domestic Space,* Routledge, London.

Tunstall, J. (1983) *The Media in Britain,* Constable, London.

Williamson, J. (1993) 'Survey of mobile communications: mobile phones and the weight of things to come', *Financial Times,* 8 Sept 1993, p. VI.

Wood, J. (1993) 'Cellphones on the Clapham omnibus: the lead-up to a cellular mass market', SPRU Research Paper, University of Sussex.

PART 5 IT FUTURES

Nick Heap, Faculty of Technology, The Open University

INTRODUCTION

The information age is barely thirty years old, but its impact on industrialised society has been profound. From everything that can be read comes the same message, that the falling cost of computing power and the digital representation of information will change the way we earn our daily bread. It might be argued that many of the changes we see are simply evolutionary, but for that fact that the changes are occurring too rapidly and it is becoming increasingly difficult for anyone to keep abreast of them.

None of this would matter but for the influence such developments have on our society, or that society has on the developments, and this brings to the fore considerations of the sort of future we want. How much personal control do you want over your life or that of your family? To what extent do you feel that technology is forcing the pace of change, dehumanising society and removing personal decision making?

Assessing the future directions of technological developments is an essential task for government and management. A technological edge over competitors may be crucial for commercial success, provided the technologies support strategic as well as commercial objectives. But the current rate of development means that products are frequently superseded before they have been fully integrated into existing systems; so selecting the wrong technology reduces its cost effectiveness, increases staff training costs and diminishes competitiveness.

Numerous writers and commentators predict a rosy future based on the use of information technology. An idyllic lifestyle of teleworking from home is forecast, one in which work can be fitted in amongst family commitments and everyone will enjoy greater leisure time. Every household interconnected by a super highway of optical fibres, permitting home shopping and banking alongside video-on-demand and interactive entertainment. Visiting friends will become a virtual activity as you don suit and headgear, embedded with sensors and activators that record your movements and convey your electronic hug. At birth you get a name-tag and personal telecommunications number, valid for life across the globe. Electronic payment systems will obviate the need for cash which, together with greater levels of video and audio surveillance, will drastically reduce the crime rate.

Such predictions appear almost weekly in the mass media, but how realistic are they? Is it possible to distinguish fact from fiction. The papers collected in this Part touch on a number of these futures, some more critically than others, but together they begin to suggest how we might approach the problem. So, for example, what questions should we ask, what are the time scales involved, are the products and services immediately available or awaiting further technological development?

The first two papers in the collection provide contrasting views of the future developments of satellite communications systems. Clarke, perhaps better known as a science fiction writer, published his ideas about geostationary satellites in 1949, some thirteen years before the introduction of a commercial satellite telecommunications service (and the same year as the announcement of the transistor). Speculation about future technological developments is not a new phenomenon, but Clarke's article is factual, supported by scientific theory and mathematics. Perhaps it is not surprising then that his forecasts were fairly accurate, albeit lacking a social context. Lockwood's paper reports on developments some forty years later, when the available geostationary orbits have been filled almost to capacity and space debris poses a hazard to future satellite systems. The Iridium system is claimed to fulfil a new need, that of mobile, global communications. The greatest market consists of those countries which lack a terrestrial telecommunications infrastructure. Lockwood does at least raise some questions for the reader. Iridium is expensive and has cheaper competitors (many not mentioned in the article), it requires international co-operation and collaboration and its primary markets may be those least able to afford such services. Will Iridium ever get off the ground?

All information and communications technologies utilise software to control and process data in an ever-increasing variety of forms. In fact software is a basic enabling technology and without it there is no IT future. Industry and government sources frequently express concern about the widening gap between our ability to supply and the demand for new software products. Various tactics have been adopted to increase productivity, reliability and compatibility. But just how successful are these measures and what will be their influence on future products and services?

The papers by Brooks and Cox provide contrasting views of the current state of affairs. Brooks argues that the very essence of software precludes any further major breakthroughs, and that the majority of enhancements and improvements will arise from incremental developments. The limiting factor is the conceptual complexity of software. Cox provides the counter argument, that productivity can and has increased with the exploitation of modular design strategies and that this represents a cultural change as significant as the industrial revolution.

Virtual reality is another technology that has captured the attention of the media with its potential for the user to immerse themselves in historical events, engage in dog-fights with the Red Baron or become the lead singer of the newest pop-group. Perhaps it is the immersive element that has caught the imagination – the ability to free oneself of the normal limitations of space and time.

Although a technology that can be traced back to the mid-1960s, virtual reality received little attention until the 1980s. So what factors led to this 'lull' of twenty years. This is one of the questions addressed by Schroeder in his article on the history, applications and projections for virtual reality technology.

Teleworking is not new, the early initiatives to permit women with young children to return to work and reduce office overheads by facilitating telework for middle and senior management occurred in the early 1980s. The growth of teleworkers and telecentres predicted then has simply not materialised, even though there have been numerous studies identifying the benefits and cost-effectiveness of this new pattern of working. Employers have been resistant to relinquish control of employees, but employees are equally concerned about the organisational changes to domestic life.

Haddon and Silverstone are well known for their studies of the domestic consumption of information and communication technologies, so they are well placed to identify the major questions relating to the potential growth of teleworking.

In this paper they examine whether the availability of appropriate technologies has furthered home-based telework, if teleworking introduces major organisation changes in domestic life, and whether the teleworking technologies are adapted and utilised by other members of the household.

Crosbie provides a snapshot of the competitive market developing for satellite mobile communications, dominated by major US corporations. His assessment makes clear that few suppliers will survive.

Extra-terrestrial Relays: Can Rockets give World-wide Radio Coverage?

Arthur C. Clarke

Although it is possible, by a suitable choice of frequencies and routes, to provide telephony circuits between any two points or regions of the earth for a large part of the time, long-distance communication is greatly hampered by the peculiarities of the ionosphere, and there are even occasions when it may be impossible. A true broadcast service, giving constant field strength at all times over the whole globe would be invaluable, not to say indispensable, in a world society.

Unsatisfactory though the telephony and telegraph position is, that of television is far worse since ionospheric transmission cannot be employed at all. The service area of a television station, even on a very good site, is only about a hundred miles across. To cover a small country such as Great Britain would require a network of transmitters, connected by coaxial lines, waveguides or VHF relay links. A recent theoretical study (Hansell, 1945) has shown that such a system would require repeaters at intervals of fifty miles or less. A system of this kind could provide television coverage, at a very considerable cost, over the whole of a small country. It would be out of the question to provide a large continent with such a service, and only the main centres of population could be included in the network.

The problem is equally serious when an attempt is made to link television services in different parts of the globe. A relay chain several thousand miles long would cost millions, and transoceanic services would still be impossible. Similar considerations apply to the provision of wide-band frequency modulation and other services, such as high-speed facsimile which are by their nature restricted to the ultra-high-frequencies.

Many may consider the solution proposed in this discussion too far-fetched to be taken very seriously. Such an attitude is unreasonable, as everything envisaged here is a logical extension of developments in the last ten years – in particular the perfection of the long-range rocket of which V2 was the prototype. While this article was being written, it was announced that the Germans were considering a similar project, which they believed possible within fifty to a hundred years.

Before proceeding further, it is necessary to discuss briefly certain fundamental laws of rocket propulsion and 'astronautics.' A rocket which achieved a sufficiently great speed in flight outside the earth's atmosphere would never return. This 'orbital' velocity is 8 km per sec. (5 miles per sec), and a rocket which attained it would become an artificial satellite, circling the world for ever with no expenditure of power – a second moon, in fact. The German transatlantic rocket A10 would have reached more than half this velocity.

It will be possible in a few more years to build radio controlled rockets which can be steered into such orbits beyond the limits of the atmosphere and left to broadcast scientific information back to the earth. A little later, manned rockets will be able to make similar flights with sufficient excess power to break the orbit and return to earth.

There are an infinite number of possible stable orbits, circular and elliptical, in which a rocket would remain if the initial conditions were correct. The velocity of 8 km / sec. applies only to the closest possible orbit, one just outside the atmosphere, and the period of revolution would be about 90 minutes. As the radius of the orbit increases the velocity decreases, since gravity is diminishing and less centrifugal force is needed to balance it. Figure 1 shows this graphically. The moon, of course, is a particular case and would lie on the curves of Figure 1 if they were produced. The proposed German space-stations would have a period of about four and a half hours.

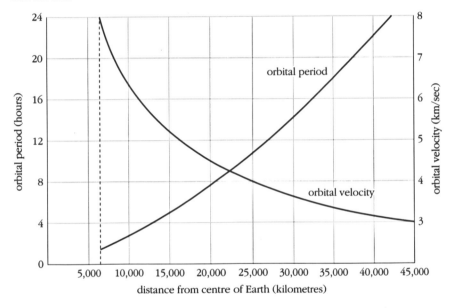

Figure 1 Variation of orbital period and velocity with distance from the centre of the earth

It will be observed that one orbit, with a radius of 42,000 km, has a period of exactly 24 hours. A body in such an orbit, if its plane coincided with that of the earth's equator, would revolve with the earth and would thus be stationary above the same spot on the planet. It would remain fixed in the sky of a whole hemisphere and unlike all other heavenly bodies would neither rise nor set. A body in a smaller orbit would revolve more quickly than the earth and so would rise in the west, as indeed happens with the inner moon of Mars.

Using material ferried up by rockets, it would be possible to construct a 'space-station' in such an orbit. The station could be provided with living quarters, laboratories and everything needed for the comfort of its crew, who would be relieved and provisioned by a regular rocket service. This project might be undertaken for purely scientific reasons as it would contribute enormously to our knowledge of astronomy, physics and meteorology. A good deal of literature has already been written on the subject (Ley, n.d.).

Although such an undertaking may seem fantastic, it requires for its fulfilment rockets only twice as fast as those already in the design stage. Since the gravitational stresses involved in the structure are negligible, only the very lightest materials would be necessary and the station could be as large as required.

Let us now suppose that such a station were built in this orbit. It could be provided with receiving and transmitting equipment (the problem of power will be discussed later) and could act as a repeater to relay transmissions between any two points on the hemisphere beneath, using any frequency which will penetrate the ionosphere. If directive arrays were used, the power requirements would be very small, as direct line of sight transmission would be used. There is the further important point that arrays on the earth, once set up, could remain fixed indefinitely.

Moreover, a transmission received from any point on the hemisphere could be broadcast to the whole of the visible face of the globe, and thus the requirements of all possible services would be met (Figure 2).

Figure 2 Typical extra-terrestrial relay services. Transmission from A being relayed to point B and area C; transmission from D being relayed to whole hemisphere.

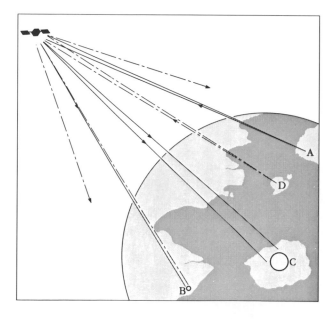

It may be argued that we have as yet no direct evidence of radio waves passing between the surface of the earth and outer space; all we can say with certainty is that the shorter wavelengths are not reflected back to the earth. Direct evidence of field strength above the earth's atmosphere could be obtained by V2 rocket technique, and it is to be hoped that someone will do something about this soon as there must be quite a surplus stock somewhere! Alternatively, given sufficient transmitting power, we might obtain the necessary evidence by exploring for echoes from the moon. In the meantime we have visual evidence that frequencies at the optical end of the spectrum pass through with little absorption except at certain frequencies at which resonance effects occur. Medium high frequencies go through the E layer twice to be reflected from the F layer and echoes have been received from meteors in or above the F layer. It seems fairly certain that frequencies from, say, 50 Mc/s to 100,000 Mc/s could be used without undue absorption in the atmosphere or the ionosphere. [N.B. cyles per second (c/s) are the equivalent of hertz (Hz).]

A single station could only provide coverage to half the globe, and for a world service three would be required, though more could be readily utilised. Figure 3 shows the simplest arrangement. The stations would be arranged approximately equidistantly around the earth, and the following longitudes appear to be suitable:

30 E – Africa and Europe.
150 E – China and Oceana.
90 W – The Americas.

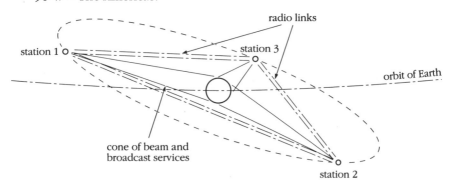

Figure 3 Three satellite stations would ensure complete coverage of the globe.

The stations in the chain would be linked by radio or optical beams, and thus any conceivable beam or broadcast service could be provided.

The technical problems involved in the design of such stations are extremely interesting (Noording, n.d.) but only a few can be gone into here. Batteries of parabolic reflectors would be provided, of apertures depending on the frequencies employed. Assuming the use of 3,000 Mc/s waves, mirrors about a metre across would beam almost all the power on to the earth. Larger reflectors could be used to illuminate single countries or regions for the more restricted services, with consequent economy of power. On the higher frequencies it is not difficult to produce beams less than a degree in width, and, as mentioned before, there would be no physical limitations on the size of the mirrors. (From the space station, the disc of the earth would be a little over 17 degrees across.) The same mirrors could be used for many different transmissions if precautions were taken to avoid cross modulation.

It is clear from the nature of the system that the power needed will be much less than that required for any other arrangement, since all the energy radiated can be uniformly distributed over the service area, and none is wasted. An approximate estimate of the power required for the broadcast service from a single station can be made as follows: –

The field strength in the equatorial plane of a $\lambda/2$ dipole in free space at a distance of d metres is (Hund, n.d.)

$$e = 6.85 \frac{\sqrt{P}}{d} \text{ volts/metre}$$

where P is the power radiated in watts. Taking d as 42,000 km (effectively it would be less), we have P = 37.6 e^2 watts. (e now in μV/metre.)

If we assume e to be 50 micro-volts/metre, which is the F.C.C. standard for frequency modulation, P will be 94 kW. This is the power required for a single dipole, and not an array which would concentrate all the power on the earth. Such an array would have a gain over a simple dipole of about 80. The power required for the broadcast service would thus be about 1.2 kW.

Ridiculously small though it is, this figure is probably much too generous. Small parabolas about a foot in diameter would be used for receiving at the earth end and would give a very good signal/ noise ratio. There would be very little interference, partly because of the frequency used and partly because the mirrors would be pointing towards the sky which could contain no other source of signal. A field strength of 10 microvolts/metre might well be ample, and this would require a transmitter output of only 50 watts.

When it is remembered that these figures relate to the broadcast service, the efficiency of the system will be realised. The point-to-point beam transmissions might need powers of only 10 watts or so. These figures, of course, would need correction for ionospheric and atmospheric absorption, but that would be quite small over most of the band. The slight falling off in field strength due to this cause towards the edge of the service area could be readily corrected by a non-uniform radiator.

The efficiency of the system is strikingly revealed when we consider that the London Television service required about 3 kW average power for an area less than fifty miles in radius (MacNamara and Birkinshaw, 1938).

A second fundamental problem is the provision of electrical energy to run the large number of transmitters required for the different services. In space beyond the atmosphere, a square metre normal to the solar radiation intercepts 1.35 kW of energy (*Journal of the British Interplanetary Society,*

1939) Solar engines have already been devised for terrestrial use and are an economic proposition in tropical countries. They employ mirrors to concentrate sunlight on the boiler of a low-pressure steam engine. Although this arrangement is not very efficient it could be made much more so in space where the operating components are in a vacuum, the radiation is intense and continuous, and the low-temperature end of the cycle could be not far from absolute zero. Thermo-electric and photo-electric developments may make it possible to utilise the solar energy more directly.

Though there is no limit to the size of the mirrors that could be built, one fifty metres in radius would intercept over 10,000 kW and at least a quarter of this energy should be available for use.

The station would be in continuous sunlight except for some weeks around the equinoxes, when it would enter the earth's shadow for a few minutes every day. Figure 4 shows the state of affairs during the eclipse period. For this calculation, it is legitimate to consider the earth as fixed and the sun as moving round it. The station would graze the earth's shadow at A, on the last day in February. Every day, as it made its diurnal revolution, it would cut more deeply into the shadow, undergoing its period of maximum eclipse on March 21st, on that day it would only be in darkness for 1 hour 9 minutes. From then onwards the period of eclipse would shorten, and after April 11th (B) the station would be in continuous sunlight again until the same thing happened six months later at the autumn equinox, between September 12th and October 14th. The total period of darkness would be about two days per year, and as the longest period of eclipse would be little more than an hour there should be no difficulty in storing enough power for an uninterrupted service.

Figure 4 Solar radiation would be cut off for a short period each day at the equinoxes.

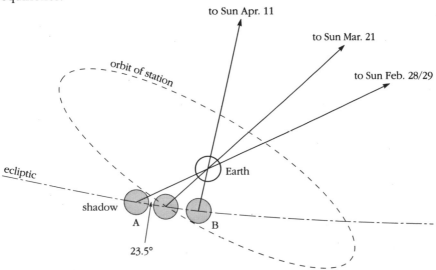

CONCLUSION

Briefly summarised, the advantages of the space station are as follows:

1 It is the only way in which true world coverage can be achieved for all possible types of service.

2 It permits unrestricted use of a band at least 100,000 Mc/s wide, and with the use of beams an almost unlimited number of channels would be available.

3 The power requirements are extremely small since the efficiency of 'illumination' will be almost 100 per cent. Moreover, the cost of the power would be very low.

4 However great the initial expense, it would only be a fraction of that required for the world networks replaced, and the running costs would be incomparably less.

APPENDIX – ROCKET DESIGN

The development of rockets sufficiently powerful to reach 'orbital' and even 'escape' velocity is now only a matter of years. The following figures may be of interest in this connection. The rocket has to acquire a final velocity of 8 km/sec. Allowing 2 km/sec. for navigational corrections and air resistance loss (this is legitimate as all space-rockets will be launched from very high country) gives a total velocity needed of 10 km/sec. The fundamental equation of rocket motion is (Ley, n.d.)

$$V = v\log_e R$$

where V is the final velocity of the rocket, v the exhaust velocity and R the ratio of initial mass to final mass (payload plus structure). So far v has been about 2-2.5 km/sec for liquid fuel rockets but new designs and fuels will permit of considerably higher figures. (Oxyhydrogen fuel has a theoretical exhaust velocity of 5.2 km/sec and more powerful combinations are known.) If we assume v to be 3.3 km/sec, R will be 20 to 1. However, owing to its finite acceleration, the rocket loses velocity as a result of gravitational retardation. If its acceleration (assumed constant) is α metres/sec^2, then the necessary ratio R_g is increased to

$$R_g = R\frac{\alpha + g}{\alpha}$$

For an automatically controlled rocket α would be about 5g and so the necessary R would be 37 to 1. Such ratios cannot be realised with a single rocket but can be attained by 'step-rockets' (Ley, n.d.), while very much higher ratios (up to 1,000 to 1) can be achieved by the principle of 'cellular construction' (Noordung, n.d.).

EPILOGUE – ATOMIC POWER

The advent of atomic power has at one bound brought space travel half a century nearer. It seems unlikely that we will have to wait as much as twenty years before atomic-powered rockets are developed, and such rockets could reach even the remoter planets with a fantastically small fuel/mass ratio – only a few per cent. The equations developed in the appendix still hold, but v will be increased by a factor of about a thousand.

In view of these facts, it appears hardly worth while to expend much effort on the building of long-distance relay chains. Even the local networks which will soon be under construction may have a working life of only 20-30 years.

REFERENCES

Abbot, C.G. 'The Sun,' Appleton-Century Co.

Hansell, C.W. (1945) 'Radio-relay systems', *Proc. IRE.*, Vol. 33, March.

Hund, A. 'Frequency modulation,' McGraw Hill.

Journal of the British Interplanetary Society, Jan., 1939.

Ley, W. *Rockets*, Viking Press, NY.

MacNamara and Birkinshaw (1938) 'London Television Service,' *JIEE*, Dec.

Noordung, H. 'Das Problem der Befahrung des Weltraums,'.

Iridium: A High Flying Phone System

Lawrence W. Lockwood
President of TeleResources

Motorola has proposed an intriguing worldwide phone communication system incorporating 77 low earth orbit (LEO) satellites. (Parenthetically the system's name is derived from the fact that the atomic number of the element Iridium is 77.) All the information on this system comes from Motorola sources including their detailed and massive December 1990 application to the Federal Communications Commission.

Satellite System

All users will need are hand-held mobile telephones or small transportable phone booths linked through a network of the LEO satellites to provide point-to-point communications between users located anywhere on Earth. Central to Iridium is the notion of the small satellite, sometimes called the light-sat (for light satellite), that could max out at 700 lbs. The concept of the light-sat is not new – more than 60 satellites lighter than 800 lbs have been built and flown by six countries since 1970. The Iridium satellites could be placed into orbit by a variety of existing launch vehicles (e.g., the U.S. Delta and Atlas, the European Ariane, the new US Pegasus air-launched vehicle and others).

Since full global coverage is essential, in theory the best solution was to use a high earth orbit so fewer satellites could cover the globe. But the network had to connect with a hand-held telephone, which meant moving the orbit down but not so far down that the drag of Earth's atmosphere would lessen orbital lifetime. The satellites could not be near manned orbital space lanes nor could they be so far above them that they might be out of reach of a Pegasus launch capability. After extensive studies, the 77 satellites will be placed in seven planes of 11 satellites each in circular polar orbits (orbits going directly north or south around the Earth passing over the North and South Poles – see Figure 1) at an altitude of 413.5 nautical miles (nmi), or 476 miles.

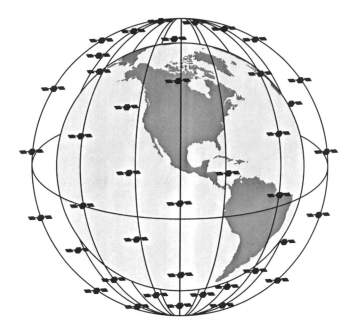

Figure 1 Iridium satellite system

A polar orbit is the one used by spy satellites because, since the Earth rotates underneath the orbit, a single satellite covers the entire surface of the Earth each 24 hours. It intuitively follows that 77 satellites in polar orbits would really blanket the Earth continuously. The satellites will all 'travel in the same direction,' which means the seven planes of satellites corotate toward the North Pole on one side of the Earth and come down toward the South Pole on the other side. The 11 satellites in each plane are evenly spaced around their planar orbit, with satellites in Planes 1, 3, 5 and 7 in phase with one another and those in Planes 2, 4 and 6 in phase with each other and halfway out of phase with 1, 3, 5 and 7. Each of the seven corotating planes is separated by slightly more than 27°.

The basic breakdown of the satellite weight would be 200 lbs for structure, 200 lbs for payload, 100 lbs for antennas and 200 lbs for enough fuel to last a five-year mission lifetime. Each satellite will have the capability of generating 37 antenna beams in the L-band (1,610 MHz).

CELL PATTERNS

The Iridium system's digital cellular design is essentially a mirror image of present-day terrestrial cellular telephone systems (see my November 1991 column in *Communications Technology*, 'PCNs – TDMA or CDMA?'). The 37-cell pattern is fixed relative to each of the constellation's 77 satellites, but moves at 16,533 mph relative to the Earth's surface. As a subscriber unit is operated, handoffs occur from cell to cell (using a 7-cell frequency reuse pattern) similar to today's terrestrial cellular telephones. However, unlike the case of terrestrial cellular telephones, Iridium's cells would be moving across the user, rather than requiring the user to move through the cells. See Figure 2.

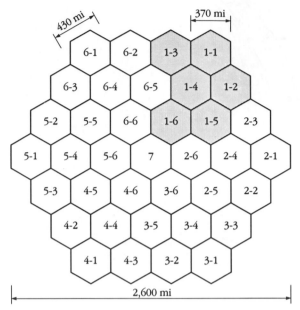

Figure 2 The 37-cell pattern

There must also be links from each satellite to others and also to earth-based telephone networks. This will be accomplished through constellation crosslinks (at 22 GHz) and gateway earth stations (20 GHz downlink, 30 GHz uplink) in various countries that would provide a link between the satellites and public switched telephone networks (PSTNs).

The typical 373 nmi (430 mi) diameter cell can simultaneously service approximately 110 users (assuming the proposed 10.5 MHz of spectrum) while individual land-based cells can handle twice that number. Thus, Motorola claims that Iridium with its limited capacity and cost structure is not designed to compete with or replace existing land-line and cellular systems. Instead Motorola says Iridium will target markets not currently served by mobile communication services, such as 1) sparsely populated locations where there is insufficient demand to justify constructing terrestrial telephone systems; 2) areas in many developing countries with no existing telephone service; and 3) small urban areas that do not now have a terrestrial mobile telecommunication structure. A graphic illustration of Iridium's worldwide coverage capabilities is shown in Figure 3.

Figure 3 Potential Iridium service areas

CURRENT ACTIVITIES

Recently, Durrell Hillis (corporate vice president of Motorola and head of the Iridium program) announced that Lockheed Corp. (Calabass, Calif.) with a $1 billion (U.S.) contract and British Aerospace (Berkshire, England) joined the design team and in the near future they expect to announce French and German participation in the program projected to cost $2.5 billion in 1991 dollars.

It is obvious that such a proposed system must have international participation. Present plans call for the Iridium constellation to be owned and operated by a consortium of international entities – such as major telecommunication companies and industrial concerns, postal telephone and telegraph (PTT) authorities and financial institutions – with expertise in telecommunications, influence of spectrum in a particular part of the world and the necessary financial resources. On the industrial team Hillis said that aside from Motorola 'we think the French and Germans will be the final additions to Lockheed and British Aerospace.'

Of the international owners and service providers Hillis said, 'We anticipate somewhere between six and 10 major owners in the Iridium program, and we have other categories of ownership, including secondary positions and minority ownership for very nominal values.'

OPERATING COSTS AND SCHEDULES

By its very nature, the Iridium system is a lower density, higher priced service than terrestrial cellular. Its per minute cost is estimated to be from three to 10 times that of conventional cellular setups. The project's financial analysis quoted a toll rate of $3 per minute for outgoing calls, which would be unaffected by distance, and a subscriber fee of $50 per month. Service costs will probably vary depending on the country and the time of day. Countries using the Iridium system as a public telephone service may choose to reduce the expense to the public through subsidies and special arrangements with the Iridium consortium such as through the leasing of bulk capacity and preleasing contracts. The worldwide total number of subscribers is estimated to exceed 1.8 million in 2001 and 2.8 million in 2006.

Motorola gave a schedule of dates of the major anticipated milestones in the development of the Iridium system:

- 1991 – Consortium formation
- 1994 – First seven satellites launched, system control facility and four Gateways operational
- 1996 – Early Iridium service available and full constellation deployed
- 1997 – The Iridium system and additional gateways are operational

COMPETITION FOR IRIDIUM

The road to system completion in a project of this scope inevitably acquires along the way a few bumps of opposition or competition. Before the World Administrative Radio Conference (WARC) '92 convenes in Torremolinos, Spain, U.S. officials are assessing concerns aired by Hughes Aircraft Co. about the Motorola plan for the Iridium frequency allocation that the State Department incorporated into its proposal. Hughes claims that the Iridium proposal is not an efficient use of the spectrum and that the frequencies requested by Motorola should not be allocated because traditional geostationary earth orbit (GEO) satellites can provide the same functionalities as Iridium without reallocating spectrum. So, in addition to its opposition, it appears that Hughes might like to be in the business itself.

A more likely and serious form of competition has recently been proposed by an international coalition – Inmarsat. The International Maritime Satellite Organization, a London-based consortium, is owned by 64 countries around the world including the United States, which is its largest stockholder. The Inmarsat proposal is called Project 21 and it would consist of about 35 LEO satellites used in combination with GEO satellites. Of course Inmarsat already has, and is launching more, GEO satellites to supply the position location service that it was formed to provide.

Inmarsat has estimated that Project 21 would cost between $500 million and $1 billion to put in place. Olaf Lundberg, Inmarsat's director general has stated the 'estimated potential mobile satellite markets, accumulated worldwide, will be significant enough by the year 2000 to support satellite investments in the neighborhood of $1 billion. But developments could stall unless significantly increased spectrum is allocated to mobile satellite services.'

CONCLUSION

To predict the end of this scenario at this time is impossible. However, there is certainly one area that requires more information: that of the business finances – capital investments, operating costs and earnings. The wide difference of projected capital costs of Iridium ($2.5 billion) and Inmarsat ($500 million to $1 billion) is enough to give one pause.

As far as earnings are concerned, the services to be offered will be, by agreement of Iridium, Inmarsat *et al.*, limited largely to undeveloped countries (communications internally and externally to and from developed countries). Thus a large portion of the earnings of an expensive system to create – and expensive to operate – must come from undeveloped countries.

Evidently, Motorola/Iridium and Inmarsat/Project 21 feel that they would profit from it. The best answer at this time seems to be 'tempus omnia revelat' – time reveals all things.

ABOUT THE AUTHOR

Lawrence Lockwood, president of TeleResources, an R&D consulting firm, is the East Coast correspondent of *Communications Technology*, the official trade journal of the US Society of Cable Television Engineers. He writes a column from Washington DC.

POSTSCRIPT

Motorola recently announced a proposal to modify the Iridium system so that instead of 77 satellites with a 37-channel capability each, the new system would have 66 satellites with 48 channels each. This would result in 11 satellites in each of six orbital planes with more powerful transmitters that, along with modified beam patterns, are expected to improve reception and reduce potential interference problems. Motorola has not yet said whether the system will be renamed from Iridium – the element with the atomic number of 66 is dysprosium – want to guess?

NO SILVER BULLET
ESSENCE AND ACCIDENTS OF SOFTWARE ENGINEERING

Frederick P. Brooks, JR.
University of North Carolina at Chapel Hill

Of all the monsters that fill the nightmares of our folklore, none terrify more than werewolves, because they transform unexpectedly from the familiar into horrors. For these, one seeks bullets of silver that can magically lay them to rest.

The familiar software project, at least as seen by the nontechnical manager, has something of this character; it is usually innocent and straightforward, but is capable of becoming a monster of missed schedules, blown budgets, and flawed products. So we hear desperate cries for a silver bullet – something to make software costs drop as rapidly as computer hardware costs do.

But, as we look to the horizon of a decade hence, we see no silver bullet. There is no single development, in either technology or in management technique, that by itself promises even one order-of-magnitude improvement in productivity, in reliability, in simplicity. In this article, I shall try to show why, by examining both the nature of the software problem and the properties of the bullets proposed.

Skepticism is not pessimism, however. Although we see no startling break-throughs – and indeed, I believe such to be inconsistent with the nature of software – many encouraging innovations are under way. A disciplined, consistent effort to develop, propagate, and exploit these innovations should indeed yield an order of-magnitude improvement. There is no royal road, but there is a road.

The first step toward the management of disease was replacement of demon theories and humours theories by the germ theory. That very step, the beginning of hope, in itself dashed all hopes of magical solutions. It told workers that progress would be made stepwise, at great effort, and that a persistent, unremitting care would have to be paid to a discipline of cleanliness. So it is with software engineering today.

DOES IT HAVE TO BE HARD? – ESSENTIAL DIFFICULTIES

Not only are there no silver bullets now in view, the very nature of software makes it unlikely that there will be any – no inventions that will do for software productivity, reliability, and simplicity what electronics, transistors, and large-scale integration did for computer hardware. We cannot expect ever to see twofold gains every two years.

First, one must observe that the anomaly is not that software progress is so slow, but that computer hardware progress is so fast. No other technology since civilization began has seen six orders of magnitude in performance-price gain in 30 years. In no other technology can one choose to take the gain in *either* improved performance *or* in reduced costs. These gains flow from the transformation of computer manufacture from an assembly industry into a process industry.

Second, to see what rate of progress one can expect in software technology, let us examine the difficulties of that technology. Following Aristotle, I divide them into *essence,* the difficulties inherent in the nature of software, and *accidents,* those difficulties that today attend its production but are not inherent.

The essence of a software entity is a construct of interlocking concepts: data sets, relationships among data items, algorithms, and invocations of functions. This essence is abstract in that such a conceptual construct is the same under many different representations. It is nonetheless highly precise and richly detailed.

I believe the hard part of building software to be the specification, design, and testing of this conceptual construct, not the labor of representing it and testing the fidelity of the representation. We still make syntax errors, to be sure; but they are fuzz compared with the conceptual errors in most systems.

If this is true, building software will always be hard. There is inherently no silver bullet.

Let us consider the inherent properties of this irreducible essence of modern software systems: complexity, conformity, changeability, and invisibility.

Complexity. Software entities are more complex for their size than perhaps any other human construct because no two parts are alike (at least above the statement level). If they are, we make the two similar parts into a subroutine – open or closed. In this respect, software systems differ profoundly from computers, buildings, or automobiles, where repeated elements abound.

Digital computers are themselves more complex than most things people build: They have very large numbers of states. This makes conceiving, describing, and testing them hard. Software systems have orders-of-magnitude more states than computers do.

Likewise, a scaling-up of a software entity is not merely a repetition of the same elements in larger sizes, it is necessarily an increase in the number of different elements. In most cases, the elements interact with each other in some nonlinear fashion, and the complexity of the whole increases much more than linearly.

The complexity of software is an essential property, not an accidental one. Hence, descriptions of a software entity that abstract away its complexity often abstract away its essence. For three centuries, mathematics and the physical sciences made great strides by constructing simplified models of complex phenomena, deriving properties from the models, and verifying those properties by experiment. This paradigm worked because the complexities ignored in the models were not the essential properties of the phenomena. It does not work when the complexities are the essence.

Many of the classic problems of developing software products derive from this essential complexity and its nonlinear increases with size. From the complexity comes the difficulty of communication among team members, which leads to product flaws, cost overruns, schedule delays. From the complexity comes the difficulty of enumerating, much less understanding, all the possible states of the program, and from that comes the unreliability. From complexity of function comes the difficulty of invoking function, which makes programs hard to use. From complexity of structure comes the difficulty of extending programs to new functions without creating side effects. From complexity of structure come the unvisualized states that constitute security trapdoors.

Not only technical problems, but management problems as well come from the complexity. It makes overview hard, thus impeding conceptual integrity. It makes it hard to find and control all the loose ends. It creates the tremendous learning and understanding burden that makes personnel turnover a disaster.

Conformity. Software people are not alone in facing complexity. Physics deals with terribly complex objects even at the ' fundamental' particle level. The physicist labors on, however, in a firm faith that there are unifying principles to be found, whether in quarks or in unified-field theories. Einstein argued that there must be simplified explanations of nature, because God is not capricious or arbitrary.

No such faith comforts the software engineer. Much of the complexity that he must master is arbitrary complexity, forced without rhyme or reason by the many human institutions and systems to which his interfaces must conform. These differ from interface to interface, and from time to time, not because of necessity but only because they were designed by different people, rather than by God.

In many cases, the software must conform because it is the most recent arrival on the scene. In others, it must conform because it is perceived as the most conformable. But in all cases, much complexity comes from conformation to other interfaces; this complexity cannot be simplified out by any redesign of the software alone.

Changeability. The software entity is constantly subject to pressures for change. Of course, so are buildings, cars, computers. But manufactured things are infrequently changed after manufacture; they are superseded by later models, or essential changes are incorporated into later-serial-number copies of the same basic design. Call-backs of automobiles are really quite infrequent; field changes of computers somewhat less so. Both are much less frequent than modifications to fielded software.

In part, this is so because the software of a system embodies its function, and the function is the part that most feels the pressures of change. In part it is because software can be changed more easily – it is pure thought-stuff, infinitely malleable. Buildings do in fact get changed, but the high costs of change, understood by all, serve to dampen the whims of the changers.

All successful software gets changed. Two processes are at work. First, as a software product is found to be useful, people try it in new cases at the edge of or beyond the original domain. The pressures for extended function come chiefly from users who like the basic function and invent new uses for it.

Second, successful software survives beyond the normal life of the machine vehicle for which it is first written. If not new computers, then at least new disks, new displays, new printers come along; and the software must be conformed to its new vehicles of opportunity.

In short, the software product is embedded in a cultural matrix of applications, users, laws, and machine vehicles. These all change continually, and their changes inexorably force change upon the software product.

Invisibility. Software is invisible and unvisualizable. Geometric abstractions are powerful tools. The floor plan of a building helps both architect and client evaluate spaces, traffic flows, views. Contradictions and omissions become obvious.

Scale drawings of mechanical parts and stick-figure models of molecules, although abstractions, serve the same purpose. A geometric reality is captured in a geometric abstraction.

The reality of software is not inherently embedded in space. Hence, it has no ready geometric representation in the way that land has maps, silicon chips have diagrams, computers have connectivity schematics. As soon as we attempt to diagram software structure, we find it to constitute not one, but several, general directed graphs superimposed one upon another. The several graphs may represent the flow of control, the flow of data, patterns of dependency, time sequence, name-space relationships. These graphs are usually not even planar, much less hierarchical. Indeed, one of the ways of establishing conceptual control over such structure is to enforce link cutting until one or more of the graphs becomes hierarchical (Parnas, 1979).

In spite of progress in restricting and simplifying the structures of software, they remain inherently unvisualizable, and thus do not permit the mind to use some of its most powerful conceptual tools. This lack not only impedes the process of design within one mind, it severely hinders communication among minds.

PAST BREAKTHROUGHS SOLVED ACCIDENTAL DIFFICULTIES

If we examine the three steps in software technology development that have been most fruitful in the past, we discover that each attacked a different major difficulty in building software, but that those difficulties have been accidental, not essential, difficulties. We can also see the natural limits to the extrapolation of each such attack.

High-level languages. Surely the most powerful stroke for software productivity, reliability, and simplicity has been the progressive use of high-level languages for programming. Most observers credit that development with at least a factor of five in productivity, and with concomitant gains in reliability, simplicity, and comprehensibility.

What does a high-level language accomplish? It frees a program from much of its accidental complexity. An abstract program consists of conceptual constructs: operations, data types, sequences, and communication. The concrete machine program is concerned with bits, registers, conditions, branches, channels, disks, and such. To the extent that the high-level language embodies the constructs one wants in the abstract program and avoids all lower ones, it eliminates a whole level of complexity that was never inherent in the program at all.

The most a high-level language can do is to furnish all the constructs that the programmer imagines in the abstract program. To be sure, the level of our thinking about data structures, data types, and operations is steadily rising, but at an ever decreasing rate. And language development approaches closer and closer to the sophistication of users.

Moreover, at some point the elaboration of a high-level language creates a tool-mastery burden that increases, not reduces, the intellectual task of the user who rarely uses the esoteric constructs.

Time-sharing. Time-sharing brought a major improvement in the productivity of programmers and in the quality of their product, although not so large as that brought by high-level languages.

Time-sharing attacks a quite different difficulty. Time-sharing preserves immediacy, and hence enables one to maintain an overview of complexity. The slow turnaround of batch programming means that one inevitably forgets the minutiae, if not the very thrust, of what one was thinking when he stopped programming and called for compilation and execution. This interruption is costly in time, for one must refresh one's memory. The most serious effect may well be the decay of the grasp of all that is going on in a complex system.

Slow turnaround, like machine-language complexities, is an accidental rather than an essential difficulty of the software process. The limits of the potential contribution of time-sharing derive directly. The principal effect of time-sharing is to shorten system response time. As this response time goes to zero, at some point it passes the human threshold of noticeability, about 100 milliseconds. Beyond that threshold, no benefits are to be expected.

Unified programming environments. Unix and Interlisp, the first integrated programming environments to come into widespread use, seem to have improved productivity by integral factors. Why?

They attack the accidental difficulties that result from using individual programs *together,* by providing integrated libraries, unified file formats, and pipes and filters. As a result, conceptual structures that in principle could always call, feed, and use one another can indeed easily do so in practice.

This breakthrough in turn stimulated the development of whole toolbenches, since each new tool could be applied to any programs that used the standard formats.

Because of these successes, environments are the subject of much of today's software-engineering research. We look at their promise and limitations in the next section.

HOPES FOR THE SILVER

Now let us consider the technical developments that are most often advanced as potential silver bullets. What problems do they address – the problems of essence, or the remaining accidental difficulties? Do they offer revolutionary advances, or incremental ones?

Ada and other highlevel language advances. One of the most touted recent developments is Ada, a general-purpose high-level language of the 1980's. Ada not only reflects evolutionary improvements in language concepts, but indeed embodies features to encourage modern design and modularization. Perhaps the Ada philosophy is more of an advance than the Ada language, for it is the philosophy of modularization, of abstract data types, of hierarchical structuring. Ada is over-rich, a natural result of the process by which requirements were laid on its design. That is not fatal, for sub-setted working vocabularies can solve the learning problem, and hardware advances will give us the cheap MIPS to pay for the compiling costs. Advancing the structuring of software systems is indeed a very good use for the increased MIPS our dollars will buy. Operating systems, loudly decried in the 1960's for their memory and cycle costs, have proved to be an excellent form in which to use some of the MIPS and cheap memory bytes of the past hardware surge.

Nevertheless, Ada will not prove to be the silver bullet that slays the software productivity monster. It is, after all, just another high-level language, and the biggest payoff from such languages came from the first transition – the transition up from the accidental complexities of the machine into the more abstract statement of step-by-step solutions. Once those accidents have been removed, the remaining ones will be smaller, and the payoff from their removal will surely be less.

I predict that a decade from now, when the effectiveness of Ada is assessed, it will be seen to have made a substantial difference, but not because of any particular language feature, nor indeed because of all of them combined. Neither will the new Ada environments prove to be the cause of the improvements. Ada's greatest contribution will be that switching to it occasioned training programmers in modern software-design techniques.

Object-oriented programming. Many students of the art hold out more hope for object-oriented programming than for any of the other technical fads of the day.(Booch, 1983) I am among them. Mark Sherman of Dartmouth notes on CSnet News that one must be careful to distinguish two separate ideas that go under that name: *abstract data types* and *hierarchical types*. The concept of the abstract data type is that an object's type should be defined by a name, a set of proper values, and a set of proper operations rather than by its storage structure, which should be hidden. Examples are Ada packages (with private types) and Modula's modules.

Hierarchical types, such as Simula-67's classes, allow one to define general interfaces that can be further refined by providing subordinate types. The two concepts are orthogonal – one may have hierarchies without hiding and hiding without hierarchies. Both concepts represent real advances in the art of building software.

Each removes yet another accidental difficulty from the process, allowing the designer to express the essence of the design without having to express large amounts of syntactic material that add noinformation content. For both abstract types and hierarchical types, the result is to remove a higher-order kind of accidental difficulty and allow a higher-order expression of design.

Nevertheless, such advances can do no more than to remove all the accidental difficulties from the expression of the design. The complexity of the design itself is essential, and such attacks make no change whatever in that. An order-of-magnitude gain can be made by object-oriented programming only if the unnecessary type-specification underbrush still in our programming language is itself nine-tenths of the work involved in designing a program product. I doubt it.

Artificial intelligence. Many people expect advances in artificial intelligence to provide the revolutionary breakthrough that will give order-of-magnitude gains in software productivity and quality.(IEEE, 1985) I do not. To see why, we must dissect what is meant by ' artificial intelligence.'

D.L. Parnas has clarified the terminological chaos (Parnas, 1985):

> Two quite different definitions of AI are in common use today. AI-1: The useof computers to solve problems that previously could only be solved by applying human intelligence. AI-2: The use of a specific set of programming techniques known as heuristic or rule-based programming. In this approach human experts are studied to determine what heuristics or rules of thumb they use in solving problems.... The program is designed to solve a problem the way that humans seem to solve it.

> The first definition has a sliding meaning.... Something can fit the definition of AI-1 today but, once we see how the program works and understand the problem, we will not think of it as AI any more.... Unfortunately I cannot identify a body of technology that is unique to this field.... Most of the work is problem-specific, and some abstraction or creativity is required to see how to transfer it.

I agree completely with this critique. The techniques used for speech recognition seem to have little in common with those used for image recognition, and both are different from those used in expert systems. I have a hard time seeing how image recognition, for example, will make any appreciable difference in programming practice. The same problem is true of speech recognition. The hard thing about building software is deciding what one wants to say, not saying it. No facilitation of expression can give more than marginal gains.

Expert-systems technology, AI-2, deserves a section of its own.

Expert systems. The most advanced part of the artificial intelligence art, and the most widely applied, is the technology for building expert systems. Many software scientists are hard at work applying this technology to the software-building environment (IEEE, 1985; Balzer, 1985). What is the concept, and what are the prospects?

An *expert system is* a program that contains a generalized inference engine and a rule base, takes input data and assumptions, explores the inferences derivable from the rule base, yields conclusions and advice, and offers to explain its results by retracing its reasoning for the user. The inference engines typically can deal with fuzzy or probabilistic data and rules, in addition to purely deterministic logic.

Such systems offer some clear advantages over programmed algorithms designed for arriving at the same solutions to the same problems:

- Inference-engine technology is developed in an application-independent way, and then applied to many uses. One can justify much effort on the inference engines. Indeed, that technology is well advanced.

- The changeable parts of the application-peculiar materials are en- coded in the rule base in a uniform fashion, and tools are provided for developing, changing, testing, and documenting the rule base. This regularizes much of the complexity of the application itself.

The power of such systems does not come from ever-fancier inference mechanisms, but rather from ever-richer knowledge bases that reflect the real world more accurately. I believe that the most important advance offered by the technology is the separation of the application complexity from the program itself.

How can this technology be applied to the software-engineering task? In many ways: Such systems can suggest interface rules, advise on testing strategies, remember bug-type frequencies, and offer optimization hints.

Consider an imaginary testing advisor, for example. In its most rudimentary form, the diagnostic expert system is very like a pilot's checklist, just enumerating suggestions as to possible causes of difficulty. As more and more system structure is embodied in the rule base, and as the rule base takes more sophisticated account of the trouble symptoms reported, the testing advisor becomes more and more particular in the hypotheses it generates and the tests it recommends. Such an expert system may depart most radically from the conventional ones in that its rule base should probably be hierarchically modularized in the same way the corresponding software product is, so that as the product is modularly modified, the diagnostic rule base can be modularly modified as well.

The work required to generate the diagnostic rules is work that would have to be done anyway in generating the set of test cases for the modules and for the system. If it is done in a suitably general manner, with both a uniform structure for rules and a good inference engine available, it may actually reduce the total labor of generating bring-up test cases, and help as well with lifelong maintenance and modification testing. In the same way, one can postulate other advisors, probably many and probably simple, for the other parts of the software-construction task.

Many difficulties stand in the way of the early realization of useful expert-system advisors to the program developer. A crucial part of our imaginary scenario is the development of easy ways to get from program-structure specification to the automatic or semiautomatic generation of diagnostic rules. Even more difficult and important is the twofold task of knowledge acquisition: finding articulate, self-analytical experts who know *why* they do things, and developing efficient techniques for extracting what they know and distilling it into rule bases. The essential prerequisite for building an expert system is to have an expert.

The most powerful contribution by expert systems will surely be to put at the service of the inexperienced programmer the experience and accumulated wisdom of the best programmers. This is no small contribution. The gap between the best software engineering practice and the average practice is very wide – perhaps wider than in any other engineering discipline. A tool that disseminates good practice would be important.

'Automatic' programming. For almost 40 years, people have been anticipating and writing about ' automatic programming,' or the generation of a program for solving a problem from a statement of the problem specifications. Some today write as if they expect this technology to provide the next breakthrough (Balzer, 1985).

Parnas (1985) implies that the term is used for glamor, not for semantic content, asserting,

> In short, automatic programming always has been a euphemism for programming with a higher-level language than was presently available to the programmer.

He argues, in essence, that in most cases it is the solution method, not the problem, whose specification has to be given.

One can find exceptions. The technique of building generators is very powerful, and it is routinely used to good advantage in programs for sorting. Some systems for integrating differential equations have also permitted direct specification of the problem, and the systems have assessed the parameters, chosen from a library of methods of solution, and generated the programs.

These applications have very favorable properties:
• The problems are readily characterized by relatively few parameters.

- There are many known methods of solution to provide a library of alternatives.

- Extensive analysis has led to explicit rules for selecting solution techniques, given problem parameters.

It is hard to see how such techniques generalize to the wider world of the ordinary software system, where cases with such neat properties are the exception. It is hard even to imagine how this breakthrough in generalization could occur.

Graphical programming. A favorite subject for PhD dissertations in software engineering is graphical, or visual, programming – the application of computer graphics to software design (Graphton and Ichikawa, 1985; Raeder, 1985). Sometimes the promise held out by such an approach is postulated by analogy with VLSI chip design, in which computer graphics plays so fruitful a role. Sometimes the theorist justifies the approach by considering flowcharts as the ideal program-design medium and by providing powerful facilities for constructing them.

Nothing even convincing, much less exciting, has yet emerged from such efforts. I am persuaded that nothing will.

In the first place, as I have argued elsewhere (Brooks, 1975), the flowchart is a very poor abstraction of software structure. Indeed, it is best viewed as Burks, von Neumann, and Goldstine's attempt to provide a desperately needed high-level control language for their proposed computer. In the pitiful, multipage, connection-boxed form to which the flowchart has today been elaborated, it has proved to be useless as a design tool – programmers draw flowcharts after, not before, writing the programs they describe.

Second, the screens of today are too small, in pixels, to show both the scope and the resolution of any seriously detailed software diagram. The so-called ' desktop metaphor' of today's workstation is instead an ' airplane-seat' metaphor. Anyone who has shuffled a lap full of papers while seated between two portly passengers will recognize the difference – one can see only a very few things at once. The true desktop provides overview of, and random access to, a score of pages. Moreover, when fits of creativity run strong, more than one programmer or writer has been known to abandon the desktop for the more spacious floor. The hardware technology will have to advance quite substantially before the scope of our scopes is sufficient for the software-design task.

More fundamentally, as I have argued above, software is very difficult to visualize. Whether one diagrams control flow, variable-scope nesting, variable cross-references, dataflow, hierarchical data structures, or whatever, one feels only one dimension of the intricately interlocked software elephant. If one superimposes all the diagrams generated by the many relevant views, it is difficult to extract any global overview. The VLSI analogy is fundamentally misleading – a chip design is a layered two-dimensional description whose geometry reflects its realization in 3-space. A software system is not.

Program verification. Much of the effort in modern programming goes into testing and the repair of bugs. Is there perhaps a silver bullet to be found by eliminating the errors at the source, in the system-design phase? Can both productivity and product reliability be radically enhanced by following the profoundly different strategy of proving designs correct before the immense effort is poured into implementing and testing them?

I do not believe we will find productivity magic here. Program verification is a very powerful concept, and it will be very important for such things as secure operating-system kernels. The technology does not promise, however, to save labor. Verifications are so much work that only a few substantial programs have ever been verified.

Program verification does not mean error-proof programs. There is no magic here, either. Mathematical proofs also can be faulty. So whereas verification might reduce the program-testing load, it cannot eliminate it.

More seriously, even perfect program verification can only establish that a program meets its specification. The hardest part of the software task is arriving at a complete and consistent specification, and much of the essence of building a program is in fact the debugging of the specification.

Environments and tools. How much more gain can be expected from the exploding researches into better programming environments? One's instinctive reaction is that the big-payoff problems – hierarchical file systems, uniform file formats to make possible uniform program interfaces, and generalized tools – were the first attacked, and have been solved. Language-specific smart editors are developments not yet widely used in practice, but the most they promise is freedom from syntactic errors and simple semantic errors.

Perhaps the biggest gain yet to be realized from programming environments is the use of integrated database systems to keep track of the myriad details that must be recalled accurately by the individual programmer and kept current for a group of collaborators on a single system.

Surely this work is worthwhile, and surely it will bear some fruit in both productivity and reliability. But by its very nature, the return from now on must be marginal.

Workstations. What gains are to be expected for the software art from the certain and rapid increase in the power and memory capacity of the individual workstation? Well, how many MIPS can one use fruitfully? The composition and editing of programs and documents is fully supported by today's speeds. Compiling could stand a boost, but a factor of 10 in machine speed would surely leave think-time the dominant activity in the programmer's day. Indeed, it appears to be so now.

More powerful workstations we surely welcome. Magical enhancements from them we cannot expect.

PROMISING ATTACKS ON THE CONCEPTUAL ESSENCE

Even though no technological breakthrough promises to give the sort of magical results with which we are so familiar in the hardware area, there is both an abundance of good work going on now, and the promise of steady, if unspectacular progress.

All of the technological attacks on the accidents of the software process are fundamentally limited by the productivity equation:

$$\text{time of task} \ = \ \sum_{i} \left(\text{frequency}\right)_{i} \times \left(\text{time}\right)_{i}$$

If, as I believe, the conceptual components of the task are now taking most of the time, then no amount of activity on the task components that are merely the expression of the concepts can give large productivity gains.

Hence we must consider those attacks that address the essence of the software problem, the formulation of these complex conceptual structures. Fortunately, some of these attacks are very promising.

Buy versus build. The most radical possible solution for constructing software is not to construct it at all.

Every day this becomes easier, as more and more vendors offer more and better software products for a dizzying variety of applications. While we software engineers have labored on production methodology, the personal-computer revolution has created not one, but many, mass markets for software. Every newsstand carries monthly magazines, which sorted by machine type, advertise and review dozens of products at prices from a few dollars to a few hundred dollars. More specialized sources offer very powerful products for the workstation and other Unix markets. Even software tools and environments can be bought off-the-shelf. I have elsewhere proposed a marketplace for individual modules (Defense Science Board).

Any such product is cheaper to buy than to build afresh. Even at a cost of one hundred thousand dollars, a purchased piece of software is costing only about as much as one programmer-year. And delivery is immediate! Immediate at least for products that really exist, products whose developer can refer products to a happy user. Moreover, such products tend to be much better documented and somewhat better maintained than home-grown software.

The development of the mass market is, I believe, the most profound long-run trend in software engineering. The cost of software has always been development cost, not replication cost. Sharing that cost among even a few users radically cuts the per-user cost. Another way of looking at it is that the use of n copies of a software system effectively multiplies the productivity of its developers by n. That is an enhancement of the productivity of the discipline and of the nation.

The key issue, of course, is applicability. Can I use an available off-the-shelf package to perform my task? A surprising thing has happened here. During the 1950's and 1960's, study after study showed that users would not use off-the-shelf packages for payroll, inventory control, accounts receivable, and so on. The requirements were too specialized, the- case-to-case variation too high. During the 1980's, we find such packages in high, demand and widespread use. What has changed?

Not the packages, really. They may be somewhat more generalized and somewhat more customizable than formerly, but not much. Not the applications, either. If anything, the business and scientific needs of today are more diverse and complicated than those of 20 years ago.

The big change has been in the hardware/software cost ratio. In 1960, the buyer of a two-million dollar machine felt that he could afford $250,000 more for a customized payroll program, one that slipped easily and nondisruptively into the computer-hostile social environment. Today, the buyer of a $50,000 office machine cannot conceivably afford a customized payroll program, so he adapts the payroll procedure to the packages available. Computers are now so commonplace, if not yet so beloved, that the adaptations are accepted as a matter of course.

There are dramatic exceptions to my argument that the generalization of software packages has changed little over the years: electronic spreadsheets and simple database systems. These powerful tools, so obvious in retrospect and yet so late in appearing, lend themselves to myriad uses, some quite unorthodox. Articles and even books now abound on how to tackle unexpected tasks with the spreadsheet. Large numbers of applications that would formerly have been written as custom programs in Cobol or Report Program Generator are now routinely done with these tools.

Many users now operate their own computers day in and day out on various applications without ever writing a program. Indeed, many of these users cannot write new programs for their machines, but they are nevertheless adept at solving new problems with them.

I believe the single most powerful software-productivity strategy for many organizations today is to equip the computer-naive intellectual workers who are on the firing line with personal computers and good generalized writing, drawing, file, and spreadsheet programs and then to turn them loose. The same strategy, carried out with generalized mathematical and statistical packages and some simple programming capabilities, will also work for hundreds of laboratory scientists.

Requirements refinement and rapid prototyping. The hardest single part of building a software system is deciding precisely what to build. No other part of the conceptual work is as difficult as establishing the detailed technical requirements, including all the interfaces to people, to machines, and to other software systems. No other part of the work so cripples the resulting system if done wrong. No other part is more difficult to rectify later.

Therefore, the most important function that the software builder performs for the client is the iterative extraction and refinement of the product requirements. For the truth is, the client does not know what he wants. The client usually does not know what questions must be answered, and he has almost never thought of the problem in the detail necessary for specification. Even the simple answer – 'Make the new software system work like our old manual information-processing system' – is in fact too simple. One never wants exactly that. Complex software systems are, moreover, things that act, that move, that work. The dynamics of that action are hard to imagine. So in planning any software-design activity, it is necessary to allow for an extensive iteration between the client and the designer as part of the system definition.

I would go a step further and assert that it is really impossible for a client, even working with a software engineer, to specify completely, precisely, and correctly the exact requirements of a modern software product before trying some versions of the product.

Therefore, one of the most promising of the current technological efforts, and one that attacks the essence, not the accidents, of the software problem, is the development of approaches and tools for rapid prototyping of systems as prototyping is part of the iterative specification of requirements.

A prototype software system is one that simulates the important interfaces and performs the main functions of the intended system, while not necessarily being bound by the same hardware speed, size, or cost constraints. Prototypes typically perform the mainline tasks of the application, but make no attempt to handle the exceptional tasks, respond correctly to invalid inputs, or abort cleanly. The purpose of the prototype is to make real the conceptual structure specified, so that the client can test it for consistency and usability.

Much of present-day software-acquisition procedure rests upon the assumption that one can specify a satisfactory system in advance, get bids for its construction, have it built, and install it. I think this assumption is fundamentally wrong, and that many software-acquisition problems spring from that fallacy. Hence, they cannot be fixed without fundamental revision – revision that provides for iterative development and specification of prototypes and products.

Incremental development – grow, don' t build, software. I still remember the jolt I felt in 1958 when I first heard a friend talk about *building* a program, as opposed to *writing* one. In a flash he broadened my whole view of the software process. The metaphor shift was powerful, and accurate. Today we understand how like other building processes the construction of software is, and we freely use other elements of the metaphor, such as *specifications, assembly of components,* and *scaffolding.*

The building metaphor has outlived its usefulness. It is time to change again. If, as I believe, the conceptual structures we construct today are too complicated to be specified accurately in advance, and too complex to be built faultlessly, then we must take a radically different approach.

Let us turn to nature and study complexity in living things, instead of just the dead works of man. Here we find constructs whose complexities thrill us with awe. The brain alone is intricate beyond mapping, powerful beyond imitation, rich in diversity, self-protecting, and self renewing. The secret is that it is grown, not built.

So it must be with our software systems. Some years ago Harlan Mills proposed that any software system should be grown by incremental development (Mills, 1971). That is, the system should first be made to run, even if it does nothing useful except call the proper set of dummy subprograms. Then, bit by bit, it should be fleshed out, with the subprograms in turn being developed – into actions or calls to empty stubs in the level below.

I have seen most dramatic results since I began urging this technique on the project builders in my Software Engineering Laboratory class. Nothing in the past decade has so radically changed my own practice, or its effectiveness. The approach necessitates top-down design, for it is a top-down growing of the software. It allows easy backtracking. It lends itself to early prototypes. Each added function and new provision for more complex data or circumstances grows organically out of what is already there.

The morale effects are startling. Enthusiasm jumps when there is a running system, even a simple one. Efforts re-double when the first picture from a new graphics software system appears on the screen, even if it is only a rectangle. One always has, at every stage in the process, a working system. I find that teams can *grow* much more complex entities in four months than they can *build*.

The same benefits can be realized on large projects as on my small ones (Boehm, 1985).

Great designers. The central question in how to improve the software art centers, as it always has, on people.

We can get good designs by following good practices instead of poor ones. Good design practices can be taught. Programmers are among the most intelligent part of the population, so they can learn good practice. Hence, a major thrust in the United States is to promulgate good modern practice. New curricula, new literature, new organizations such as the Software Engineering Institute, all have come into being in order to raise the level of our practice from poor to good. This is entirely proper.

Nevertheless, I do not believe we can make the next step upward in the same way. Whereas the difference between poor conceptual designs and good ones may lie in the soundness of design method, the difference between good designs and great ones surely does not. Great designs come from great designers. Software construction is a *creative* process. Sound methodology can empower and liberate the creative mind; it cannot inflame or inspire the drudge.

The differences are not minor – they are rather like the differences between Salieri and Mozart. Study after study shows that the very best designers produce structures that are faster, smaller, simpler, cleaner, and produced with less effort (Sackman, Erikson and Grant, 1968). The differences between the great and the average approach an order of magnitude.

A little retrospection shows that although many fine, useful software systems have been designed by committees and built as part of multipart projects, those software systems that have excited passionate fans are those that are the products of one or a few designing minds, great designers. Consider Unix, APL, Pascal, Modula, the Smalltalk interface, even Fortran; and contrast them with Cobol, PL/I, Algol, MVS/370, and MS-DOS. (See Table 1.)

Table 1   Exciting vs. useful but unexciting software products.

Exciting Products	
Yes	No
Unix	Cobol
APL	PL/1
Pascal	Algol
Modula	MVS/370
Smalltalk	MS-DOS
Fortran	

Hence, although I strongly support the technology-transfer and curriculum-development efforts now under way, I think the most important single effort we can mount is to develop ways to grow great designers.

No software organization can ignore this challenge. Good managers, scarce though they be, are no scarcer than good designers. Great designers and great managers are both very rare. Most organizations spend considerable effort in finding and cultivating the management prospects; I know of none that spends equal effort in finding and developing the great designers upon whom the technical excellence of the products will ultimately depend.

My first proposal is that each software organization must determine and proclaim that great designers are as important to its success as great managers are, and that they can be expected to be similarly nurtured and rewarded. Not only salary, but the perquisites of recognition – office size, furnishings, personal technical equipment, travel funds, staff support – must be fully equivalent.

How to grow great designers? Space does not permit a lengthy discussion, but some steps are obvious:

- Systematically identify top designers as early as possible. The best are often not the most experienced.

- Assign a career mentor to be responsible for the development of the prospect, and carefully keep a career file.

- Devise and maintain a career-development plan for each prospect, including carefully selected apprenticeships with top designers, episodes of advanced formal education, and short courses, all interspersed with solo-design and technicalleadership assignments.

- Provide opportunities for growing designers to interact with and stimulate each other.

ACKNOWLEDGMENTS

I thank Gordon Bell, Bruce Buchanan, Rick Hayes-Roth, Robert Patrick, and, most especially, David Parnas for their insights and stimulating ideas, and Rebekah Bierly for the technical production of this article.

REFERENCES

Balzer, R. (1985) 'A 15-Year Perspective on Automatic Programming,*IEEE Trans. Software Engineering* (special issue on artificial intelligence and software engineering), J. Mostow, guest ed., Vol. 11, No. 11, Nov., pp. 1257-1267.

Boehm, B.W. (1985) 'A spiral model of software development and enhancement', TRW tech. report 21-371-85, TRW, Inc., 1 Space Park, Redondo Beach, CA 90278.

Booch, G. (1983) 'Object-Oriented Design,' *Software Engineering with Ada*, Benjamin/Cummings, Menlo Park, Calif.

Brooks, F.P. (1975) *The Mythical Man-Month*, Addison-Wesley, Reading, Mass., New York, Chapter 14.

Defense Science Board, *Report of the Task Force on Military Software*, in press.

Graphton, R.B. and Ichikawa, T. (1985) *Computer* (special issue on visual programming), R.B. Graphton and T. Ichikawa, guest eds., Vol. 18, No. 8, Aug.

Mills, H.D. (1971) 'Top-Down Programming in Large Systems,' in *Debugging Techniques in Large Systems*, R. Ruskin, ed., Prentice-Hall, Englewood Cliffs, N.J.

Mostow, J. (1985) *IEEE Trans. Software Engineering* (special issue on artificial intelligence and software engineering), J. Mostow, guest ed., Vol. 11, No. 11, Nov.

Parnas, D.L. (1979) 'Designing software for ease of extension and contraction,' *IEEE Trans. Software Engineering, Vol.* 5, No. 2, Mar., pp. 128-138.

Parnas, D.L. (1985) 'Software aspects of strategic defense systems,' *American Scientist,* Nov.

Raeder, G. (1985) 'A survey of current graphical programming techniques,' *Computer* (special issue on visual programming), R.B. Graphton and T. Ichikawa, guest eds., Vol. 18, No. 8, Aug., pp. 11-25.

Sackman, H., Erikson, W.J. and Grant, E.E. (1968) 'Exploratory experimental studies comparing online and offline programming performance,' *CACM*, Vol. 11, No, 1, Jan., pp. 3-11.

To slay the werewolf

Why a silver bullet? Magic, of course. Silver is identified with the moon and thus has magic properties. A silver bullet offers the fastest, most powerful, and safest way to slay the fast, powerful, and incredibly dangerous werewolf. And what could be more natural than using the moon-metal to destroy a creature transformed under the light of the full moon?

The legend of the werewolf is probably one of the oldest monster legends around. Herodotus in the fifth century BC gave us the first written report of werewolves when he mentioned a tribe north of the Black Sea, called the Neuri, who supposedly turned into wolves a few days each year. Herodotus wrote that he didn' t believe it.

Sceptics aside, many people have believed in people turning into wolves or other animals. In medieval Europe, some people were killed because they were thought to be werewolves. In those times, it didn' t take being bitten by a werewolf to become one. A bargain with the devil, using a special potion, wearing a special belt, or being cursed by a witch could all turn a person into a werewolf. However, medieval werewolves could be hurt and killed by normal weapons. The problem was to overcome their strength and cunning.

Enter the fictional, not legendary, werewolf. The first major werewolf movie, *The Werewolf of London,* in 1935 created the two-legged man-wolf who changed into a monster when the moon was full. He became a werewolf after being bitten by one, and could be killed only with a silver bullet. Sound familiar?

Actually, we owe many of today's ideas about werewolves to Lon Chaney Jr.'s unforgettable 1941 portrayal in *The Wolf Man.* Subsequent films seldom strayed far from the mythology of the werewolf shown in that movie. But that movie strayed far from the original mythology of the werewolf.

Would you believe that before fiction took over the legend, werewolves weren' t troubled by silver bullets? Vampires were the ones who couldn' t stand them. Of course, if you rely on the legends, your only salvation if unarmed and attacked by a werewolf is to climb an ash tree or run into a field of rye. Not so easy to find in an urban setting, and hardly recognizable to the average movie audience.

What should you watch out for? People whose eyebrows grow together, whose index finger is longer than the middle finger, and who have hair growing on their palms. Red or black teeth are a definite signal of possible trouble.

Take warning, though. The same symptoms mark people suffering from hypertrichosis (people born with hair covering their bodies) or porphyria. In porphyria, a person's body produces toxins called porphyrins. Consequently, light becomes painful, the skin grows hair, and the teeth may turn red. Worse for the victim's reputation, his or her Increasingly bizarre behavior makes people even more suspicious of the other symptoms. It seems very likely that the sufferers of this disease unwittingly contributed to the current legend, although in earlier times they were evidently not accused of murderous tendencies.

It is worth noting that the film tradition often makes the werewolf a rather sympathetic character, an innocent transformed against his (or rarely, her) will into a monster. As the gypsy said in *The Wolf Man*,

> Even a man who is pure at heart,
> And says his prayers at night,
> Can become a wolf when the wolfbane blooms,
> And the moon is full and bright.

Nancy Hays

THERE IS A SILVER BULLET

Brad J. Cox

Of all the monsters that fill the nightmares of our folklore, none terrify more than werewolves, because they transform unexpectedly from the familiar into horrors. For these, one seeks bullets of silver that can magically lay them to rest. The familiar software project, at least as seen by the nontechnical manager, has something of this character; it is usually innocent and straightforward, but is capable of becoming a monster of missed schedules, blown budgets, and flawed products. So we hear desperate cries for a silver bullet – something to make software costs drop as rapidly as computer hardware costs do. Brooks (1987)

Two centuries after its birth in the industrial revolution, the age of manufacturing has matured and is showing signs of decline. And a new age, the information age, is emerging, born of the phenomenal achievements that the age of manufacturing brought to transportation, communication, and computing.

By eliminating time and space as barriers, however, the very achievements that put us within reach of a truly global economy are burying us in irrelevant and useless data, in mountains of low-quality ore that must be laboriously refined for relevant information – the signal hidden in the noise. The critical resource for turning this raw data into useful information is computer software, as strategic a resource in the information age as petroleum is today.

More than 20 years ago, the NATO Software Engineering Conference of 1968 coined the term *software crisis* to indicate that software was already scarce, expensive, of insufficient quality, hard to schedule, and nearly impossible to manage.

For example, in *The Mythical Man-month,* one of the seminal works of these two decades, Fred Brooks observed that adding more people to a late software project only makes matters worse. And in 'No Silver Bullet: Essence and Accidents of Software Engineering,' he argues that the difficulties are inevitable, arising from software's inescapable essence – not from accident, but from some deficiency in how programmers build software today.

But if you view these same facts from a new perspective,a more optimistic conclusion emerges. The software crisis is not an immovable obstacle but an irresistible force – a vast economic incentive that will grow toward infinity as the global economy moves into the information age.

To turn Brooks' own metaphor in a new direction, there *is* a silver bullet. It is a tremendously powerful weapon, propelled by vast economic forces that mere technical obstacles can resist only briefly. But as Brooks would agree, it is not a technology, a whiz-bang invention that will slay the software werewolf without effort on our part or vast side effects on our value systems and the balance of power between software producers and consumers.

The silver bullet is a *cultural* change rather than a technological change. It is a paradigm shift – a software industrial revolution based on reusable and interchangeable parts that will alter the software universe as surely as the industrial revolution changed manufacturing.

OBJECT-ORIENTED TECHNOLOGIES

The term *object-oriented* keeps turning up. There are object-oriented environments, object-oriented applications, object-oriented databases, architectures, and user interfaces, and object-oriented specification, analysis, and design methods. And, of course, there are object-oriented programming languages, from conservative Ada to radical Smalltalk, with C++ and Objective-C somewhere in between. You may well wonder what, if anything, all these different technologies have in common. What does the adjective *object-oriented* really mean?

Who can say with certainty what *any* adjective means? No one is confused when an adjective such as *small* means entirely different things for cars, molecules, and galaxies. But in the software domain, words often cloud as much as they illuminate.

Object-oriented fails to distinguish between the low-level modularity/binding technologies of Ada and C++ and the higher-level ones of Smalltalk, and between these three languages and a hybrid environment like Objective-C. Moreover, purists summarily exclude ultra-high-level modularity/binding technologies like Fabrik or Metaphor (Ingals *et al.*, 1988) from the object-oriented domain because they are iconic rather than textual and because they do not support inheritance, forgetting that the same is true of things like tables and chairs that are indisputably 'objects.'

The confusion is understandable. The inhabitants of the software domain, from the simplest BASIC statement to a million-line application program, are as intangible as a ghost. And because programmers invent and build them all from first principles, everything in the software domain is unique and therefore unfamiliar, composed of modules and routines that have never been seen before and will never be seen again.

These component parts of the domain of software obey laws – promulgated by the programmers – that are specific to a unique instance. There are no general guidelines to bring order to the software domain. As Brooks put it, software is a world of werewolves and silver bullets. When all a programmer knows for certain is what he or she put there in the last few days, mystical belief will always win out over scientific reason. Thus, terms like *computer science* and *software engineering* remain oxymorons, tripping up those who don't recognize their inherent contradictions.

To get a grip on *object-oriented* means coming to the realization that it is an end, not a means – an objective rather than the technologies for achieving it. It means changing how we view software, shifting our emphasis to the objects we build rather than the processes we use to build them. It means using all available tools, from COBOL to Smalltalk and beyond, to make software as tangible – and as amenable to common-sense manipulation – as are the everyday objects in a department store. *Object-oriented* means abandoning the process-centric view of the software universe where the programmer-machine interaction is paramount in favor of a product-centered paradigm driven by the producer-consumer relationship.

But since reverting to this broader meaning might confuse the terminology even further, I use a separate term, *software industrial revolution,* to mean what *object-oriented* has always meant to me: transforming programming from a solitary cut-to-fit craft, like the cottage industries of colonial America, into an organizational enterprise like manufacturing is today. It means *enabling* software consumers, making it possible to solve your own specialized software problems the same way that homeowners solve plumbing problems: by assembling solutions from a robust market in off-the shelf, reusable subcomponents, which are in turn supplied by multiple lower level echelons of producers.

The problem with the old paradigm is illustrated with a simple question. When building a house, would you consider buying a plumbing system built entirely from unique, customized parts?

Yet this is just what the software community, with its infatuation with process and the pursuit of perfection from firm principles, expects programmers to do whenever they build software. This would be considered ludicrous in a mature domain such as plumbing, yet it is business as usual in software.

To illustrate further, contrast the enormous interest that is generated by advances in process-oriented technologies – for example, structured programming, object-oriented programming CASE, and Cleanroom – with the woeful lack of interest in the development of a robust market of fine-grained reusable software components.

The key element of the software industrial revolution is the creation of such a standard-parts marketplace, a place where those who specialize in the problem to be solved can purchase low-level pluggable software components to assemble into higher-level solutions. The assemblers, of course, have as little interest in the processes used to build the reusable components as plumbers have in how to manufacture thermostats.

Clearly, software products are not the same as tangible products like plumbing supplies, and the differences are not minor. However, I shall avoid dwelling on the differences and emphasize a compelling similarity. Except for small programs that a solitary programmer builds for personal use, both programming and plumbing are organizational activities. That is, both are engaged in by ordinary people with the common sense to organize as producers and consumers of each other's products rather than reinvent everything from first principles. The goal of the software industrial revolution in general, and object-oriented technologies in particular, is to bring common sense to bear on software.

THE COPERNICAN REVOLUTION

> Let us assume that crises are a necessary precondition for the
> emergence of novel theories, and next ask how scientists respond to
> their existence. Part of the answer, as obvious as it is important, can
> be discovered by noting first what scientists never do when
> confronted by even severe and prolonged anomalies. Though they
> may begin to lose faith and then to consider alternatives, they do not
> renounce the paradigm that has led them into crisis. They do not, that
> is, treat anomalies as counter-instances, though in the vocabulary of
> philosophy of science, that is what they are. The decision to reject
> one paradigm is always simultaneously the decision to accept
> another, and the judgement leading to that decision involves the
> comparison of both paradigms with nature and with each other.
> Kuhn (1962)

Aristotle's universe had the earth and mankind at the center, with the sun,
moon, planets, and stars circling around on ethereal spheres. The second-
century astronomer Ptolemy amended this model by adding *epicycles* to
account for observed discrepancies in planetary motion. By the sixteenth
century, 90 such epicycles were needed, and the resulting complexity
created an astronomy crisis.

The Aristotelian cosmological model as extended by Ptolemy was once
as entrenched and 'obvious' as today's process-centered model of software
development. Given any particular discrepancy, astronomers were
invariably able to eliminate it by making some adjustment in Ptolemy's
system of epicycles, just as programmers can usually overcome specific
difficulties within today's software-development paradigm.

But like today's software engineers, the astronomers could never quite
make Ptolemy's system conform to the best observations of planetary
position and precession of the equinoxes. As increasingly precise
observations poured in, it became apparent that astronomy's complexity
was increasing more rapidly than its accuracy and that a discrepancy
corrected in one place was likely to show up in another. The problem
could not be confined to the astronomers and ignored by everyone else,
because the Julian calendar, based on the Ptolemaic model, was several
days wrong – a discrepancy that any believer could see from the behavior of
the moon.

This was as serious a problem for that era as the software crisis is today,
since missing a saint's day lessened a worshipper's chances of salvation. By
the sixteenth century, the sense of crisis had developed to the point that you
can well imagine an early astronomer, frustrated beyond limit with keeping
Ptolemaic models up to date, venting his despair in an article titled 'No Silver
Bullet: Essence and Accidents of Astrophysics.'

In 1514, the Pope asked Copernicus to look into calendar reform, and
over the next half century, Copernicus, Galileo, Kepler, and others obliged
by eliminating the astronomy crisis, once and for all. But their silver bullet

was not what the church had in mind. It was not a new process, some whiz-bang computer or programming language for computing epicycles more efficiently. It was a cultural change, a paradigm shift, a 'mere' shift in viewpoint as to whether the heavens rotate around the earth or the sun.

The consequences to all the beliefs, value systems, vested interests, and power balances of that era were anything but minor. The astronomer's silver bullet removed mankind from its accustomed place at the center of the universe and placed us instead at the periphery, mere inhabitants of one of many planets circling around the sun.

The software industrial revolution involves a similar paradigm shift, with a similar assault on entrenched value systems, power structures, and sacred beliefs about the role of programmers in relation to consumers. It is also motivated by practical needs that an older paradigm has been unable to meet, resulting in a desperate feeling of crisis.

Just as the church's need for calendar reform escalated the astronomy crisis to where change became inevitable, the need for reliable software in the information age is escalating the software crisis to where a similar paradigm shift is no longer a question of whether, but of when and by whom.

THE INDUSTRIAL REVOLUTION

It does not diminish the work of Whitney, Lee, and Hall to note the relentless support that came from the government, notably from Colonel Wadsworth and Colonel Bomford in the Ordnance Department and from John C. Calhoun in Congress. The development of the American system of interchangeable parts manufacture must be understood above all as the result of a decision by the United States War Department to have this kind of small arms whatever the cost. Hawke (1988)

The cottage-industry approach to gunsmithing was in harmony with the realities of colonial America. It made sense to all parties, producers and consumers alike, to expend cheap labor as long as steel was imported at great cost from Europe. But as industrialization drove materials costs down and demand exceeded what the gunsmiths could produce, they began to experience pressure for change.

The same inexorable pressure is happening in software as the cost of computer hardware plummets and the demand for software exceeds our ability to supply it. As irresistible force meets immovable object, you experience the pressure as the software crisis: the awareness that software is too costly and of insufficient quality, and its development is nearly impossible to manage.

The software industrial revolution will occur, sometime, somewhere, whether programmers want it to or not, because it will be the software consumers who determine the outcome. It is only a question of when and by whom – whether the present software development community will be able to change its value system quickly enough to service the relentless pressure for change.

Contrary to what a casual understanding of the industrial revolution may suggest, it didn't happen overnight, and it didn't happen easily. In particular, the revolutionaries were not the cottage-industry gunsmiths; they actually seem to have played no role whatsoever, for or against. They stayed busy in their workshops and left it to their consumers to find another way.

Judging from a letter written by Thomas Jefferson in 1785, it was actually he who found the solution in the workshop of a French inventor, Honoré Blanc. Key technical contributions were made by entrepreneurs (e.g., Eli Whitney, John Hall, and Roswell Lee) attracted from outside the traditional gunsmith community by incentives that the gunsmiths' consumers laid down to foster a new approach.

Those with the most to gain, and nothing to lose – the consumers – took control of their destiny by decisively wielding the behavioral modification tool of antiquity: money. They created an economic incentive for those vendors who would serve their interest (i.e., the ability to reuse, interchange, and repair parts) instead of the cottage-industry gunsmiths' interest in fine cut-to-fit craftsmanship.

Although it took consumers nearly 50 years to make their dream a reality, they moved the center of the manufacturing universe from the process to the product, with the consumers at the center and the producers circling around the periphery. Of course, the gunsmiths were 'right' that interchangeable parts were far more expensive than cut-to-fit parts. But high-precision interchangeable parts ultimately proved to be the silver bullet for the manufacturing crisis: the paradigm shift that launched the age of manufacturing.

REUSABLE SOFTWARE COMPONENTS

A crucial test of a good paradigm is its ability to reveal simplifying structure to what previously seemed chaotic. Certainly, the software universe is chaotic today, with object-oriented technologies fighting traditional technologies, Ada, fighting Smalltalk, C++ fighting Objective-C, and rapid prototyping fighting traditional methods, such as Milspec 2167 and Cleanroom.

Only one process must win and be adopted across an entire community, and each new contender must slug it out with older ones for the coveted title, 'standard.' Different levels of the producer-consumer hierarchy cannot seek specialized tools and reusable components for their specialized tasks, skills, and interests, but must fit themselves to the latest do-it-all panacea.

By focusing on the product rather than the process, a simpler pattern emerges, reminiscent of the distinct integration levels of hardware engineering (see Figure 1). On the card level, you can plug off-the-shelf cards to build custom hardware solutions without having to understand soldering irons and silicon chips. On the chip level, vendors can build cards from off-the-shelf chips without needing to understand the minute gate- and block-level details that *their* vendors must know to build silicon chips. Each modularity/binding technology encapsulates a level of complexity so that its consumer needn't know or care how components from a lower level were implemented, but only how to use them to solve the problem at hand.

Building software applications (rack-level modules) solely with tightly coupled technologies like subroutine libraries (block-level modules) is logically equivalent to wafer-scale integration which is something that hardware engineering can barely accomplish to this day. Yet this is just what every software developer must do.

So, seven years ago, I cofounded The Stepstone Corp. to play a role analogous to that of silicon chip vendors by providing chip-level software components, or Software-ICs, to the system-building community. The goal was to create an enabling technology for a multilevel marketplace in reusable software components. (It is called the Objective-C System-building Environment.)

Stepstone's experience amounts to a large-scale study of the reusable-software-components-marketplace strategy in action. With substantial Software-IC libraries now in the field and others on the way, the chip-level software-components-marketplace concept has been tried commercially and proven sound for an amazingly diverse range of customer applications.

However, this study has also revealed how difficult it still is, even with state-of-the-art object-oriented technologies, to design and build components that are both useful and genuinely reusable, to document their interfaces so that consumers can understand them, to port them to an unceasing torrent of new hardware platforms, to ensure that recent enhancements or ports haven't violated some pre-existing interface, and to market them to a culture whose value system, like that of the colonial gunsmith, encourages building everything from first principles to avoid relying on somebody else's work.

A particularly discouraging example of this value system is that, in spite of the time and money invested in libraries and environmental tools like browsers, Objective-C continues to be thought of as a language to be compared with Ada and C++, rather than as the tiniest part of a much larger environment of ready-to-use software components and tools.

Another lesson of the last few years is that chip-level objects are only a beginning, not an end. The transition from how the machine forces programmers to think to how everyone expects tangible objects to behave is not a single step, but many, as shown in Figure 1. Just as there is no universal meaning for adjectives like *small or fast,* there is no single, narrow meaning for *object-oriented.*

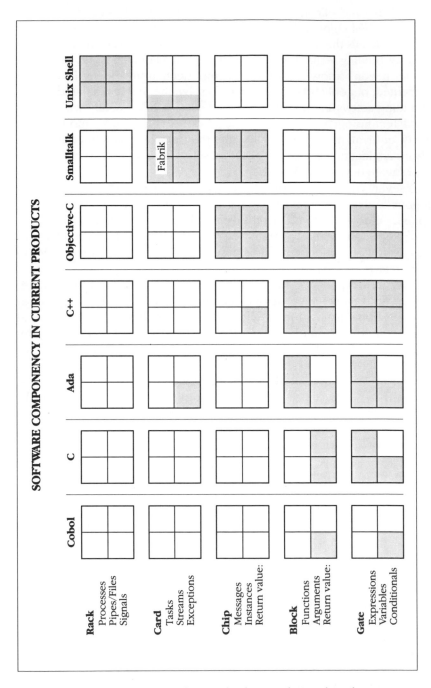

Figure 1 A product-centered view discloses relationships between languages that were not obvious from the traditional process-centered view. It implies a multilayered architecture of reusable, interchangeable software components analogous to the multilayered architecture of hardware engineering. It also implies that the critical path to escaping the software

crisis does not involve discovering new modularity/binding technologies, but integrating those that are already known.

At the gate and block levels of Figure 1, *object-oriented means* encapsulation of data and little more. The dynamism of everyday objects has been relinquished in favor of machine-oriented virtues, such as computational efficiency and static type checking. At the intermediate (chip) level, objects also embrace the open-universe model of everyday experience where all possible interactions between the parts and the whole are not declared in advance, as opposed to the closed universe of early binding and compile-time type checking.

But on the scale of any large system gate-, block-, and even chip-level objects are extremely small units of granularity: They are grains of sand where bricks are needed. Since even chip-level objects are as procedural as conventional expressions and subroutines, they are just as alien to nonprogrammers. Until invoked by passing them a thread of control, these objects are as inert as conventional data, quite unlike the objects of everyday experience.

WHAT NEXT?

In the stampede to force the world's round, dynamic objects into square, static languages like Ada or C++, you must never forget that such low-level languages – and even higher-level environments like Objective-C and Smalltalk – are highly unlikely to be accepted by mainstream information-age workers. They are more likely to insist on nontextual, nonprocedural visual 'languages' that offer a higher-level kind of 'object,' a card-level object, of the sort that programmers know as coroutines, lightweight processes, or data-flow modules. Since these objects encapsulate a thread of control alongside whatever lower-level objects were used to build them, they admit a tangible user interface that is uniquely intuitive for nonprogrammers.

By definition, these systems are more fundamentally 'object-oriented' than the procedural, single-threaded 'object-oriented' languages of today. Like the tangible objects of everyday experience, card-level objects provide their own thread of control internally. They don't 'communicate by messages'; they don't 'support inheritance'; and their user interface is iconic, not textual.

By introducing these and probably many other architectural levels, where the modularity/binding technologies at each level are oriented to the skills and interests of a distinct constituency of the reusable-software-components market, the programmer shortage can be solved as the telephone-operator shortage was solved, by making every computer user a programmer.

REFERENCES

Brooks, F. (1987) 'No Silver Bullet: Essence and Accidents of Software Engineering.' *IEEE Computer,* April 1987.

Hawke, D. F. (1988) *Nuts and Bolts from the Past: A History of American Technology 1776-1860,* New York, Harper and Row.

Ingals, D., Scott W., Yu-Ying Chow, Ludolph, F. and Doyle, K. (1988) 'Fabrik: a visual programming environment,' *OOPSLA '88 Proceedings.*

Metaphor is an office automation product of Metaphor Computer Systems, Mountain View, CA.

Kuhn, T. (1962) *The Structure of Scientific Revolutions,* The University of Chicago press.

Virtual Reality in the Real World: History, Applications and Projections

Ralph Schroeder
Department of Human Sciences, Brunel University

Since the late 1980s, there has been a rapid take-off in the development of virtual reality (VR) technologies. This article presents an outline of the events leading up to this take-off phase and explores two of the first applications of VR, in education and entertainment games. Against this background, it is possible to examine some ideas about the future of VR and its social implications.

Virtual reality (VR) technology and its antecedents were almost unknown outside those working on computer displays and related technologies until the late 1980s. Since then, VR has become widely known and a number of applications, albeit in the early stages of use, are receiving a lot of attention. Moreover, the computer-generated simulated worlds created with this technology have become associated with the future promise of current advances among information and communication technologies, particularly in the light of the widely predicted convergence among digitized electronic media.

In order to think about the kinds of social changes that may be attendant on the further development of VR technologies, it is necessary, first, to examine the emergence of this technology. This will put the recent 'take-off' of VR in context. Next, it is useful to look at some applications of this technology. Here, the focus is on education and entertainment games as these are currently among the most important and well known uses of VR (apart from scientific visualization and battlefield simulations). Finally, we can survey some ideas about the future implications of VR and the issues that are likely to arise.

THE PRE-HISTORY OF VR

The term 'virtual reality' was coined by Jaron Lanier in the late 1980s, but the origin of VR technologies can be traced back to Ivan Sutherland's work on interactive computing and head-mounted displays in the mid-1960s [1]. Sutherland's research at MIT and Harvard University was partly funded by the Advanced Research Projects Agency of the US Department of Defense. In a paper he contributed to the International Federation of Information Processing Congress in 1965, entitled 'The ultimate display', he outlined the model for a human-computer interface that has continued to inspire the thinking about computer-generated virtual environments ever since [2]. Sutherland's idea was that a computer display could create a simulation of the physical world with which the operator could interact directly by means of the senses. Such a display would offer new possibilities for displaying information. In a subsequent paper presented at the Fall Joint Computer Conference in 1968, 'A head-mounted three dimensional display', he explained how this device could be built using a position sensor and computer graphics to generate a three-dimensional world [3].

By 1 January 1970, Sutherland, then at the University of Utah, and a team of researchers had developed the first operational interactive head-mounted display system [4]. From this point onwards, several strands can be identified which would eventually lead to the take-off of VR technology in the late 1980s. These lie broadly in three areas: art, flight simulation and robotics, and military and space-related research .

In art, the first person to explore the potential of VR-like interactive computing devices was Myron Krueger, although he prefers the label 'artificial reality' [5]. In the early 1970s, Krueger created a gallery installation which allowed users to interact with a two-dimensional computer-generated environment. The difference between Krueger's 'artificial reality' and immersive VR systems is that he is not attempting to create a simulation which gives the user the impression of bodily 'presence' in a virtual world. Instead, Krueger's system projects silhouette images on to a wall-sized screen with which users can interact when they move in front of these 'worlds'. Interactivity is achieved in this case by recording the user's movements with a videocamera so that the user's silhouette image can interact with the projected 'world'. This system also allows a number of users to interact with each other in the projected screen 'world'.

Flight simulators and robotics have also contributed to VR, particularly in the areas of human factors and input devices. Flight and other types of vehicle simulation have been developed since the 1960s, mainly for training purposes [6]. In this way, techniques for simulating the aeroplane's controls, for example, could carry over into the design of joystick computer controls. Or again, research on simulator sickness can be related to the psychological issues arising from virtual environment displays [7]. The same is true of research on robotics or teleoperations, where the use of robot arms, for example, overlaps with VR problems such as the input of the user's commands and conveying the machines' operations back to the user.

While there has also been work in these areas for military uses, the military research that is more directly related to VR is the work on head-mounted displays and training that has been carried out for the US Air Force and for NASA. Two research sites are particularly important here: one is the Wright-Patterson Air Force base near Dayton, Ohio, where flight simulation has been ongoing since the 1960s and head-mounted displays have been produced for pilots. The other is the NASA Ames Research Center in Mountain View, California, where research has focused, again, on head-mounted displays, partly with a view to carrying out remote operations in space.

The extent to which these and other sources influenced the take-off of VR technology in the late 1980s is difficult to assess [8]. A number of those who developed VR systems in the 1980s, including Lanier, were partly aware of existing research, but came from the completely different background of computer games, and especially the firm Atari, which supplied many of the people who were involved in Silicon Valley computer developments in the 1980s. Apart from the research background and the personnel, an important precondition for this take-off was the rapid increase in affordable computing power in the 1980s, which was required especially for generating the computer graphics to create a 'realistic' three-dimensional world. Another was the enhanced sophistication of human-computer interaction techniques, including joystick control and the use of icons. Thus, while the conceptual groundwork had been laid much earlier by Sutherland, it was only during the 1980s that the technical means became available to produce systems that were more than prototypes.

In the late 1980s, Jaron Lanier was the first to start attaching the label 'virtual reality' to interactive computer-generated three-dimensional immersive displays. Together with a number of colleagues, he put together the first fully immersive system of the type that has since come to be widely identified with VR – headmounted display, body suit and glove. The story of how this system was put together, by tinkering with and cobbling together various artefacts in a garage (or in this case, living room), and how this amateur effort rapidly became a successful business enterprise (VPL Inc) which was the first to sell VR systems commercially, has all the makings of the typical – if often somewhat mythologized – story of the emergence of new technologies. Even the denouement of the story, of how Lanier came to be tired of the commercial aspect of VR, withdrew from this part of VPL and was eventually ousted from the company he founded, has a familiar ring [9].

But while this sequence of events can be compared with the pattern of other innovations, what is remarkable in this case (though far from unique) is the 'lull' of more than 20 years between Sutherland's ideas and the take-off phase of VR on the one hand, and the speed with which this technology, once it had received the label 'virtual reality', gained widespread recognition on the other. In the early 1990s, R&D efforts have mushroomed so that there are now dozens of institutions devoted to VR research and to commercial projects in what has become a multi-million dollar industry [10]. One point that emerges even from this cursory account of the sources which came together in the making of VR, however, is that the developmental path of VR has been varied and does not give any straightforward indication of the direction in which this technology may be headed.

VR APPLICATIONS: EDUCATION

If the military uses of VR, and especially battlefield simulations, are considered under the rubric of education and training, then these must be counted among the most important uses of VR to date. Here we are concerned with education in the more narrow sense and briefly look at the first two schools which have used VR in a classroom setting [11].

The first experiment with VR as a learning tool was undertaken at the Human Interface Technology Laboratory (HITL) in Seattle, one of the institutions at the forefront of VR research. The first summer school, for pupils aged between 10 and 15, took place in 1991, and a second was held in 1992. Both consisted of a number of self-contained one-week sessions during which pupils would build their worlds on a desktop computer from Monday to Thursday, and go to the lab itself on Friday to experience their world with an immersive VR system. The aim of the project was to take 'a first step in evaluating the potential of VR as a learning environment' [12].

At the West Denton High School in Newcastle, VR was introduced to classroom teaching in March 1992. Unlike the HITL project, at West Denton VR was integrated into the standard curriculum, especially in computer science and art and design. The pupils were aged between 13 and 19 years and would spend several hours per week building virtual worlds. A further difference is that West Denton used only desktop VR systems, ie personal computers which allow the creation of three-dimensional 'worlds' with interaction by means of a 'mouse' or a 'spaceball'. One of the main projects in this case was the creation of the 'Dangerous Workplace' world, a factory with moving machines and vehicles with which users could interact and intended as a means of learning about safety at the workplace.

There are many interesting phenomena associated with the introduction of this technology into the classroom. For our purposes here, we concentrate on two: the first is that both uses of VR in the classroom encouraged pupils to work independently from teachers. Pupils found it easy to learn how to create virtual worlds and worked together to explore the capabilities of the system and to build worlds. This was partly because these systems were as new to teachers as they were to pupils, but also because of the ease of use of the equipment and the imagination and skills involved in the task of world building. At both schools, teachers commented that pupils were often more adept at learning to use VR and more creative in using it than they were.

The second is that pupils not only enjoyed the use of VR, but an overwhelming majority also said, when asked in a questionnaire, that they would rather build their own worlds than use ready-made ones. Here it is notable that a higher proportion of the HITL pupils preferred to build their own worlds than those at West Denton, which may reflect the use of an immersive system, but may also be related to the fact that, unlike at West Denton, HITL pupils built their own worlds from start to finish [13]. In any case, the worlds they built and those which, when asked, they said they would like to build – ranging from mediaeval space stations to utopian future neighbourhoods – showed that they were able to identify the potential uses of the technology in an imaginative way.

If these two points relate to the ways in which this technology introduced changes into the classroom setting, both in terms of the roles of teachers and pupils and in as much as the technology offers new possibilities for learning with interactive virtual worlds, this application of VR also demonstrates the limitations of introducing new technology into the classroom. One feature observed in both cases was that, as in the case of other uses of computers in the classroom, there seemed to be lot of time idly spent, either because the systems did not work as they should have done, because the tasks required were routine or time-consuming, or because of difficulties in organizing the tasks among a number of users or for individual users.

Second, although the potential of VR as a classroom tool or as a creative activity for pupils was clearly illustrated in both cases, it is not yet clear in what way this potential can be fully exploited. What kind of skills, for example, can best be taught by means of using VR as opposed to other means, and how is VR best used as a learning tool? The two projects have not yet provided answers to these questions, and as long as this is the case, it is possible that VR may become like other uses of information technology in the classroom – either gadgets which detract from rather than enhancing the learning process, or used by pupils for playing games. In this light, it is uncertain whether the positive aspects introduced by VR, the teacher-independent, cooperative and creative process of world building, would in the long run yield to more routine uses of technology or become integrated into the curriculum in such a way that the advantages would be lost or outweighed by disadvantages.

VR APPLICATIONS: ENTERTAINMENT

VR entertainment games are poised to become one of the main uses of this technology [14]. In April 1993, Jonathan Waldern, founder and director of the first company to manufacture immersive VR games, could announce that 3 million people had used his company's games [15]. Other manufacturers are following suit. Here we can concentrate on Waldern's 'Virtuality' games since these are currently the only immersive games available to the public.

One immediately interesting point is that the label 'virtual reality' only became attached to Waldern's W Industries game *after* the term had become popularized by Jaron Lanier. Waldern's first Virtuality game was just getting ready for launch in 1990/91 when Lanier drew media attention to the new technology. Henceforth it became known as a VR game [16]. The same is true, incidentally, of the firm Dimension's desktop VR games, which had been using the name 'Superscape Alternate Realities'. This became labelled a VR game in the early 1990s [17].

The Virtuality games consist of a head-mounted display system and joystick control (or in some cases a steering wheel) used in a stand-up or sitting-down coin-operated arcade game. Inside their helmets, players see and hear a three-dimensional world and they navigate and shoot things by means of the joystick control. The basic devices used are therefore similar to the immersive VR system used at the HITL summer school (apart from the use of a glove at HITL), although the technical specifications of the two systems are quite different. The content of the Virtuality games, however, is similar to other computer- and videogames. The games involve racing cars, spaceship battles, flight simulation, battles with armoured dinosaur-like creatures, and Dungeons and Dragons.

Likewise, the response to these games has been a mixture of recognizing that VR may offer new possibilities in entertainment on the one hand, and the use of the technology to promote existing forms of entertainment in a new guise on the other. So, for example, the Virtuality game 'Legend Quest', akin to Dungeons and Dragons, allows several players to interact with each other within the virtual world, a world in which players can choose their characters and which consists of many rooms or environments. This new level of interaction and the unusually high degree of narrative content is attractive to players. One player commented: 'You forget where you are. You actually feel like you're in that dungeon and fighting. You panic. If something starts killing you, you try and get away. There are some rooms I dread going back to'. According to another: 'In Virtual Reality, you're not controlling a character. You are the character. The interaction is brain to brain, person to person. It's just the visual aspect of the person that's different' [18]. In other words, both the 'realism' of the game and the ability to interact with other users set this game machine apart from others.

These reactions of players can be compared with reactions of a different type. First, that of a VR researcher: Warren Robinette was among the early and very successful developers of computer games who subsequently became a VR researcher at the University of North Carolina at Chapel Hill, again one of the foremost institutions in the field. On the occasion of his first encounter with a stand-up game of the dinosaur-fighting type, instead of engaging with the game, he immediately explored the display standard and navigational flexibility of the machine. He moved his helmetted head and the joystick vigorously to discover the responsiveness of the tracking device and the way in which the virtual world could be explored. Unlike other users, he was not interested in the content of game, but clearly impressed with the machine's technical capabilities [19]. Being able to make this distinction between the technical aspects of the machine and the content of the virtual world, however, may become important when we think about the direction in which VR might be developed.

This can be illustrated by comparing these responses with the responses to a different, non-immersive game. Vincent John Vincent's 'Mandala' game is not immersive, but similar to Krueger's 'artificial reality' in using a videocamera to record a silhouette of the user which interacts with the image of an environment on a screen (either television- or wall-sized). The games that can be played include a virtual drum kit, where the user can play the instruments on the screen, and different ball games, as well as interactive dance routines. The game is often used by two or more users since they are able to step directly into the environment. The machine on which the game runs is put together from several low-cost components and it is possible for an amateur to learn how to program environments, create different sound-effects and reconfigure the system's devices.

A marked difference can be observed between the reactions of users on their first encounter with Mandala as against those with an immersive VR system: Mandala users typically express delight at being able immediately to 'play' music or play with other objects in the various environments. The system allows a form of interaction that can be grasped quickly and intuitively, and the focus here is on interaction. This also leads to their surprise and delight at the content of the game. On the other hand, users are for the most part not impressed by the technology as such, which is more like the technology with which they are already familiar, such as videorecording, videogames and synthesized music.

The reactions to immersive environments, by contrast, typically focus on the novelty value of the technology. Users are often disoriented by their first immersive experience and disappointed by the quality of the display, but express amazement at the new technology. In short, one simple (and no doubt simplistic) contrast that can be made is that users consider immersive VR technically impressive, whereas the Mandala systems are more fun to explore [20].

At this point we can return to the Virtuality games. In several respects, they can be seen as an extension of patterns in the use of existing computer- and videogames. They are similar to other arcade games in so far as they are sold as complete units to be used in public spaces, as well as by being coin-operated. They are designed so that new W Industries games can be loaded on to the arcade units, thus reproducing the mechanisms whereby console videogames currently operate, with profit expected not so much from the sale of the machines but from the subsequent purchase of games from the same manufacturer. At the same time, and again like other video- and computer games, the themes of the W Industries games are mainly action-oriented, i.e. speed and violence. This application of VR concentrates on the realism of the computer graphics, rather than making use of the features that are unique to this, as opposed to other entertainment technologies, such as the ease of use in creating virtual worlds, or the engagement in exploring interactivity. The same applies to the multi-user experiences of the two types of games. Virtuality machines thus seem designed for the most part to intensify the type of experience that is possible with other, existing technologies.

The same goes for the content of the games. Apart from the game themes already mentioned and which are, again, similar to other games, Waldern presented a preview of a W Industries game in March 1993 to be released later in the same year. This game will be technically superior to previous ones in featuring a lighter helmet and more detailed and more 'realistic' computer graphics. The content of the game allows the player to 'become' a robot-like creature with a large arm that consists of a powerful gun. This figure looks and acts like a cross between the Robocop and Terminator characters in the successful Hollywood films bearing their names, violent and powerful. The thudding steps of the figure, throbbing sound-effects and the 'realism' of the explosions are designed to reinforce this impression. VR technology, and the sense of presence in an immersive environment created with it, is thus used here to imitate the content from another medium and to make it appealing by other means.

BACK TO THE FUTURE

VR has precipitated many ideas regarding the possible impact of the technology. One of the reasons for this is the possibility of extensive VR use. As Biocca puts it:

'...time spent in using this immersive medium may be higher than for any previous medium. Kubey and Csikszentmihalyi estimated that people spend approximately 7 years of their life watching television. If people eventually use VR technology for the same amount of time that they spend watching television and using computers, some users could spend 20 or more years 'inside' virtual reality' [21].

A second and related reason is the question of how this new technology will fit into a range of technologies that look set to transform a number of fields, especially information display and communications media. NASA Ames researcher Stephen Ellis formulates this cautiously: 'It is difficult to foretell the future practical mass-market applications for virtual environments...possibly, once the world is densely criss-crossed with high bandwidth, public access, fiber-optic 'information highways', mass demand will materialize for convenient, virtual environment displays of high resolution imagery' [22]. In the light of the potential significance of VR, let us look at some ideas about its future, its relation to other technological developments and its impact on society. Al Gore and Jaron Lanier provide two good examples here.

As US Vice-President and informally the administration's science and technology 'czar', Al Gore's ideas about information and communication technology and about VR may be of some importance. Gore chaired a US Senate subcommittee hearing on VR in May 1992 at which Jaron Lanier, Tom Furness (director of HITL) and Fred Brooks (of the University of North Carolina at Chapel Hill) were among the expert witnesses. Much was made at the hearing about the competition between the USA and Japan, with Gore suggesting that without government action, the economic benefits of the US lead in research would be lost to other countries which developed practical applications, as had happened in other instances [23]. On a different occasion, Gore likened distributed computer networks to the positive aspects of capitalism and presented communism as a 'large and powerful central processor, which collapsed when it was overwhelmed by ever more complex information' [24].

Gore has also linked his well publicized idea of an information-network infrastructure for the USA, which is in his view essential to the nation's future wellbeing [25], to VR: 'If the users of virtual reality could be at some distance from these [graphics] engines and use them by means of an information superhighway, a network in other words, then that would potentially speed up the introduction of new applications for this new technology' [26]. At the same time, Gore's vision of the future relies on finding the appropriate uses for these 'highways' or 'networks' which, as he put it, 'would enable a child to come home from school and, instead of playing Nintendo, use something that looks like a video game machine to plug into the Library of Congress' [27]. Needless to say, the technological optimism of these ideas is perhaps more revealing about US politics and culture than about the role of information and communication technology in society.

Similarly with our second example, Jaron Lanier. Lanier is a well known figure among VR developers and the person most closely identified with the technology in the mass media. He, too, devotes a great deal of attention to the possibility of networked or shared virtual environments. Indeed, two years after Lanier's VPL presented the first full-body-suit immersive VR system, VPL demonstrated a shared immersive system in 1989 called 'Reality Built For Two' [28]. One point he made at the US Senate hearings was that the importance of VR would come with its use as a mass medium, like the telephone [29].

Lanier thinks that VR has an 'infinity of possibility . . . it's just an open world where your mind is the only limitation . . . it gives us this sense of being who we are without limitation; for our imagination to become shared with other people' [30]. This, however, may have its positive and negative aspects, allowing human beings to share their ideas and dreams on the one hand, or absorbing them within their own private world, like television or videogames, on the other [31]. Hence he thinks that one possibility might be that VR could recreate a sense of community that has been lost. This would replace the isolation of the individual – he mentions 'California [which] is the worst example of this. Individuals don't even meet on the sidewalks any more. We live in our cars' – with the 'English commons, where there's a shared community space' [32]. Mixed with this optimism is a sense of the dangers of VR so that, for example, he advocates that children up to the age of eight or ten should in future not be allowed to use VR, although this 'could be framed positively. There could be a nice sort of ritual for kids when they get old enough to use simulators' [33].

At this stage we can return to relating these ideas back to the emergence of the technology and its current applications. Gore and Lanier may be prescient in focusing on the implications of VR as a shared medium. Large multinational communications firms which have their sights set on dominating the emerging global communications markets are among those with the strongest interest in VR: the French firm Thomson, which is a member of one of the rival consortia bidding to establish a standard for high definition television (HDTV), has recently gained control of VPL, and with it the patents on key components of VR. US West Communications, which has teamed up with Time-Warner to exploit new cable and telecommunications technologies, is a HITL consortium member, in addition to making generous contributions to the HITL summer school project. In the UK, BT, which aims at becoming a global telecommunications provider, is pursuing a number of VR projects.

VR is thus clearly at a crossroads in its development: there seems to be a large gap between projections about how the technology will affect the future and the current applications of VR. The geopolitical concerns, utopian ideas about ritual and community and strategic plans of multinational firms seem to be at some remove from arcade games and classroom settings. Yet this gap could fill within a short space of time. A prognosis made by Lanier in September 1991, for example, that a high-quality VR machine for home use at $10 000 (1992 $) would only become available by the turn of the century [34], seems conservative a year-and-a-half later.

At the same time, from a technical viewpoint, there are many possible directions and options for VR technology: whether, for example, fully immersive systems with head-mounted displays and body suits or desktop systems become most widespread, which of the senses are to be used as input and output, how navigation in virtual worlds takes place and how the user's position is tracked, whether the display is projected on to the retina or surrounds the user in a room-size environment, whether VR systems are mainly for single users or for use as shared virtual environments, and finally what kind of content the virtual worlds themselves will have – all these are questions which are open and difficult to foretell. Moreover, the diverse origins and sources of the technology, ranging from the military to computer games, do not present a clear pattern which could be extrapolated into the near future. If anything, the background to the technology itself suggests that a number of directions are possible and a variety of paths may be taken.

There is as yet little experience with VR and limited evidence about how advances in VR technology translate into practical applications. From the two examples of current applications given (and several others could have been presented to strengthen this case), it is nevertheless clear that the social settings of VR machines as well as their technical features and content are quite diverse and make an important difference to users and to the purposes to which the machines are put, some opening up the possibility for exploring innovative uses of this technology while others foreclose them. This article has only provided some brief perspectives on the past and present of VR. Its future lies in the open and contested space between various technical options, the social forces shaping VR and the ideas about its possible uses.

NOTES AND REFERENCES

1 Ellis, S. (1991) 'Nature and origin of virtual environments: a bibliographic essay', *Computing Systems in Engineering*, 2(4), page 325; Palfreman, J. and Swade, D. (1991) *The Dream Machine – Exploring the Computer Age*, London, BBC Books, pages 95-97. There were a number of forerunners to Sutherland's work, both in science fiction and in entertainment and other technologies. Sutherland's work, however, was to provide the foundation for much of the subsequent research related to VR.

2 Sutherland, I. (1965) 'The ultimate display', *Proceedings of International Federation of Information Processing Congress*, pages 506-508.

3 Sutherland, I. (1968) 'A head-mounted three dimensional display', *Proceedings of the Fall Joint Computer Conference*, pages 757-764.

4 Rheingold, H. (1991) *Virtual Reality*, London, Secker and Warburg, page 106.

5 Krueger, M. (1991) *Artifcial Reality II*, Reading, MA, Addison Wesley, 2nd edn.

6 Vince, J. (1992) 'Virtual reality techniques in flight simulation' in *Virtual Reality Systems*, British Computer Society Conference proceedings.

7 The perceptual and psychological issues in relation to VR use have yet to be fully investigated. See, for example, Rushton, S. and Wann, J. (1993) 'Problems in perception and action in virtual worlds', *Proceedings of the Third Annual Conference on Virtual Reality*, London, Meckler, pages 43-55; for earlier research on motion sickness see Oman, C. (1991) 'Sensory conflict in motion sickness: an Observer Theory approach', in Ellis, S. (1991) (editor) *Pictorial Communication in Virtual and Real Environments*, London, Taylor and Francis, pp. 362-377.

8 Another important centre of VR research which predates the recent take-off is the Department of Computer Science at the University of North Carolina at Chapel Hill. Rheingold, *op cit* [4], provides an overview of this and other early VR work.

9 This pattern of invention in America is described by Hughes, T. (1989) *American Genesis – A Century of Invention and Technological Enthusiasm*, New York, Viking Penguin, especially chapters 1-3.

10 For example, Helsel, S. and Doherty, S. D. (1992) *Virtual Reality Marketplace 1993*, Westport, CT, Meckler.

11 Further details of the two schools' projects can be found in Schroeder, R., Cleal, B. and Giles, W. (1993) 'Virtual reality in education: some preliminary social science perspectives', in *Interface to Real and Virtual Worlds*, Paris, EC2, pp. 147-158.

12 Bricken, M. and Byrne, C. (1990) 'Summer students in virtual reality: a pilot study on educational applications of virtual reality technology' (mimeo, 1992); see also Bricken, M. (1990) 'A description of the virtual reality learning environment', Human Interface Technology Laboratory Technical Report No HITL-M-90-4.

13 However, the questionnaires at HITL (carried out by Bricken and Byrne, *op cit.* [12]) and at West Denton (carried out by Schroeder, Cleal and Giles, *op cit.* [11]) were pilot studies with small pupil samples, and the findings are therefore far from conclusive.

14 As in the case of games for microcomputers, many VR developers and manufacturers are distancing themselves from the games application of VR because it is felt to be not 'serious'. This phenomenon is discussed in relation to microcomputers by Leslie Haddon, 'Interactive games', in Hayward, P. and Wollen, T. (1993) (eds), *Future Visions – New Technologies of the Screen*, London, British Film Institute, pp. 123-147.

15 At the Virtual Reality '93 conference in London, April 1993.

16 Interview with Jonathan Waldern in *Black Ice*, Issue 1, January 1993, page 16.

17 Author's interview with Ian Andrew, managing director of Dimension, 16 July 1992.

18 Players interviewed by Amanda Whittingdon in 'Fun with Eric the Spider', *New Statesman and Society*, 29 May 1992, page 33.

19 Author's conversation with Warren Robinette in London 16 July 1992.

20 This is not to say that they are mutually exclusive: a 'virtual drum kit', for example, can also be played as part of an immersive VR system. Bob Stone, a prominent VR researcher in Britain, was interviewed playing an immersive virtual drum on the BBC Radio 4 programme 'One Step Beyond: Virtual Valerie' (21 November 1992), and again commented favourably on his enjoyment of the game.

21 Biocca, F. (1992) 'Communication within virtual reality: creating a space for research', *Journal of Communication*, 42, (4), Autumn, page 14, where the study cited is Kubey, R. and Csikszentmihalyi, M. (1990) *Television and the Quality of Life: How Viewing Shapes Everyday Experience*, Hillsdale, NJ, Lawrence Erlbaum and Associates.

22 Ellis, *op cit.* [1], where the term 'information highways' refers to the use of this term by Al Gore, which is described below.

23 Although the link between scientific research, technological innovation and economic benefits is perhaps more complex than Gore allows for. A review of recent analyses can be found in Inkster, I. (1991) 'Made in America but lost to Japan: science, technology and economic performance in the two capitalist superpowers', *Social Studies of Science*, 21, (1), pp. 157-178.

24 Gore, A. (1991) 'Infrastructure for the global village', *Scientitic American*, September, page 108.

25 *Ibid*, page 111.

26 Senate hearings of May 1992, quoted in the *HIT Lab Review*, No 1, Winter 1992, pp. 8-9.

27 Gore, *op cit.* [24], page 110. Japanese videogame manufacturers are rumoured to be set to market a home VR game in late 1993.

28 Rheingold, *op cit.* [4], pp. 168, 170. See also Blanchard, C. *et al.* (1990) 'Reality built for two: a virtual reality tool', *Computer Graphics*, 24, (2), March, pp. 35-36.

29 Lanier interviewed by Frank Biocca in 'An insider's view of the future of virtual reality', *Journal of Communication*, 42, (2), Autumn 1992, pp. 156-157.

30 Jaron Lanier, panel session 'Virtual environments and interactivity: windows to the future', *Computer Graphics*, 23, (5), December 1989, page 8.

31 *Ibid*, page 9; see also Lanier's interview with Biocca, *op cit.* [29], page 156.

32 *Ibid*, page 157; see also page 168.

33 *Ibid*, page 168.

34 *Ibid*, page 153.

TELEWORK AND THE CHANGING RELATIONSHIP OF HOME AND WORK

Leslie Haddon and Roger Silverstone

INTRODUCTION

This paper deals with the following three questions:

1 Has the availability of telecoms-related and computer-related technologies been a significant factor encouraging and enabling home-based telework?

2 Is teleworking likely to introduce major changes into the organisation of domestic life, and with what implications for all Information and Communication Technologies (ICTs) in the home?

3 Will the introduction into the home and use of ICTs for work purposes lead to these technologies being used by household members other than the teleworker and used for purposes other than telework?

These questions indicate straight away that our aims are different from the existing literature on telework. They are different in two ways. Much of the research on telework has focused on reasons for and factors affecting the success of this working arrangement. Although our own research may provide insights into these issues our main concern is with the way in which telework could potentially have implications for home life. Second, we address what we regard as the key questions concerning the technologies used by teleworkers, since this study is part of a larger programme of research which examines how ICTs are experienced by different social groups. Hence, the organisation of telework is dealt with in so far as it has ramifications for these technologies. A more detailed analysis of both telework and the ICTs used in teleworking is currently being prepared as a separate document.

A few preliminary points need to be made about the scope of our research. [This research was hased on extremely detailed interviews with the adults in 20 households where one or more partners worked at home using ICTs.]. Since the focus of our general research programme is on ICTs in the home, our operational definition of teleworkers included people working at home using, as a minimum requirement, microcomputers and the telephone in the course of their work. This definition includes, therefore, the self-employed and individual employee initiatives as well as teleworking schemes initiated and organised by employers. We are aware of definitional controversies concerning the term 'telework' (Huws, 1988), and clearly our sample will fit in with some the definitions and not others. But those very definitions have been developed in relation to issues around and theories about the organisation of work. For us, the interesting questions emerge from the effects of the entry of paid labour into the home. and the way in which work provides a route for ICTs to enter the home.

Throughout this paper we will demonstrate that it is not appropriate to simply talk about the 'impact' of these new working arrangements on home life. Domestic life has its own rhythms and routines, its temporal and spatial patterns, its shared values and rules as well as its domestic conflicts. These all shape how teleworking can enter the home and whether and how it can be accommodated. Hence, although the arrival of telework can have a bearing on those domestic patterns, telework also has to be adjusted to fit in with home life.

Finally, both telework and domestic life have their own dynamic. Telework can change in terms of such matters as its content, the necessity for contactability, the balance of work inside and outside the home, the spatial requirements of work and the times when work has to take place. In households, the fact that children are born and grow up introduces constantly changing demands on domestic space and time. Relationships also change, with tensions, conflicts, the negotiation of new ways of organising household life, the break up of households and the formation of new ones. There is also material change, with the introduction of new goods, including ICTs, and indeed, the acquisition of new homes and hence opportunities for new spatial arrangements.

The consequence of these dynamics is that the experience of telework changes. It can take place at different times in different places. At times it can become more stressful, as new problems constantly emerge - at other times it can be easier to accommodate. As a result, we can talk of teleworking careers and telework trajectories, whereby people come to telework from a variety of routes, their experience of it changes over time and, after longer or shorter periods, some give it up and return to office-based work - or else cease to be part of the labour force.

KEY QUESTIONS

While the introductory questions give an instant overview of the content of this paper, they require some further elaboration. The first question addresses the extent to which the growth of teleworking has been technologically driven and is technologically determined. The answer can in part be drawn from the existing telework literature, but the emphasis here is on the variation which our own study of teleworkers reveals. Basically, teleworkers are a very heterogeneous group who have come to telework for different reasons. In addition, the status of telework varies in different households. What we are specifically interested in here is the centrality of ICTs in different forms of telework. Some patterns can be identified.

The second question derives from our general interest in ICTs' role in domestic life. For example, in principle telework offers flexibility in temporal and spatial patterns: if they do not have to go into an office, teleworkers can work at any time and anywhere. This could well have a bearing on the use of all ICTs - not only work-related technologies, but also patterns of media consumption. So how does the dialectic between telework and home life structure where ICTs are located, and hence how they can be displayed and accessed by others? How does it structure how ICTs are regulated and used? Finally, how are ICTs implicated in the actual process of managing telework, and coping with the problems which telework throws up?

The third, related, set of questions concerns the way in which telework can provide a route for new ICTs to enter the home as well as transform the meaning of technologies already present. What new meaning do technologies take on and what are their careers? In what circumstances can the presence of these ICTs create new skills and competences? How might technologies acquired or used for work purposes also start to take on a domestic role, finding applications relating to the home or being used by others in the home?

ICTs ENABLING TELEWORK

There are some forms of telework where ICTs play an essential role. Examples from our research include a software designer, someone programming on a distant mainframe computer via a modem, a researcher conducting data analysis using a software package and a computer conference mediator. In all these cases, which predominantly consists of employees, the tasks would have been impractical without ICTs. Either the telecoms link for programming, receiving or sending data is vital, or else the growth of microcomputers in the workplace has meant that computer staff can now bring their essential tools home - they are no longer tied to work because of the need to access a centralised facility.

These types of telework can be contrasted with cases where the work could have been conducted from home without ICTs. Examples include a secretary doing wordprocessing at home, various report writers, a media researcher, an editor, an accountant, an administrator for a book distribution business, a systems analyst who produces feasibility reports, someone running a childcare agency and an abstract writer. In other words, these teleworkers, predominantly self-employed, are involved in text production or else clerical or professional forms of administration.

Many of these possess only computers but also have a wide range of other ICTs, such as photocopiers, faxes and modems, which no doubt facilitate their work. These ICTs make the work easier and quicker and they offer some new options (e.g. consulting distant databases without needing to travel). Indeed, ICTs might have become more essential given clients' expectations about the speed of production or their desire for electronic output. Yet, this work could have taken place in the past without the aid of new ICTs. In fact, in our sample, both the editor and abstract writer had worked for nearly 20 years at home, only starting to use new telecoms and electronic technology as they appeared in the 1970s and 1980s. Before this the only technologies they used were the typewriter and basic phone. These examples represent forms of professional and clerical work - not captured in literature on traditional manufacturing homework - which have always been conducted at home by a few.

In between these two sets of teleworker, there are some people for whom ICTs are more than just a facilitator because of the magnitude of the task and time pressures involved. For these, mostly but not exclusively self-employed, ICTs make telework more of a feasible option. Examples include an executive managing director, a publisher trading in international book rights, and various consultants producing substantial reports and packages at short notice. In these cases, communication is a significant element in their work, or else they are producing major texts in a short time span which require a professional appearance. The existence of ICTs providing the kind of personalised technological back-up that they might expect in an office had made teleworking viable.

In sum, there are different degrees to which technology is a facilitator of telework, with one key variable being employment status. But even where ICTs have been relatively more important for conducting the telework, it is important to appreciate that they act as an enabling force rather than a driving one. For companies, the social-economic factors driving telework, such as the need to reduce building overheads or to retain staff, have already been well documented in the telework literature. Equally, social considerations shape individuals' decision to telework. For example, they do so in order to spend more time with or better manage children, or to cut down commuting. For some, it is a positive lifestyle choice. For others it is merely the best or only option available. Lastly, to the extent that there have been macro changes in the number of teleworkers in the country, this is also the result of social causes. This includes a greater awareness of this option, the fact that working at home has become more acceptable to employers or clients, the rise of teleworker organisations offering various kinds of support and - more negatively - the massive restructuring of companies in the recession which for some means telework is the only alternative to unemployment or early retirement.

TELEWORK AND CHANGE IN EVERYDAY DOMESTIC LIFE

Any temporal flexibility which telework may offer is in practice constrained by social factors. First, there are the demands of work. These include the requirement of employees to co-ordinate activities with others who are working core hours in an office or the need to be contactable at certain times. Our case studies reveal instances of managers regularly having to face crises at times not of their own choosing, and of clerical and professional self-employed teleworkers working longer hours than they would like because of rush jobs, the need to bring new products to market, consultancy deadlines, or short-term notice of work.

At the same time, teleworkers often experience pressures to synchronise their non-work with others both inside and outside the home.

Female clerical teleworkers, and some professionals, who cannot afford to pay for childcare can often only work when the children are not around or when their partners can look after them. In cases where young children are present, this means working in the evenings and at weekends. Or some teleworkers try to keep weekends free to retain a place in the community - since that is when social activities are most likely to occur. In addition, many teleworkers prefer to stick to the approximate times when they used to work in offices because this routine helps their self-discipline.

In response to these pressures of work and domestic life, key temporal patterns emerge. In one, work is relatively more imposed upon domestic life and, if necessary, household routines have to be adjusted. For example, many employees on telework schemes continue to work in the day and so that time is blocked out for work: they do not suddenly take on more domestic tasks by virtue of being home nor do they make themselves totally accessible to others in the household. Alternatively, the demands of work may mean it takes place outside traditional office hours - but again, work takes precedence. This appears to be a more masculine style, but one also adopted by some women, particularly professional employees. In contrast, a more common female pattern, especially clear where the telework is part-time, involves fitting work into domestic rhythms, fitting it in around the times when the children or partners are absent and hence not making demands, or fitting it in between other domestic responsibilities.

In terms of when work takes place, the pattern whereby telework is imposed on home life is more often associated with virtually no change from core office hours. There may be just a little more flexibility than flexitime offers, which is often useful for child management. The contrasting pattern involves working non-standard hours - either when work is fragmented and fitted in and/or performed in the evenings at weekends. For those working long hours, of course, prioritising work may mean working both the core day and evening and weekend work. Clearly any pattern which involves working outside normal office core time has implications for the use of all ICTs in the home - for example, patterns of TV-watching, video use and radio listening can also change for these teleworkers

Social constraints also affect the location of telework. Although regular commitments to visit one or more worksites may limit teleworkers' choice of where they would want to live, of far more significance is domestic inertia. Teleworkers are established in houses, are part of communities, the children have friends at local schools and have partners whose own work commitments have to be considered. In our sample, only one household, where both partners teleworked, was considering relocating in the south of France. On the whole, the flexibility offered by telework does not lead people to radically relocate and decamp to the countryside.

The spatial location of telework within homes is also constrained by domestic considerations. One common image of teleworking is that where telework is conducted in a home office - and hence, work-related ICTs are based in a separate defined work space. This does happen, although it is more likely in the case of professional teleworkers because they tend to have bigger homes. But even professional teleworkers and certainly clerical ones often operated in a shared space: multi-purpose rooms, guests rooms, dining rooms, often bedrooms, caravans and even in kitchens. The point is that both work and, especially, children made competing demands on space. Because these demands change over time, as work changes, as children grew older, telework sometimes has to move around the house, at one point taking place in a dining room, at another in a bedroom, at another, if a larger house is acquired, in a study. Such constraints on space become significant for the teleworker's scope for impression management, for creating an image of their telework both to other household members and to outsiders. This includes constraints on the manner in which they can display their technology as a means to identify with high-tech images of telework.

Making time and finding space for telework involves some negotiation within households - albeit negotiation where some household members may well be able to mobilise more power than others. In particular, teleworkers have the problem of boundary maintenance: to greater or lesser extents, separating work and home life and preventing the mutual interference. One level at which boundary maintenance operates involves creating rules and understandings about the accessibility of teleworkers to other household members or contactability for either work or social purposes.

This form of boundary maintenance may involve ICTs to the extent that both incoming work and social phone calls are directed to certain time spots, or to different phones or are controlled by the use of answerphones. Here we have an instance of using ICTs to manage telework. Teleworkers mainly used the answerphone, and to some extent the fax, to control the timing of communication, taking and responding to different types of message when it suits them. This allows them to better control interruptions - from work or social calls - to whatever task is at hand. In addition, technologies such as the answerphone enable teleworkers to control the impression they give to the public world of work, allowing them to disguise their location and distance themselves from the domestic setting which threatens to intrude if the phone is answered by other household members or through extraneous noise

Another dimension of boundary maintenance also involves impression management: being able to convey to outsiders - clients, employers and others contacted in the course of work - the image of being in a workplace. This often means regulating how telephones are answered and who can answer them under what conditions. It can also mean regulating the sound regime of the home in general or at least the spaces in proximity to telework - so that domestic noise neither interferes with work nor creates the wrong impression for outsiders. This also includes regulating sound for ICTs such as the TV.

The final dimension of boundary maintenance involves the use of work-related ICTs: stipulating whether and when different household members can have access to ICTs. There are sometimes tensions, for example, over the use of computers by children where teleworkers fear it may damage the hard- or software. And certainly, access to shared micros by others in the household is likely to take second priority to the teleworker's own use. Similarly, multiple use of a single phone line can lead to conflicts over the way domestic calls may block the line and hinder incoming work-calls. In cases where ICTs like microcomputers or phone lines are shared, this again means potential conflict and trying to establish rules about use: rules which may be accepted or flouted. Alternatively, for those such as teleworking employees where equipment is supplied by employers or professional self-employed teleworkers, the solution is avoid sharing ICT resources and instead acquire a second (or third) computer dedicated to work or one or more extra phone lines specifically for work.

Beyond issues of time, space and boundary maintenance, teleworking also has a bearing on and is affected by a range of social relationships within the household. Not only do the responses of other household members, particularly partners, have to be taken into account when considering telework. Others in the household can support or resist telework in a variety or ways and may be enrolled in the actual work itself. Partners can support telework in practical terms, by taking over childcare or keeping children away from teleworker, as well as by enforcing boundaries and regulations. This appears to be far more significant, for example, than doing more to help with routine domestic tasks: telework apparently makes little difference to gendered division of labour in more households.

In addition, partners and sometimes children literally help with the work. Sometimes this assistance as auxiliary labour involves no particular help with the actual technology of production: it may, for instance, involve picking up and delivering work material or acting as a sounding board for ideas. However, sometimes others in the household take part in the production process, either acting as a technical support or else using ICTs and hence developing new computer and telephone skills.

Finally, social networks outside the home can play a role in supporting telework. Most often, such support has no bearing on actual technologies: it may be in the form of networks who can help take on some of the workload, provide additional childcare back-up or offer social contact to overcome any sense of isolation. But that support also includes networks which, like partners, can provide technical advice and assistance relating to the teleworker's ICTs.

In some cases, ICTs enter the home for the first time because of telework. Examples include the microcomputer itself and related scanners, modems, new software, faxes, answerphones, photocopiers. Telework undoubtedly provides a route for such ICTs to enter the home for the first time, with the possibility that both teleworkers and other household members will use them within new patterns of activities, and that they will spill over into home life.

But an equally likely consequence of telework's arrival is the further multiplication of ICTs which are already possessed: i.e. a second or third micro, another telephone line or two, a second answerphone, etc. This too is an important dimension of the way ICTs diffuse to homes - and within homes, since a process of technological inheritance sometimes takes place whereby children or partners acquire, for example, the old microcomputer when a new one arrives for telework. The fact that other household members now have individual rights of possession and access to a technology, compared to the previous situation of conflicting demands on a shared household resource, can make a difference to their usage of the technology.

The third process, already discussed at some length in the previous section, involves not the acquisition of new ICTs so much as change in the regulation and pattern of use of existing technologies. The status of ICTs such as computers and phones may change: using that equipment for work purposes leads to new rules, tensions, conflicts and changes in claims of possession.

So far, we have discussed the possible pattern of ICT acquisition and regulation. But it is important to also examine the actual process by which ICTs enter the home, since this too has a bearing on their meaning and subsequent usage. For example, many ICTs are supplied by employers, but sometimes also by clients. In such cases, rules about use may be laid down by the supplier, restricting usage to work. In our sample, for example, the work phone was not used for social purposes - although children were often allowed some, albeit heavily supervised, access to the computer. Of course, some, usually small, ICTs such as answerphones are acquired by a variety of means: for example, as gifts or through points gained in special offers. However, the most common alternative to supply by an employer is buying ICTs - which is usually the course of action taken by self-employed teleworkers.

This immediately raises the question of finance. Clearly, the absolute amount of money available to the teleworking household is an important consideration - with wealthy households having to deliberate less about the purchase of ICTs. But even in many professional households, disposable income is subject to competing demands and questions of priorities. For example, in our study, some self-employed teleworkers wished to upgrade their microcomputers and knew that they might or indeed were losing, business through not doing so. But they did not upgrade because of other priorities - the desire for new TV technologies in one case and in another case the desire to continue using disposable income to finance their children's private education.

Although partners often negotiate over the disposal of joint household funds, it appeared that males in our study were more likely to make successful demands on funds. One key factor in this exercise of power is that they were more likely to aspire to be primary earners, to have a commitment to a career and to want to work full-time. Although this was true of a number of female teleworkers, many women were secondary earners in the household. Many worked part-time and although they had career aspirations, being primarily responsible for childcare they were satisfied to be bringing in some income and keeping in touch with work in a period when it was difficult to manage an office based career. On the whole, therefore, they were more cautious as regards the purchase of ICTs and less likely to take risks.

In the examples above it was possible to identify where teleworkers were losing business through the level of ICT they possessed. However, in many instances, it is actually difficult to discern before purchase whether a particular ICT, such as a cordless phone or a fax, is 'necessary' for the telework, or even to ascertain exactly how 'useful' it will be. Similar difficulties can arise when trying to determine if the technology possessed, such as a microcomputer, is 'adequate' or whether an upgrade should be acquired. At times, teleworkers are explicit about their uncertainty. But at other times, claims about technology are the subject of controversy, where teleworkers argue for an acquisition but their partners resist. In other words, 'need' is negotiated.

In such instances it appears that telework can act as a catalyst for purchasing ICTs already desired. For example, where a number of the teleworkers, mainly male, were already early adopters of ICTs, telework could justify acquisition of extra technology. Furthermore, once acquired, telework could also justify the pleasurable activity, especially but not uniquely for males, of exploring that technology, making time free from other obligations. These teleworkers were not general hobbyists, but they could argue that the hours spent experimenting on their equipment would assist their work. Sometimes their partners were sceptical.

Turning to the question of ICT use in the household, a first general point needs to be made about power and empowerment. Telework can lead to, or enhance, the development of technological expertise: not only with computers but also with telecoms, now that a considerable amount of telecoms-related equipment is available beyond the basic phone. And expertise means not only being able to literally use technology but becoming aware of its social dimension: examples from telecoms being when to use the fax, what the fax was useful for, the advantages and disadvantages of E-Mail and how to organise phone calls and present oneself on the phone. Not only the teleworker, but others in the household often developed some of these new competences.

But apart from being a source of pride and self-esteem, a teleworker's expertise could also be exercised as power - as when a teleworker would tell other household members how they should be using the technology and what mistakes they were making. On the other hand, empowerment through technology could be more positive. This was best illustrated in one case study where a female researcher who teleworked had an uncertain future with her clients and an uncertain future in the relationship with her partner. Following long-standing conflicts in the marriage, there was the prospect of splitting up and her having to find full-time work again. Her purchase of an Apple Mac, which was itself very controversial in the household, enabled her to feel much more secure, since she then possessed an important tool which might help her acquire more work if she needed it.

As regards actual usage, in our study the degree to which telecoms equipment was used by others in the household depended in part on how much the ICT was already seen as a home technology. The answerphone and cordless phone were not seen as specifically 'work' technologies and were used by others. Although there was some social use of the fax and mobile phone, these were more likely to find exclusive or mainly work applications and be used solely by the teleworker. There were signs among the more confident users that this may change over time - some children had begun to use the fax as a photocopier and had faxed a few messages to relatives abroad.

There were few cases where use of the computer was absolutely contained to telework with no seepage into the rest of the household: partners may not have used the machines but children usually had some access. Of course, a particular machine might be dedicated to work where several were available in the home. When we look at partners' use, gender differences were apparent. Female partners of male teleworkers often had some word-processing skills and were likely to use their partner's machine for the occasional letters, for educational purposes or for their own work. This was less the case with male partners of female teleworkers. One consideration here is that a number of these males worked in skilled manual occupations that did not require experience of micros and so they had neither the skills for nor interest in using them.

Older children were also likely to use, and be encouraged to use, work computers for wordprocessing. While general computer literacy was welcomed in many homes, parents recognised that keyboard literacy was a particularly useful practical skill - and that wordprocessed school work was likely to receive better marks. While some older children nevertheless rejected the computer, all the younger ones showed some interest and were allowed access. These parents were quite proud of the way that their children were gaining early familiarity with computer technology and envisaged buying the children their own machines when they grew older. In many cases, then, telework had introduced a technological resource into the home which was helping children in the household to develop both familiarity with ICTs and new competences.

Lastly, we have the question of what these ICTs are used for - their application. We have already noted the limited use of the fax for social messages. But at least one teleworker used the fax for domestic arrangements such as dealing with banks, and another received articles via fax for the vintage car newsletter of which he was an editor. In contrast, there was little use of the modem to participate in electronic networks other than for work purposes: modems rarely provided a new window to the outside social world

Various ICTs found some role in terms of keeping records: the photocopier and photocopying facility on fax machines were often used to retain copies of domestic correspondence to outside officials. Meanwhile, the computer kept electronic copy of word-processed letters.

Apart from its use for games, the computer was mostly used for word-processing - and certainly few partners or children used other software. The computerisation of domestic life in terms of, for example, keeping electronic household accounts, was very rare and then usually in part only attempted in the process of experimenting with the machine.

ICTs and ICT skills acquired for telework could also find a use for and by those outside the home. This could happen at a number of levels. Friends, neighbours and relatives sometimes requested access to the equipment - e.g. to send a fax or photocopy a document. Here we have the technological equivalent of, perhaps, asking to borrow a cup of sugar! Second, the teleworker's own expertise with ICTs could become an asset, where teleworkers' advice was sought or else teleworkers helped other people set up equipment or overcome problems. Third, teleworkers often used their ICTs on behalf of or even at the request of outside organisations in which they were involved: for instance, writing newsletters for voluntary bodies, producing tickets for events at sports clubs, or word-processing school reports. Lastly, teleworkers, often acting as earlier adopters of certain equipment, simply created awareness of the technology - through having people visit the home or talking about their experiences of ICTs. Clearly, the acquisition of work ICTs provided several new bases for interaction and these technologies became in part a community resource.

TELEWORK, DOMESTIC LIFE AND ICTS

This paper has addressed some of the key questions that might be asked about technology and telework. Summarising the answers to these questions:

1 Certainly some forms of telework have been made more viable by ICTs, and some could not have been accomplished without these technologies. However, a range of especially self-employed clerical and professional work, perhaps accounting for the majority of teleworkers, has been conducted at home for some time - ICTs have not enabled this so much as facilitated it. Moreover, socio-economic factors are more significant than technology in shaping employers' and employees' decision to move to telework and in any trends regarding teleworking.

2 The potential of telework and ICTs to allow teleworkers temporal and spatial flexibility is always constrained by social factors. The different temporal and spatial patterns that emerge, and the efforts to maintain the boundaries between home and work, have a bearing upon the time when ICTs are used, the access of others in the household to ICTs and how ICTs can be displayed. Some telecoms ICTs play a significant role in helping to maintain these boundaries. The introduction of telework has also involved enlisting the support of others inside and outside the

home, including technical support and enrolment of others in the production process using ICTs.

3 While new ICTs are sometimes acquired, we needed to also pay attention to the other processes whereby existing ICTs are multiplied and/or experience new patterns of regulation. The process of acquisition often involves the negotiation of 'need' and household priorities, a negotiation where male teleworkers can be more successful, and at times telework can be a catalyst for purchases already desired. Telework ICTs can not only provide the basis for new competences, self-esteem, and the creation of expertise, but can also be empowering. As regards usage, there were few cases where ICTs were only used for work. Telecoms products which already had a domestic identity were more likely to be used by other households members. The pattern of computer use by partners was noticeably gendered, while children often used the equipment to develop keyboard literacy or, in the case of younger children familiarity with the machine. As regards applications, there were early signs of the fax finding non-work uses. Within the home, the main use of computers apart from games remained word-processing although various ICTs were also used to keep records of official communications. ICTs and ICT-skills could act as a community resource.

We end this paper on a broader set of observations. In the course of answering our initial questions, this paper has illustrated how important it is to look beyond the data on possession and usage that are routinely collected in quantitative data. To make sense of and go beyond that data, we must appreciate the meanings which these technologies initially have and later take on within the home - meanings which are negotiated and struggled over. This was a key theme of our earlier work (Silverstone, 1991; Haddon and Silverstone, 1992) and has now, more concretely, been examined in this paper. Hence, our stress on the significance of attempts to regulate technologies, and on the role which ICTs come to play for individuals and households: in helping to maintain or regain control of various aspects of their lives, and in helping them to forge identities.

Second, this paper raises questions about how we might conceptualise the diffusion of new ICTs. Traditionally, studies of diffusion focus on when technologies cross the threshold into the household. In contrast, we want to understand not only the process of acquisition, but the subsequent career of those technologies - in terms of 'diffusion' to others, and changes in the identity and role of those technologies from being work machines to finding domestic or community applications.

Finally, there is the significance of telework. At one level, telework provides a very useful case study for exploring some of the above points. Although it does not make such a radical difference to daily life as its potential flexibility promises, it nevertheless makes a considerable difference to people's lives. It is a sufficiently new way of working that it throws up new issues, conflicts and ways of organising life in the home -

in which ICTs are involved. But teleworking also serves as more than an illustration. There is very little research on the consequences of ICTs entering the home for work purposes, and clearly telework, as well as work which spills over from the office, is one, perhaps increasingly, important route into the home for these new technologies. This research has a made a start in charting the consequences of this mode of entry and showing where telework does, and for the moment does not, make a difference to the technological culture of the home.

REFERENCES

Haddon, L. and Silverstone, R. (1992) *Information and Communication Technologies in the Home: The Case of Teleworking*, CICT, Working Paper 17, Science Policy Research Unit, University of Sussex.

Huws, U. (1988) 'Remote possibilities: some difficulties in the analysis and quantification of telework', in Korte, W. et.al.(eds.), Telework: Present Situation and Future Development of a New Form of Work Organisation, Amsterdam, Elsevier Science Publishers.

Silverstone, R. (1991) *Beneath the Bottom Line: Households and Information and Communication Technologies in the Age of the Consumer*, PICT Policy Research papers, 17.

THE NEW SPACE RACE

David B. Crosbie

SATELLITE MOBILE COMMUNICATIONS

Geostationary orbits have long been the most valued positions for communications satellites. Since *Intelsat 1* was launched in 1965, this band of space has become almost cluttered with satellites providing direct TV broadcasting telecoms relays, international video links and other services. Other orbital patterns have been largely ignored – at least as far as communications are concerned – since the early days of space technology.

The first satellites occupied low Earth orbits by technological default – the rockets of their day could not lift them any higher. The first two-way voice and television communication by satellite took place in August 1960 using a passive, reflective inflatable 'balloon' named *Echo 1* which orbited every 2 hours at an altitude of 1500 km At that time, the common vision of satellite telecoms was that long-distance telephone calls would be relayed by a fleet of LEO satellites, each taking over as its predecessor passed out of sight; Intelsat was first formed with this scheme in mind, although it soon became obsolete.

Today Intelsat provides fixed intercontinental links with a fleet of geostationary satellites. However, there is another branch of telephony that is just starting to take advantage of space technology: mobile.

The only existing major operator of mobile telephony by satellite is Inmarsat (the International Maritime Satellite Organisation), which has progressed from providing systems for large ocean-going vessels to the suitcase-sized Earth stations that allowed reporters to give vivid live accounts of allied air attacks on Baghdad in 1991 This sort of advance has helped Inmarsat grow at over 40% per year for the past 4 years, earning US$300 million revenue in 1992 from just 12,000 terminals, whose owners pay over $10 per minute to use their phones.

This success, together with the more general takeoff of mobile telephony services, has drawn other competitors into the market.

In the past few years, a number of large US companies – many of them hoping to recycle expertise gained from the SDI (President Reagan's Strategic Defense Initiative, or 'Star Wars' programme) – have come to realise that LEOs could allow a cheaper service to attract a much larger market.

The great advantage of LEO over geostationary orbits is that the satellite is much closer to the user's terminal. The shorter signal path reduces transmission delays from 230 ms to around 40 ms, and the signal loss by around 21 dB. This allows a hand-held terminal and omni-directional antenna to work without microwaving the user's brain.

On the other hand, the system becomes quite complicated: to guarantee uninterrupted communications requires enough satellites to ensure that, when one sets over the horizon, there is always another rising

Table 1 Major LEO services planned for launch within the next 10 years.

Description	Iridium	Globalstar	Odyssey	Aries	Ellipso
Sponsor	Motorola Brazilian Government, United Comms of Thailand, Raytheon	Loral Qualcomm, Aerospatiale Alenia Alcatel, DASA	TRW Inc. Matra Marconi Space	Defense Sciences, International Microspace Pacific Comms Sciences	Mobile Communications Holdings Inc. Matra Group, Fairchild
Operator	Iridium Inc.	Globalstar	TRW	Constellation	Ellipso
Constructor	Lockheed	sponsors	sponsors	sponsors	Fairchild
Service	voice, radiopaging	voice, GPS, radiopaging	voive, GPS	voice, data, radiopaging	voice, data, radiopaging for USA only
No. of satellites	66	48	12	48	24

Table 1 Major LEO services planned for launch within the next 10 years.

Description	Iridium	Globalstar	Odyssey	Aries	Ellipso
Orbit	polar circular, 765 km inclined 87°	circular, 1389 km inclined 52°	elliptical, 10,000 km inclined 55°	polar circular 1000 km inclined 90°	elliptical 429-2903 inclined 64°
Switching and Processing	onboard cellular switching inter-satellite links	ground-based switching	ground-based switching	ground-based switching	ground-based switching
Multiplexing	FDMA/TDMA	CDMA	CDMA	CDMA	FDMA/CDMA
Investment	$3400 million	$1500 million	$800 million	$500 million	$280 million
Operational	1998	1999	1997	1998	1997

to take over the call. This handover is not simple to manage. However, unlike handover in cellular networks, it is very predictable; the satellites are moving at roughly 7500 m/s, making even aircraft appear practically stationary in comparison.

SERVICES

It is possible to distinguish two types of LEO system in the present batch of proposals: 'little' LEOs, for data services, and 'big' LEOs for both voice and data service, aiming to serve millions of terminals at a call charge of a few dollars per minute.

Obviously, a major attraction of such a service would be its global nature, which means that a terminal will use the same frequencies regardless of where it is. Under US pressure, the international radio-frequency conference WARC 92 allocated worldwide frequencies to both types of LEO system: frequencies around L6 and 25 GHz for big LEOs, and a VHF allocation (140 MHz) for little LEO services. The latter carries only secondary status in Europe, which will effectively prevent it from being used there.

Two companies, Orbcomm and Starsys, have gained initial regulatory approval from the US Federal Communications Commission (FCC) and plan to test prototype systems this year, with commercial services planned for 1995/96. Services will include global two-way messaging and the tracking of terminals; these would be most useful for relaying research data from remote locations, and for tracking people and animals. The terminals are very small and simple, operate at VHF frequencies and should not cost more than a few hundred dollars. If continuous coverage is not required, these systems can start with a few satellites and work up to about 24 for full coverage.

Of big LEO systems, the biggest is Motorola's Iridium; Iridium satellites will each contain something akin to a cellular base station. Other systems will use regional Earth stations, with the satellites acting as repeaters (dubbed the 'bent pipe' configuration): Qualcomm/Loral's Globalstar, Constellation's Aries and TRW's Odyssey will work in this way.

All the systems are to use digital transmission technology. Most systems have opted for code-division multiple access (CDMA), which allows several lightly-loaded systems to coexist in the narrow frequency band currently assigned to this application.

CDMA technology was developed for the military as an inherently encrypted method that can overcome interference or jamming. The technique involves multiplying the signal by a high-bit-rate pseudorandom code. To recover the data, the receiver must know the pseudorandom code: without it, the signal looks like relatively low-level noise. Because the average power is low, many CDMA transmitters can share the same frequency band, each using a different (orthogonal) pseudorandom code. The total number of users is limited by the total power-spectrum for the band.

CDMA's capacity is not necessarily greater than that of TDMA, but it avoids the need for synchronisation between transmitters, so one band can simply be shared between several rival networks.

CDMA signals must be decoded before they are switched, which requires more processing complexity than a small satellite can easily carry at present.

The exception is Iridium, which has chosen time-division multiple access (TDMA) because of its unique decision to relay calls directly by inter-satellite microwave links before handing them to the Earth station nearest their destination. This allows international calls to be handled entirely by the constellation, but means that each satellite must contain a cellular switch, rather than just receiving and retransmitting the signal back to the regional earth station. Iridium satellites have been criticised for being too complicated.

It is difficult for both TDMA and CDMA systems to share the same narrow frequency allowance, so Iridium is arguing against the other system proponents about how this resource should be split. The judge and jury is the FCC which strictly governs US coverage only, but its decision will probably have international consequences. The European Commission, among other bodies, is clearly unhappy that the rest of the world is having no say in this decision; one suggestion is to extend the International Telecommunication Union to become a global regulator, but it seems likely that the FCC will act before any international rival is established, presenting the world with a *fait accompli*.

Satellite systems are seen as complementing rather than competing with, existing cellular services; one idea is to combine both into one handheld phone such that the celestial system can be used if the user is outside cellular coverage, or the local system is incompatible. It is therefore desirable that the two systems have as much in common as possible.

Iridium's TDMA multiplexing standard is similar to that of the European digital cellular standard (GSM), which will also be implemented in Australia, Singapore, Hong Kong and possibly China. The future US standard is less clear: there are four contenders, and although the Cellular Telephone Industry Association recently endorsed a CDMA-based standard, the battle will go on for some time.

ORBITS

Geostationary satellites orbit around the equator (0° inclination) at an altitude of 36,000 km, to a European observer, they appear stationary at about 40° above the southern horizon.

LEO satellites orbit at altitudes of between 200 and 1600 km, generally completing an orbit in something under 2 hours.

Most of the proposed LEO satellite orbits are inclined by about 60° to the equator, an exception is Motorola's 66 Iridium satellites, which have 90° inclination and so orbit via the poles.

The Earth rotates independently of the satellites' orbit, so each satellite scans the Earth's surface in a series of broad north-south cycles. To a ground observer satellites will appear to rise from one horizon and set over the other some 15 minutes later.

Little-LEO satellites weigh around 120 kg – much less than the 2-4 tonnes of a geostationary satellite. This means that they can be launched on relatively small launchers, based on missile technology.

Big-LEO satellites weigh from 150 to 700 kg; the plan is to launch five to eight of these at a time with a conventional rocket such as *Ariane 4*, although small launchers may be used to replace individual satellites if they are light enough.

Because both big and little LEO satellites will come off a production line, rather than being built individually by hand, they should be considerably cheaper than conventional satellites. This technique could fundamentally change the satellite industry.

Also included under the general heading of LEOs are highly elliptical orbit (HEO) satellites: these swoop to within 200-500 km of the Earth before soaring to 10,000-40,000 km. HEO satellites may be used for communications for between 2 and 8 hours in the higher portion of their orbit. TRW intends to use 12 large satellites in a HEO, rather than 48 to 66 small satellites in a LEO, as proposed by the other would-be operators. This configuration sacrifices some of the advantage of the short signal path; on the other hand, fewer satellites make for a simpler and cheaper system.

ECONOMICS

All the big LEO systems are likely to cost between US$2 billion and $4 billion, while a regional mobile system using two geostationary satellites, such as that of American Mobile Satellite Corporation, would cost $400 million. To justify such a large investment in satellites and ground stations requires a global market with over a million users.

To raise these billions of dollars, the systems' proponents are now negotiating with the world's PTTs and other operators for equity and banks for debt. They are in a difficult position: projected returns of 35 per cent compare well with investment in cellular networks, but the technology is commercially unproven and market size is difficult to forecast. Cellular services are rapidly spreading into rural areas and developing countries. To complicate matters, service providers must obtain permission to operate separately in each country they cover; individual governments will be looking to protect their own service providers and raise revenue from any new service in their territory.

For political reasons, Inmarsat, as an international organisation, may have an advantage in gaining approval to operate in various countries. It also has more experience than most of its rivals. On the other hand, its plans for handheld voice terminals are some way behind those of some other companies. It is still conducting studies to determine the most suitable satellite configuration.

Maritime services are Inmarsat's core business, worth over $200 million a year in revenues. Complete worldwide marine coverage from a LEO system requires inter-satellite links because of the remoteness of the 'local' ground station. Coastal shipping and pleasure craft are particularly interesting markets. Some boats already carry cellular radios, as the UK cellular system can sometimes be used as far away as Calais.

Little LEO systems face less of a challenge, if only because they are simpler and therefore cheaper. The short-term market is likely to come from existing users of satellite data systems such as Argos, Inmarsat-C and AMSC: applications such as remote data collection, users including small boats, journalists and aid agencies. Their relative cheapness may allow usage to expand rapidly, and there is probably enough demand for both systems.

Big LEOs are a more doubtful proposition; most market forecasts suggest that there is room in the market for just a few satellite systems. Hence there is intense competition to attract international investors – particularly those that would help in the hunt for operating licences. These are granted by the governments of each country, but the local telephone operator often has a major influence and therefore makes an ideal partner. Market momentum will be important: the greater the potential market accessible to an operator, the more attractive it becomes to investors and other licensing authorities and the lower the commercial risk As a result, some systems may never even get off the ground.

INDEX

Abbey National, 186, 190
Abrams, Philip, 60
access
    to books (visually impaired
        learners), 10, 179, 224–35
    differential (material resources),
        270–3
    to education (ISDN), 211–22
    to education (RBL), 10, 216–17,
        237–47
    to ICTs (telework), 342, 395, 400–12
    inequality and, 90–8
    in information society, 63, 67–8
    to IT devices (ownership patterns),
        10, 268, 311–39
    to telephone, 37–9
    to telephone networks, 268, 284–306
    universal, 37–9, 98
accessible material, 231
accidents (of software systems), 359,
    361–3, 364
Acorn, 275–6, 277
active construction, 250–1
active learning, 242
actor network approach, 42–3, 49
ACTT (Association of Cinematograph
    and Television Technicians), 168,
    169
Ada (software language), 363–4,
    411, 415, 417–19
advanced countries, 139–40
Advanced Research Agency, 387
advertising, 49
aged (telephone usage), 295–7
Akrich, M., 85
Alaska Instructional Communications
    Consortium, 200
Algol software, 374
Allied Carpets, 186
Allott, M., 97
Alvey Programme, 27, 59
American Bell Telephone, 36, 38
American Mobile Satellite Corporation,
    408
American Telephone and Telegraph,
    36–7, 39, 64, 182
AMSC satellite data system, 409
Amstrad, 271
Annual Abstract of Statistics, 330
answer machines (telephone), 312, 318,
    405–7
APL software, 374
Apple Computers, 49, 182, 281, 334, 409

Appleyard, B., 336
appropriation (of technology for social
    ends), 50
Argos satellite data system, 419
Ariane 4 (satellite launcher), 418
Aries satellite system, 414–15, 416
Aronson, Sidney, 289
artificial intelligence, 25–7, 65, 364–5
    robotics, 103–12
artificial reality, 388, 392
Ascherson, N., 45
ASLEF, 166
Association of Cinematograph and
    Television Technicians (ACTT), 168,
    169
Association for Progressive
    Communication, 93, 95
Association of Southeast Asian Nations,
    111
AT&T (American Telephone and
    Telegraph), 36–7, 39, 64, 182
Atari, 278, 280, 389
Atkinson, J., 154
atomic power, 350–1
attitudes (adoption of technology-based
    training), 190–1
audio-conferencing, 193, 198–9, 204,
    206
audio-graphics, 198–9, 213–14, 218–19
Audio Visual Centre (Dublin), 215
Australia (telephone survey), 268,
    284–306
automatic programming, 366–7
automation , 9, 103–12
axial principle, 55, 66

B & Q retail, 183
Bacsich, P.D., 200
Baldry, C., 173
Ballistic Missile Office, 23
Balzer, R., 365, 366
Barbay, Dr., 38
Barclaycard, 186
Barker, B., 214
Barme, L., 205
Barnard, J., 218
Barnes, B., 21
basic knowledge phase
    product cycle model, 18–26, 28
    telephone system development, 11,
        33, 36
batch production, 24
Bates, A.W., 218
Batstone, E., 150, 152–3, 167, 172–4
Baudrillard, J., 49

BBC project (computer literacy), 267, 275–6, 277
Beard, R., 196
Bedaux system, 172
Bell, Alexander Graham, 11, 33–7, 39, 40, 207
Bell, Daniel, 55–7, 59, 63, 65–6
Bell, Diane, 285–6
Bell, Melville, 33
Bell Company, 11, 35
Bellcore Laboratories
  Cruiser videotelephony system developed at, 203
Benford, S., 205
Beniger, James, 58
Bennett, N. 253
Berg, A.-J., 74–5
Bessant, J., 151
Bijker, W.E., 16, 42, 83
binary code, 12
Biocca, Frank, 394
biological engineering, 22
biotechnology, 135, 138–41, 146
Birkinshaw, 348
'black box' technology, 14, 15, 19
Blanc, Honoré, 415
blind learners, 10, 179, 224–35
Bloor, D., 21
Bly, S.A., 198, 203
Boalt, C., 74, 86
Boddy, D., 143, 149–50, 173–4
Boder, A., 202
Boehm, B.W., 372
Bolter, David, 66
Booch, G., 363
books for visually impaired learners, 10, 179, 224–35
Boots (the Chemist), 183–4
bottom-up approach (to managing change), 163–4, 167–8, 170–1
boundary maintenance, 405–6, 410
Bowser, D., 217
BPI, 337
Braid, M., 338
braille, 224–7, 229, 231–5 *passim*
Branscomb, A., 97
Braverman, H., 43, 114, 120, 126, 151, 154, 172
Britain, 63
  computerized machine tools, 126–33
  flexible specialization, 144–7, 121–4
  telephone access, 39, 40
British Aerospace, 355
British Airways, 184, 187
British Gas South East, 190

British Market Research Bureau, 319–22, 323–4, 326–8, 329, 331–2, 335
British Radio and Electronic Manufacturers (BREMA), 327
British Rail, 62, 165–6, 170–1, 174–5
British Telecom, 166–8, 170–1, 174–5, 186, 193, 312, 316–7, 396
British Videogram Association, 327
Brooks, F.P., 367, 394, 377, 378
Brown, J.S., 255, 256
Brown R.H., 98
Bruner, J.S., 196, 260
Bubble Dialogue, 206, 249, 257–61, 263
Buchanan, D.A., 143, 149–50, 163, 171, 173–4
bulletin-board system, 34, 40
Burdene, P.A., 93
business IT, technology-based training, 186–8
business telephones, 312–13, 316–17
Butterworth, G., 255–6
buy *versus* build (software), 369–70

C++ language, 378, 382, 384–6
Callon, M., 42
capitalism, 114, 119–20, 172
  future of work, 141, 144–6
  information society, 56–7, 60, 68
  information technology and, 91–3
'Capitalism Triumphant', 135, 147
Caro, Robert, 19
Carr, E.H., 136
Carter, M., 336
CASE software, 379
case studies (social shaping), 21–6
Cash Cow, 11, 35–40
CD-ROM
  ownership pattern, 10, 268, 311, 336–8
  visually impaired learners, 10, 179, 224–35
CDMA technology, 406–7
cell patterns (Iridium system), 353–5
Cellnet, 318
Cellular Telephone Industry Association, 407
changeability (software), 360–1
charging policy (telephone use), 303–6
Charles Stark Draper Laboratory, 23
Child, J., 43, 152–5, 162, 163, 173
Chrysler
  comparative productivity, 109
Chute, A., 213
Cincinnati Milacron, 105

Clark, J., 150, 167, 168, 174
Cleanroom, 379, 382
Clegg, C., 159, 160
'closure' of technology, 42, 46, 50
Cobol software, 370, 374, 379, 384
Cockburn, C., 49, 75, 326
code-division multiple access, 416–17
cognitive approach, 250–3, 255–6, 262
Cold War, 65
CoLearn system, 202, 205, 213
collaboration, 246–7
collaborative learning, 253–4, 256, 262
    computer supported, 10, 192–207
Collins, A., 255, 256
Collis, B., 202
commoditization of information, 97
Commodore, 271, 272, 275, 277
communication technologies
    (consumption of), 42, 44–9
communications, satellite mobile, 403–6
Communications Act (1934), 98
communications systems, 198–203
compact disc player (ownership
    pattern), 10, 268, 311, 336–8
compact disc technology, 224–35
company training needs, 182–91
compatibility
    conformity of software, 360
    off-the-shelf software, 370, 382–3
    standardization of training, 138,
        185–6, 190
complexity (software systems), 359–60
CompuServe, 34
computer conferencing, 180, 193,
    198–204, 206, 212, 257
computer games, 277–9, 281
computer games console (ownership
    patterns), 10, 268, 311, 335–6
computer numerical control, 102, 183
    British/German firms, 126–33
    social shaping case study, 23–4
computer supported collaborative
    learning, 10, 192–207
computerized machine tools, 126–33
computers
    access and inequality, 90–8
    Fifth Generation project, 27, 65
    group working with, 252–4
    home (contextualising), 267–8,
        269–81
    home (ownership patterns), 10, 268,
        311, 329–35
    home micro (multiple meanings),
        274–9
    for teleworking, 402, 406–11 passim
    for visually impaired learners, 224–6

see also software engineering
Conceptual Change in Science project,
    261–3
conflicts (role), 253, 262
conformity (software systems), 360
Connolly, A., 173
Constellation Aries, 414–5, 416
constructivist learning theories, 249–63
consultants, 188–9
consumers
    ownership patterns, 10, 311–39
    'prosumers', 92–3
    sovereignty, 48
    women as, 83–5
consumption of
    information/communication
    technologies, 42, 44–9
contingency approach, 16, 17, 164
control
    cues/signal, 205
    of labour, 9, 114, 150–62, 174, 342
    by learner, 238, 244–5
    objectives, 150, 165, 167, 173–5
    search activities, 230–1
    selection and intervention, 229–30
    social, 63, 206–7
    structure of, 115–17
    system (in smart house), 78, 80
'control revolution', 58
Control of Space Invaders (and other
    electronic games) Bill (1981), 279
convergence
    CNC application, 128–9
    telework, 400–12
    virtual reality, 387–96
    see also group work; integration;
        networks
Coombs, N., 204
cooperation (in groups), 194–6, 197
Copernican revolution, 380–1
Corbusier, 85
cost-effective training, 184–5
costs
    CD-ROM material, 231–2
    charging for telephone use, 303–6
    of labour, 9, 43, 101, 151–3, 162
    operating (Iridium system), 356
    software, 369–70
Cowan, R.S., 49, 74–5, 83, 86
Cringley, R.X., 92
Crompton, R., 43
Cronberg, Tarja, 74
Cruiser videotelephony system 203
Cullen, M., 95
cultural and media studies, 42, 44–9,
    267

cultural practices (CNC operations), 127–8
culture of information, 65–7
Cunningham, D., 261
Curien, N., 200
current activities (Iridium system), 355
cyberspace, 91

Damon, W., 196
Daniel, W., 122, 151, 161
Danko, W.D., 269
Davies, A., 163, 164
Davis, A., 251
Day, Alice, 297
de-skilling, 9, 43, 101–2, 116–17, 126, 130–1, 141–4, 151–2, 154–5, 172, 175
death stage (product life cycle), 40
decentralized training, 186
decision-making, 102, 151, 157
    see also management choice
Dede, C.J., 192
Defense Science Board, 369
deferred time, 201
'defining technology', 66–7
deindustrialization, 64
DeLamarter, R.T., 92
Department of Education and Science, 267, 275
Derycke, A.C., 202, 205
design, 48, 83–4
    of products/services, 18–26, 28
    telephone system development, 33–40
'design space', 167, 171, 175
designers
    great (of software), 372–4
    of smart house developments, 78–80
desktop conferencing, 180, 193, 198, 204, 212
'desktop metaphor', 367
desktop virtual reality, 390, 391
developing countries, 140–1
developmental theories of learning
    Bubble Dialogue, 257–61
    cognitive approach, 250–2
    Conceptual Change in Science, 261–3
    social context of learning, 254–5
    use of information technology, 255–7
    working in groups with computers, 252–4
Diamond, John, 238
Dickerson, M., 269
diffusion of innovation, 270–3
diffusion of technology

material resources, 270–3
product-cycle model, 18–26, 28
telephone system development, 33–40
Digital Equipment Corporation, 183
Digital Radio Concentrator Scheme, 302
Dilic, R.F., 49
Dimension
    virtual reality software producer, 391
direct numerical control, 183
disabled learners (access to education), 10, 179, 224–35
disconnections (social resources), 273–4
discrimination in recruitment, 144–5
discursive resources (home computers), 274–9
distance learning, 10, 180, 192–3, 212
distancing, 261
distribution of incomes/wealth, 96–7
distribution of infrastructure, 94–6, 98
division of labour
    international, 114
    responsible autonomy, 115–17, 122
    sexual, 74, 76, 81–2, 85–6
    Taylorist, 9, 101, 104, 115–19, 121, 123–4, 138, 172–3
DM3 program, 262
'Dog' stage (product life-cycle), 40
domestic consumption of information, 42, 47–9
domestic responsibilities, telework and, 401, 403–12
Donaldson, M., 251, 254, 260
Douglas, M., 46–7
Draper, 262
Drayson, P.R., 25, 26
Drexel, I., 120
Driver, R., 261–2
Duguid, P., 255, 256
Düll, K., 118
'Dungeons and Dragons', 392
Dutton, W.H., 270, 271

E-Mail, 408
Eastman Kodak, 185, 186
Echo 1 (satellite), 413
economic activity (location), 139–41
economics (satellite systems), 418–19
Edge, D.O., 22
Edgeworth, 21
Edigo, C., 200
Edinburgh case studies, 14, 21–6
Edison, Thomas Alva, 17, 20
education, 9
    access to (ISDN), 211–22
    access to (RBL), 10, 216–17, 237–47

access to (visually impaired), 10,
    179, 224–35
applications of virtual reality 389–91
distance learning, 10, 180, 192–3,
    212
home computer use, 267, 275–7,
    280–1
inequalities, 96
Micros in Schools scheme, 267,
    275–7
National Curriculum, 228, 231, 234–5
see also learning; learning and
    information technology
educators (technology mediation),
    206–7
Edwards, A.D.N., 226
'effects' (social shaping), 18–20
Einstein, Albert, 360
electronic
    funds transfer, 184
    news gathering, 168–71
    point of sale, 184
Ellipso satellite system, 414–15
Ellis, Stephen, 394
Ellus, Jacques, 69
embedded training, 187–8
employee qualifications (CNC), 130–2
employment skills, 235
encoding, 47–8, 50
ENG technology, 168–71
ENIAC, 56
entertainment
    application of virtual reality, 391–4
    see also leisure
environments (software), 368
epicycles
    in planetary motion, 380–1
equality, 63
    access and inequality, 90–8
    access for visually impaired, 10,
        224–35
    equal opportunities legislation, 144
    telephone charging policy, 303–6
Erickson, J., 92
Erikson, W.J., 373
ESPRIT, 27
essence of software systems, 358–76
ethnic minorities (discrimination), 145
eugenics, 22
EUREKA, 27
European Commission, 417
expert systems, 364, 365–6
extra-terrestrial relays, 344–51
Exxon, 64
Fabrik, 378, 384
factory system, 103–4

Fahlén, L., 205
Fall Joint Computer Conference (1968)
    origins of virtual reality, 388
Family Expenditure Survey, 271
Family Spending, 314–16, 319, 323, 325,
    330, 333–4
FANUC plant, 24, 107–8
fax machine, 405–6, 408–11
Featherstone, M., 45, 47
Federal Communications Commission,
    352, 416, 417
feedback loops, 19–21, 24, 26, 27
Feigenbaum, Edward, 65
feminine culture of telephone, 284–306
feminism, 74, 75
feminization of American telephone, 39
Fiat, 109
Fifth Generation project, 27, 65
financial aspects (telework), 407–8
Fine, D., 253
Fish, R.S., 203
Fleck, J., 18, 24, 25
flexibility of innovation process, 14
flexible education, 192
flexible firms, 154–5
flexible manufacturing system, 159, 183
flexible specialization, 114–24
flight simulators, 388
Ford, Henry, 172
Fordism, 104, 124, 137–8
forecasting (future work), 136, 139
Fortran, 374
Forty, Adrian, 48
Foulkes, George, 279
France
    history of telecommunications, 38
    telematique system, 63
France Telecom, 193
Francis, A., 150, 163
Fransman, M., 23
Frederick, H., 95
Freeman, C., 137–8
Friedman, A., 43, 116
Fujitsu, 24, 110, 111
full life-cycle of technology, 12, 42,
    49–50
functional encoding, 48, 50
Furness, Tom, 394
further education (skills), 235
future use of virtual reality, 394–6
futures, *see* information technology
    (futures)
futurism, 57, 58, 59

GABe, Frances, 83
Gale, S., 199
Galileo Galilei, 380
Galton, M., 21, 253
gender discrimination, 144–5
gendered
  inequalities, 96
  innovation process, 85–6
  socio-technical construction (smart
    house), 74–86
  technology, 85–6
General Household Survey, 324, 331,
  338
General Motors, 136, 186
Genie, 34
Gensollen, M., 200
Gentry, J., 269
geostationary satellites, 343–51, 356,
  413–9
Germany
  computerized machine tools, 126–33
  flexible specialisation, 114–21, 123–4
Gershuny, J., 16
Gibson, W., 91
Gill, C., 173
globalisation, 193
  access and inequality, 93–7 *passim*
  geostationary satellites, 343–51, 356,
    413–9
  information society, 62–5, 68
  robotics, 110–12
  satellite mobile communications,
    413–9
  telephone system, 40
  virtual reality, 395–6
Globalstar, 414–5, 416
Golden Vapourwate, 11, 33, 36
Golding, P., 271
Goodal, P., 44
Goodwin, R., 214
Goofy Prototype, 11, 33–5
Gore, Al, 98, 394–5
Gorz, A., 74
Gourlay, S.,150
Graham, J., 279
Grant, E.E., 373
graphical programming, 367
Graphton, R.B., 367
Gray, A., 47, 326
Griliches, Z., 19
group process support systems, 198,
  202
group technology, 138
group work
  collaboration/cooperation, 194–7

with computers, 252–4
resource-based learning, 246–7
groupware development, 205–6
grow don't build (software), 371–2
Grudin, J., 207
GSM (digital cellular standard), 417
Gullestad, M., 74, 85
Gunawardena, C., 216, 220
Gunter, B., 328

Hacker Crackdown (US telephones),
  33–40
Haddon, L., 45, 47, 49, 274, 277, 411
Hagelskjaer, E., 74, 86
Hall, John, 381, 382
Hall, P.H., 269
Hall, Stuart, 45, 46
Hamelink, Cees, 68
Handy, C., 90
Hansell, C.W., 344
Harasim, L., 201
Harding, S., 75
Harrison, M.R., 157, 159, 160
Hartley, J., 196
Hawke, Bob, 64
Hawke, D.F., 381
Hawkridge, D., 224
Healy, L., 253
Heeren, E., 202
Henwood, Felicity, 144
Heppell, S., 242
'heterogeneous engineering', 43
Hewlett Packard, 183
high-level languages, 362, 363
highly elliptical orbit satellites, 408
Hill, S., 49
Hillis, Durrell, 355
Hirsch, E., 47
HITL project, 390, 392, 396
home
  feminine culture of telephone,
    284–306
  ownership of IT devices, 10, 311–39
  smart houses, 74–86
  telework in, 10, 400–12
home computers
  contextualising, 267–8, 269–81
  multiple meanings, 274–9
  ownership patterns, 10, 268, 311,
    329–35
Home Office, 144
Honeywell house, 76–7
  housework in, 78
  technologies, 78
Hooper, S., 196

Hounshell, D.A., 17
housework, 267
   in smart houses, 74–6, 78, 79, 80–4
   telework and, 401, 403–12
Hoyles, C., 253
Hughes, T.P., 17, 18, 20, 42
Hughes Aircraft Company, 356
Human Interface Technology
   Laboratory, 390, 392, 396
human technology interface
   actor network approach, 42–3, 49
   HITL project, 390, 392, 396
   Information Finder interface, 233
   resource-based learning, 242–7
   training, see training
   virtual reality, 387–96
   for visually impaired learners, 10,
      224–35
Hund, A., 348
Huws, U., 400
hypertext, 202, 226–7

IBM, 64, 92, 187, 200, 271, 281
Ichikawa, T., 367
identification, 261
ideology, 48, 69
IEEE, 364, 365
Illich, I.D., 196
image recognition, 364–5
implementation (social shaping), 17–18
income distribution, 96–7
incremental development (software),
   371
Independent Broadcasting Authority,
   168
industrial relations, 16–17, 62, 115,
   121–2, 151–2, 156–62, 165–71
Industrial Relations Research Unit, 151,
   161
industrial revolution (new), 103–12
industrial revolution (software), 377–82
INECO, 337
inequality, 13
   access and, 90–8
inference-engine technology, 365, 366
information
   access, 216–17, 237–47
   commoditization, 97
   culture, 65–7
   dissemination systems, 241
   economy, 55, 61–2, 97–8
   -handling skills, 240–1, 245, 247
   management, 97
   superhighway, 98, 394–5
   transfer, 64
   workers, 61–2

Information and Communications
   Technologies, telework and, 10, 341,
   342, 395, 400–12
Information Finder disc, 233
information ownership
   control by learners, 238, 244–5
   home computing, 267–8, 269–81
   IT devices in home, 10, 268, 311–39
information society, 12, 54
   critiques, 67–70
   global aspects, 62–5, 68
   postindustrialism, 55–7
   problematic status, 59–61
   social forecasters/planners, 57–9
   themes, 61–7
information system design, 41
information technology
   capitalism and, 91–3
   domestic consumption of, 42, 44–9
   future of work and, 135–47
   impact, 9–10
   production processes, 138
   product and services, 139–40
   skills, 234–5
   society and (theorising), 41–50
information technology
   (developments), 9
   access and inequality, 90–8
   differing perspectives, 11–13
   information society, 54–70
   smart house, 74–86
   social shaping, 14–28
   society and, 41–50
   US telephone network, 33–40
information technology (futures), 10,
   341–3
   extra-terrestrial relays, 344–51
   Iridium, 352–7
   software engineering, 358–76,
      377–86
   space race (new), 403–9
   telework, 390–402
   virtual reality, 377–86
information technology (in the home),
   267–8
   contextualizing home computing,
      269–81
   devices (ownership), 10, 268, 311–39
   feminine culture of telephone,
      284–306
information technology and learning,
   9–10, 179–81
   books for visually impaired learners,
      224–35
   computer supported collaborative
      learning, 192, 207

constructivist learning theories,
249–63
educational value of ISDN, 211–22
resource-based learning, 237–47
technology-based training 182–91
information technology in workplace, 9,
101–2
computerized machine tools, 126–33
flexible specialization, 114–24
robotics, 103–12
technological change, 135–47,
149–75
infrastructure, distribution of, 94–5, 96,
98
Ingals, D., 378
Inmarsat, 356–7, 413–5, 418–9
innovation, diffusion of, 270–3
innovation process, 14, 15, 85–6
innovations in labour regulation,
156–62
Institute of Manpower Studies, 122–3,
154–5
institutional context (ISDN), 211–12
instrumental technology, 56
instrumental telephone calls, 268, 285,
286–8, 297–9, 305
integrated services digital networks, 68,
193, 200
educational value of, 211–22
integration, 219, 235
of new technologies, 241–3
smart house, 78–80, 86
intellectual property rights, 97
Intelsat, 413
interaction
electronic networks, 62–3
learning through, 217–20, 242–4
mode, 242–3
virtual reality, 387–96
Interlisp, 362
internal labour market, 154, 157
internal services, 189
international division of labour, 114
International Federation of Information
Processing Congress, 387
International Maritime Satellite
Organization, 356–7, 413
International Telecommunication
Union, 417
Internet, 93
'interpretative flexibility', 16, 42
'interval variables', 21
intervention (NCET project), 229–30
intrinsic telephone calls, 268, 285–9,
292, 294, 297, 299–301, 305

invention (social shaping), 17–18
investigation skills, 240, 242
invisibility (software system), 361
Iowa School District, 199
Iridium, 343, 352–7, 414–18
Irvine Interactive Television System, 200
ISDN, 68, 193, 200
educational value of, 211–22
Isherwood, B., 46–7
ITU (International Telecommunication
Union), 417

Jacobs, A., 168
Jaguar, 186
Jameson, Fredric, 46
Japan, 27, 58–9, 65, 81, 104–9, 111,
139–40
JAROL, 105–6
Jefferson, Thomas, 382
job performance, 186
Johansen, R., 203
Johnson, Richard, 47
Johnson-Laird, P.N., 47
Joiner, R., 253, 262
Jonassen, D., 194
Jones, B., 150–1
Jones, G., 43
Jouet, J., 271
Jürgens, U., 118
'just-in-time' production, 23, 24, 104,
105
JVC, 311

Kaplinsky, R., 138
Kawasaki Heavy Industries, 106
Kaye, A.R., 195, 201, 202, 203
Kearfott, 23
Keen, B., 45
Kehoe, L., 334
Kemp, N., 159, 160
Kepler, Johannes, 380
Kerbrat, C., 203
Kern, H., 117–18, 119–20
Kiesler, S., 220
Kirvan, P., 211
knowledge, 196
constructivist theories, 250–1, 256
scientific, 21–6, 42
see also basic knowledge phase
Knowles, M.S., 196
Kramarae, Cheris, 303, 304
Krueger, Myron, 388, 392
Kuhn, T., 380
Kumar, Krishan, 62, 65

labour
  control, 9, 114, 150–62, 174, 342
  costs, 9, 43, 101, 151, 152–3, 162
  information workers, 61–2
  internal market, 154, 157
  polyvalency, 115–16, 212, 122–3, 154
  see also skills; training
labour process, 172
  flexible specialization, 114–24
  industrial relations, 16, 17, 62, 115,
    121–2, 151–2, 156–62, 165–71
labour regulation
  innovations in, 156–62
  technological change and, 152–5
language
  social context of learning, 254–5
  of telephone calls, 298–300
language (software)
  Ada, 363–4, 378, 382, 384–6
  high-level, 362, 363
  object-oriented, 363–4, 378–9, 385–6
Lanier, Jaran, 387, 389, 391, 394–5, 396
Larsen, J.K., 270
Latour, B., 42
Laure, L., 203
Laurillard, D., 243
Law, J., 42–3
learners
  visually impaired, 10, 179, 224–35
  see also students
learning, 9, 179
  approaches to, 180–1
  barriers, 224–35
  collaborative, see collaborative
    learning
  constructivist theories, 249–63
  developmental theories, 250–63
  distance education, 10, 180, 192,
    193, 212
  educational value of ISDN, 211–22
  resource-based, 10, 216–217, 237–47
  social context, 254–5
  through interaction, 217–20, 242–4
  virtual reality in classroom, 390–1
learning and information technology,
    9–10, 179–81
  books for visually impaired learners,
    224–35
  computer-supported collaborative
    learning, 192–207
  constructivist theories, 249–63
  educational value of ISDN, 211–22
  resource-based learning, 237–47
  technology-based training, 182–91
'learning webs', 196
Lee, Roswell, 381, 382

'Legend Quest', 392
Leiss, W., 46
leisure, 267, 277–9
  ownership of computer games
    console, 10, 268, 311, 335–6
  ownership of IT devices, 10, 311–39
  virtual reality application, 391–4, 396
Levy, M., 328
Ley, W., 346
liberal critique (information society),
    69–70
Lie, M., 74, 75, 85
linear model (innovation), 14, 18–20
Littler, C., 115, 172
Littleton, K., 252
Livenet, 200
location of economic activity, 139–41
Lockheed Corporation, 355
Lockwood, Lawrence, 357
LOGO, 249, 251–2, 263
long-distance telephones, 37
Loral Globalstar, 414–5, 416
Lovell, Bernard, 22
low earth orbit satellites, 352, 356,
    413–19
Luddite critique (information society),
    69–70
Lundberg, Olaf, 356–7
Lyon, D., 90

McCorduck, Pamela, 65
McGrath, J.E., 198
machines/machine production, 137
Mackay, Hughie, 49, 311
MacKenzie, Donald, 16, 19, 21–2, 23,
    26, 27, 41, 44
MacLachlan, J.M., 269
McLoughlin, I.P., 150, 162, 165, 168, 174
McMahon, H., 204, 206, 257, 260–1
MacNamara, 348
management choice
  implementing new technology,
    162–71
  objectives and, 149–52
  operation of new technology, 171–5
  in robotics, 102, 103–12
management objectives, 149–52
management sub-strategies, 162, 163–5
managerial practice (postwar), 115–17
Mandala (virtual reality game), 392–3
Marginson, P., 151
market research, 49
marketing, 48–9
Martin, James, 57
Martin, R., 151, 156, 161
Marx, Karl, 67

Marxism, 9, 56, 57, 101, 142, 146
Mason, R.D., 200, 201
Mason, Roy, 77, 82, 83
mass production, 114, 115–16
  Fordism, 104, 124, 137–8
Masuda, Yoneji, 58
material resources (computers), 270–3
materials
  new, 135, 139, 140
  role (resource-based learning),
    245–6
mathematical statistics (social shaping),
  21–2
Matsushita, 311
Meager, N., 154
media and cultural studies, 42, 44–9,
  267
Mercer, 255
Mercury, 312
meta-communicative signals, 205
Metaphor, 378
metaphors (in CSCL), 205
Mevarech, Z., 253
microelectronics, 55, 59, 61, 64, 68, 153,
  160–1
Micros in Schools scheme, 267, 275–7
Microsoft, 92–3, 187, 227
Midland Bank, 190
migrant women (telephone use),
  297–300
Miles, I., 80, 86
military technology, 65, 68, 388, 396,
  416
Miller, D., 46
Mills, H.D., 372
Milspec 216–7, 382
Mintel, 313–14, 317, 319–24, 326–32,
  334–6
missile guidance systems (social
  shaping), 23
Mitchell, J., 204
Mitsubishi, 64
mobile communications, 403–6
mobile telephone, 312–13, 317–18
mobilisation, 41
modern technologies (significant),
  137–8
Modula software, 364, 374
Moore, George, 93
Moores, S., 47
Mooser, J., 115
moral economies, 280–1
Morgan, J.P., 36
Morley, David, 45, 46
Morris, M.E., 201
Moses, Robert, 19, 20

Motorola, 110, 111, 352, 354–7, 414–6,
  418
MS-DOS software, 374
Mulkay, M.J., 22
multimedia conferencing, 180, 193,
  198–204, 206, 212, 214, 219
multinational companies, 110–12, 395–6
Mumford, Lewis, 66
Murdock, Graham, 269, 271, 273
Musco, Vincent, 305
MVS/370 software, 374
MX/Peacekeeper Advanced Inertial
  Reference Sphere, 23
MX missile, 64

NAHB smart house system, 77
  housework in, 81
  technologies in, 79
Naisbitt, J., 90, 93
NASA, 378, 384
National Association of Home Builders,
  77, 79, 81
National Cash Register, 92
National Council for Educational
  Technology, 227, 228–35
National Curriculum, 228, 231, 234–5
National Economic Development
  Office, 54
national institutions (CNC operation),
  127–8
national sovereignty, 64
National University Teleconferencing
  Network, 220
NATO Software Engineering
  Conference (1968), 377
navigational skills, 240, 245
NCET project, 228–35
neo-Marxism, 43
networks, 192–3
  social resources, 273–4
  telephone (women's), 268, 289–94
new materials, 139
newly industrializing countries
  (economic activity), 140–1
Nintendo, 281, 335, 336
Nissan, 107, 109
Noble, D.F., 16, 17, 44
Noble, Grant, 284, 292
'nominal variables', 21–2
Noording, H., 347
Norman, Don, 256
Northcott, J., 151, 156
Nyberg, A., 74–5

object-oriented programming, 363–4
object-oriented technologies, 378–79,
    385–6
Objective-C language, 378, 382, 384–6
objectives (resource-based learning),
    244–5
Odyssey satellite system, 414–5, 416
OECD countries, 140, 141
OECD report (biotechnology), 139
Olgren, C., 199
O'Neill, W., 204, 206, 257, 260–1
open learning, 192
    resource-based, 10, 216–17, 237–47
openness of technology, 45–6, 50
Opening up the Library for Visually
    Impaired Learners project, 228–35
operating costs (Iridium), 356
operating objectives, 150, 165, 167, 174
operational skills (resource-based
    learning), 240, 245
Orbcomm, 416
orbits (satellites), 417–18
organizational structure (CNC), 129–30
Orrod, S., 49
ownership patterns
    IT devices in the home, 10, 268, 311,
        339
    of products/services, 145

pace of change, 93–4
    diffusion of innovation, 270–3
    geostationary satellites, 344–51
    Iridium satellite system, 352–7
    software development, 342, 358–76,
        377–86
    teleworking, 341–2, 400–12
    virtual reality, 342, 387–96
Papert, Seymour, 251–2, 263
parallel processing, 206
Parker, L., 199
Parnas, D.L., 361, 364, 366
Pascal software, 374
Pearson, Karl, 22
peer collaboration, 10, 192–207
personnel management (role), 156–62
personnel structure (CNC process), 132
Peugeot, 109
Phelan, A., 215
Philips, 64, 337
Piaget, Jean, 250–6 passim, 263
Pike, Robert, 305
Pinch, T.J., 16, 42, 83
Piore-Sabel thesis, 114–15, 118, 119, 123
PL/1 software, 374
pleasure search (NCET project), 230–1
Plowman, L., 242, 245, 247

Policy Studies Institute, 151
political aspects (of information
    society), 62–5
Pollert, A., 154
polysemy, 46
polyvalency, 115–16, 121, 122–3, 154
Pool, I. de Sola, 45, 317
Porat, Marc, 61
Poseidon missile, 23
post-war managerial practice, 115–17
Post Office, 167
postal telephone and telegraph, 355,
    418
Poster, Mark, 57
postindustrialism, 55–9, 61–2, 64–6
Potter, S., 166
Powell, W.W., 16–17
Prais, S.J., 127
Preece, D.A., 154, 157, 159, 160
printed text (access for blind learner),
    226
privacy, 39, 63, 260–1, 286, 416
privatisation, 41, 312
pro-active policies, 27, 157
process innovation, 153
Prodigy, 34
product-cycle model, 18–26, 28
    telephone system development,
        33–40
product innovation, 153
production
    costs, 153
    processes (based on IT), 138–9
    see also flexible specialization;
        Fordism; mass production; Taylorism
products (information technology), 139
program verification, 368
Project 21, 356–7, 414–15
Prokopi, V., 85
prototypes
    product-cycle model, 18–26, 28
    smart houses, 74–86
    software system, 370–1
    telephone system development, 11,
        33–5
pseudorandom code, 406
Ptolemy, 386
PTTs, 355, 418
public service broadcasting, 60
public switched telephone networks,
    354
Purcell, J., 157

Qualcomm Globalstar, 414–15, 416
quality of working life, 141–4

Rada, Juan, 65
radio
     astronomy, 22
     globalisation, 344–51
     telephone, 302
Raeder, G., 367
Rajasingham, L., 212
Rakow, Lana, F., 294, 303–4
Rank Xerox, 189–90
reactive technology policies, 26–7, 157
Reagan administration, 271, 413
real time, 199–201
recruitment (discrimination), 144–5
reflection skills, 241, 242
Reinhardt, A., 193
remote access to information , 216–17
Report Program Generator, 370
requirements refinement (software),
     370–1
research
     findings (CNC), 127–32
     findings (telephone use), 287–95
     issues (collaborative learning), 196–8
     policy (social shaping), 26–8
     shaping/effects model, 18–20
     strategy (telephone use), 285–8
     research and development, 62, 68,
          139, 140
Research Machines, 275
residential telephones, 312–18
resource-based learning, 10, 216–17,
     237–47
resources sharing systems, 198, 201–2
resources (home computing), 269–81
responsible autonomy, 115–17, 122
reusable software components, 382–6
Rising Star, 11, 33–5
risk reduction, 189–90
Robinette, Warren, 392
Robins, K., 49, 90
robotics, 103–12, 388
     social shaping case study , 24–6
rocket design, 350
rockets, 344–51
Rogers, C., 196
Rogers, Everett, 270
Rogers, P., 156
Romiszowski, A., 212, 241
Rothwell, Sheila, 156–7, 158, 159
Rover, 186
Royal National Institute for the Blind,
     227
rule base (expert system) 365–6
rural women (telephone use), 300–3
Russell, S., 43

Saba, F., 217, 219
Sabel, C., 114–15, 118, 119, 123
Sackman, H., 373
Salaman, G., 172
Sangregorio, I.-L., 74
satellite systems
     geostationary satellites, 343–51, 356,
          413–19
     Iridium, 343, 352–7, 414–18
     mobile communications, 413–19
Scanlon, E., 261–2
Schiller, J., 204
Schofield, J., 92, 94
schools
     Micros in Schools, 267, 275–7
     National Curriculum, 223, 231, 234–5
     supporting resource-based learning,
          243–7
     see also education
Schrage, M., 194, 195
Schumann, M., 117–118, 119–20
Schumpeter, J.A., 137
science, 21–6
     conceptual change in, 261–3
scientific knowledge, 21–6, 42
scientific management, 49, 171–2
screen readers, 225–7, 232, 234
SDI, 413
search process (CD-ROM), 230–4
     passim
security
     anti-piracy devices, 278
     pseudorandom codes, 416
     role of telephone, 38–9, 296–7, 300,
          318
     in smart house, 78
     surveillance, 63, 341
Sega, 281, 311, 335–6
selection (NCET project), 229–30
Sengenberger, 119
Servan-Schrieber, Jacques, 64
services, 139, 416–17
sexual division of labour, 74, 76, 81–2,
     85–6
Shaiken, H., 17, 18
Shallis, Michael, 69
Shapin, S., 16
'shaping' studies, 18–20
Shepherd, D., 217
Shepherd, S., 335–6
Sherman, Mark, 363
Siemens, 64
Silber, O., 253
Silicon Valley, 389
silver bullet analogy, 358–76, 377–86

Silverstone, R., 47, 280, 411
Simula-67, 364
Sinclair, Clive, 275
Sinclair computers, 271–2, 275, 277–8
Sisson, K., 157
situated cognition, 255, 256–7, 263
skills
    de-skilling, 9, 43, 101–2, 116–17,
        126, 130–1, 141–4, 151–2, 154–5,
        172–3, 175
    flexible specialization, 114–24
    information-handling, 240–1, 245,
        247
    information technology, 234–5
    responsible autonomy, 115–17
    up-skilling, 123–4, 142–4, 174
    utilization (CNC), 126–33
Skirrow, G., 279
Slack, Jennifer, 69
SLANT project, 255
Slavin, R.E., 197
Sloanism, 49
Smalltalk, 374, 377–8, 382, 384, 386
smart house, 74–86
Smart House Development Venture Inc.
    (SHDVI), 77, 79
Smith, Adam, 137
Smith, C., 43
Smith, K., 220
Smith, S.L., 173
Smith, T., 213
Smith, T.W., 199
social change, 9, 14–28, 41, 60, 67
social constructivism, 42, 43, 49
social context, 192–3, 254–5, 260
social control, 63, 206–7
social engineering, 28
social forecasters, 57–9
social impacts, 14–15, 54, 57
social networks (teleworking), 406
social planners, 57–9
social resources (networks), 273–4
social shaping of technology, 14–28
    IT/society relationship, 41–50
Social Trends, 315, 322, 324, 327, 331,
    338
society/IT relationships, 41–50
Society of Cable Television Engineers
    (USA), 357
socio-cognitive conflict, 253
socioeconomic conditions (CNC), 128–9
sociology of scientific knowledge, 42
Software-ICs, 385
software engineering, 342, 358–76
    industrial revolution, 377–82
    reusable components, 382–6

Software Engineering Institute, 372
solar radiation, 348–9
Solzhenitsyn, Alexander, 38
Sony, 311
Sørensen, K., 75
Soviet Union, 38, 109
space race (new), 413–19
space station, 346, 347–50
special sectors (telephone use),
    295–303
Spectrum, 280
speech recognition, 364–5
stages of development, 250–1, 253
Stalin, Joseph, 38
standardization, 235
    conformity of software, 360
    off-the-shelf software, 370, 382–3
    of training, 138, 185–6, 190
standards, 92
Star Wars programme, 413
Starsys, 416
state (political aspects), 62–5
Steadman, S., 243
Steffens, J., 151
Steiner, I.D., 197
Stepstone Corporation, 385
Stone, H., 216
Stonier, Tom, 57, 61, 64
storage (on CD-ROM disc), 232
strategic choice, 153, 162
Strategic Computing Plan, 27
Strategic Defense Initiative, 403
strategic objectives (management), 150,
    165, 167, 174
Strategic Systems Program Office, 23
strategies for technology-based training,
    188–90
Streeck, 119
Strowger system, 166–7
structuring knowledge, 250–1,
students
    aims/objectives (RBL), 244–5
    in resource-based learning, 239–40
    visually impaired, 10, 224–35
'Superscape Alternate Realities', 391
support material (CD-ROM project),
    233–4
supporting resource-based learning,
    243–7
surveillance, 63, 341
Sutherland, Ivan, 387–8, 389
Sutherland, R., 253
symbolic encoding, 47–8, 50
symptomatic technology, 41
systems approach, 42, 43

T/Maker, 187
Take Five system, 189–90
Target Group Index, 314, 319–20, 324, 326–7, 331
task specialisation approach, 196
Taylor, F.W., 171, 172
Taylor, J., 201
Taylor, M.E., 228–9
Taylorism, 9, 101, 104, 114–19 *passim*, 121, 123–4, 138, 172, 173
TDMA technology, 407
teachers, 234, 244–6
technocracy, 62, 91
technological change
    future of work, 135–47
    at work, 149–75
    see also pace of change
technological context of CSCL, 192–3
technological determinism, 12, 14–15, 41, 43–4, 50, 59, 101, 118
technological developments (in smart houses), 78–80
technological systems, 42, 43
technologies
    communication (consumption of), 42, 44–9
    for computer-supported collaborative learning, 198–9
    modern (significant), 137–8
    object-oriented, 378–9, 385–6
technology
    -based training, 182–91
    black box, 14, 15, 19
    changing (quality of working life), 141–4
    closure, 42, 46, 50
    defining, 66–7
    diffusion of, *see* diffusion of technology
    full-life-cycle of, 12, 42, 49–50
    gendered, 85–6
    mediation, 203–7
    military, 65, 68, 388, 396, 416
    new (management choice), 162–75
    new (sub-strategies), 163–5
    new (uses for resource-based learning), 241–3
    openess, 45–6, 50
    policy, 26–8
    social shaping, 14–28
    society and, 41–50
Telecom (Australia), 285, 287
telecommunications, 55–6, 58, 63
    globalisation, 94–5
    policy (Australia), 284–306
    see also satellite systems; telephone

teleconferencing, 180, 193, 198–202, 203–4, 206, 212, 301–2
Telefon Hirmondó, 34
telegrams, 35
telegraphy system, 34–5
telematique system (France), 63
telephone
    BT, 166–8, 1701, 174–5, 186, 193, 312, 316–17, 396
    feminine culture, 268, 284–306
    infrastructure, 94–5
    Iridium system, 352–7, 414–18
    networks, 11–12, 33–40
    ownership patterns, 10, 268, 311–18
    satellite communications, 413–19
Telephone Interpreter Service, 298
'telepresence', 205
TeleResources, 357
television, 45, 46
    electronic news gathering, 168–71
    globalisation, 344, 348
    ownership patterns, 10, 268, 311, 318–23
telework, 10, 341, 342, 400–12
Texaco Tankerships, 185
Texas Instruments, 183
Thatcherism, 90
Third Wave concept, 54, 59, 60
Third World, 54, 109–10, 141, 270, 328
Thomas, R., 97
Thomason, G., 157
Thomson (VPL control), 396
time-division multiple access, 417
time-reading (CD-ROM), 232
time-searching (CD-ROM), 232–3
time-sharing (software), 362
Time-Warner, 396
timed local calls, 285
Tinnell, C.S., 269
Toffler, Alvin, 54, 64, 74, 90, 92
Toles, T., 278
Tolkien, J.R.R., 279
top-down approach, 163–8 *passim*, 170–1
TOPS project, 165–6
Touraine, Alain, 57
Toyota, 106, 109
training, 9–10
    CNC application, 130–2
    costs, 186
    embedded, 187–8
    standardization, 138, 185–6, 190
    supported material (CD-ROM project), 233–4
    technology-based, 182–91
transnational corporations, 64, 68

Trident missile, 23
TRW, 414–15, 416, 418
Tuana, N., 75
Tunstall, J., 322
Turkle, S., 45, 47
Twain, Mark, 303

unemployment, 90, 119, 122, 271
unified programming environments,
    362–3
Unimation, 105
United Nations Development
    Programme, 96
United States, 63, 104–7, 108–9, 139–40
    Air Force, 23, 388
    NASA, 388, 394
    Navy, 23
    telephone network, 33–40
universal access, 37–9, 98
Unix, 362, 369, 373, 384
up-skilling, 123, 124, 142–4, 174
usability
    double life of technology, 45–6
    home computers (contextualizing),
        269–81
    resource-based learning, 243–7
    telephone (by women), 268,
        284–306
usage levels
    IT devices in home, 10, 268, 311–39
    telephone (patterns/needs), 295–303
    telephone (survey), 287–9
users, see consumers

vaccination data (variables), 22
Vail, Theodore, 11, 36–8, 39
Vallee, O., 199
van Eijkelenburg, K., 198
Vanek, J., 74–5, 86
VARILAB program, 262
vendors (technology-based training),
    188, 189
Venkatesh, A., 270
Verne, Jules, 105
VIC 20 computer, 275
video-conferencing, 193, 198, 200,
    203–4, 206, 214–16
video cassette recorders, 10, 268, 311,
    323–9
Video Recording Act (1985), 279
Vincent, Tom, 224
Vincent, Vincent John, 392–3
Virtual Reality, 10, 342, 387–96
visiting other companies (for
    technology-based training), 189

visually impaired learners (use of CD
    technology), 10, 179, 224–35
Vitalari, N.P., 270
Vodaphone, 318
VPL Inc., 379, 395–6
Vygotsky, L.S., 196, 254–6, 260, 263

Waggoner, M., 201
Wajcman, J., 16, 41, 44, 75
Waldern, Jonathan, 391, 393
Wallace, J., 92
Wang, 183
WARC, 356, 416
Warwick, M., 221
Wason, P.C., 254
Watson, D., 243
Watson, T.J., 157
Watson, Thomas, 92
Watzlawick, P., 205
wealth distribution, 96–7
Webb, N.M., 197
Weber, Max, 58
Webster, F., 49, 90
werewolf legend, 375–6, 377
West Communications, 396
West Denton High School, 390
Western Union, 34, 37
Wharf, B., 95
Wheelock, Jane, 274
White, B., 18
White, L., 45
Whitney, Eli, 381, 382
Wield, D., 173
Wiener, Norbert, 284
Wilkinson, B., 150–1, 173
Williams, Raymond, 12, 41, 48
Williamson, J., 318
Willman, Paul, 150, 152–3, 156
Wilson, P., 202
Winch, G., 150, 156
Windolf, P., 127
Winner, L., 18, 19, 20, 41, 43–4
WIRS, 151, 160, 161
women
    feminine culture of telephone, 268,
        284–306
    feminism, 74, 75
    feminization of American telephone,
        39
    migrant (telephone use), 297–300
    rural (telephone use), 300–3
    as social group (consumers), 83–5
Wood, J., 318
Wood, S., 114, 116, 126
word processors, 234–5, 409–10

work
  future of, 135–47
  -home relationship (telework),
      400–12
  industrial relations, 16–17, 62, 115,
      121–2, 151–2, 156–62
  see also labour; labour process;
      labour regulation; skills; training
working life, quality of, 141–4
workplace, 9, 16–17, 101–2
  computerized machine tools, 126–33
  flexible specialisation, 114–24
  robotics and automation, 103–12
  technological change, 135–47,
      149–75
Workplace Industrial Relations Survey,
      151, 160, 161
worksheets, 239, 246, 247
workstations, 154, 206–7, 228, 234–5,
      367, 368, 369
World Administration Radio
      Conference, 356, 416
Wozniak, Steve, 54
Wriston, Walter, 64

Xanadu (smart house), 77–8
  housework in, 81–2
  technologies in, 79
Xerox, 183
Xerox PARC, 198, 203

Yule, George Udny, 22

zero-defects policy, 23
Zimmerman, J., 74
ZX 80 computer, 275
ZX 81 computer, 275